THE PEOPLES AND CULTURES
OF ANCIENT PERU

LUIS G. LUMBRERAS

Translated by BETTY J. MEGGERS

SMITHSONIAN INSTITUTION PRESS

CITY OF WASHINGTON · 1974

© Francisco Moncloa Editores, S.A.
1ra. edición: Agosto de 1969
Translation copyright © 1974 by Luis G. Lumbreras.
All rights reserved.
Published by the Smithsonian Institution Press.
Second printing, 1976
Third printing, 1977
Fourth printing, 1979
Fifth printing, 1981
Sixth printing, 1983
Seventh printing, 1987

Designed by Crimilda Pontes.
Printed in the United States of America.

PHOTO CREDIT ABBREVIATIONS

NMHN	National Museum of Natural History, Smithsonian Institution, Washington, D.C.
MHRA	Museo Histórico Regional de Ayacucho
MNAA	Museo Nacional de Antropología y Arqueología, Lima
MUA	Museo de la Universidad de Arequipa
MUSCH	Museo de la Universidad de San Cristóbal de Huamanga, Ayacucho
MUSM	Museo de Arqueología y Etnología de la Universidad Nacional Mayor de San Marcos, Lima
MRLH	Museo Rafael Larco Herrera, Lima

LIBRARY OF CONGRESS CATALOGING IN PUBLICATION DATA

Lumbreras, Luis Guillermo.
The peoples and cultures of ancient Peru.

Translation with revisions of De los pueblos, las culturas y las artes del antiguo Perú.
Bibliography: p. 237
1. Peru—Antiquities. 2. Indians of South America—Peru—Antiquities. I. Title.
F3429.L8813   980.4'5   74-2104
ISBN-0-87474-146-7 (cloth)
ISBN-0-87474-151-3 (paper)

PREFACE

The Peruvian edition of this book was written in 1964–1965, although it was not published until 1969. It originated as a text for a course in Andean archeology, taught first at the Universidad de San Cristóbal de Huamanga in Ayacucho and later at the Universidad Nacional Mayor de San Marcos in Lima. As a result of this background, defects and omissions will be evident to specialists. Some of them are attributable to the present state of knowledge about Andean cultures, which makes it impossible for a single archeologist to achieve detailed command over all of the aspects treated; others reflect the necessity of keeping the text within manageable length. This is not a book for specialists, however, but for students who are interested in a panoramic view of Central Andean archeology. Hopefully, it will also be useful to anthropologists specialized in other areas, who seek information on Andean prehistory but cannot afford the time to search through the numerous scientific sources published all over the world.

The many notable advances since the publication of the original edition have made it necessary to revise the text prior to translation. New information on the Lithic and Archaic periods is so extensive that these chapters had to be rewritten entirely. The remaining chapters have been corrected and expanded without significantly altering their previous structure with two exceptions: (1) Huarpa, a new culture in Ayacucho, has been added to the chapter on the Period of Regional Developments and (2) the Lake Kingdoms of the Titicaca altiplano, which were not discussed in the original edition, expand the chapter on the Regional States to include the regions of Puno, Arequipa, Tacna, Arica, and part of Bolivia, on the frontier between the Central and Southern Andes. Although I do not feel that the Inca Empire has received adequate coverage, few additions have been made because numerous books on this subject are available in English for those readers interested in greater detail.

This edition contains a different set of illustrations from the Spanish original, in which the criterion for selection was esthetic rather than scientific. The maps are more detailed and the chronological charts cover more areas and include a larger number of complexes.

I should like to conclude by thanking Betty J. Meggers for proposing this translation and making useful suggestions during the preparation of the revised version of the text, George Robert Lewis for drawing the maps and charts, and Joan Horn for undertaking the important but unobtrusive editorial tasks required to convert a manuscript into a finished book.

L.G.L.

Universidad Nacional Mayor de San Marcos
Lima, Peru
February 1972

CONTENTS

3 INTRODUCTION

3 The Environmental Setting
7 History of Andean Archeology
12 Development of a Period Framework

21 THE LITHIC PERIOD: 21,000–4000 B.C.

21 Old World Antecedents
22 The Andean Quaternary
23 The Peopling of the Americas
24 The Andean Undifferentiated Gatherers
27 The Earliest Advanced Hunters
29 The Early Postglacial Hunters
30 Hunter-Gatherers of the Middle Neothermal

35 THE ARCHAIC PERIOD: 5000–1300 B.C.

36 The Lower Archaic: Appearance of Agriculture
40 The Upper Archaic: Village Horticulturalists

49 THE FORMATIVE PERIOD: 1800 B.C.–A.D. 100

50 The Lower Formative
57 The Middle Formative: Spread of Chavín Culture
81 The Upper Formative

95 THE REGIONAL DEVELOPMENTAL PERIOD: 100 B.C.–A.D. 700

96 The Gallinazo Culture
99 The Moche Culture
111 The Recuay Culture
119 The Lima Culture
122 The Nazca Culture
133 The Huarpa Culture
139 The Tiahuanaco Culture
145 Little-Known Cultures

151 THE WARI EMPIRE: A.D. 700–1100

159 The Wari Culture
165 The "Tiahuanacoid" Expansion

179 THE REGIONAL STATES: A.D. 1100–1470

180 The Kingdom of Chimú
191 The Chancay Culture
195 The Inca-Chincha Culture
198 The Chanka "Confederation"
200 The Lake Kingdoms of the Altiplano
214 The Kingdom of Cuzco

217 THE EMPIRE OF TAWANTINSUYU: A.D. 1430–1532

237 LITERATURE CITED

245 INDEX

THE PEOPLES AND CULTURES
OF ANCIENT PERU

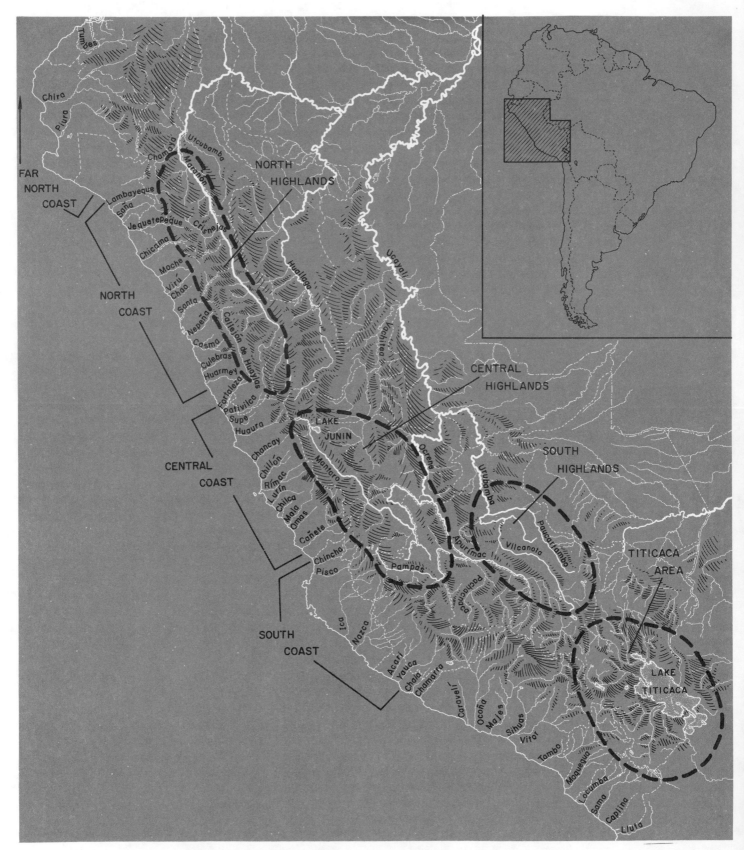

Figure 1. Topography and major environmental divisions in the Central Andes.

INTRODUCTION

The Environmental Setting

In anthropological terms, a culture area is a territory possessing a set of distinctive environmental conditions that tend to produce cultural uniformity. The Andean area is consequently that portion of western South America occupied by Andean culture. The cordillera of the Andes, the dominant geographic feature, extends from the Caribbean coast of Colombia in the north to the Cabo de Hornos in the south; on the west, it rises from the Pacific Ocean and on the east it descends and dissipates into the Amazonian forest and the Argentine plains. The chain of mountains forming the cordillera originates as three small branches in Colombia, which unite near the Ecuadorian border before bifurcating into two parallel segments that fuse in Loja. From this region southward through Peru, varying numbers of ranges are formed, reunited, and separated, until they are reduced to two in Bolivia and to one in southern Chile. Although the term "Andean" is often restricted to the mountainous portion, the Andean culture area is more extensive, embracing both the coastal lowlands and the margin of the Amazonian forest.

The extreme differences in altitude create zones with distinctive characteristics, which can be simplified into three classes: the coast, the highlands, and the margin of the forest (often termed the *montaña*). The reality, of course, is much more complicated. Pulgar Vidal (1946) recognizes eight climatic regions, Tosi (1960) speaks of ten life zones, and Troll (1958) identifies some twelve Andean landscapes.

Since the Andes traverse the tropics, they might be expected to exhibit the ecological characteristics of tropical regions. Because of their altitude, however, tropical conditions are not only modified but often replaced by different environmental types. The Andean cordillera generally exceeds 3000 meters average elevation, creating a formidable physical barrier between the Pacific Ocean and the Amazonian lowland forest. Sporadically, the summit rises to 4000 meters and Huascaran reaches 6768 meters. Perpetual snows begin around 4500 meters and higher elevations are characterized by coldness and aridity.

When the southeasterly winds originating from the Atlantic reach the cordillera, all moisture is removed, creating a sharp distinction between rainfall intensity east and west of the barrier. The eastern lowland is humid and hot, a climate suited to tropical forest vegetation. These conditions extend up the eastern slopes of the cordillera, culminating in a region of permanent clouds where relative humidity exceeds 90 percent. In the highlands, humidity is lower and precipitation is not only less but also confined to shorter periods of time, averaging about 3 months each year. West of the cordillera, rainfall is very low, whereas temperature exceeds that in the highlands. On the narrow coastal fringe, aridity increases under the combined effect of oceanic winds and temperatures. A cold marine current, known as the Humboldt Current, parallels the Central Andean coast. Hot winds approaching the coast are cooled by this current, causing the formation of low-lying clouds that seldom dissolve into rain.

The Andean region is differentiated latitudinally as well as altitudinally into three major zones, which are also distinguished by special combinations of heat and humidity. The north, which includes Colombia, Ecuador, and a small portion of northern Peru, has the highest precipitation, compressed into an annual rainy season, and, as a consequence, the most dense vegetation. The center, which will be described later in more detail, has lower average temperature and humidity, while the south is the driest and coolest of the three zones.

In the far north, where altitude is lowest, a páramo environment prevails in the highlands and tropical forest covers both the eastern and western lowlands. On the coast of Ecuador, climatic conditions become more variable and this is reflected in the appearance of xerophytic vegetation and savannas, which sometimes occur as enclaves in the forest. Proceeding southward, coastal aridity becomes increasingly pronounced, culminating in the bleak Atacama desert of northern Chile. At this latitude, the western cordillera expands into an extensive puna covered with salt flats, where little vegetation can survive. Adjacent to it is a large dry puna, which is nearly uninhabitable. On the eastern cordillera, the puna zone resembles that of the Central Andes but receives lower rainfall. It is bordered by a narrow band of subtropical páramo, where precipitation is higher.

Within the Central Andes, the subject of this volume, there are important regional variations in environment. The coast is divisible into three principal sectors (Figure 1): (1) a semitropical zone extending south to the vicinity of Lambayeque, with characteristics intermediate between those of the North and Central Andes; (2) a misty subtropical zone between Lambayeque and Cañete; and (3) a dry subtropical desert zone between Cañete and Majes. Of these three zones, the latter two

played the most important roles in the development of Central Andean civilization. Cultural considerations have led to the designation of the northern zone as the "Far North," the southernmost as "South," and division of the central zone into "North" and "Central." The principal valleys of the North coast (the misty zone) are from north to south: Lambayeque, Saña, Jequetepeque, Chicama, Moche, Virú, Chao, Santa, Nepeña, Casma, Culebras, and Huarmey; those of the Central coast are Fortaleza, Pativilca, Supe, Huaura, Chancay, Chillón, Rímac (Lima), Lurín, Chilca, Mala, Omas, and Cañete. On the South coast, corresponding to the subtropical desert zone, are the valleys of Chincha, Pisco, Ica, Nazca, Acarí, and Yauca.

The coastal desert (Figure 2) is interrupted periodically by rivers that descend the western slopes of the Andes (Figure 3). During the rainy season in the highlands, these rivers increase their flow and create oases that support plant, animal, and consequently also human life. In the misty subtropical zone, a common phenomenon is the existence of "lomas," a term applied to low hills that support a special type of vegetation as a consequence of continuous exposure to misty air, making them suitable for grazing but of little use for cultivation. Furthermore, they are verdent only during the seven months of the year when the mist is present.

The Central Andean highlands are also divisible into three primary altitudinal regions. These are: (1) the cordilleran; (2) the pre-cordilleran or "puna" (Figure 4), including the highland savannas; and (3) the interandean valleys and ravines (Figure 5). The eastern margins of the cordilleran region incorpo-

Figure 2. Typical coastal desert.

Figure 3. The Pisco Valley on the South coast.

Figure 4. Alpacas on the puna at an elevation above 4000 meters.

Figure 5. The interandean valley of Ayacucho.

rate a zone of "páramo," which has grassy vegetation resembling that of the puna, and is the most favorable environment for the South American cameloids (Figure 6), especially the llama *(Lama glama),* alpaca *(Lama pacos),* and vicuña *(Vicugna vicugna).* On its eastern slope, the páramo is perpetually covered by low clouds.

The principal highland river drainages are, from north to south, the Marañon, which flows northward and is the source of the Amazon; the Santa, which forms the Callejón de Huaylas that divides the Cordillera Blanca from the Cordillera Negra; the Mantaro and Apurímac, tributaries of the Amazon; the Vilcanota, and the Titicaca, the latter running south into the Southern Andes. During the course of the following discussion, these basins have been grouped into larger regions. The Marañon and Santa belong to the North highlands, the Mantaro and Apurímac to the Central highlands, and the Vilcanota to the South highlands. The Titicaca is frequently referred to as the "Altiplano de Titicaca."

The interandean valleys and highland savannas were favorable to cultural development, although it is notable that the largest populations did not coincide with the major valleys. Generally speaking, local characteristics promoted cultural differentiation during periods of intense regionalism, and the major river basins facilitated the transmission of the expansive cultural currents that recur during the history of the Central Andes.

The quantity of water that the highland rivers normally contain is insufficient for the irrigation of large areas. As a consequence, highland agriculture was less dependent on the rivers than on rainfall, which normally occurs between the months of December and March. The short period of natural precipitation led to the search for supplementary means of meeting agricultural requirements, which ultimately led to the construction of impressive hydraulic works. Both in the highlands and on the dry coast, competition for water control became a primary factor in conflict and social progress.

While the behavior of societies is always in part explainable by the environment in which they evolve, history is not made by the physical environment, but by the people who exploit it to satisfy their needs. Each society obtains material products

Figure 6. A llama and its owner traveling on the páramo.

from its habitat, thereby modifying the landscape while at the same time adapting to it. This intimate relationship between culture and environment leads to the development of culture areas.

A culture area represents the expansion of a relatively homogeneous culture over a particular region at a particular time. Cultures are not eternal and, since they are constantly changing, their area of dispersion also fluctuates. For this reason, a reconstruction of the history of an area generally reveals distinct cultural patterns at different stages. This is the case in the Central Andes, where several millennia of human occupation manifest themselves in a complex web of regional cultural variations. The fact that the various local groups maintained permanent communication favored extensive horizontal mobility and stimulated a notable cultural advance. A similar situation prevailed in the northern and southern Andes, although it took a somewhat different form. Because of this regional and chronological diversity, it is difficult to define Andean culture in terms of a set of unique or diagnostic characteristics. As used herein, the term "Andean culture" refers to a generalized pattern of adaptation to the Andean environment, while "Andean cultures" are the special manifestations that distinguish and identify regions and periods.

The term "civilization" will be applied to that level of culture that begins with the development of cities and which is characterized by the appearance of the state and by changes in economic pattern. When the Spaniards arrived in Andean territory, they encountered the Inca Empire and until the beginning of this century it was believed that this was the only high culture that had existed in the Andes in precolumbian times. Archeological investigations during the past 50 years have revealed a different picture, however, in which the Inca represent the final episode in a long and complicated history of cultural development.

History of Andean Archeology

The chroniclers who accompanied the Spanish conquistadores were the first Europeans to manifest an interest in ancient Peru. Many commented on the legendary history of the Inca Empire and some provided information on aboriginal customs of the contact period. A few, notably Pedro Cieza de León, spoke of pre-Inca times as reflected in the monuments of Tiahuanaco in the Titicaca Basin and of Wari near Ayacucho in the Central highlands. The difficulty in conceiving of a human society different from that described in the Bible led to identification of these monuments with early European immigrants or white-bearded Semites, who thus represented the ancestors of the Incas. Rejection of any explanation not provided in the sacred book of Christianity meant acceptance of a static picture of the world, in which the earliest man was no different from ourselves.

The idea of a stable human society still predominated during the 19th century, but new information was beginning to emerge to challenge this view. After a year and a half of travel throughout Peru, the Englishman Ephraim George Squier (1877) published an important book in which he expressed the opinion that the archeological monuments he had seen were of different ages. The German geologists Reiss and Stübel (1880–1887) subsequently undertook excavations in the Ancón region near Lima, and other travelers—among them Charles Wiener (1874), Thomas J. Hutchinson (1873), and E. W. Middendorf (1873–1895)—visited many archeological sites and recorded information on their condition and character. Middendorf appears to have conceived the idea of a pre-Inca expansion of Chavín culture in the highlands and North Peruvian coast. During the final years of the 19th century, the spectacular ruins of Tiahuanaco east of Lake Titicaca were the focus of investigations by Adolf Bandelier (1911), Erland Nordenskiold (1906), and Max Uhle (1892).

Although Andean archeologists were still concerned principally with beautiful buildings and rich tombs during the early part of this century, the existence of epochs preceding the Incas began to be discerned. Mysterious megalithic empires were a topic of much speculation, inspired by the Tiahuanaco complex of buildings, which was attributed to the Aymara of the altiplano of Titicaca rather than to the Inca. Ignorance of methods already widely employed in Europe led historians into flights of literary imagination, enriched by incautious use of philology. Place names in languages such as Runa Simi (Quechua), Hake Aru (Aymara), Muchik (Yunga), and others of lesser importance served as points of departure for debate on cultural problems, on the assumption that languages identified races and races were synonymous with cultures. Some scholars devoted their efforts to the search for evidence for the Aymara origin of Tiahuanaco. The antiquity of a building was often established on the basis of the name by which it was known.

The arrival of the German archeologist, Max Uhle, was a milestone of particular significance in the history of scientific studies in the Andes because he introduced scientific methodology, particularly the systematic registration of archeological remains and the interpretation of data on the basis of relative stratigraphic position—that is, as a function of the sequence in which objects occur in the ground, the deepest being older and those above increasingly more recent. Uhle's preference for excavation of cemeteries led him to rely principally on stylistic seriation for chronological orientation, however, since stratigraphic evidence seldom occurs in such sites. Contemporary with Uhle or slightly later, Baessler, Means, Nordenskiold, d'Harcourt, Latcham, Posnansky, Jijón y Caamaño, Villar Córdoba, and others undertook investigations that later served as a basis for cultural classifications.

Uhle's archeological work not only penetrated into the nebulous pre-Inca world, but did so in a sufficiently systematic manner that he was able to propose subdivision of Central Andean history into six periods: The Inca Empire, Local Cultures, Tiahuanaco Epigonal Styles, Tiahuanaco Culture, Protoid Cultures, and Primitive Coastal Fishermen.

According to Uhle (1920), Andean culture stemmed from the two earliest periods, the first represented by the insignificant remains of primitive fishermen encountered in the sites of Ancón and Supe, and the second by a group of well-developed cultures, such as Proto-Nazca and Proto-Chimú. These "Protoid" cultures not only served as a point of departure for the subsequent Andean development, but also provided a means of connecting the origin of Peruvian civilization with that of other advanced peoples, such as the Maya of Mesoamerica. Currents originating from the Protoid cultures created the Tiahuanaco culture, which for a time dominated the Central Andes from a nucleus on the Titicaca altiplano. The end of Tiahuanaco supremacy led to an upsurge of innovations on the Peruvian coast, reflected particularly in a ceramic style that Uhle labeled "Epigonal." The Chimú, Chancay, and Chincha cultures are among the local developments derived from the Protoids but influenced by Tiahuanaco.

The fact that Uhle's investigations were mainly on the coast inevitably influenced his interpretations. Partly in reaction to this bias, Julio C. Tello (Figure 7), a highland Peruvian Indian, concentrated his archeological efforts in the highlands, although he descended to the coast whenever he

suspected the impact of highland influence. Tello's tireless search made him so popular and legendary a figure that even today the highest accolade that can be offered the discoverer of a site is: "These ruins are totally unknown; not even Tello succeeded in visiting them."

Tello must be credited with the discovery of the Chavín culture. Although Middendorf had previously spoken of a culture in northern Peru resembling Chavín, its significance escaped him. Uhle also had encountered Chavín remains at Supe and Ancón, which he attributed to primitive fishermen of considerable antiquity. Tello (1929), however, identified a culture, or more accurately a cultural current, that not only expanded over a very extensive area but did so at such an early date that it served as the foundation for subsequent Andean cultural development. The Chavín of Tello is equivalent to the Proto-Nazca and Proto-Chimú of Uhle.

Tello's discoveries opened new avenues to the interpretation of Andean prehistory. Uhle had proposed a Mesoamerican origin for Central Andean cultures and suggested that the Protoid cultures of the coast served as the forgers of civilization. Tello (1942) argued that the location of the most important center of Chavín culture in the eastern highlands and the presence of Chavín elements at the site of Kotosh in the Huallaga region, implied derivation from the Ucayali Basin or the tropical forest. Tello's reconstruction of prehispanic Peruvian culture stemmed from this highland-eastern lowland orientation. He recognized four major epochs. The earliest was the "Civilization of the Eastern Andes," followed by the "Civilization of the Western Andes," the "Civilization of the Pacific Coast," and the "Civilization of Tawantinsuyu." Although his eagerness to find support for his theories led to some exaggeration, several of his ideas remain valid and some of the evidence that he postulated is beginning to materialize.

While Uhle and Tello energetically pursued their opposing positions and attracted the attention of most other Andean experts, young Luis E. Valcarcel calmly emerged from the shadows of the legendary Sacsahuaman to assume direction of the Museo Nacional in Lima. Valcarcel withdrew slightly from the emotional topic of origins and directed his attention toward the reconstruction of Andean prehistory as a whole, extending it backward into the distant millennia of the Paleoandean and forward into the better known Neoandean. Sacsahuaman, where he began his archeological career, served as his focus. This Inca fortress was founded in the Mesoandean period, flowered in the Neoandean, and declined with the Spanish conquest. Valcarcel (1924, 1934–1935, 1939) studied the Central Andes in terms of Sacsahuaman—its origins, its mythology, its florescence, its decadence, its oblivion. Here, he dealt with the essence of the history of Peru: a remote and nebulous beginning, the legendary early periods, the founding of great confederations, and the ultimate florescence encountered by the Spaniards. In this perspective, the decline brought about in 1532 was only one more historical event. The subsequent progressive decadence followed by oblivion were more serious phenomena, however, and the effort to understand them led Valcarcel to attempt to combine the data from archeology, history, and ethnology into a single historical thread. Uhle, Tello, and Valcarcel constitute the founding trilogy of the early history of the Central Andes, today known as Peru.

Following the era of Uhle and Tello, a new generation composed partly of their followers initiated the second epoch in Andean prehistory, in which less emphasis was placed on fieldwork and more on techniques of analysis and interpretation. Louis A. Kroeber of the University of California at Berkeley, with his disciples William D. Strong (Figure 8) and Anna Gayton, applied a typological method based on the detailed classification of pottery form and decoration to collections excavated by Uhle in the effort to construct chronological sequences. Eugenio Yacovleff and Jorge C. Muelle studied Peruvian art and confirmed some of Uhle's ideas.

Wendell C. Bennett (Figure 9) was the precursor and participant of the third epoch, characterized by the excavation of refuse accumulations by North Americans. Uhle had worked principally with graves and Tello on monuments; Bennett initiated the era of middens. He excavated the first stratigraphic pits in Tiahuanaco and published his results in 1934. From that time onward, habitation refuse assumed documentary value in the precolumbian history of Peru.

A project sponsored between 1941 and 1943 by the Institute of Andean Research covered a major part of the Andean area. William Duncan Strong, Gordon R. Willey, and John M. Corbett worked on the Central coast in the valleys of Chancay, Chillón, and Lurín; Tello was responsible for the Paracas culture on the South coast; John H. Rowe studied in Cuzco; Theodore McCown investigated Huamachuco and Cajabamba; Alfred Kidder II and Marion H. Tschopik worked on the boundary between the Central and Southern Andes, reconstructing the history of the western Titicaca Basin. Rowe traced the origin of Cuzco culture to earlier complexes, among which the one he named Chanapata extended back to the Chavín period. Kidder and Tschopik demonstrated that the Bolivian variant of Tiahuanaco culture exerted influence over a very limited area, requiring revision of Uhle's concept of a widespread Tiahuanaco epoch. Peruvian and Bolivian variants of Tiahuanaco were distinguished, as well as coastal and highland variants, but the concept of an expansion from the altiplano into the Central Andes was retained.

On the coast, Uhle's sequence was confirmed and

Figure 7. Julio C. Tello.

Figure 8. William Duncan Strong.

Figure 9. Wendell C. Bennett.

augmented. During the 1940s, Rafael Larco Hoyle (Figure 10) contributed significantly to the interpretation of Chavín with the discovery of a major center of development on the North coast, which he designated as Cupisnique. His archeological investigations of this region are fundamental because of their scope and clarity of presentation.

During 1946, one of the most comprehensive projects ever undertaken on the Peruvian coast was carried out with the participation of a group of North American and Peruvian archeologists, ethnologists, and geographers. This "Virú Valley Project" initiated the modern approach to the study of the aboriginal past in the Andes. Archeological fieldwork was conducted by Wendell C. Bennett of Yale University, William Duncan Strong of Columbia University, Gordon R. Willey of the Bureau of American Ethnology, Smithsonian Institution, Junius Bird of the American Museum of Natural History, James A. Ford and Clifford Evans of Columbia University, and Donald Collier of the Chicago Museum of Natural History. The Project was planned by the Institute of Andean Research and financed by various North American institutions. Survey and intensive excavations in the North coastal valley of Virú produced the most complete chronological and cultural information available for any comparable Andean region. As a consequence, this work has served as a basis for elaboration of interpretations concerning the nature and development of Andean culture in general.

The past two decades have also brought significant discoveries concerning the earliest human occupation of the Andes. In 1946, Junius Bird encountered on the North coast the remains of agriculturalists who had no pottery. Frederic Engel (1957b, 1958, 1964) subsequently reported similar evidence throughout coastal Peru. Augusto Cardich (1958, 1964) excavated caves in the highlands and expanded knowledge of cultural development during earlier millennia, previously documented only by sporadic finds, such as those of Harry Tschopik in the Central highlands and Larco Hoyle on the North coast.

During the 1960s and early 1970s, investigation of the paleoindian and subsequent preceramic periods proliferated greatly. Edward Lanning, Thomas Patterson, and Michael Moseley have done significant work on the Central coast between Ancón and the Lurín Valley, resulting in establishment of a sequence extending from the Pleistocene

Figure 10. Rafael Larco Hoyle.

to the recent pottery-producing periods. Rosa Fung of the Universidad de San Marcos and Josefina Ramos de Cox of the Universidad Católica de Lima have contributed additional information on the preceramic and ceramic periods, particularly the Formative. Other investigations of Formative remains have been undertaken by Hugo Ludeña, Carlos Williams, Lorenzo Roselló, and Cirilo Hyapaya M.

Data on the Lithic Period have been provided by several long-term projects. Some are individual in nature, such as those organized by Thomas Lynch in the Callejón de Huaylas, by Rogger Ravines in Huanuco (Ambo site) and in Toquepala (extreme south of Peru), and by Máximo A. Neira of the Universidad de Arequipa in the latter area. Collaborative projects have been more characteristic in recent years, however. The largest is the Ayacucho Archaeological-Botanical Project directed by Richard MacNeish of the R. S. Peabody Foundation. It was concerned particularly with the Lithic and Archaic periods and the staff included a large number of specialists from the United States, France, Mexico, and Peru—not only archeologists, but also botanists, archeozoologists, microbiologists, geomorphologists, paleontologists, and other kinds of experts. Fieldwork was restricted to an interandean valley and lasted from 1969–1971; analysis of the results will require several more years. This project has extended the knowledge of Andean prehistory backward for several millennia, since carbon-14 determinations in excess of 20,000 years have been obtained.

Another major recent tendency has been emphasis on the Formative Period. In the early 1960s, Seiichi Izumi and Toshihiko Sono of the University of Tokyo conducted an intensive excavation at the site of Kotosh near Huánuco and subsequently extended their work to other early ceramic sites in the region. The project lasted several seasons and trained a number of Japanese specialists in Andean archeology. Their efforts supplement those of Yoshitaro Amano, who has worked in the Chancay Valley for many years and founded a museum in Lima to preserve his extensive collections.

Subsequently, the Universidad de San Marcos in cooperation with governmental agencies organized a project for intensive investigation at Chavín de Huantar under the direction of Luis G. Lumbreras and Hernán Amat. The Smithsonian Institution also initiated a long-range project concentrating on the Formative Period in the North and Central Peruvian highlands, with the participation of Ramiro Matos Mendieta, Hernán Amat, Hermilio Rosas, and Ruth Shady, coordinated by Clifford Evans and Betty J. Meggers. Matos Mendieta has conducted important investigations on early periods in the Junín region, Amat is working in the Chavín zone, and Rosas and Shady on the middle Río Marañon.

All of these projects are oriented toward securing stratigraphic sequences, although there are differences of opinion concerning the relative merits of "natural" and "arbitrary" stratigraphy. Excavation by arbitrary levels serves as a basis for detecting relative chronology by permitting recognition of quantitative differences in artifact representation through time. This method was developed principally by James Ford (Ford and Willey 1949, Ford 1962) and amplified by Meggers and Evans (1969). Excavation by stratigraphic layers predominates among those concerned with the preceramic period, who have been more strongly influenced by European prehistorians, but this method has also been used in more recent sites.

Another technique for obtaining a relative chronology that has also been used extensively during the past decade, especially by John Rowe and his students from the University of California at Berkeley, is stylistic seriation. This approach does not employ information from stratigraphic excavation, although a few of Rowe's students have excavated; it is based instead on associations of elements of pottery form and decoration in "closed" contexts, such as grave lots or sites of short occupation. A sequence is constructed by observing stylistic changes in these elements, a procedure that was followed by Menzel, Rowe, and Dawson (1964) to reconstruct the Formative chronology of Ica (Ocucaje style).

Fieldwork during the past ten years has broadened the coverage of the Central Andes in space as well as time. Investigations initiated by Donald Lathrap and his students in the 1950s in the lowlands adjoining the eastern cordillera have been amplified and intensified, providing information on this area from which only ethnographic and linguistic data were previously available. The eastern part of the cordillera has produced peculiar remains of a culture known as "Abiseo" (Bonavia 1968) or "Pajatén," with an advanced type of architecture that appears to be contemporary with the Inca.

Finally, the revival of interest in what can be called "Inca archeology" deserves mention. Although Valcarcel (1934–1935) and Rowe (1944) conducted pioneer investigations in Cuzco, fieldwork was subsequently neglected in favor of research on the documents provided by the Spanish chroniclers of the 16th, 17th, and 18th centuries. In 1963, John Murra and a group of specialists representing various disciplines, among them archeologists Craig Morris and Donald Thompson and ethnologists Gordon Hadden and César Fonseca, began a survey of the population of the Huánuco region during Inca domination that combined documentary evidence with archeological investigations. A comparable neglect has prevailed with regard to sites contemporary with or slightly antecedent to the Inca Empire. During the past several years, however, a Spanish team under the direction of Manuel Ballesteros has conducted fieldwork at the site of Chincheros in Cuzco. More recently, Chan-chan and the Moche Valley have been the locus of a Harvard University project under the direction of Michael Moseley and Carol Mackey, which is designed to reconstruct the history of the valley from its initial occupation to contact times.

Other investigators are pursuing diverse fields of interest. Heinrich Ubbelöhde-Doering worked in the Moche zone between 1962 and 1963, concentrating on the earliest "classic" sites. The city of

Cajamarquilla in the Rímac Valley has been the object of long-term research sponsored by the Museo Pigorini in Rome and directed by Claudio Sestieri. Mention should also be made of the work of Carlos Ponce Sanginés at Tiahuanaco, a site basic for the understanding of Andean prehistory. In addition, several individuals are working in the extreme south of Peru, among them Máximo Neira, Eloy Linares, and Isabel Flores of Peru, and Hermann Trimborn and Hans Disselhoff of Germany.

Development of a Period Framework

In 1946, Bennett presented the following chronological framework* for the Andean area:

1532	Spanish Conquest
1500	Inca Periods
1300–1400	Late Periods
900–1200	Middle Periods
700– 800	Early Periods
A.D. 400– 600	Chavín Periods

The fact that Bennett's scheme preserves the terminology employed in the first publications on the Uhle collections by Kroeber and Strong in 1924 is a reflection of the insignificant increase in knowledge during the intervening decades. The influence of Uhle and Tello is also discernible. The Chavín periods are represented by Paracas Cavernas, coastal Chavín sites (Ancón, Supe, Cupisnique), and Chavín de Huantar. The Early Periods equate with the Protoid of Uhle and include Nazca, Interlocking, Early Lima (Proto-Lima), Mochica, Tiahuanaco, and other local cultures. The Middle Periods correspond to the expansion of Tiahuanacan influence over Peru, while the Late Periods incorporate local pre-Inca cultures such as Chimú, Chancay, Ica (Chincha), and Early Inca (Killke).

The Virú Project developed a new approach to archeological data, and an evolutionary and functional orientation toward the interpretation of Andean cultural development. These ideas, first formulated at a meeting in 1946 at the Hacienda Chiclín near Trujillo, were elaborated the following year during a conference at the Wenner-Gren Foundation for Anthropological Research in New York. In the publication resulting from these discussions, Bennett (1948a:6) recognized six major periods:

* In this and succeeding chronological frameworks, the periods are listed to conform to stratigraphic ordering from early (bottom) to late (top).

6. Imperialists (Inca)
5. City Builders (Ica, Chancay, Chimú, etc.)
4. Expansionists (Tiahuanaco, etc.)
3. Master Craftsmen (Mochica, Nazca, Recuay, etc.)
2. Experimenters (Salinar, Chanapata, Cavernas, etc.)
1. Cultists (Chavín, Cupisnique, etc.)

In 1949, in *Andean Culture History* co-authored with Junius Bird, Bennett added two periods at the lower end of the sequence, which he called Hunters and Early Agriculturalists.

Based primarily on refuse stratigraphy, Strong (1948:98) proposed a different terminology for the Virú Valley cultural sequence:

Colonial
Imperial (Inca, Chimú)
Fusion (Coastal Tiahuanaco)
Florescent (Mochica)
Formative (Gallinazo, Salinar, Cupisnique)
Developmental (Cerro Prieto)
Preagricultural

Willey (1948:9) utilized the concept of "horizon style" as a basis for still another formulation, which combined evolutionary criteria with the spatial distribution of ceramic styles, designated as "horizons."

INCA HORIZON
Expansionistic
TIAHUANACO HORIZON
Regional Classic
NEGATIVE HORIZON
WHITE-ON-RED HORIZON
Formative
CHAVÍN HORIZON
Preceramic

The papers presented at a symposium on irrigation civilizations organized by Julian H. Steward were published in 1955. The goal of this symposium was to compare the development of civilizations in Mesoamerica, the Central Andes, the Near East, and China as a test of the validity of the theories of Steward and other neo-evolutionists that comparable conditions would lead independently to the following general sequence of cultural development:

Militaristic Expansion: Empire
                        Local Kingdoms
                        Initial Conquests

Regional Florescence
Formative: Late
           Early
Incipient Agriculture

At a Roundtable held in 1958 at the Universidad de San Marcos in Lima, Jorge C. Muelle, Eugene Hammel, and Edward Lanning returned to the horizon concept that had been employed since Uhle's time. Over the years, this concept has been used in many different ways. Muelle has proposed that it be applied to a specific complex of traits distributed over a given area during a restricted period of time. Rowe, by contrast, emphasizes the chronological aspect, so that a horizon becomes a band of time within which certain cultural manifestations occur. The existence of groups of widely distributed traits at three different periods in the Central Andean area has led Rowe (1960) to construct the following chronological framework:

Late Horizon (Inca)
Late Intermediate Period
Middle Horizon (Tiahuanacoid)
Early Intermediate Period
Early Horizon (Chavinoid)
Initial Period
Preceramic Period

These generalized sequences inferred from relative temporal relationships have been supplemented by absolute chronologies since the advent of carbon-14 dating. Interpretation of archeological remains has also been enriched by improved methods of data recovery and interpretation, which permit a more reliable and detailed reconstruction of the content and evolution of prehistoric Andean society. A milestone was the publication in 1953 of Willey's analysis of settlement pattern as a basis for reconstructing the social history of the Virú Valley. Among other important efforts are those of Emilio Choy (1960) to interpret Andean civilization by the application of Marxist theory in conjunction with the methodology developed by the European archeologist, Gordon Childe (1936).

New information on the chronology and distribution of Andean cultures gathered during the past two decades permits the formulation of yet another developmental scheme. Since the goal of this volume is to summarize the chronology and characteristics of the area as they are now known, arrangement will follow a temporal order that begins with the initial population and ends with the Inca Empire. The terminology combines several of the period designations most commonly used by Peruvianists (Figure 11). The first three periods have been called "Lithic," "Archaic," and "Formative," which are the terms proposed by Willey and Phillips (1958) for the hunter-gatherer, incipient agricultural, and early pottery-making village epochs. The succeeding periods have been labeled "Regional Developmental" for early localized cultures; "Wari Empire" for the "Military Expansionistic" or "Middle Horizon"; "Regional States" for the "Late Intermediate" period; and "Empire of Tawantinsuyu" (Inca Empire) for the Inca epoch or "Late Horizon." The names of the three most recent periods employ political terms to emphasize that consolidation of the state is considered to be their most significant aspect.

overleaves

Figure 11 *a–e*. Chronological correlation between regional sequences in the Central Andes.

EPOCHS		LAMBAYEQUE – JEQUETEPEQUE	CHICAMA – MOCHE	VIRU	SANTA	CASMA	TIME SCALE
INCA EMPIRE		INCA – CHIMU ↑	INCA – CHIMU ↑	ESTERO ↑	INCA ↑	INCA ↑	1500
REGIONAL STATES		CHIMU – LAMBAYEQUE LAMBAYEQUE GEOM. TRICOLOR	CHIMU	CHIMU – LA PLATA ↑	CHIMU – SANTA	CASMA (?)	1000
WARI EMPIRE		(TIAHUANACOID) ?	SANTA WARI	TOMAVAL	SANTA	SANTA	
REGIONAL DEPARTMENTAL		?	M O C H E — LATE MIDDLE EARLY GALLINAZO	HUANCACO III GALLINAZO II I	RECUAY (GALLINAZO) ?	?	500 AD BC
FORMATIVE PERIOD	UPPER	? CHONGOYAPE	SALINAR	PUERTO MOORIN		PATASCA	500
	MIDDLE	(JEQUETEPEQUE)	CUPISNIQUE	LATE GUAÑAPE		MOQEKE	1000
	LOWER		PLAIN POTTERY	MIDDLE GUAÑAPE EARLY GUAÑAPE		CERRO SECHIN HALDAS ?	2000
		TOLON (?)				CULEBRAS	
ARCHAIC PERIOD	UPPER		HUACA PRIETA	CERRO PRIETO			3000
	LOWER		?				4000
LITHIC PERIOD	ADVANCED HUNTERS		PAIJAN				6000 8000
	UNDIFFER-ENTIATED GATHERERS						10,000 15,000 20,000

A

EPOCHS		CHANCAY	ANCON-CHILLON	RIMAC	LURIN	CHILCA	CAÑETE	TIME SCALE
INCA EMPIRE		↑	↑	INCA	INCA-PACHACAMAC	INCA	INCA-HUARCO	1500
REGIONAL STATES		CHANCAY — BLACK-ON-WHITE GEOMETRIC — TRICOLOR EPIGONAL	CHANCAY — BLACK-ON-WHITE GEOMETRIC — TRICOLOR EPIGONAL	?	PUERTO VIEJO (?)	PUERTO VIEJO	LATE CAÑETE	1000
				EPIGONAL	EPIGONAL			
WARI EMPIRE		TEATINO (WARI)	TEATINO WARI	WARI — CAJAMARQUILLA	WARI — PACHACAMAC	?	HUACA DEL ORO	
		?		← NIEVERIA	NIEVERIA		?	500
REGIONAL DEVELOPMENTAL		LIMA	LIMA	LIMA	LIMA			
		MIRAMAR	MIRAMAR	MIRAMAR		?	?	AD
FORMATIVE PERIOD	UPPER	BAÑOS DE BOZA	BAÑOS DE BOZA	?	FRIJOLOID (?)		TOPARA	BC
								500
	MIDDLE	CHAVINOID	ANCON	CHAVINOID	CHAVINOID	(CHAVINOID) ?		
								1000
	LOWER		COLINAS CHIRA	GARAGAY LA FLORIDA	MINA PERDIDA CURAYACU			
					?	?		2000
ARCHAIC PERIOD	UPPER		GAVIOTA CONCHAS PLAYA HERMOSA	CHIRA — VILLA (?)	TABLADA DE LURIN (?)	PRE-CERAMIC WITH COTTON ?		3000
	LOWER		ENCANTO			CHILCA		4000
					?			6000
LITHIC PERIOD	ADVANCED HUNTERS		CANARIO			LATE TRES VENTANAS		
			LUZ – ARENAL CHIVATEROS II		CONCHITAS	EARLY TRES VENTANAS ?		8000
			CHIVATEROS I		?			
			OQUENDO		CERRO ACHONA			10,000
	UNDIFFERENTIATED GATHERERS		RED ZONE		CERRO TORTUGA			15,000
								20,000

B

EPOCHS			CHINCHA	PARACAS-PISCO	ICA		NAZCA	ACARI	TIME SCALE
INCA EMPIRE			INCA-CHINCHA	INCA	INCA-TACARACA		INCA	INCA	1500
REGIONAL STATES			CHINCHA	ICA	ICA	SONICHE	POROMA	ACARI	
						CHULPACA			
						PINILLA	EPIGONAL		1000
WARI EMPIRE			?	?	ICA-PACHACAMAC			?	
					WARI-ATARCO ROBLES MOQO		WARI-ATARCO ROBLES MOQO-PACHECO		
				?	NAZCA 9				500
REGIONAL DEVELOPMENTAL			(LA ESTRELLA)	LATE NAZCA	NAZCA	IV (PHASES 7-8)	HUACA DEL LORO	LATE NAZCA (CHAVINA)	
						III (PHASES 5-6)	LATE NAZCA		
			(EL CARMEN)	DOS PALMOS		II (PHASES 2-4)	EARLY NAZCA (CAHUACHI)	TAMBO VIEJO	AD
						I (PHASE 1)	PROTO NAZCA		BC
FORMATIVE PERIOD	UPPER		TOPARA	NECROPOLIS	OCUCAJE	LATE PARACAS			
	MIDDLE			CAVERNAS		CALLANGO ISLA	EARLY PARACAS		500
				↓			?	?	
	LOWER					CERRILLOS (CHIQUERILLO)	?		1000
				DISCO VERDE		ERIZO		HACHAS	
				?		?	?		
ARCHAIC PERIOD	UPPER			OTUMA	(CASA VILCA)				2000
	LOWER			CABEZA LARGA					3000
							? ↑ (SAN NICOLAS) ↓ ?		4000
				↑ SANTO DOMINGO ?					6000
LITHIC PERIOD	ADVANCED HUNTERS								8000
	UNDIFFER-ENTIATED GATHERERS								10,000
									15,000
									20,000

C

EPOCHS		EXTREME N.	NORTH HIGHLANDS			CENTRAL HIGHLANDS			S. HIGHLANDS	TIME SCALE
		UTCUBAMBA	CAJAMARCA	HUAYLAS	HUANUCO	JUNIN	MANTARO	AYACUCHO	CUZCO	
INCA EMPIRE		PAJATEN / INCA	INCA– CAJAMARCA V	INCA	INCA YACHAS– CHUPAICHOS	INCA	INCA (WANKAS)	INCA– AYA ORQO (CHANCAS)	INCA	1500
REGIONAL STATES		(REVASH)	?	LATE LOCAL STYLES		SAN BLAS RED-ON-BUFF	PATAN QOTO	ARQALLA	KILLKE	
			CAJAMARCA IV				MANTARO	MANTARO		1000
WARI EMPIRE		(CHIPURIC)	WARI CAJAMARCA III	WARI–HONCO	?	?	WARI	WARI (VIÑAQUE) ROBLES MOQO CONCHOPATA	WARI–LUCRE	
		(KUELAP)								500
REGIONAL DEVELOP- MENTAL		?	CAJAMARCA II	RECUAY	HIGUERAS		HUANCAYO	HUARPA	WARU (?)	
						?				AD
										BC
FORMATIVE PERIOD	UPPER		CAJAMARCA I	HUARAS	KOTOSH– SAN BLAS	?	?	RANCHA	PAQALLAMOQO	
						?				
	MIDDLE			RAKU	SAJARAPATAC	?	ATAURA	CHUPAS	CHANAPATA	500
			KUNTUR WASI	CHAVIN-ROCAS		?		KICHKAPATA		
					KOTOSH– CHAVIN		?	(WICHQANA)		1000
				CHAVIN- OFRENDAS	KOTOSH				(MARCA VALLE)	
	LOWER		PACOPAMPA	TORIL (?)	WAYRA-JIRCA	SAN BLAS I	?	(ANDAMARCA)		
			?	?			?	?	?	2000
ARCHAIC PERIOD	UPPER				MITO		CUNAS	CACHI		
					LAURICOCHA III					3000
	LOWER			(QUISHQUI PUNCO) II						
								CHIHUA		4000
								PIKI		
LITHIC PERIOD	ADVANCED HUNTERS			QUISHQUI PUNCO I	LAURICOCHA II –AMBO	TILARNIYOQ			JAYWA	6000
				GUITARRERO II	(PACHAMACHAY)					8000
					LAURICOCHA I				PUENTE (HUANTA)	
	UNDIFFERENTIATED GATHERERS			?					?	
				GUITARRERO I		(PANALAGUA)			AYACUCHO	10,000
										15,000
								PACCAICASA		20,000

D

EPOCHS	CHUQUIBAMBA	AREQUIPA	TACNA-ARICA	PUNO	TIAHUANACO	ORURO	TIME SCALE
EMPIRE OF TAWANTINSUYO	INCA ↑	INCA ↑	INCA ↑	INCA {LUPAQAS COLLAS}	INCA {OMASUYOS PACAJES}	(INCA)	1500
REGIONAL STATES	CHUQUIBAMBA	CHURAJON	II(GENTILAR) (MAYTAS, COLLAO, CHIRIBAYA, ETC.) I(SAN MIGUEL)	SILLUSTANI COLLAO—ALLITA AMAYA	(MOLLO)	BLACK-ON-RED	
WARI EMPIRE / TIAHUANACO EXPANSION	WARI-QOQOPA ↓ ?	? ↓	TIAHUANACO	TIAHUANACO EXPANSION	TIAHUANACO Ⅴ	TIAHUANACO	1000
FORMATIVE PERIOD — UPPER	?		?	?	TIAHUANACO Ⅳ	LATE WANKARANI	500
					TIAHUANACO Ⅲ		AD
FORMATIVE PERIOD — LOWER			FALDAS DEL MORRO	PUKARA	TIAHUANACO Ⅱ TIAHUANACO Ⅰ		BC
					CHIRIPA		500
				QALUYU		WANKARANI ↑	
				?	PRE-MOUND ?		1000
ARCHAIC PERIOD	?	ARCATA (?)	CHINCHORRO Ⅱ				2000
			CHINCHORRO Ⅰ			?	3000
			QUIANI Ⅰ				4000
LITHIC PERIOD — ADVANCED HUNTERS		HUANAQUEROS (?)				VISCACHANI ↓	6000
			TOQUEPALA Ⅰ				8000
LITHIC PERIOD — UNDIFFERENTIATED GATHERERS							10,000
							15,000
							20,000

E

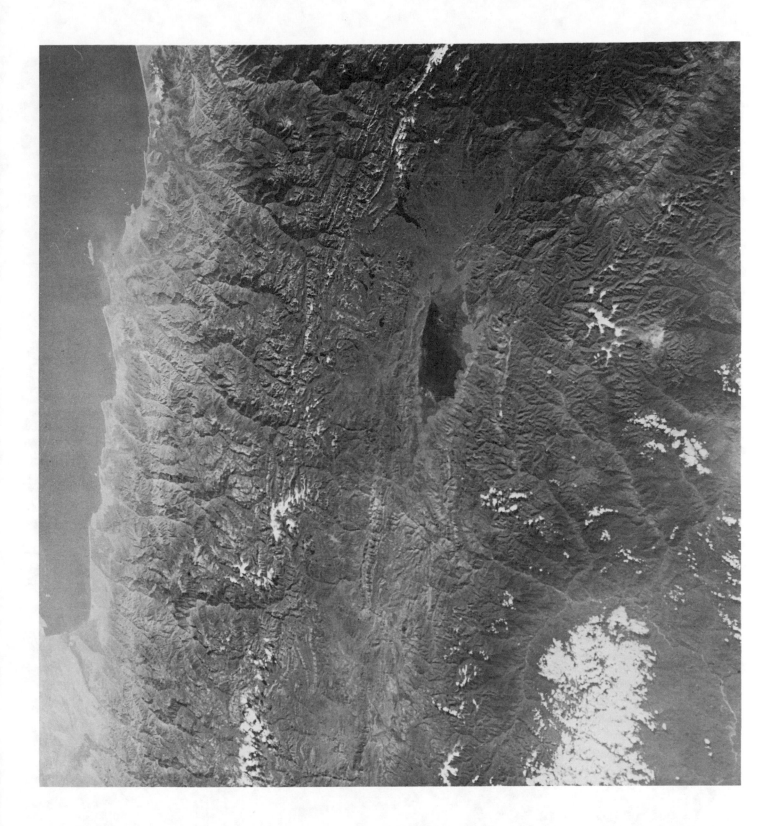

The narrow coastal desert, the deep ravines of rivers descending from the cordilleras, Lake Junin and the Mantaro Basin, and the snow-capped peaks of the Central Andes as photographed from the Gemini IX satellite at an altitude between 146 and 157 nautical miles. Lima is located opposite the elongated island at the upper left (courtesy National Aeronautics and Space Administration).

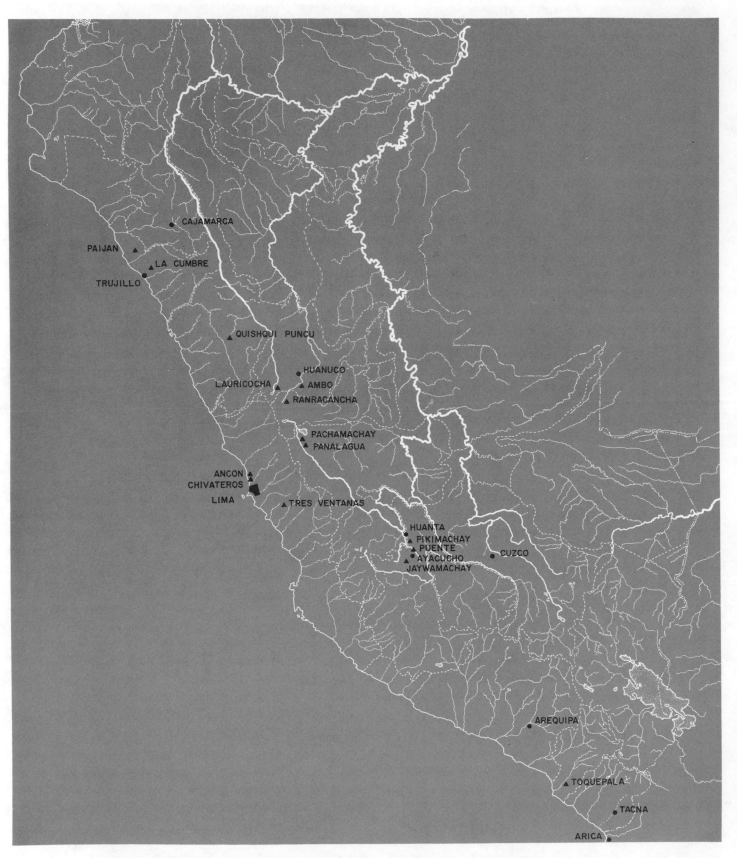

Figure 12. Location of the principal sites of the Lithic Period (▲ archeological site; ● modern town).

THE LITHIC PERIOD

21,000–4000 B.C.

Old World Antecedents

Many remains testify to the existence of primitive hominids, such as *Australopithecus,* in south and east Africa some two million years ago. The increasing ability to employ tools for the satisfaction of basic needs reflects the gradual development of progressively more intelligent and more generalized types of human beings. Eventually, culture attained sufficient flexibility that it not only liberated *Homo sapiens* from the arboreal life of his Tertiary primate ancestors, but permitted him to populate the most distant and environmentally diverse portions of the earth.

The simplest manner of satisfying requirements for food and shelter is by collecting natural products, and all species of animals have evolved special biological capacities for exploiting their environments. The possession of tools expanded man's acquisitive abilities far beyond their innate capacity, however, and the history of the earliest stages of human life is the history of perfection of methods of food gathering. These advanced from reliance on biological faculties to the invention of tools that enhanced strength and skill, and culminated in the discovery of methods of control over food production.

The earliest humans lived in a changing environment. During the Tertiary, the earth entered a period of progressive cooling, which led to the so-called glacial era or Pleistocene epoch. Periodically, the frigid climate of the polar regions "advanced" toward the equator, creating glacial periods that have been distinguished with considerable precision in the northern hemisphere; during the intervening "interglacials," the ice sheets withdrew toward the poles. In Europe and North America, at least four major advances and recessions have been recognized, extending over some two million years. The final glaciation was a small-scale replica of the Pleistocene as a whole. It is known in the Alps as "Würm," in northwestern Europe as "Weichsel," and in North America as "Wisconsin." In Argentina, it is called "Atuel" and in Peru "Lauricocha" or "Negritos." During this interval, there were four advances and three interstadials or recessions, but climatic changes were less pronounced than during earlier glaciations and interglacials. The short time interval since the final regression, which ended some 10,000 years ago and concerns us most directly here, is termed the "Holocene" or "Recent" epoch. Together, the Pleistocene and Recent epochs constitute the Quaternary period.

During the Quaternary, climatic alterations must have affected human existence as drastically as they did the conditions of life for other species. Paleontologists have shown that cold-adapted animals living during glacial epochs were replaced by a "warm" fauna during interglacials. The primitive human beings must have been forced by these climatic fluctuations to adopt increasingly complex modes of subsistence, but specialization to a particular environment carried with it the danger of extinction for man as it did for other animals when the food resources changed.

Faunal alterations observed by paleontologists during successive geological periods generally reflect natural selection for the most successful species, and this process operated on hominids. A more highly evolved species, *Homo erectus* (formerly known under other names, such as Pithecanthropus and Sinanthropus), appeared during the interval between the two earliest glaciations at the end of the Lower Pleistocene. His cranial capacity was greater than that of his predecessors, and he was capable of producing tools of superior although still rudimentary types, which have been designated as the Lower Paleolithic industries. During the third glaciation, in the Upper Pleistocene, *Homo sapiens* evolved. All human beings today belong to this species, as did our most recent fossil ancestors, Neanderthal and Cro-Magnon man. *Homo sapiens* was the first type of man to populate the Americas, but the time of his arrival is still a matter of uncertainty. In the southern hemisphere, the problem is complicated by conflicting interpretations of the Pleistocene time scale.

The Andean Quaternary

Although the glacial periods in North America and Europe appear to be synchronous, it is not yet certain whether the same chronology also applies to the Central Andes, which are located south of the equator. Based on studies in the Ayacucho Basin of the Central Peruvian highlands, MacNeish (1971) has in fact proposed an inverse correlation, in which each glacial advance in the northern hemisphere would correspond to a recession in the Andes and vice versa. He recognizes three Andean advances during the last glaciation, contemporary with the three interstadials or warm periods in North America and Europe. These interpretations are still preliminary and speculative; nevertheless, efforts to establish regional chronologies and correlations with North America must take them into account.

In the Central Andes, the study of the Quaternary and its climatic changes dates back only a few years. Among those who have interested themselves in this problem are Augusto Cardich, as a result of his excavations in Lauricocha (Huánuco), and Olivier Dollfus, who worked in the Central highlands. Cardich (1964) postulates the existence of a "Lauricocha" glaciation, which corresponds to the Würm, Weichsel, and Wisconsin periods in the northern hemisphere. He also tentatively establishes seven phases (four advances and three regressions) equating with the same number of advances and regressions in the north. The advances have been called, from early to late, "Antacallanca," "Agrapa," "Magapata," and "Antarragá." This sequence is valid for the highlands, where altitude permitted

glacial conditions in spite of the tropical latitude; the future, however, will determine whether the direct correlation with events in the northern hemisphere proposed by Cardich or the inverse correlation postulated by MacNeish is correct. Resolution of this conflict will become increasingly important as archeological investigations bring to light more information on human activities during the Andean Pleistocene, which is still poorly known.

The termination of the Antarragá stage, which concludes the Pleistocene, has been dated by Cardich (1964:21) on the basis of his excavations in the caves of Lauricocha and associations with nearby moraines. He believes that the earliest human occupation, termed Lauricocha II and dated about 7566 ±250 B.C. by carbon-14, occurred as soon as the glacier receded sufficiently to make the caves habitable. As evidence, he cites the fact that the human remains rest directly on glacial deposits. If this interpretation is correct, it favors a synchronic correlation between the northern and southern hemispheres with respect to the end of the Pleistocene and the beginning of the Holocene. In Europe, the postglacial began about 8300 B.C.; in North America, it is dated about 8000 B.C.; both of these dates agree closely with that for the initial occupation at Lauricocha.

Among studies in other parts of the Central Andes are those by Kalafatovich (1956) in the Cuzco zone, where he has designated the last glaciation as "Andina," and by Suter, who has recognized a pluvial period on the coast, which he has called "Negritos" (cf., Steinmann 1930:265) and which correlates with the Monastiriano of the Mediterranean and the Würm and Riss-Würm of the Alps. Suter also mentions the Máncora, Talara, and Lobitos advances, corresponding to the European Gunz, Mindel and Riss, respectively, and a Post-Negritos period called "Salina," which may correlate with the beginning of the Holocene.

In general, the Central Andean Pleistocene as now known is characterized by a downward extension of the perpetual snows for about 600 or 700 meters, that is to some 4000 to 4500 meters above sea level, and in some cases to 3700 or 3400 meters. Much of the cordillera from Cajamarca (?) to the Titicaca Basin was consequently covered (Steinmann 1930:267–276). During glacial periods, the displacements of masses of snow and the accumulation and transportation of debris, sands, and clays must have had a notable effect on the river drainages. Although the coastal desert surroundings were probably essentially the same as today, the number of rivers may have been greater and those still in existence probably were broader. Such differences would have resulted from the fact that the coastal rivers originate in the highlands, where snow fields are now fewer in number, extent, and volume. Cardich (1964:36) has cited evidence for differences in drainage patterns on the Central coast, where "the ancient valley of Chillón must have incorporated also the desert valley of Ancón, according to the investigations of Harold Conkling . . . , a conclusion that is supported by the presence today of subterranean water at Ancón derived from the Chillón basin."

It is clear that the environment in some parts of the Central Andes differed from that of today, since Pleistocene fauna adapted to humid and wooded conditions has been encountered in regions that are now desert. In Ayacucho, MacNeish and his associates found stone artifacts associated with the remains of giant herbivores that could not survive under modern climatic conditions; among them are megatheria (giant sloths), mastodons, horses, cameloids (paleo-llama), saber-toothed tigers, and canids (MacNeish, Nelken-Terner and García Cook 1970: 33).

Remains of mastodon and horse dating to about 8500 B.C. have been found in a desert north of Trujillo (Moseley and Ossa, pers. comm.). In the Chilca canyon, which today is uninhabited desert, Engel (1970) discovered megatherium bones dated at 40,000 years ago in prehuman levels of a cave. The fauna included several species ancestral to modern ones, as well as a considerable number of large mammals that have been referred to as "megafauna." According to Steinmann (1930:277), the following species are most characteristic: *Megatherium americanum* and *Mylodon* (giant sloths); *Mastodon andium* and *Mastodon bolivianus* (resembling elephants); *Scelidotherium leptocephalus, Cerfus brachyceros,* and *Cervus dubius* (deer); *Parahipparion saldesi, Onohippidium peruanum,* and *Equus curvidens* (horses). To these can be added the *Smilodon* (saber-toothed tiger), paleo-llama, and various species of canids, all now extinct.

The Peopling of the Americas

During this period and under these conditions, the peopling of the Americas and of the Andes took place. We will refer briefly to the former as a basis for understanding the latter.

The origin of the New World population has been a matter of general interest since the arrival of the Spanish conquistadores, in part because the sacred books that were supposed to contain everything known about mankind made no specific mention of it. Consequently, the initial explanations were attempts to reinterpret biblical passages referring to "lost tribes" or to find other "loopholes." During the 19th century, interpretations began gradually to deviate from religious dogma, although the incipient state of scientific investigation kept the debate on a speculative level until a few decades ago.

In spite of the abundance of information accumulated during the past 20 years, the problem of American Indian origins remains largely in the realm of hypothesis. Modern theories differ from earlier ones in being based more on archeological and geological data and less on linguistic and ethnographic inference. Furthermore, since the general history of mankind on a world scale is known, the problem of New World origins has been reduced to identifying the groups that populated the continent, the date or dates at which they came, and the routes that they followed. Although there has not been a significant increase in specific data on the earliest immigrants, great progress has been made in framing problems and especially in the methodology applied to their resolution, with a resultant reorientation in archeological investigations.

Several early populations are now recognized and those of greatest antiquity are found in North America, indicating that the principal route must have been from eastern Asia via the Bering Strait or the Aleutian Islands. During certain parts of the Pleistocene, a terrestrial bridge linked Siberia and Alaska, so that hunters and gatherers could have crossed from one continent to the other on foot, as did many kinds of animals. This bridge was not permanent, however, so that entry in this manner was restricted to specific periods. The land bridge existed whenever expansion of the glaciers impounded sufficient water to lower the sea level and expose the continental connection in the vicinity of Bering Strait and the Aleutians. During the Iowa and Tasewell advances of the Wisconsin glaciation, there were at least two intervals when a bridge existed. It also reappeared during the last advance (Mankato, Cory-Valders), but during a considerable part of this time a continuous barrier of ice impeded passage southward across Canada.

When the archeological data are combined with these glaciological findings, several important coincidences are evident that affect the probable date of peopling of the Americas. New World archeologists agree that there were several immigrations rather than a single entry and that some were more significant than others. In general terms, two principal entries can be postulated: One of hunter-gatherers with a very rudimentary stone and bone industry, which will be designated as "Undifferentiated Gatherers," and another of hunters who made finely chipped stone tools, including projectile points, which we will call "Advanced Hunters." It is possible that more detailed information will reveal sufficient differentiation within each of these "currents" to permit the recognition of subgroups, as some archeologists have already suggested.

If we accept the available carbon-14 dates and assume that the associations are correct, we can identify the first great "wave" into the Americas with the Undifferentiated Gatherers, since Lewisville (38,000 years ago) and Friesenhahn in Texas, Tlapacoya in Mexico (24,000 years ago), and other sites with crude stone tools are the oldest reported to date and can be included in this stage. MacNeish (1971) has suggested that there were at least two distinct currents during this period and possibly three, which he has designated as the "Core Tool Tradition," the "Flake and Bone Tradition," and the "Blade, Burin and Leaf-Point Tradition." Each tradition is believed to have a different origin in Asia and a distinct history in the Americas. Presumably, these migrations occurred during the Iowa advance, between about 50,000 and 30,000 years ago.

The second great migratory current may have entered via the second Wisconsin bridge, between 18,000 and 15,000 B.C., and was composed of Advanced Hunters or Paleoindians who made finely chipped projectile points. The best-known component is the Clovis population, whose fluted points are associated with the Pleistocene megafauna during the end of the last glacial advance, about 8000 B.C. A considerable variety of Plano (ovate) and Llano (fluted) points has been described, some of which define temporal or regional manifestations during this period. This heterogeneity has led some archeologists to suggest that more than one "wave" occurred. Nevertheless, the Clovis industry appears to be one of the most important ancestors of the "point technology" on a hemispheric level, if not the only parent. Bosch-Gimpera (1943) has suggested that the Llano complex, to which Clovis

belongs, is an expression of the eastern Solutrean, an industry of the European Upper Paleolithic that diffused toward the Asiatic continent. In support of this proposition, he points to similarities between Sandia points of western North America and Solutrean ones. Other archeologists have suggested the alternative hypothesis of an indigenous development of Paleoindian technology, in which case Clovis, for example, would be a local invention. Although much remains to be learned before either explanation can be accepted as final, the immigration hypothesis appears the most probable at the present time.

Both the Undifferentiated Gatherers and the Advanced Hunters drifted southward and their presence in the Andes is our next concern (Figure 12).

The Andean Undifferentiated Gatherers

A considerable amount of data has accumulated to document the existence in the Andes during the Pleistocene of lithic industries corresponding to Krieger's "Pre-Projectile Point Stage" (1964) and designated in this volume as "Undifferentiated Gatherers." The oldest of these industries discovered so far in the Andes is a phase that MacNeish (1971) has called "Paccaicasa," encountered in the lowest levels of Pikimachay Cave, 24 kilometers north of the city of Ayacucho. The cave (Figure 13) is about 55 meters wide, 25 meters deep, and 10 meters from floor to ceiling, and is located some 2900 meters above sea level in a zone that is now semiarid and dominated by spiny vegetation. The Paccaicasa phase has been estimated by MacNeish to have lasted from about 21,000 B.C. until 14,000 B.C. on the basis of a carbon-14 date of 17,650 B.C., which equates with a relatively late part of the phase (MacNeish, Nelken-Terner, and García Cook 1970:13). He places this industry within his Core Tool Tradition, corresponding to the first wave of immigrants into the New World.

During the seven thousand years that the Paccaicasa phase persisted, the Andean highland environment underwent at least three climatic changes associated with different types of vegetation. The replacement of páramo by forest and the subsequent diminution of the forest correlate with a glacial advance, an interstadial, and the beginning of a second advance. These changes should equate with the Agrapa stadial, an interstadial, and the initiation of the Magapata stadial in the Lauricocha sequence.

Figure 13. Pikimachay Cave in the Ayacucho Basin (courtesy R. S. MacNeish).

Figure 14. Artifacts of the Ayacucho complex (after MacNeish 1969, fig. 11).

The Paccaicasa industry is characterized by the absence of projectile points and a notable technological simplicity. In the words of MacNeish (1970: 31), "The artifacts themselves are a nebulous lot, in the main manufactured from volcanic tufa probably from the walls of the cave itself, but even our most skeptical colleagues were willing to admit that some, if not all, of these tools were man made." More detailed examination of the examples from Pikimachay Cave has substantiated their authenticity and also that of other lithic remains not initially considered to have been artifacts. All were utilized for the preparation of food or the working of animal skins, tree bark [?], and other raw materials; none appear to be specialized for hunting. At least 11 tool types have been distinguished, among them flakes, denticulated slabs, and hammers of volcanic tufa; ellipsoidal core choppers of tufa, basalt, or pebbles, and crude scraper-planes of basalt.

In Zones h and h1 of the same cave, MacNeish identified a second stage of Undifferentiated Gatherers, which he has called "Ayacucho" (Figure 14) and which he suggests may be a late variant of Paccaicasa (or Paccaicasa may be an early phase of Ayacucho). More recently, he has offered the hypothesis that Ayacucho marks the introduction of a new cultural tradition designated as the Flake and Bone Tool Tradition. The most important distinction between the two complexes is the appearance in the Ayacucho complex of unifacial stone points and triangular points of bone from extinct species of animals. Both types are restricted to the upper levels, implying that they were introduced during the latter part of the period. The Ayacucho complex also employs a greater variety of raw materials, several of which must have been obtained at some distance from the cave. MacNeish (1969:33) has divided the lithic industry into five major categories: unifacial knives or scrapers and points; denticulate instruments; pebble tools, represented principally by choppers; implements with burin blows and bifacial tools. The first group is the largest. Bone tools are nearly as common as stone ones and include antler punches or flakers, scrapers and polishers, as well as large triangular points.

The only carbon-14 date available for the Ayacucho complex is 12,200 B.C. Since this corresponds to a late part of the period, MacNeish estimates it to have existed between 14,000 and 11,000 B.C. (MacNeish, Nelken-Terner, and García Cook 1970: 15). During this interval, the climate changed from frigid (supporting a páramo type of vegetation) to temperate (associated with forest). Correlation with the Lauricocha sequence (modified) would align the beginning of the Ayacucho period with the end of the Magapata advance, making it contemporary with the entire third interstadial. Horse bones are abundant, and remains of saber-tooth tiger, puma, extinct species of deer, paleo-llama, and possibly mastodon also occur.

Recent investigations by Ramiro Matos Mendieta (1970) in Panalagua Cave near Lake Junín indicate that remains comparable to the Ayacucho phase occur in this region also. This cave is in the páramo, more than 3000 meters above sea level.

Another important site is Guitarrero Cave in the Callejón de Huaylas in northern Peru (Lynch and Kennedy 1970). The cave lies at the base of the Cordillera Negra, about 3000 meters above sea level. It has an area of approximately 100 square meters and remained sufficiently dry throughout its history for the preservation of organic materials. A lithic industry associated with human skeletal remains recovered from the lowest levels has been dated at 10,610 ± 360 B.C. The Guitarrero I industry is composed almost exclusively of flake tools (Figure 15)

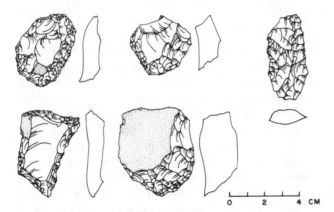

Figure 15. Artifacts of the Guitarrero I industry from Guitarrero Cave in the Callejón de Huaylas (after Lynch and Kennedy 1970).

and lacks both the bifaces and burins present in other contemporary complexes. There are scrapers, a few choppers, hammerstones, and lamellar flakes, along with other cruder tools. Both Lynch and MacNeish consider Guitarrero I related to the Ayacucho phase in spite of the presence of a single projectile point, which they believe to be intrusive from an upper and more recent level. The human skeletal remains consist of the mandible of a 30 to 40 year old female (?), an adult premolar (not from the same mandible), and a phalanx (finger bone).

Another long preceramic sequence has been established by Lanning and Patterson (1967) on the Central coast in the Chillón Valley, which includes the Bay of Ancón and neighboring sand hills, now a desert environment. This sequence begins with three Pleistocene industries: Chivateros Red Zone, Oquendo, and Chivateros I, the first two of which belong to the Undifferentiated Gatherer stage. Their chronological order was established initially by inference from surface samples, and carbon-14 dates and stratigraphic evidence have since supported its validity. Patterson (1966) has shown the physical superposition of Red Zone, Chivateros I, and Chivateros II, and has proposed that the Oquendo complex intervenes between Red Zone and Chivateros I, with which it shares various features. MacNeish (1971:45) has suggested that Red Zone should be included in his Flake and Bone Tool Tradition, along with the Ayacucho phase; we would add the Oquendo phase, although its chronology is not yet firmly established. Both Chivateros and Oquendo are workshops in open locations on desert outcrops, where fauna and other kinds of perishable evidence have not been preserved. They are now several kilometers from the sea and also from the valley, but both the shore and the valley vegetation were undoubtedly closer at the time of occupation.

The Red Zone artifacts were made from flakes produced by direct percussion either from unprepared cores or from naturally fractured pieces of quartzite, which are common in the region. Cores are abundant and some of them are reminiscent of the polyhedral cores characteristic of early lithic complexes elsewhere in the Americas. Burins, scrapers, and other objects of "crude" appearance also occur. Projectile points are not mentioned.

The Oquendo industry, according to Patterson (1966:146), employs a fine-grained, gray-green quartzite, which was flaked by the direct percussion technique, utilizing beach or river cobbles as hammers. The cores have an unprepared striking platform and were generally discarded after the flakes had been removed, although some were adapted for use as scrapers or even burins. A burin is an artifact formed by a special kind of blow, which creates a cutting edge in the process of detaching a flake from the core. This cutting edge generally is at a 90-degree angle to the striking platform. A scraper is a tool with edges or margins (lateral or terminal) that have been retouched to produce a cutting blade similar to that of a modern carpenter's plane. Oquendo flakes usually retain a small section of the original striking platform on the proximal end, near the bulb of percussion. The artifacts are typically unifacial and burins are abundant. A variety of types occurs, some of which serve multiple functions; one artifact, for example, has three burin blows and an edge used as a scraper. Other implements include asymmetrical denticulate tools, side scrapers, and end scrapers.

The only carbon-14 date obtained so far for this early coastal sequence is from the boundary between Chivateros I and II; it is 8480 ± 160 B.C. and thus falls between the Pleistocene and the Neothermal. Patterson (1966:150) believes that Chivateros I, Oquendo, and Red Zone equate with the Pleistocene:

The radiocarbon measurement obtained from the wood incorporated into the salitre at the top of the second soil zone at Chivateros suggests that the formation may be contemporary with the Vanders Readvance and Younger Dryas in the northern hemisphere and that the eolian deposit underlying the salitre was formed during a slightly warmer, drier interval that corresponds to the Two Creeks Interstadial and the Allerod Oscillation. The salitre layer covering the fourth soil zone at Chivateros would represent a wet phase corresponding to the Port Huron or Older Dryas glacial advance in the northern hemisphere. If this is the case, then the Chivateros Red Zone assemblage would have an age of slightly more than 12,000 radiocarbon years, and the Oquendo complex would date between 11,000 and 12,000 radiocarbon years [9000 to 10,000 B.C.].

This discussion assumes contemporaneity between climatic events in the Andes and the northern hemisphere, whereas acceptance of the "inverted correlation" of MacNeish would lower the beginning of Chivateros I to about 11,000 B.C. and Red Zone to 15,000 B.C. We have followed the latter correlation (Figure 11), although Patterson (1966) and Lanning (1967) rely on more "direct" evidence.

A little to the south, in the Lurín Valley also on the Central coast, Patterson (1966:150) encountered the Cerro Tortuga complex, which shares traits with Red Zone and Oquendo. He has also identified a later complex related to Oquendo and Chivateros I, which he has called "Cerro Achona."

In summary, existing evidence clearly shows that the initial wave of New World immigrants is represented in the Andes. The earliest inhabitants lived in association with fauna now extinct, manufactured very rudimentary tools from cores and/or flakes, and lacked weapons specialized for hunting.

The Earliest Advanced Hunters

Events between about 11,000 and 8000 B.C. are obscure in every respect. Climatically, this was the time of transition from the Pleistocene to the Holocene or Postglacial epoch, with the concomitant extinction of numerous species of animals. Culturally, the ancient "undifferentiated" industries were replaced by lithic complexes specialized for hunting. In the Ayacucho Basin sequence, this period is represented by only three artifacts from levels h and gl at Pikimachay, consisting of a prismatic flake and two scrapers.

Toward the end of the Pleistocene, a new phase appeared in the Ayacucho area. Initially called "Huanta," it was later included in the "Puente" complex of the early Postglacial epoch (MacNeish, pers. comm.). The most distinctive artifact is a stemmed projectile point similar to fluted "fish-tail" examples from El Inga near Quito in highland Ecuador (Figure 16) and Fell's Cave in southern Patagonia (Figure 17). The distribution of these points raises the possibility of a third or fourth intrusion from the north, coincident with the termination of the Pleistocene and perhaps related to this climatic change. Although a few Pleistocene

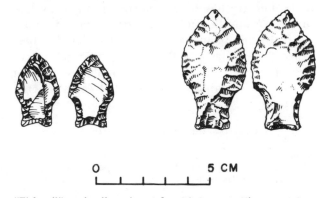

"Fish-tail" projectile points (after Bird 1969): Figure 16 (*left*). From El Inga in the Ecuadorian highlands. Figure 17. From Fell's Cave in Southern Patagonia.

species are associated with Huanta or Early Puente, as far as is now known only "modern" animals existed in the Andes after about 8000 B.C. Support for interpretation of the finds at El Inga, Ayacucho, and Fell's Cave as evidence of a southward migratory current is provided by the discovery of a similar point in the Lake Madden region in Panama (Bird, 1969).

Although probably affiliated with the North American Clovis industry, it seems clear that the South American expression is both distinctive and widespread. Isolated projectile points have been reported from southern Brazil, Los Toldos in

Argentina, and the Department of Flores in Uruguay. In Patagonia, they also occur in Palli Aike cave. Dates obtained from associated organic materials range between 9040 ± 170 and 8760 ± 300 B.C. for the Patagonian points. If distributional evidence continues to expand, the fish-tailed point tradition may require a chapter of its own in the future; at present, however, it is represented in the Central Andes only by the meager remains from the lower levels of Jaywamachay Cave in the Ayacucho Basin.

Phase II of Guitarrero Cave can also be assigned to the Advanced Hunters tradition, since its date and artifact characteristics place it between early and middle Postglacial complexes. The superposition of Guitarrero II on Guitarrero I, which appears to represent the Undifferentiated Gatherers of the terminal Pleistocene, implies an abrupt invasion by the Advanced Hunters if the cave remained continuously occupied.

On the Central coast, a hunting-gathering tradition apparently related to the Undifferentiated Gatherers prevailed. The already mentioned Chivateros industry has been reported from many sites in the Ancón-Chillón area (Patterson and Lanning 1964). In the Lurín Valley, a local variety has been called "Conchitas" by Patterson (1966:150). Chivateros has been divided into two phases. Phase I, which is superimposed over the Red Zone-Oquendo

complex, is characterized by bifacial ovoid tools of quartzite made by direct percussion (Figure 18). Most of the information on this tradition comes from Argentina and Chile, although similar industries have been found in Ecuador and Venezuela. Associated with the bifaces are crude flake implements resembling scrapers, large well-chipped spear points, and more poorly finished tools. These artifact types continue into Chivateros II, which is differentiated primarily by the introduction of a new and more finely chipped variety of projectile point.

The "Paleolithic" appearance of these bifaces has led some people to consider them derived from the European Lower Paleolithic; for example, Le Paige (1963) interprets the Ghatchi industries of the Atacama desert as an American expression of Chellean-Acheulean. The fact that this industry appears to date from the terminal Pleistocene and is known so far only from workshop sites has led other archeologists to consider the artifacts to be cores prepared for use in making points or knives rather than finished tools. This opinion, however, is as speculative as opposing "protolithic" origin.

Moseley and Ossa (pers. comm.) have recently obtained a carbon-14 date of 8585 ± 280 B.C. for an advanced hunting industry that has been known for many years by the name of "Paiján," and is characterized by large, triangular, stemmed points with a flat base (Figure 19). Although these have

Below
Figure 18. Artifacts of the Chivateros industry of the Central coast (MUSM).

Right
Figure 19. Projectile point of the Paiján type from the type site; actual size (courtesy César Rodríguez Razzetto).

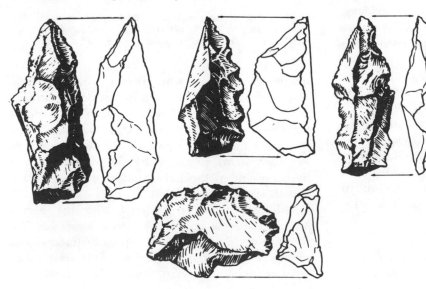

generally been considered early or middle post-glacial in age, it now appears that they may be related to the fish-tailed stemmed type and ancestral to the stemmed points prevalent throughout the succeeding early Neothermal.

The Early Postglacial Hunters

With the tapering off of the Pleistocene, living conditions in the Andes changed markedly. At least three Neothermal phases can be recognized.

During the earliest postglacial phase, called "Jalca" by Cardich (1964:31), a cold climate with intermittent warmer oscillations prevailed, to judge from the abundance at Lauricocha of deer (*Hippocamelus* sp.) that prefer cold habitats but generally remain below the snow line. Cardich has recognized three oscillations, which he has designated as Jalca 1 (a marked glacial regression), Jalca 2 (an advance, also known as the Sheguel Huamán stadial), and Jalca 3 (a pronounced deglaciation). He also indicates that humidity (rain and cloudiness) must have been greater than today.

During the succeeding phase, known as "Yunga," Cardich (1964:32) says that "temperature was warmer, producing a climatic optimum that is a world-wide Holocene phenomenon confirmed by investigations in both hemispheres. In Lauricocha, and throughout the Andean highlands, this oscillation would have created benign and optimum conditions since the improvement in temperature was accompanied by higher rainfall than at present, although still within a moderate range." Similar conditions characterize the North American "Altithermal" and the European "Atlantic" and "Late Boreal" (7000 to 5500 B.C.). Faunal changes noted by Cardich at Lauricocha include a decline in the frequency of cervids and an increase in Andean cameloids (*Lama guanicoe* and *Vicugna vicugna*). Glacial regression must have reached its maximum during this stage. Dollfus (1965:228–229) adds:

This "climatic optimum" is characterized in the Andes by the alternation between a warm and rainy period and a dry one with pronounced fluctuations in daily temperature. . . . On the coast, this phase is marked by rising sea level (glacial and thermostatic), culminating in a transgression beginning about 5000 years ago and corresponding to the maximum of the Flandrian transgression. In tectonically stable parts of the coast, the sea level was 3 to 4 meters above that of the present time.

Dollfus (1964:4) also mentions that during this period the coast was covered with fog, which favored the expansion of the grass-covered hills or lomas.

The succeeding postglacial stage, called "Quechua" by Cardich (1964:38), was characterized by moderate climate "although small oscillations appear to have occurred." Lower temperature was accompanied by a diminution in relative humidity tending toward drought. Concomitant changes in the fauna are of primary importance and must reflect significant changes in the flora. The process of deglaciation increased the number of life zones in the highlands; areas previously covered with snow became dominated by woodlands composed of plants like the *queñales* (*Polylepis* sp.) or by grasslands. The larger species of Andean mammals were reduced to cervids (*Hippocamelus antisensis*), deer (*Odocoileus* sp.), and two cameloids: the guanaco (*Lama guanicoe*) and vicuña (*Vicugna vicugna*). Rodents and birds were also hunted. Prominent among the former are the viscacha (*Lagidium* sp., *Lagostomus crassus*), various kinds of guinea pig (*Cavia aperea*, etc.), and field mice.

The Lauricocha caves were first occupied during this epoch, according to Cardich. The same is true of the Toquepala caves excavated by Muelle in the extreme south of Peru, the caves of Jaywamachay and Puente in the Ayacucho area, and a large number of other rockshelters in the highlands and open sites on the coast. Generally speaking, all these sites represent a single tradition, in which unstemmed projectile points are the most diagnostic feature.

In the Ayacucho sequence, the hiatus during the terminal Pleistocene ends with the advent of the Puente phase, which may have originated during the Pleistocene, but which belongs primarily to the postglacial Jalca period. There are a number of sites in the Ayacucho region with Puente occupations, the most important being the cave of Jaywamachay, about 40 kilometers southwest of the town of Ayacucho and 3400 meters above sea level.

The Puente phase is characterized principally by three types of stemmed projectile points (Puente Stemmed, Lauricocha Stemmed, and Tuina Triangular), although Ayampitín Lanceolate, Ayamachay Stemmed, Puyenca Rhomboid, and other forms occur, especially during the latter part of the phase (Figure 20). Also very common are terminal scrapers, particularly an elongated variety with a well-chipped convex end. Artifacts have generally been retouched by pressure and exhibit a mastery of both technique and material that implies a long tradition, perhaps derived from the fish-tailed point industry or an earlier one related to El Jobo in Venezuela, Lerma in Mexico, and Chivateros on the Peruvian coast.

The best-known complex in the Northern highlands is that at Lauricocha (Figures 21, 22), excavated by Cardich (1958). Lauricocha is at an elevation of 3800 to 4100 meters above sea level, near the perpetual snows of the Cordillera of Waywash. The earliest occupation dates from about 7500 B.C. and is characterized by the presence of a few lanceolate and stemmed projectile points reminiscent of those from Ayacucho and Ancón-Chillón (Arenal).

Paiján stemmed points appeared during the Pleistocene on the North coast and must have persisted for a considerable time, since examples from the Central coast, found by Lanning and called "Luz" (Figure 23), are dated well into the Neothermal. The industries of Toquepala 1 in the extreme south, early Tres Ventanas in Chilca, and Viscachani near Lake Titicaca also correspond to this period.

Lanning (1963c) has interpreted the sites of Arenal-Luz on the Central coast as seasonal camps rather than workshops and has suggested that the hunter-gatherers may have followed a pattern of seasonal nomadism or transhumance, moving from one place to another within a prescribed area according to a fixed annual schedule. This kind of pattern would be well adapted to exploitation of the coastal lomas, given the fact that these formations are barren desert for nearly six months each year and become verdent only with the advent of the seasonal mists. Since these coincide with the dry season in the highlands, deer and guanaco feeding on highland pastures would have been attracted to the coast during such periods, as they are today, and the hunters probably followed them. On the coast, large game was supplemented by land mollusks, burrowing owls, lizards and other small animals, along with seafood and wild plants.

A pattern of transhumance does not imply only a coastal-highland exchange, however; it also could have developed within the highlands, where a variety of ecosystems exist in close proximity as a consequence of abrupt changes in altitude. Seasonal movements into the ravines and valleys with permanent water and continuously available plant and animal food could have alternated with exploitation of game at higher elevations.

It is important to note that both on the lomas and in the intermontane valleys, the diet emphasized plants. Lanning's excavations in refuse of the Arenal phase produced remains of *Lagenaria* (cucurbits), as well as manos and mortars indicating the production of flour and/or dough from grain or tubers.

Although information on physical type is sparse, we know from several skeletons associated with Lauricocha 1 that the population of this period was dolicocephalic. Cardich (1964) assigns it to the "Lagoide" race, which is considered by some anthropologists to be the most primitive immigrant type. It differs from modern Andean peoples in having a long narrow skull, pentagonal when viewed from the front, and a relatively broad and square face. Body proportions appear to have been short and stocky. Most of the individuals seem to have been interred, but only children were provided with artifacts and ornaments.

Hunter-Gatherers of the Middle Neothermal

As has been noted, the end of the early postglacial period about 6000 B.C. was characterized by an increase in temperature and humidity. There is no cultural disruption indicative of a population invasion; rather, it appears that local evolution from the preceding stage took place under the influence of diffusion. Perhaps the hunters living in Peru at the beginning of the Neothermal had adapted to the diverse conditions of the highlands and the coast by remaining "unspecialized." At a certain time and by methods as yet unknown, they were exposed to and adopted new technological patterns, notably the manufacture of the lanceolate points that are the hallmark of the hunter-gatherer cultures of the middle Neothermal. The combination of favorable climatic conditions and cultural innovations improved living conditions and permitted a notable increase in population, which is expressed both in a greater abundance of sites and the enlargement of those already inhabited. For example, the most intense occupation in the caves of Lauricocha correlates with this period; on the Central coast, the Canario group alone is composed of some 21 sites.

The total extension of the lanceolate projectile point "horizon" has not been established, but evidence has been encountered from the northern Andes to the southern tip of the continent. In Peru, the best known sites are Quishqui Puncu in the Callejón de Huaylas, Ambo and Lauricocha in Huánuco, Ranracancha in Cerro de Pasco, Pachamachay and Tilarniyoq in Junín, Canario in Ancón-Chillón, the Jaywa phase in the Ayacucho

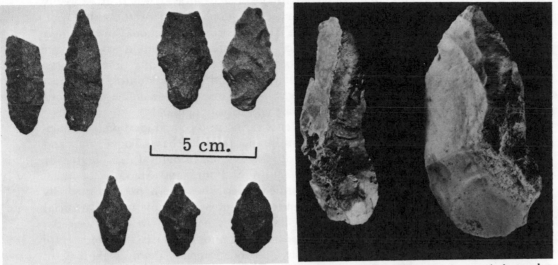

Figure 20. Projectile points of the Puente type from the Ayacucho Basin (courtesy R. S. MacNeish).

Figure 21. Artifacts of the Lauricocha 1 industry; length of right object 6.25cm (MUSM).

Figure 22. Artifacts of the Lauricocha II industry; length of upper right object 6.5cm (MUSM).

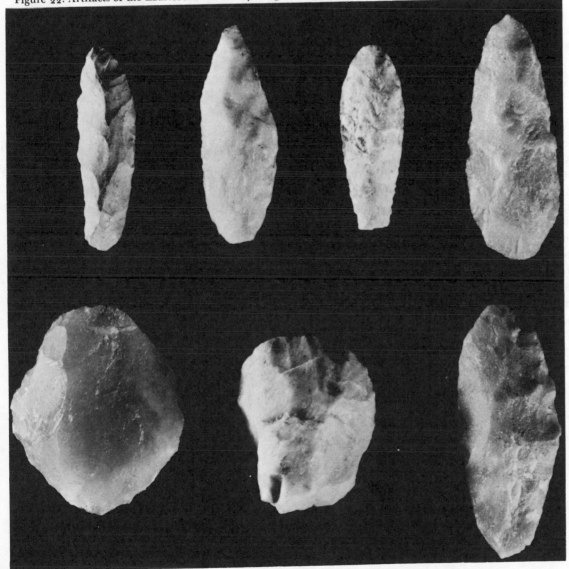

Figure 23. Projectile point of the Luz type from the Central coast.

area, the most recent phases in the caves of Quiqché and Tres Ventanas in Chilca, Huamaqueros in Arequipa, and Viscachani (phase of fine points) in Bolivia; many others have been only superficially studied. Numerous finds in Chile and Argentina are also assignable to this "tradition"; in fact, its name derives from the Argentine site of Ayampitín.

Figure 24. Laurel leaf-shaped projectile points from the Jaywa phase, Ayacucho Basin (MUSM).

The unifying element of the Ayampitín industry is a simple, pressure-retouched, laurel leaf-shaped point, averaging 4 to 5 centimeters long, but varying greatly in dimensions and proportions (Figure 24). Associated artifacts include scrapers, knives, and bone tools, as well as other forms of points, all of which exhibit significant local variations. In Lauricocha, for example, Cardich (1964) found long and narrow triangular points with a convex base, as well as a few "scraper-knives" and asymmetrical knives with one straight and one curved side. At Quishqui Puncu in the Callejón de Huaylas, Lynch (1970) has reported fluted and fish-tailed points, although these may be intrusive or survivals from the preceding period.

The subsistence economy of these bands was basically the same as that of the Early Postglacial Hunters, but gathering activities appear to have diversified. At Canario on the Central coast, mortars were employed for the preparation of seeds. Greater emphasis on plant collection has also been observed in the Ayacucho area, where it probably reflects dry-season exploitation of the valley bottoms. On the coast, shell fishhooks make their appearance, and represent a notable advance over the harpoons that were until this time the only implements for catching fish. Hunting also continued to be a fundamental economic activity both on the coast and in the highlands.

Settlements varied in type and location. In Lauricocha, Intihuasi, Jaywamachay, Toquepala, and other places, bands lived in natural rock shelters or caves. At Quishqui Puncu and Ambo by contrast, they occupied open sites, perhaps protected by brush lean-tos or some other simple type of artificial shelter. Climate does not seem to have been the determining factor since Ambo is in a temperate zone while Quishqui Puncu is almost at the base of the snow line. On the coast, open-air camps were universal, but the possibility cannot be ruled out that the principle of construction with nonperishable materials such as stone or clay may have been in the process of discovery.

Rock paintings have been reported at Ranracancha, Lauricocha, Jaywamachay, Toquepala, and various other sites. They generally show hunting of guanacos (Figure 25) or scenes combining human and animal elements (Figure 26). At present, it is difficult to associate them with any particular artifact complex and some may date from before the Middle Neothermal.

Cranial deformation was practiced, perhaps because the results were considered beautiful, perhaps as a means of personal adornment, or perhaps because of beliefs that were not purely esthetic. The Lauricocha skulls exhibit deformation of the tabular erecta type, produced by pressure on the frontal and occipital regions by means of boards firmly bound to the skull during infancy. Skull deformation was also practiced at Intihuasi in Argentina, but there it was the circular type and slightly more recent in time.

During the Lithic Period, one of the most important discoveries in Andean history seems to have occurred; namely, the means of controlling the life and reproduction of flora and fauna by agriculture and animal domestication. This topic will occupy us in the following chapter.

Figure 25. Pictograph from the Lauricocha regions showing men hunting cameloids.

Figure 26. Pictographs of men and animals from Toquepala.

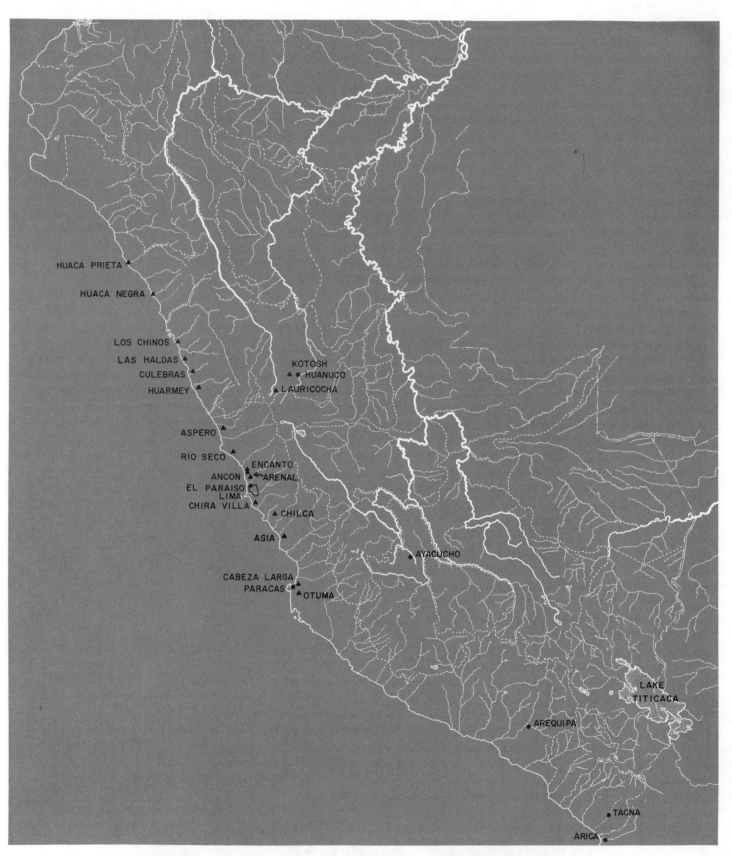

HUACA PRIETA ▲

HUACA NEGRA ▲

LOS CHINOS ▲
LAS HALDAS ▲
CULEBRAS ▲
HUARMEY ▲

KOTOSH
▲ ● HUANUCO
▲ LAURICOCHA

ASPERO ▲

RIO SECO ▲
ENCANTO
ANCON ▲ ←ARENAL
EL PARAISO ◻
LIMA
CHIRA VILLA ▲
▲ CHILCA

ASIA ▲

AYACUCHO ●

CABEZA LARGA ▲
PARACAS ▲ OTUMA

LAKE
TITICACA

AREQUIPA ●

TACNA ●

ARICA ●

Figure 27. Location of the principal sites of the Archaic Period (▲ archeological site; ● modern town).

THE ARCHAIC PERIOD

5000–1300 B.C.

Knowledge of the prehistory of the Central Andes was still limited to the pottery-making and agricultural periods, with the exception of slight information on preceramic highland sites, until the 1946 investigations of Bird (1948) at Huaca Prieta and Strong and Evans (1952) in the Virú Valley established the existence of coastal populations with an economy based on plant cultivation, fishing, and shellfish gathering preceding the first ceramic groups. The characteristics of the sites also indicated a form of agriculture, but neither the methods of cultivation nor the plants involved suggested strong dependence on domesticated foods. Subsequently, Engel (1957b) showed not only that the entire Peruvian coast was occupied by preceramic groups of this general type between about 5000 B.C. and 1800 to 1300 B.C., but that they represented more than one stage of cultural development. More recently, work in the Callejón de Huaylas (Lynch 1967), Ayacucho (MacNeish 1969), and Huánuco (Izumi and Sono 1963) has amplified our knowledge of this period in the highlands (Figure 27).

Like the biological process of human origins, the cultural transition from a hunting-and-gathering way of life to one dependent upon domesticated plants and animals has provoked a variety of interpretations. Many are not supported by adequate data, while others are based on hypothetical models rather than empirical observations. This is an inevitable consequence of the perishable nature of the primary evidence; namely, the plant remains.

One of the first to concern himself with these problems was Alphonse de Candolle (1886). Utilizing ethnobotanical information, he postulated three major centers of plant domestication: China, southwest Asia (including Egypt), and tropical America,

and attempted to reconstruct the probable origin of the principal cultivated plants in each region. Following a similar procedure, Vavilov (1932) recognized seven centers: China, India, the Near East, the Mediterranean, Abyssinia, Mexico-Central America, and South America. Sauer (1936, 1952) initially accepted Vavilov's reconstruction, but subsequently developed a different and strongly diffusionistic thesis. The failure of archeology to provide adequate data has encouraged the formulation of hypotheses based primarily on studies of modern plants. Among botanists who have employed this line of reasoning is Anderson (1952), who has suggested that cotton (*Gossypium* sp.) originated in India, maize (*Zea mays*) in southeast Asia, and peanuts (*Arachis hypogaea*) in China, although all these plants are generally considered native to the Americas.

New World archeologists speculated rather freely about the problem until 1946, when the first archeological evidence of cultivated plants was discovered almost simultaneously at Huaca Prieta in Peru and at Bat Cave in New Mexico. Since that time, improvements in archeological field techniques, growing interest among archeologists in recovering noncultural evidence from prehistoric sites, and recognition of the importance of interdisciplinary cooperation have greatly increased the quantity and quality of data. From the standpoint of archeologists, the social context is as significant as the specific process of domestication and its place of origin. As a result, efforts have been concentrated on "centers of domestication," where research can be expected to shed light on the relative importance of diffusion and independent invention in explaining the character of the transition from

35

food collecting to food production. Specifically social questions have been raised concerning the impact of the adoption of plant cultivation on the cultural development of a region.

In this respect, the formulations derived by Childe (1936) from his investigations in the Near East and Europe have much to offer. He visualized the transition from Paleolithic hunters to Neolithic cultivators as a revolutionary change, both in duration and consequences, rather than a slow evolution. In terms of the total span of human existence, the transition from a gathering to a food-producing economy was remarkably rapid compared with the length of time during which mankind lived on wild foods; furthermore, concomitant economic, social, and technological changes were of such magnitude that many more millennia would have been required for their development by the kind of gradual evolutionary process prevalent during the Paleolithic. These points are supplemented by archeological evidence of marked population increase, which according to Childe resulted from and is consequently indicative of the success of the species in the struggle for survival.

The present status of investigations in the Andes does not permit a detailed description of the transition from food gathering to food production; we can only present some of the current hypotheses and the evidence on which they are based. Plant cultivation may have evolved as a consequence of seasonal transhumance, during which the survival of hunting groups depended on observation of how plants reproduce and when and where this occurs. The instructions are provided by nature itself, which established the process. Emphasis on certain kinds of fruits and seeds inevitably affected the equilibrium of the ecosystem, and gatherers must have noticed that uncontrolled collecting led to impoverishment or even elimination of subsistence resources. Recognition of the consequences of intensive use could have led to selective exploitation, perhaps expressed in incomplete harvest that left a portion of the crop for reproduction during the following season, or in elimination of competing elements to encourage the proliferation of desirable plants. From this point to true agriculture is only a short step. In the case of animals, the situation is comparable since excessive killing of females and young leads to extermination of the species. Here, however, conservation could be accomplished by keeping useful animals in captivity, where selective breeding could take place.

The crucial event was not the discovery of domestication, however, but the possibility it offered for substitution of a sedentary way of life for a wandering existence, a change that became increasingly significant as food production became the focus of community activity and assumed a determining role in the economic and social relations within the group. This obviously did not occur everywhere, nor was agriculture essential for settled life, since this can be based on other subsistence resources, in particular fishing and shellfish gathering. The latter, however, never supported a level of social development as advanced as that attained by sedentary agricultural communities. All agricultural communities are not alike either; many remained little more advanced culturally than hunter-gatherers while others progressed to civilization. Although the former became sedentary, their primary focus of subsistence activity continued to be hunting, fishing, and gathering; agriculture remained a supplementary food resource that did not significantly influence social relations. On the coast between Arequipa and Arica such sedentary maritime communities attained more advanced levels of social organization only under the impact of intrusive agricultural societies, while in the forest east of the Andes societies based primarily on gathering persisted into this century.

The Lower Archaic: Appearance of Agriculture

The process of plant and animal domestication may have begun during the period of the Early Postglacial Hunters, although the first evidence comes from the middle postglacial. Grinding stones, which are generally interpreted as indicating a technology specialized for the preparation of seeds or other plant foods, are sporadically represented at coastal sites such as Arenal, but become more common and widely distributed around 6000 B.C. Engel (1966c: 83) has reported remains of gourds, "tomatillo," and a plant resembling sweet manioc at Santo Domingo in Paracas. Llama remains, assigned by MacNeish to the Jaywa period in Ayacucho, imply that a similar process was underway simultaneously in the highlands. It has not been possible as yet to prove that either the plants or animals were domesticated, although MacNeish (1969:29) states:

Interestingly enough in Zone B2 were burned feces of llama, as well as llama bones, indicating that even in the Jaywa period llama were living on the same floors with man. Therefore there is the possibility that llama was domesticated in this period, somewhere between 6300 and 5000 B.C. Also in the Jaywa levels we did find one seed of Achiote, a domesticate which is native in elevations below 2,000 meters. This may be an early domesticate or early import in the Ayacucho region.

Clear evidence for domestication appears about 5000 B.C. both in the highlands and on the coast. In the highlands, the best documented finds are from Ayacucho, where the "Cordilleran complex" of highland plants and animals (Lumbreras 1967) had begun to take form about this time. Andean domesticated animals are the llama (*Lama glama*) and alpaca (*Lama pacos*), the guinea pig (*Cavia porcellus*), the duck (*Cairina* sp.), and the dog (*Canis familaris*). The last is apparently of non-Andean origin and does not appear until the Formative epoch, around 1200 B.C. The antecedents of the duck are unclear, but the preceding three species seem to be of highland origin. On the coast, domesticated llamas date between 1500 and 1000 B.C. and the earliest coastal remains of guinea pig also come from Formative contexts. Although MacNeish believes that he has evidence for the process of domestication in Ayacucho, this was certainly not a primary center; more probable areas are Lake Junín or particularly Lake Titicaca, which is the preferred habitat of these animals.

Present information seems to indicate that the llama diverged by selective breeding from the guanaco (*Lama guanicoe*) or a closely related extinct wild form. The ancestry of the alpaca is still disputed. While some authorities consider it also derived from the guanaco, certain morphological similarities to another wild cameloid, the vicuña (*Vicugna vicugna*), have suggested the possibility that the alpaca might be a hybrid between the llama and the vicuña; it has even been proposed that this hybridization was intentionally undertaken to obtain an animal with fine and abundant wool. The earliest known alpaca remains are associated with the Pukara culture on the west side of Lake Titicaca and date about 200 B.C. The llama,

which produces not only wool and hide but meat as well, was one of the major Andean dietary ingredients for a much longer period of time.

The guinea pig has several potential wild ancestors, all of which inhabit lacustrine environments. One of the most likely candidates lives around Lake Titicaca and is called "cochacuy" (*Cavia aperea*) or "lagoon guinea pig" for this reason.

Quinoa (*Chenopodium quinoa*) is a component of the "Cordilleran complex," along with other grains and tubers for which archeological evidence is still missing. These include cañiwa (*Chenopodium pallidicaule*), a grain resembling quinoa; and tubers such as the potato (*Solanum tuberosum*), olluco (*Ullucus tuberosum*), oca (*Oxalis tuberosa*), and mashwa (*Tropaelum tuberosum*). Quinoa is one of the most nourishing of foods and its role in Andean society was of vital importance, second only to that of the potato and maize, which were the most valued cultigens. The time of potato domestication is still unknown and will be difficult to detect because of the perishability of the tubers. On the coast, where conditions for preservation are better, it has not been found in Archaic contexts, implying that its center of domestication lies in the highlands, an inference that agrees with botanical evidence.

MacNeish (1969:39–40) has stated that the llama and guinea pig were definitely domesticated by his Piki phase, which he dates between 5500 and 4300 B.C. Associated with these animals are remnants of gourds and squashes, as well as quinoa, amaranth, and probably chili peppers.

On the coast, a larger number of Lower Archaic refuse middens has been excavated, the most important being Chilca and Encanto. Encanto, which is on the Central coast near the bay of Ancón, is a complex of about 13 sites. Subsistence depended heavily on the lomas, which change profoundly with the seasons (Lanning 1963c). During the winter, they are covered with lovely meadows and even small patches of trees, while in summer they are barren of vegetation. The lomas not only underwent annual alterations, they were also subject to cyclical modifications. At intervals of about 20 years, the vegetation disappeared completely from certain areas, whereas humidity increased in others. A transhumant or seasonally changing way of life was consequently mandatory. During the summer, the representatives of the Encanto phase must have abandoned the lomas and moved to the nearest river valley or up to the highlands. The absence of

Encanto sites in the Chillón and Rímac Valleys favors the latter alternative; there, activities probably centered on hunting, although a few plants such as cucurbits could have been raised.

On the coast, subsistence must have been essentially marine oriented, with strong emphasis on mollusks, although the refuse contains bones of small fish that could have been taken with nets (the existence of which has not as yet been directly demonstrated) and with shell or cactus hooks. Seals (*Otaria* sp.) were another marine resource. Remains of terrestrial animals occur sporadically, among them bones of cameloids. Their scarcity contrasts with the abundance of lanceolate projectile points, which were presumably produced for use in hunting. Gathering and incipient agriculture were complementary activities during occupation of the lomas, with emphasis on cucurbits and zapallos. In

Chilca, some 100 kilometers to the south, beans have also been found.

Evidence for the use of certain types of cucurbits during the Lower Archaic is highly significant because it supports the thesis of the American origin of this cultigen. The bottle gourd (*Lagenaria siceraria*) has been found in Tamaulipas, Mexico (Cutler and Whitaker 1961) in contexts dating back 7000 years. Remains of gourds have been reported by Lanning (1963c) from Peruvian sites of the Arenal period, and Engel (1964) has also found evidence of cultivated plants, including squashes (*Cucurbita moschata*), in other sites of equivalent age. Although there is a tendency to consider Mexico or Central America as the area of cucurbit domestication, the possibility of an independent domestication in the Andean area cannot yet be discounted. It is reasonable to assume that gourds

Figure 28. Reconstruction of the type of dwelling used at the site of Chilca on the Central coast (after Donnan 1964).

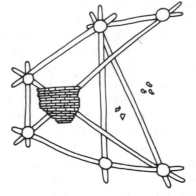

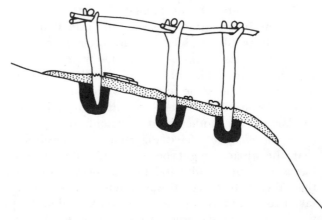

Figure 29. House construction at Río Grande de Nazca (after Engel 1964).

0 20 60 100 CM

were used by hunting peoples from an early time, a hypothesis that would also account for their wide distribution in the Americas. The common bean (*Phaseolus vulgaris*) and the jack bean (*Canavalia* sp.) are other early cultigens that may have been domesticated independently since *Canavalia* seems to be Andean, while *Phaseolus* may be of Central American origin. New evidence, such as the recent discovery that *Phaseolus* had been domesticated by 6000 B.C. in the Callejón de Huaylas (Kaplan, Lynch, and Smith 1973), should permit better evaluation of such speculations in the near future.

These alterations in subsistence emphasis produced a change in population concentration. The Chilca community may have contained 100 families, which occupied small circular semisubterranean dwellings or perishable surface structures (Engel 1966a). One of the former, dated at 3407 ± 120 B.C. (Donnan 1964), has been described as conical, 2.4 meters in diameter, and constructed over a circular pit 35 centimeters deep. The walls were of interlaced canes joined together at the tips and completely covered with rushes (Figure 28). Several burials were found inside. At Encanto, by contrast, although living quarters were larger than those of the preceding period, the pattern of dispersed and seasonal camps continued to prevail. At another site described by Engel (1964), some 400 kilometers south of Chilca on the sloping bank of the Río Grande de Nazca, groups of houses were constructed of willow or acacia posts (Figure 29). Although Engel's population estimate of 100 families for Chilca may be high, the emergence of a true village settlement pattern during this period cannot be denied.

Another significant change occurred in the treatment of the dead. Although interments remained simple, they began to be accompanied by distinctive mortuary goods, such as two mats woven from rushes or, occasionally, nets or a mantle with a wide fringe terminating in knots. Special ritual practices may be reflected in the discovery beneath a layer of ashes at Chilca of eight mortuary bundles, in which the bones had been partially burned and mixed with numerous human and marine mammal remains. Although this is not conclusive evidence of cannibalism, the possibility cannot be ruled out. At Río Grande, burials have been encountered in trenches excavated in the sand dunes; the individuals were clothed and provided with articles of daily use. This type of burial was also found at Cabeza Larga, a site of the same period near Paracas (Engel 1960).

The burials also indicate advances in textile technology, which appears to have been limited to basketry prior to this time. Twined fabrics utilizing bast fibers, especially rushes, now become common (Figure 30). This technique, which does not involve the loom, was employed to make wrappings for the dead (leather was sometimes substituted), small baskets, bags, and other kinds of storage containers. At Cabeza Larga, a short skirt of rushes was worn.

Although a more reliable food supply is associated with increased life expectancy, this effect is not evident during the initial period of plant domestication. Only one of the individuals buried at Chilca lived to an age of 50 to 60 years. The majority died between ages 20 and 30 and many did not survive early childhood.

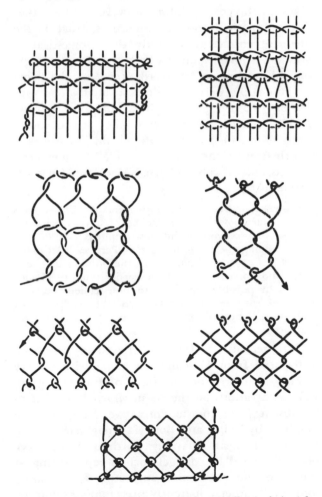

Figure 30. Textile techniques of the Middle Archaic (after Engel 1957b, figs. 7–11).

The Upper Archaic: Village Horticulturalists

Experimental plant domestication was variable in emphasis and sporadic in distribution until about 2500 B.C., when the process had become widespread. Information on events in the Central Andes between approximately 2500 and 1500 B.C. is much greater than on earlier periods and most of it comes from the coast (Engel 1957b, Lanning 1963c, Patterson and Moseley 1968). Little is known of the highlands except in the Ayacucho (MacNeish 1969; MacNeish, Nelken-Terner, and García Cook 1970) and Huánuco areas (Izumi and Sono 1963).

MacNeish has recognized two Upper Archaic phases in the Ayacucho region, which he calls "Chihua" and "Cachi." Chihua has been dated between 4300 and 2800 B.C., making it contemporary with the Lower Archaic Encanto and Chilca complexes on the coast. Chihua, however, has a rather advanced agricultural subsistence, so that if the dates are correct they imply that domestication became a primary food resource earlier in the highlands. According to MacNeish (1969:42), the llama and guinea pig were fully domesticated, along with such plants as the gourd, quinoa, amaranth, zapallo, lucuma (*Lucuma bifera*) and other fruits, cotton (*Gossypium* sp.), possibly tubers, and "in two very disturbed areas there were a single common bean and a couple of cobs of corn." MacNeish (1970:38) comments,

The corn is extremely interesting for W. C. Galinat's study so far shows the cobs to be of a very primitive ancestral or prototype of the most primitive type of corn known among the modern races of Peru called Confite Morocho. . . . Dr. Galinat was of the opinion that such a corn did not come out of the earlier types in Mexico and might possibly represent an independent domestication of corn in the highlands of the Andes. Much study is still needed before this speculation is turned into fact.

Until recently, maize was believed to have been introduced from Mesoamerica along with pottery making, primarily on the basis of Engel's (1957b, 1960) excavations on the coast, which showed it to be absent prior to the Formative. Samples since obtained by Kelley and Bonavia (1963) from a nonceramic site near Huarmey, north of Lima, have been identified by Mangelsdorf as representing at least two different strains, suggesting two separate sources. Another apparently preceramic sample reported by Willey and Corbett (1954) at Aspero in

Supe has been shown by Towle (1961:119) to correspond in all characters to Formative maize from the Cupisnique period; also, pottery has been collected in the vicinity. Clearly, the problem of a possible independent Andean origin for maize domestication will remain unsolved until information from Peru is more complete. Perhaps it was a highland cultigen and the few preceramic coastal occurrences represent colonies of highlanders of the kind that existed later in Andean history (pp. 202, 210). An alternative hypothesis is the suggestion by MacNeish (1969:42) that the preagricultural pattern of seasonal transhumance continued during the Chihua period and into later times. Noting that contemporary sites occupy distinct environments, he has stated that "our superficial comparison of materials from these sites seems to indicate that the artifacts and probably the subsistence was rather different in each of the zones. This may be the result of some sort of seasonal round of agriculture and collecting and herding." This pattern could well have been expanded to encompass the coast.

The succeeding Cachi period is characterized by the presence of cotton and an increase in emphasis on edible plants, although hunting was not abandoned. Villages occurred during both periods, but the more transitional nature of the Chihua settlement pattern is reflected in the judgment by MacNeish (1969:40) that "these are the remains of either an extremely large macroband camp or an actual village."

Cotton (*Gossypium barbadense*), which became important during the Cachi period, is another cultigen of uncertain origin. As far as is now known, only four cultivated species exist, two of which occur in the Old World (*G. arboreum* and *G. herbaceum*) and two in the New World (*G. hirsutum* and *G. barbadense*). The origin of the New World cottons has been of great interest to botanists since the discovery that the species are haplopolyploid combining the chromosomes of an Asiatic cultivated cotton with those of a New World wild cotton. The present tendency appears to be to consider that a Peruvian wild plant (*G. raimondii* or an equivalent) hybridized with an Asiatic cultigen (probably *G. arboreum*). Cotton was present on the Peruvian coast by 2500 B.C., when its use and probably also its cultivation were already well developed. In Mexico, *G. hirsutum* appeared in the Tehuacán region around 1500 B.C. The fact that the Mesoamerican and Andean species are different, however, suggests that their occurrence may not be attributable to simple diffusion.

Most of the information on the Upper Archaic comes from the coast. In spite of the great variation between sites, there is a degree of homogeneity that suggests a pattern of autonomous groups whose basic culture developed in a framework of interregional contacts. Sites tend to be near the shore, in locations where springs provided a supply of fresh water. The fact that they are always far from torrential streams has led Engel (1957b) to infer that accessibility to fishing and shellfish resources took precedence over availability of water for crops, and consequently that domestication was still at an incipient level of development.

The earliest site identifiable with the Upper Archaic village horticulturalists is Huaca Prieta on the North Peruvian coast, which has an initial carbon-14 date of around 2500 B.C. Huaca Prieta is an artificial hill composed of refuse and other habitational remains on the margin of a former bed of the Río Chicama, about four kilometers from the present course (Figure 31). A modern beach now intervenes between the mound and the sea. The combination of a debris-covered beach, rough water, and exposure to the wind makes the location appear poorly suited for settlement by fishermen.

Bird (1948) conducted systematic excavations at Huaca Prieta, but unfortunately only preliminary reports have so far been published. He was able to detect little cultural change from the initial occupation until abandonment of the site, which coincided approximately with the introduction of pottery, maize, and other features associated with a well-developed agricultural society. Nor was it possible to determine whether the 12-meter accumulation resulted from permanent residence or intermittent (perhaps seasonal) occupation. The upper half of the mound contained small, semisubterranean, oval or quadrangular houses, up to 1.6 meters in depth, with walls composed of rounded cobbles. These habitations were haphazardly arranged and consisted of one or two rooms. A stairway facilitated access to the surface. Traces of wooden beams provided the only indication of the form and composition of the roof.

The residents of Huaca Prieta cultivated several types of cucurbits (*Cucurbita ficifolia, C. moschata,* and *Lagenaria siceraria*) and beans (*Phaseolus lunatus, Canavalia* sp.), along with cotton (*Gossypium barbadense*), chili pepper (*Capsicum* sp.), and a tuber known as achira (*Canna edulis*). Remains of fruits, including lúcuma (*Lucuma* sp.) and green plum (*Bunchosia armeniaca*), have also been identified (Towle 1961:105).

Farther to the south, at the mouth of the Virú Valley, Strong and Evans (1952) investigated another large mound known as Huaca Negra. The preceramic refuse contained remnants of houses with walls made with lumps of clay and then plastered with a thin layer of salt-impregnated clay to give a smooth, hard surface. They were semisubterranean and had hard clay floors. The Huaca

Figure 31. Huaca Prieta in the Chicama Valley of the North coast (courtesy Clifford Evans).

Negra cultural complex differs from that at Huaca Prieta in house construction and in other cultural details, partly because of local differences in raw materials. Nevertheless, when these northern sites are compared with others of the same period elsewhere on the Peruvian coast, the similarities loom larger than the differences. It is notable that neither site has produced ceremonial structures or features suitable for community use.

Engel has examined a large number of Upper Archaic sites and has supplied much of the evidence now available for reconstruction of the way of life between 2000 and 1300 B.C. in the coastal valleys, many of which are now too arid for habitation. The most important known sites, in addition to Huaca Prieta and Huaca Negra, are Las Haldas, Culebras, and Huarmey near the Casma and Huarmey valleys; Aspero and Río Seco near Supe and Chancay; Ancón and Chillón north of Lima; Chira Villa near the Río Rímac; Chilca near the Río Mala south of Lima; Asia in the valley of the Río Omas north of Cañete; and Otuma near the peninsula of Paracas. Although the culture is characterized in general by the absence of pottery, the presence of cotton, a similar textile technology, a common subsistence pattern, and a tendency for sites to be located near the shore, it is becoming increasingly clear that the epoch can be subdivided on the basis of refinement in agricultural methods, growing sedentism, and progressive addition of new traits.

The changing nature of the economy and way of life has been emphasized by labeling these settlements as horticultural villages, but the contribution from cultigens was small in relation to that from other subsistence sources. Excavations have produced remains of terrestrial fauna, including cervids, canids, and possibly nutrias, but some mammals common during earlier periods, among them cameloids native to the highlands, have not been found. The relatively low representation of land species contrasts with a marked increase in the proportion of large marine mammals, especially seals (*Areto cephalus australis* or *Otaria byronia*). Although whale bones occur, the small quantity suggests that they probably represent occasional individuals washed up on the beach. Seal hunting, on the other hand, is an activity detectable as early as Chilca times. The technique is unknown, but clubbing may have been employed, as it was in later periods. Terrestrial animals were probably killed with projectiles. Fish remains are sparse, although

shell and bone hooks and nets with gourd floats and stone weights were available. The most commonly exploited fish were anchovy and robalo.

Shellfish gathering must have been a daily activity, to judge from the abundance of mollusks. Engel (1963a) has noted that the earliest levels at Asia contain a larger quantity of seal remains than of shells, while the proportions are reversed in the upper levels, indicating a gradual decline in the exploitation of large marine fauna at this site. In some areas, terrestrial mollusks were collected in addition to marine invertebrates. The latter included sea urchins, crabs and other crustacea, as well as shellfish.

The most common cultivated plants, in addition to those already listed from Huaca Prieta, were the bean (*Phaseolus vulgaris*) and possibly jíquima (*Pachyrrhyzus tuberosus*) (Engel 1957b:145–146). Fruits often consumed were the guava (*Psidium guajaba*) and the pacae or guaba (*Inga feuillei*). Plants considered by Engel of doubtful utility as foods are arracacha (*Arracacia esculenta, A. stenocephala,* or *A. xanthoriza*), tarwi (*Lupinus tauris*), berro (*Mimilus glabratus*), oca (*Oxalis tuberosa*), and a legume (*Polymnia sinchifolia edulis*). He mentions several other species possibly associated with this period, among them the tomato (*Solanum lycopersicum*), tree tomato (*Cyphomandra splendens, Solanum muricatum*), and ground cherry (*Prunus capulli, Physalis peruviana*).

Little is known about methods of cultivation. Trunks of small trees have been found that may have been used for turning the earth. There is no evidence of irrigation and agriculture was limited to areas naturally watered either by rivers or by subsurface moisture. The fact that all food was not consumed immediately is indicated by the presence at Asia of rows of storage pits along the base of patio walls, near or inside each house (Engel 1963b). Large buried gourds, some of them covered with straw, have been unearthed at the same site. Information on food preparation is also minimal. Chili was probably used as a seasoning and the calcified stones found at Huaca Prieta and other sites may have been used in cooking. The presence of manos and metates indicates that some foods were pulverized before being eaten. Plates and cups must have been most commonly made from gourds, although vessels of whale bone and basketry were also employed. Some metates resemble polished stone plates.

These horticulturalists tended to settle near the

beach, and sites now located farther inland reflect changes in the shoreline subsequent to abandonment. The majority consist of refuse accumulations on slopes or rises or on rocky outcrops. Many contain no vestige of dwellings, while others preserve remnants of a great variety of construction techniques. At Los Chinos in the Nepeña Valley, for example, stone houses, the majority of them subterranean, are arranged haphazardly on the hillsides bordering the valley. Both isolated houses and complexes of dwellings were built of large irregular stones set in clay in such a way that the interior wall surfaces were even. The houses were circular, rectangular, or square, up to 1.5 meters in depth, and averaging 1.5 by 1.8 meters in area. There was a tendency to arrange the stones in the walls so as to produce ornamental geometric patterns.

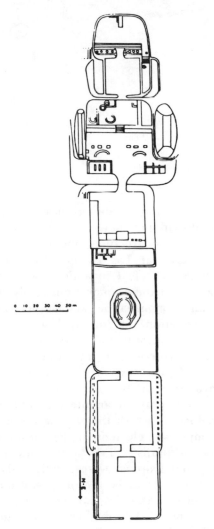

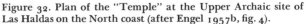

Figure 32. Plan of the "Temple" at the Upper Archaic site of Las Haldas on the North coast (after Engel 1957b, fig. 4).

The site of Las Haldas near the Casma Valley is a vast complex of living quarters and community and ceremonial centers, including some of the oldest known pyramids (Figure 32). The houses are not subterranean; they were constructed on the rocky surface with walls sufficiently strong that they have withstood the weight of the refuse that now covers them. The most important pyramid, which occupies a central location, is 465 meters long and composed of seven platforms. Las Haldas has been carbon-14 dated at 1844 ± 80 B.C. and although pottery has been found in the vicinity, Rowe (1963:5) believes that the ceramic occupation was limited in extent and that the site was a preceramic urban complex with several thousand inhabitants.

Another important site is Culebras, on the south side of a bay near a small river that is now almost dry. Architectural remains also include both habitations and public buildings. Some small quadrangular and rectangular structures, probably family dwellings, were constructed of irregular field stones laid with the flat surface toward the interior, as at Los Chinos. A slightly larger variant usually has architectural ornamentation in the form of rectangular niches on the interior walls. A third category consists of buildings of diverse forms placed on terraces faced with rocks, including large erect stones that create an ornamental effect. The terraces extend from the middle to the top of the slope surrounding the bay; at the center are large stone steps that descend from the upper terrace to the ground level. In addition, there are passages and structures of unknown use. Some houses have traces of plaster on the walls, as well as superimposed floors that indicate sequential occupations.

The site of Río Seco, north of the Chancay Valley, contains isolated groups of houses arranged in no apparent pattern. There are several mounds, but only a few contain structures. Mound 6 is the largest and is constructed of large stones, blocks of coral, and whale bones. Mound 7 is composed of various buildings, the central one being the most attractive. The wall has a rubble and clay core faced on both surfaces with clay. The entrance has a lintel composed of five beams of what appears to be maguey (*Agave americana*) and remnants indicate that the roof may also have been of beams. The interior walls are ornamented by combining adobes and stones into a patterned arrangement. Generally speaking, the site represents "a cluster of quadrangular rooms and patios joined by wide and solid walls of large stone blocks brought from the neighboring hills. . . . These walls were laid on the refuse; they are high, some measuring about 3 meters; some rooms are connected by doors with lintels of wood and stone" (Engel 1958:24). A similar type of architecture has been observed at Chira Villa near Lima, but Engel does not believe the structures here are Upper Archaic since the associated cultural remains are later.

Intensive investigations on the Central coast have permitted the recognition of three phases, differentiated primarily by changes in textiles, at several sites in the Ancón-Chillón zone (Moseley and Barrett 1969). The Playa Hermosa and Conchas phases existed between 2500 and 1900 B.C. and the Gaviota phase lasted from 1900 to 1700 B.C., the period during which pottery made its appearance in the region. All the sites are near arid beaches except El Paraíso or Chuquitanta, which is near the mouth of the Río Chillón, about two kilometers inland. Sites are small during the earliest phases, covering only a few hundred square meters; later, they occupy several hectares. Patterson (1971a, b) estimates that the population living in the area increased from about 100 persons at the beginning of the period to some 1500 by the time it ended.

The largest site yet excavated, El Paraíso, represents the Gaviota phase (Engel 1966b). It is a vast architectural complex covering 50 to 60 hectares, with agglutinated rooms and enclosures apparently used for community purposes. The constructions are of field stone laid in clay and the walls were often covered with a clay plaster. Some have simple designs incised when the plaster was dry.

Asia, another site investigated by Engel (1963b), has a carbon-14 date of 1314 ± 100 B.C. Before excavation, the portion designated as Unit I had the appearance of a small mound some 15 meters in diameter and about one meter high. Clay walls, only the lower 80 centimeters of which remained intact, formed a rectangle about 12.5 meters square, with interior rooms and an entrance toward the north (Figure 33). Burials were encountered in the subsoil. Surface evidence indicates that the total inhabited area was much larger than the excavated portion.

Generally speaking, then, the coastal horticultural villages were composed of habitations and community centers, which certainly served a ceremonial purpose. Architectural uniformity did not exist, and stone, adobe, or simple lumps of clay were employed indiscriminately. Walls were sometimes straight, sometimes curved. Houses were

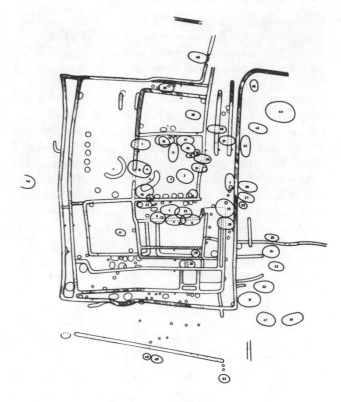

Figure 33. Plan of dwellings at the site of Asia on the Central coast (after Engel 1963b, fig. 4).

either above ground or subterranean. Most were irregularly distributed, but planning is evident in some of the public structures, among them a symmetrical building at Las Haldas that may have been a temple. The first pyramids also date from this period. All of these innovations imply changes in community organization and leadership that laid the foundation for increased social controls necessary for the production of really large labor-consuming constructions in later times.

During the Upper Archaic, the principal distinctive characteristics of Andean civilization began to take shape, not only in architecture but also in textile production, which the acquisition of cotton made an important element in the culture of the village horticulturalists. Two techniques, twining (Figure 34) and looping, were greatly elaborated. The former appears to be the older and died out at the end of the Archaic, making it an excellent diagnostic element. Looping survived into later times and was the principal technique for making nets. Spindles with wooden or stone whorls were

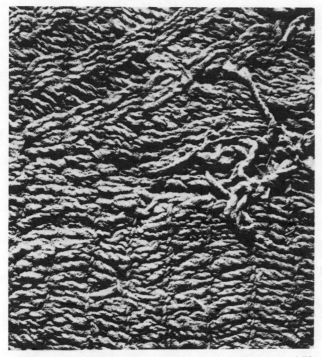

Figure 34. A twined fabric from the Upper Archaic site of El Paraíso (MUSM).

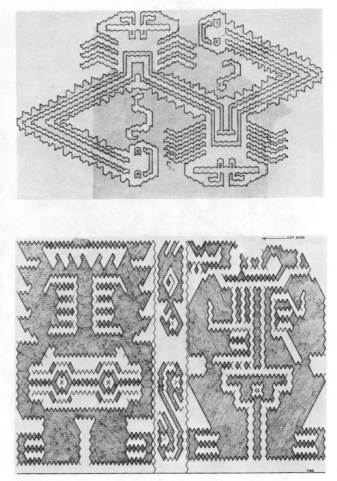

Figure 35 (*above right*). Snake-like pattern on a textile from Huaca Prieta (after Bird 1963, fig. 4).

Figure 36. Anthropomorphic design on a textile from Huaca Prieta (after Bird 1963, fig. 3).

used in the preparation of cotton fibers, and weaving tools included needles and shuttles. For twining, a bar was used to anchor the warp threads.

Varying functions are reflected in the types of textiles, which included fishing nets, blankets, bags, small mantles, and cloths resembling skirts. Turbans were made from junco fibers. Many fabrics were decorated, some by combining threads of different colors during manufacture and others by painting the finished cloth. Feathers were an additional decorative element. Geometric motifs or stylized representations of birds and snake-like creatures were most common, but figures resembling human beings or felines also occur (Figures 35, 36).

Aside from textiles, the technology of the village horticulturalists was rudimentary. Stone working declined in quality in spite of the introduction of new techniques, among them abrasion, polishing, pecking, and incising. Small axes, hammers, knives, scrapers, grinding stones, and other instruments were manufactured. Projectile points decreased in frequency and were absent in some regions. Pressure retouch was rare north of Ica. In Chicama and Virú, pebbles flaked into crude choppers were common. Metal working was unknown, but bone, shell, and wood were extensively used for a variety of implements and ornaments. Local availability of most raw materials made trade unimportant. Most of the wood that has been identified is of coastal origin rather than imported from the Amazonian forest, as some investigators have asserted. Gourds were employed as containers and sometimes decorated by incision or pyro-engraving. Basketry was well developed but less common than other kinds of weaving.

Little information is available on other forms of art. A flute associated with the body of a child at Asia gives a hint of musical development. Earrings, necklaces, bracelets, anklets, rings, mirrors, and other objects of personal adornment were abundant and attractive.

Burials provide a few insights into religious beliefs and life expectancy. The body was normally

Figure 37. Typical Mito phase structures at the site of Kotosh in the Central highlands (courtesy Seiichi Izumi).

Figure 38 (*below left*). The Temple of the Crossed Hands at Kotosh (courtesy Seiichi Izumi).

Figure 39. Wall of the Temple of the Crossed Hands, showing the hands in relief below a niche (courtesy Seiichi Izumi).

interred in a horizontal position, but occasionally flexed, and was wrapped in mats or mantles. Mummification was not practiced. Burial was near or inside the dwelling, in a shallow pit sometimes lined with stones or adobes; there was no preferred orientation. Some graves contain only skulls, while others have headless bodies. At Asia, where several skulls were found together, one had a perforation suitable for attachment of a cord possibly indicating that the trophy head concept common in later periods was already in existence. Some burials were provided with bags containing strange objects that Engel (1963a) has suggested may have had magical significance. Prominent among them are "charm stones," which may have been endowed with curative powers because of their spherical form and other peculiar characteristics. Physically, the population differed little from earlier or later groups. There are few remains of old people and many of young children, implying that death came at an early age.

Little information is available from the highlands, but excavations at the site of Kotosh in the vicinity of Huánuco have revealed a complex of ceremonial constructions associated with artifacts for hunting and gathering indicative of a Middle or Lower Archaic type of subsistence pattern (Izumi and Sono 1963). The chipped-stone industry of this Mito phase is typologically related to Lauricocha II and III, and lanceolate points are common. Unfortunately, no plant remains have been encountered, but guinea pigs were domesticated and may have been kept in the niches found in some of the walls.

Mito phase architecture is known only from the ceremonial or communal structures, which are quadrangular enclosures walled with field stone laid in clay or erect stones with straightened sides and a flat outer surface (Figure 37). In the Temple of the Crossed Hands, the walls are preserved to a sufficient height to reveal the presence of narrow vertical rectangular niches, some of which contain fragments of bones or other things that might be interpreted as offerings. Beneath two of the niches, hands—or more accurately, arms—had been modeled in clay, one crossed over the other (Figures 38, 39). At the center of each enclosure was a kind of raised frame surrounding a small patio with a central hearth, which was provided with a subterranean tube or ventilator extending from the base of the pit horizontally through the exterior wall. A trench excavated across one of these hearths revealed that it was used for long periods of time and then restored and reused. Whether the hearths served to preserve fire because of the difficulty of producing it, or were the focus of community or family gatherings, or were truly sanctuaries dedicated to fire or other powers remains unknown. Whatever the case, these structures foreshadow the appearance of sacred buildings.

The finds at Kotosh are important not only because of what they add to our general knowledge of the Archaic period, but because they are the only remains of this type yet known from the highlands or the coast. Among the distinctive features are a more integrated type of public or community architecture combined with emphasis on hunting of large animals, which caused the survival of a lithic technology characteristic of earlier periods, such as Chilca and Encanto on the coast and Chihua in the Southern highlands. No carbon-14 dates have been obtained for the Mito culture, but those for the succeeding Waira-jirka period indicate that it should be placed prior to the beginning of the second millennium B.C. Kotosh-Mito raises special problems relevant to the origin of agrarian society in the Andes, since it is certainly derived from earlier manifestations not yet discovered in the region. The proximity of the site to the eastern lowland forest and the evidence of contacts with that area during subsequent periods suggest that more attention should be paid to the possibility of interrelations with the Amazonian region at an early date than hitherto has been the case.

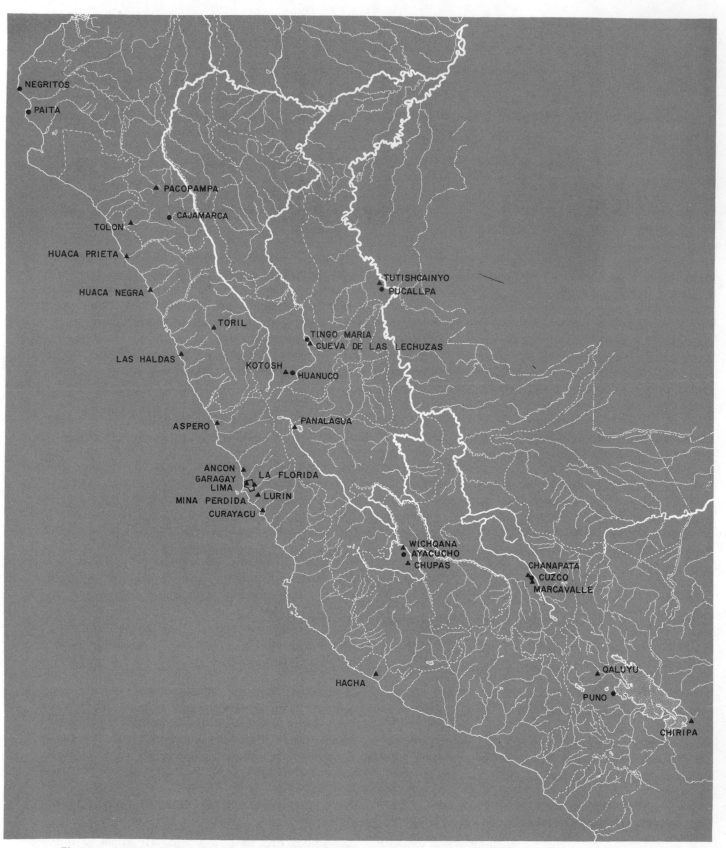

Figure 40. Location of the principal sites of the Lower Formative Period (▲ archeological site; ● modern town).

THE FORMATIVE PERIOD

1800 B.C.-A.D. 100

Before preceramic remains were discovered, reconstruction of Andean culture history began with the earliest pottery-making tradition, which was believed to have originated either from a process of independent invention or by diffusion from north of the Andes. This pottery was associated with an art style known as Chavín and appeared to have dispersed from a center in the Northern highlands. Additional discoveries produced alternative hypotheses and the interpretation that the earliest regional manifestations were similar to, but not necessarily derived from, Chavín received greatest acceptance among Peruvianists. It was recognized, however, that there was sufficient unity between regional manifestations to indicate a pan-Peruvian diffusion of certain basic general traits.

The discovery of Lithic and Archaic remains caused reappraisal of the idea of a single origin for Andean pottery, but the concept of a widespread Chavinoid epoch immediately following the Archaic was retained. It included not only complexes with Chavín elements but also certain non-Chavín manifestations superimposed on the preceramic remains on the North coast. More recently, the hypothesis of a general Chavinoid horizon in the Central Andean area has been reexamined as a result of the identification of various additional ceramic complexes that predate the diffusion of the Chavín style. As a consequence, many pottery types once labeled Chavinoid (that is, similar to or derived from Chavín) are now considered either pre-Chavín (in regions where influence from this style subsequently penetrated) or simply non-Chavín.

The complex known as Chavín is a relatively advanced Formative manifestation, which includes a group of stylized art motifs clearly associated with a highly elaborated religious cult and a number of elements closely related to Mesoamerican occurrences of approximately equivalent age. The non-Chavín or pre-Chavín Formative groups, by contrast, are stylistically and technologically heterogeneous. In the following discussion, the Formative has been divided into three stages: Lower, Middle, and Upper. The adjectives "early" and "late," which are more common in the literature, have been avoided because of their chronological implications. The Lower stage includes both pre-Chavín complexes, which are earlier than Chavín, and non-Chavín complexes, which may be pre-Chavín but are not necessarily so; the Middle stage corresponds to the diffusion of the Chavín complex and is consequently not represented where Chavinoid traits did not penetrate; the Upper stage incorporates complexes derived from both Chavín and non-Chavín antecedents.

The Lower Formative

The Lower Formative, as here defined, is not a stylistic or chronological horizon. It represents the recognition that much of the Andean area was occupied by groups possessing varying kinds of Formative culture before the spread of Chavín influence (Figure 40). Where Chavín influence did not penetrate, existing chronological data are often insufficient to differentiate pre-Chavín from non-Chavín complexes, and some of the groups in this category may turn out to be later in time. They are more comparable to pre-Chavín manifestations than to Chavinoid ones, however, and for this reason have been included in the Lower Formative. To complicate the situation further, many complexes have been described only in terms of ceramic features. Furthermore, the pottery is variable and often has been incompletely studied. As a consequence, discussion of this period is necessarily directed more toward specific finds than to the cultural context that they represent.

Toward the end of the Archaic, the first indications of pottery making began to appear on the Peruvian coast and existing evidence indicates that this introduction did not, initially at least, create a significant change in the way of life. Groups such as Valdivia (Ecuador) and Puerto Hormiga (north coast of Colombia) were manufacturing relatively simple pottery by about 3000 B.C., suggesting a center of diffusion between the Guayas coast of Ecuador and Panama. Speculations about the origin of these early ceramics are beyond the scope of this book, but it should be noted that the hypothesis of an Asiatic derivation via transpacific contact is receiving increasing support.

Although the possibility of influences from Valdivia or Puerto Hormiga on the Central Andes cannot be reliably assessed until more data are available, a ceramic complex apparently related to Valdivia has recently been encountered in the Jequetepeque Valley on the North coast. Called "Tolón" after the type site, it is characterized by crude jars with incised decoration closely similar to that from Valdivia both in technique and motif (Figure 41). In the Piura Valley, north of Chicama

Figure 41. Pottery of the Tolón style from the Jequetepeque Valley (MUSM).

and Virú, Lanning (1963b) has reported another complex he calls "Negritos," and although the evidence is limited to a handful of fragments from the surface of two sites, he postulates a relationship to Valdivia; if so, this would imply a movement from Ecuador to the south. Another early complex from the same area, called "Paita" and represented by only a few crude fragments with incised decoration, has also been assigned to the pre-Chavín period.

Other finds have been made on the eastern slopes of the Central Andes. In the Ucayali region, Lathrap (1970) has encountered ceramics that exhibit strong resemblances to the earliest complexes of northern South America. The oldest phase, Early Tutishcainyo, has been assigned an antiquity of some 3000 years based on the occurrence at the site of Kotosh in Huánuco of trade pieces associated with Kotosh period, which dates about 1000 B.C. Another type of pottery from the Cueva de las Lechuzas near Tingo María has been correlated with the pre-Kotosh Waira-jirka period (Lathrap and Roys 1963). This evidence suggests the possibility of at least two diffusional currents or origins for the pottery of the Central Andes, one along the coast and the other along the eastern slopes of the cordillera. Whatever their antecedents, all the Lower Formative complexes that will be mentioned herein belong to a fully developed ceramic stage, in spite of the fact that Rowe and his disciples classify them in their "Initial" ceramic period.

The Coast

The best-defined coastal complex is Guañape, found in the small valley of Virú on the North coast (Strong and Evans 1952). Early Guañape is characterized by predominantly plain, dark reddish brown or black pottery. As time passed, simple decoration appeared, including fingertip impressions, punctation, and incisions on applique ribs (Figure 42). Vessel shapes are few and consist principally of two varieties of rounded jars, one with a thickened rim and the other with a short, everted rim. Both have elongated bodies and rounded or conical bases; handles do not occur.

The subsistence remains and other aspects of Early Guañape culture indicate that these pottery makers were still incipient agriculturalists, and the pottery from the site of Huaca Prieta in the Chicama Valley is so primitive that it is tempting to attribute it to independent invention. Although the carbon-14 date for Early Guañape is about 1250 B.C., considerably later than dates for pottery in Ecuador, Colombia, and Panama, comparison between these complexes and Guañape reveals only very general shared features, such as fingertip impressions or poorly controlled firing, and considerably less technological control over the clay medium. Evidence for relationship is strengthened, however, by the fact that all of these complexes possess an Archaic type of subsistence economy.

Middle Guañape is characterized by a larger variety of pottery types, many of which are continuations from the preceding period and others that are new. Some of the latter are closely related to developments on the South coast and around Ancón near Lima. The ware tends to be thinner and ornamentation is more frequent; typical decoration consists of alternating plain and punctated zones separated by incised lines. Incision is a common technique and motifs are geometric; the absence of biomorphic elements differentiates this pottery from that of later periods. The few designs that have been reconstructed consist of combinations of lines delimiting abstract figures that show no affinity to the Chavín style.

Although few other Middle Guañape features are known, several suggest important differences from the preceding phase. Community structures, which were in use farther to the south during the Archaic, appear in Virú during this time to judge from the investigations by Strong and Evans (1952) at the Temple of the Llamas. This very simple rectangular structure on the summit of Huaca Negra was built of irregularly arranged field stones

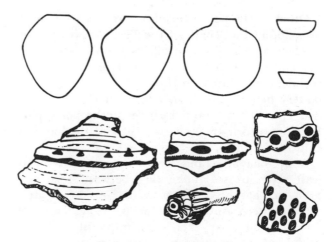

Figure 42. Vessel shapes and decorative techniques of Early Guañape pottery (after Strong and Evans 1952, figs. 45, 47, 48).

(Figure 43). Llama burials were encountered and interpreted as offerings. This marks the initial appearance of llamas on the coast, and implies close relations with the highlands. The economy may have been enriched by the addition of maize, but remains of this plant were not found in the Virú excavations.

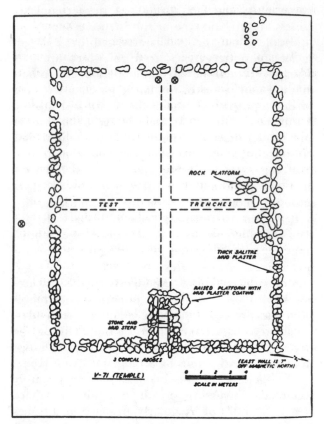

Figure 43. Plan of the Temple of the Llamas in the Virú Valley (after Strong and Evans 1952, fig. 5).

Other early pottery-making groups have since been found the length of the Peruvian coast. The most notable site on the north-central coast is Las Haldas, which also contains a large preceramic, incipient-agricultural occupation (pp. 42–43). The pottery here differs slightly from that of Guañape and Huaca Prieta, and includes anthropomorphic figurines, which are a characteristic of the Valdivia culture of Ecuador.

A pre-Chavín ceramic sequence composed of at least seven phases and dating between 1750 and 1175 B.C. has been reconstructed on the Central coast between Ancón and Lurín. More than one diffusion source appears to be responsible for the initial pottery in this zone, since sites separated by only a little more than 100 kilometers, as is the case with Ancón (Figures 44, 45) and Curayacu (Figure 46), exhibit different ceramic traditions, one decorated with incision and punctation and the other by painting. A third current is implied by the presence of polished pottery with deep groove-like incisions at La Florida in the central Rímac Valley (Patterson and Moseley 1968:119). The incised and punctate tradition, which appears at Ancón and other sites, has been called "Chira." The one with painted decoration is known as "Curayacu," while the last is termed "La Florida." A late phase of the Lower Formative in the Ancón region is identified with pottery called "Colinas." The earliest phase, known only from Ancón and characterized by crude pottery, is superimposed on remains of the Gaviota preceramic stage. The pottery from the spectacular ceremonial center of La Florida is approximately contemporaneous, dating between 1750 and 1600 B.C.

The Central coast is a region of great importance for the reconstruction of the history of ceremonial centers, since it contains both late Archaic sites such as El Paraíso and a number of important Lower Formative centers, including La Florida in Rímac, Garagay between the Rímac and Chillón valleys, Malpase and Mina Perdida in Lurín. All are artificial hills constructed of clay and irregularly shaped stones in the form of an animal, possibly a feline (Ludeña 1970). The "body" is some 10 meters in elevation, and the "head" and "tail" are lower lateral platforms. The head is toward the west, the tail toward the east, and the abdomen toward the north. The latter, which constitutes the most important part of the ceremonial center, is a region of stairways and terraces at the end of a large plaza bounded by elongated platforms that represent the legs. If the chronological placements are correct, these structures should be ancestral to Middle Formative ceremonial centers such as Chavín de Huantar, which follows the same general pattern. This type of construction continues into later times on the Central coast.

Lower Formative sites have also been identified on the South coast. The initial pottery from Hacha, with carbon-14 dates between 1297 and 997 B.C. (Rowe 1963:5), has very unusual characteristics that give it a highly elaborated aspect. Among them is negative painting, which becomes common in later periods. This term derives from the technique by which contrasting tones were produced; namely, the application of wax, grease, clay, or some other impermeable material to the surface to create the

Figure 44. Refuse stratigraphy in the Tank sector at the site of Ancón on the Central coast (courtesy Ramiro Matos Mendieta).

Below

Figure 45. Bichrome olla from Ancón (MUSM).

Right

Figure 46. Pottery figurine from Curayacu (MNAA).

motifs, after which the vessel was covered with paint, smoked, or dipped in a pigment darker than the original surface. When the resistant substance was removed, the protected areas were a lighter color than the rest of the design.

Rowe (1963:5–6) describes Hacha as a habitation site of irregular form measuring about 800 by 200 meters. There are remnants of clay-walled structures, perhaps public buildings, one of which is considered earlier than 1279 B.C. Dwellings were probably constructed of perishable materials. Shellfish were a common food, and cotton, gourds, lima beans, guava, squash, and peanuts were being cultivated by 1000 B.C. No trace of maize has been found.

In the Ica Valley, a type of pottery called "Erizo" seems to antedate Ocucaje, which developed during the Middle and Late Formative.

The Highlands

At Kotosh in the Huánuco area, near the headwaters of the Huallaga, at least three pre-Chavín phases have been recognized, the latter two of which are ceramic (Izumi and Sono 1963). The pottery of the earliest phase, called "Waira-jirca," differs both in decoration and vessel shape from the other Formative complexes known in the Andean area, and carbon-14 dates of about 1800 B.C. make it the oldest so far discovered in Peru. Open vessels, resembling cups and vases, predominate, but stirrup-spout jars also occur and constitute the first appearance in the Cenral Andes of this form, which was later to become highly popular. Tripods and tetrapods are also represented. Bands of fine parallel incised lines filled with red, white, or yellow pigment after firing are the diagnostic type of decoration (Figure 47). Another method of achieving contrast was through excision, in which part of the surface was removed to produce differences in elevation. Waira-jirca architecture follows the pattern of earlier periods at Kotosh, which featured platforms with walls of field stone or cobbles covered with mud plaster. Houses were semicircular or rectangular.

The Kotosh period, which follows Waira-jirca, is characterized ceramically by decoration emphasizing broader incisions and large punctates filled with red, white, or yellow pigment after firing (Figure 48). Another common technique was painting with graphite on a red-slipped surface. Figurative motifs begin to appear, principally anthropomorphic rep-

resentations. During this period, at least two major currents can be detected. The most recent contains a number of Chavín elements, among them wide-necked bottles and a type of incised decoration exemplified by a depiction of a maize ear, which Coe (1962) has compared with Olmec designs from Mesoamerica. Kotosh pottery is associated with architecture similar to that of the preceding Waira-jirca period.

Little is known of the subsistence economy of either complex, but it could well have been sedentary agriculture. It is assumed that maize was grown during the Kotosh period, at least in its latter part (a deduction based on the pottery design just mentioned). The studies of faunal remains by Wing and Ueno (Wing 1972) indicate an increase in domesticated animals in proportion to game, especially evident in the relative abundances of cameloids and cervids.

Waira-jirca pottery is too highly elaborated to be considered an initial stage and presupposes the existence of earlier complexes. Its discoverers (Izumi and Sono 1963) attribute it to a forest affiliation, a hypothesis that has also been supported by Lathrap (1958) on the basis of discoveries at Pucallpa and Tingo María, both forested localities. Tutishcainyo pottery, encountered in the lowest levels at Pucallpa, resembles Waira-jirca-Kotosh ceramics stylistically and technologically, and Tutishcainyo trade pieces are associated with these pre-Chavín phases at the Kotosh site. Pottery from the Cueva de las Lechuzas near Tingo María also exhibits a number of close resemblances to Waira-jirca. The most notable similarities are in vessel shape, techniques of incision, and post-fired painting in several colors, and emphasis on geometric motifs (Figure 49).

North of Huánuco in the Cajamarca region, the Reichlens (1949) have reported a Formative occupation that they call "Torrecitas-Chavín." Although the remains are qualitatively and quantitatively limited, they apparently constitute a complex different from Chavín. Post-fired painting in several colors, predominantly geometric decoration, and plate and cup shapes are ceramic features possibly related to the pre-Chavín complexes at Kotosh, although with the notable difference that Torrecitas painting covers large areas rather than fills the incisions. Recently, Rosas LaNoire and Shady Solís (1970) have found a ceramic complex at Pacopampa, east of Cajamarca, that they assign to the pre-Chavín period in spite of the presence of some

Chavín stylistic features. If they are correct in their interpretation, Pacopampa may represent an incipient expression of the Chavín complex.

At least two phases apparently antecedent to Chavín have been encountered in the Ayacucho region of the Central highlands and tentatively designated as "Andamarca" and Wichqana." Wichqana is characterized by thin, brown, pebble-polished pottery with little decoration. Andamarca pottery is orangeish, thick, and shows vestiges of red paint. (For additional comments on these tentative complexes, see pp. 70, 80).

Two Formative cultures are also known from the Southern Peruvian highlands: Chanapata in Cuzco and Qaluyu in Puno. Both have been considered late on the supposition that they were derived from Chavín. Neither shows any relationship to Chavín, however, and a carbon-14 date for Qaluyu places it about 1000 B.C. Chanapata pottery is black or red and thick; straight-walled vessels and rounded,

Figure 47. Waira-jirca pottery with zoned-hachure decoration.

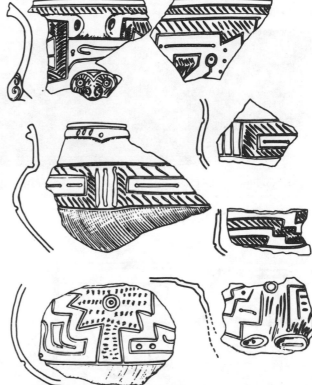

Figure 49. Pottery with zoned-hachure decoration from the Cueva de las Lechuzas (after Lathrap and Roys 1963).

Figure 48. Kotosh bowls with incised and punctate decoration.

neckless jars with flat bottoms are typical shapes (Rowe 1944). Decoration is by burnishing, painting, or incisions filled with pigment after firing (Figures 50, 51). Motifs consist principally of circles and other geometric forms, animal figures resembling the fox, the frog, and the monkey, and occasional human representations. Large zoomorphic adornos were employed for decoration of the vessel surface, rims, or handles. Pottery figurines occur (Figure 52). The dead were interred in a flexed position in circular pits dug in village refuse. During excava-

tions, a llama burial reminiscent of the Middle Guañape find on the North coast was encountered.

Marcavalle, a site in the province of Cuzco, is considered to be anterior to Chanapata (Rowe, pers. comm.). Excavation was conducted by Luis Barreda Murillo and a group of students from the University of Cuzco, who encountered pottery related to Chanapata but with more emphasis on painted decoration, including a metallic paint reminiscent of the graphite-painted pottery from Kotosh. Associated with Marcavalle and Chanapata

Figure 50. Bowl of the Chanapata style (collection of J. Yábar, Cuzco).

Figure 52. Pottery figurine from Chanapata; height about 6 cm (MUSM).

Figure 51. Incised and relief decoration of the Chanapata style of Cuzco (after Rowe 1944).

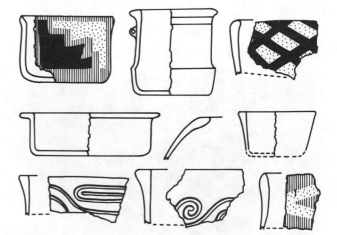

Figure 53. Vessel shapes and decorative techniques of the Qaluyu style (after Lumbreras and Amat 1968, fig. 1).

is a type of pottery painted with cream on a reddish surface; it is known as "Paqallamoqo" and believed to be later than the other two styles.

Farther south, on the west side of Lake Titicaca, Manuel Chávez Ballón has reported a relatively early complex known as Qaluyu. According to Rowe (1956), its distribution extends nearly to Cuzco. Bowls and plates are embellished with broad incisions forming geometric patterns on a coarse, dark-red or black surface. Other vessels are painted with black bands on a cream or red surface. Motifs are also geometric and resemble those from Cuzco (Figure 53). Shapes of plain vessels are like those of Chanapata and Marcavalle pottery. The type site appears to have been an agglutinated village.

In the interior of Bolivia, between La Paz and Oruro, there developed a very important complex known as "Wankarani" (Ponce Sanginés 1970). In addition to a rather coarse kind of plain pottery, it possesses an important new element: copper. The

date of 1200 to 1000 B.C. makes this the oldest copper-using region in South America. Small solid pottery figurines are another distinctive feature. They are very crude, flattened, and have anthropomorphic features indicated by incisions and low relief. In some examples, the eyes are of the "coffee-bean" type; in others, both eyes and mouth are incised. The hands are sometimes in relief, with incisions defining the fingers. The feet and legs may be separated or barely suggested. The sites producing these elements are small peasant villages in the páramo, a zone that seems better suited for stock-raising than agriculture. Hunting was important, to judge from the abundance of projectile points. Form is predominantly triangular, with a pronounced basal notch, although some are stemmed; the majority are very small. Stones bearing the sculptured figures of cameloids have been found, but their association with these sites is not clear as yet. Stone hoes have also been found.

The Middle Formative: Spread of Chavín Culture

By the end of the still obscure Lower Formative stage, the inhabitants of the Andean region had developed a stable agricultural economy that permitted the establishment of more cohesive villages, a religious system associated with pyramidal ceremonial centers, and a notable advance in all aspects of technology. About 800 B.C., a highly developed art style and cult, known to archeologists as Chavín, diffused over most of the Central Andes (Figure 54).

The appearance and expansion of Chavín raises serious problems for the reconstruction of Peruvian prehistory. The first to perceive this was Tello (1929, 1942), who considered it to be a culture of forest origin that had achieved its full development on the margins of the Río Marañon before expanding throughout the Andean area. As subsequent work by many archeologists in Mexico and Peru increased our knowledge, first Spinden (1917) and later Strong (1943) suggested the possibility of Mesoamerican-Andean relationships, an interpretation that is meeting with increasing acceptance. In Mesoamerica, there was a similar cultural expan-

sion during the Formative Period, during which Olmec elements were superimposed on Lower Formative groups. The fact that many of the traits characteristic of Olmec also occur in Chavín and the general contemporaneity of the Mesoamerican period of expansion (around 1000 B.C.) with the emergence of Chavín strengthen the case for influence from the north.

On the subsistence level, the Middle Formative probably represented a continuation of earlier practices, including intensification of dependence on agriculture. Maize became the basic ingredient in the diet and, although emphasis on marine resources remained strong on the coast, cultivated plants became increasingly popular there as well as in the highlands. The many varieties of cucurbits and gourds, along with chili peppers, lima beans, common beans, cotton, and other cultigens known since the Archaic, persisted and increased in diversity. New plants introduced at this time include sweet manioc (*Manihot utilissima*) and peanuts (*Arachis hypogea*), which may have been brought from the eastern forested region. The tree tomato (*Solanum muricatum*,

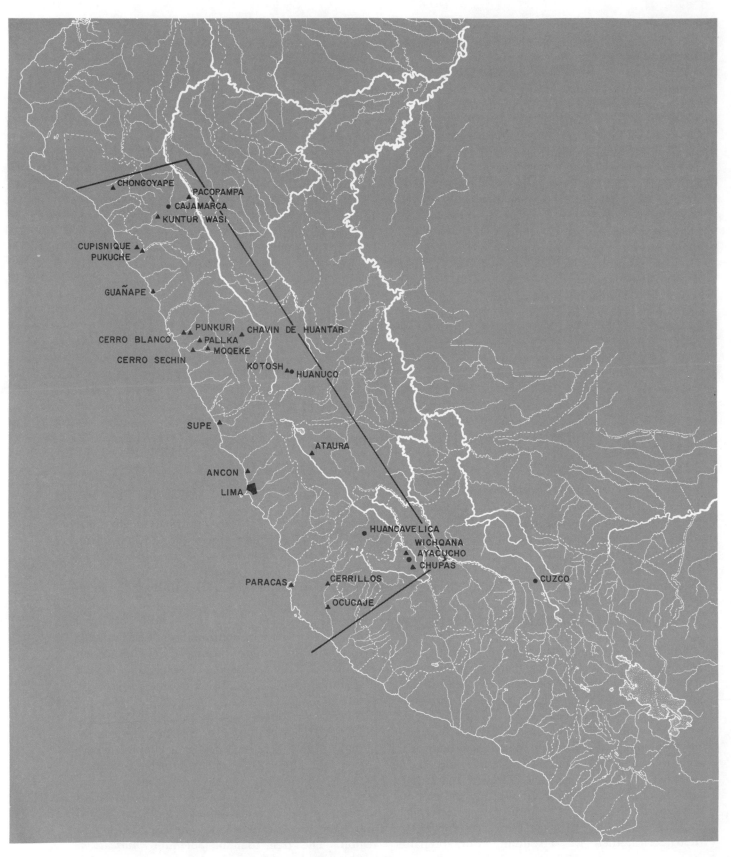

Figure 54. Location of the principal sites of the Middle Formative and the geographical extent of Chavín influence (▲ archeological site; ● modern town).

Cyphomandra splendens) and jíquima (*Pachyrryzus tuberosus*), whose presence during the Archaic is still doubtful, were also well established. Highland plants, such as the potato (*Solanum tuberosum, Solanum goniocalyx*), olluco (*Ullucus tuberosus*), mashwa (*Tropaeolum tuberosum*), oca (*Oxalis tuberosa*), quinoa (*Chenopodium quinoa*), and cañiwa (*Chenopodium pallidicaule*), became integrated with other domesticates, notably enriching the diet of both highland and coastal populations. The sweet potato (*Ipomoea batatas*) was probably cultivated by this time, although this remains to be proved. Unfortunately, traces of these plants in the archeological record are few, so that the time of their domestication is often conjectural. In general, however, the Middle Formative population appears to have utilized most of the plants being consumed when the Spanish arrived in the Andean area. Methods of cultivation are poorly known, but the possibility that some form of irrigation was practiced cannot be discounted. The large number of cultivated plants alone implies that agricultural techniques were more advanced than in earlier periods.

Agriculture continued to be supplemented by hunting, gathering, and fishing. Chavinoid refuse at Cerrillos contains bones of llama, highland fox, dog, and guinea pig (Wallace 1962:312), and marine mollusks, sea urchins, and other produce of the sea are characteristic of many Chavinoid sites near the shore. Certain shells of the genera *Mytilus* and *Pecten* were apparently highly valued, perhaps for magic purposes, to judge from their occurrence in places as far inland as Chavín and even Kotosh, some 300 kilometers from the ocean. The earliest evidence of the domesticated dog comes from this period.

Projectile points are highly variable both in form and technique of manufacture. Obsidian was employed in some areas, while chalcedony or slate was preferred in others. Both stemmed and unstemmed forms occur, although the majority tend to be triangular or lanceolate, with or without a basal notch. Manufacture is generally by coarse pressure retouch.

The population appears to have increased considerably as a consequence of the diversification in subsistence resources and nearly all the coastal and highland valleys were settled. Dwellings of perishable materials were generally constructed near the fields, on the slopes bordering the valleys, and a typical village consisted of 20 to 30 irregularly spaced houses. In the Virú Valley, some dwellings

have up to six rooms, but those with one or two are most common (Figure 55). Rooms were rectangular or semicircular and walls were constructed of irregular stones set in mud. Adobes were also used, a conical form being characteristic. Gabled roofs are shown on pottery vessels, implying a highland origin for this architectural feature, since the absence of rain makes it unnecessary on the coast.

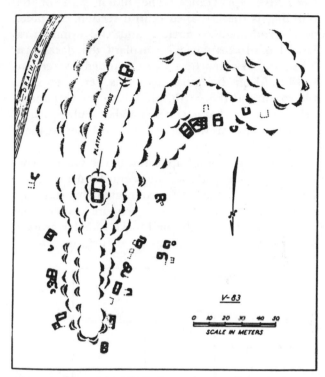

Figure 55. Plan of the Middle Formative site of V-83 in the Virú Valley (after Willey 1953, fig. 7).

The distinctive innovation in settlement pattern was not village location or architecture, neither of which differ notably from those of earlier times, but rather the appearance of large centers with magico-religious functions. It was during the Middle Formative that the most important of these were developed, from the standpoint both of architectural beauty and the amount of labor that must have been involved. This statement remains valid in spite of the possibility that ceremonial centers antedated the appearance of Chavín in the strict sense of the term.

Chavín de Huantar

The best known ceremonial center is Chavín de Huantar, located 3177 meters above sea level at the junction of the Mosna and the Wacheksa, two small tributaries of the Río Marañon. (Figure 54). The central building, known as the Castillo, is made up of four sections that appear to have been constructed during different periods. It is 15 meters high and consists of superimposed platforms. Beam-like stone blocks worked into a parallelepiped form were set horizontally in clay mortar. Alternating rows of large and small stones give the walls a distinctive appearance. The oldest part of the building is the U-shaped central section, composed of a quadrangular nucleus and two symmetrical lateral platforms enclosing a plaza that faces east. This primary structure was expanded by sections until solid quadrangular platforms were created on the south and the north, producing the asymmetrical form that characterizes it today. Subsequently, a final platform was added east of the northern structure (Figure 56).

In spite of its solid appearance, the Castillo contains numerous galleries and compartments at different levels, which are connected by stairways (Figure 57). The space between one gallery and another was filled with small rocks and clay, worked stones being reserved for exposed surfaces. The in-terior galleries were provided with square tubes that could have served for ventilation since they link the galleries with one another and with the exterior. Rectangular niches of different sizes also occur. The ceilings consist of large stone blocks; generally, one or more rows of stones project from the upper wall for improved support, giving some of the galleries a pseudo-gothic aspect (Figure 58). Most passages are narrow, measuring slightly over a meter, although some larger compartments occur. Many of the walls must have been plastered and painted, since clearing along the base has revealed earth with traces of red and yellow pigment. Some of the beams in an isolated cell corresponding to a phase subsequent to the construction of the initial U-shaped temple are decorated with incised and red-painted figures. One is a fish with felinic characteristics and there are four examples of another animal, which may be shrimp.

The temple was originally adorned with sculptures on both exterior and interior and a large number of carvings have been found in the vicinity (Figure 59). All undoubtedly had religious significance and some appear to have been executed for

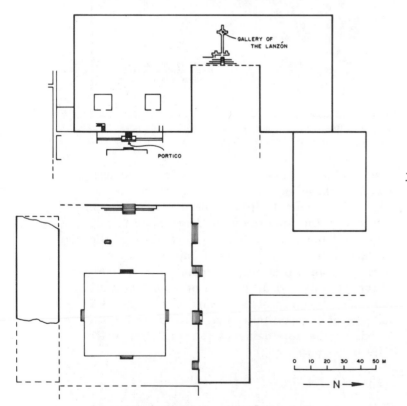

Figure 56. Plan of the site of Chavín de Huantar (after Lumbreras 1970).

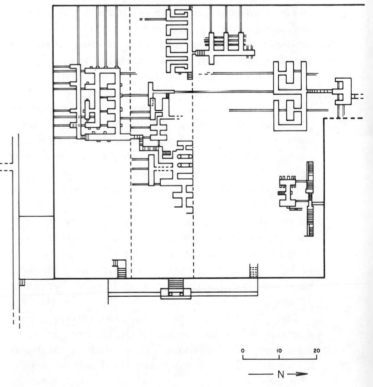

Figure 57. Plan of the galleries in the Castillo at Chavín de Huantar (after Lumbreras 1970).

Figure 58. Views of the galleries inside the temple at Chavín de Huantar.

Figure 59. Cornice with a feline design in Chavín style.

this purpose alone; the majority, however, were an integral part of the architectural context, serving either as ornament on the wall or as a functional part of the building. In addition, some of the galleries served as depositories for offerings of artifacts and animal bones. During exploration of the Gallery of the Offerings, for example, several hundred pottery vessels, llama, guinea pig, and fish bones, and marine shells (transported at least 150 kilometers, over a route requiring the crossing of two cordilleras) were discovered. The pottery, which was mostly in fragments, is extremely well made and exquisitely decorated.

In the most ancient sector are two groups of superimposed galleries laid out in the general form of a cross. The center of the lower gallery contains a sculptured stone 4.53 meters long with a peculiar shape resembling a lance or a knife, leading to its designation as the "Lanzón." The surface is almost completely covered with the highly stylized figure of an anthropomorphized feline, which must have represented an important deity in the Chavín cult (Figure 61). The creature is standing with the right arm raised and the left one along the side. Fingers and toes terminate in claws and the face is markedly felinic. The thick lips are elevated toward the corners, a large tusk protrudes over the lower lip, and the nose projects only slightly. The eyebrows and hair are depicted as serpents, while each ear bears a large ornament. The costume terminates in a fringe that does not completely cover the legs. Both the waist and the "handle" of the Lanzón are ornamented with the heads of felines, all of which have the pupils looking upward in typical Chavín style. The deity faces eastward, toward the entry to the chamber. The "handle" projects into the ceiling and must protrude into the second floor, if the channel that passes through the whole eastern portion of the structure and terminates in a small hole just above the head of the god can be assumed to have had some associated function. Although this image has been referred to as the "Smiling God" (Rowe 1962:19), it is more probably a "Cruel God" since, as Tello (1960:176) once noted, the treatment of the mouth suggests the threatening snarl of a wild beast. It is best, consequently, to

Figure 60 (left). The Raimondi Stela from Chavín de Huantar (after Lumbreras 1970:51). Figure 61 (center). The Lanzón in its original position in one of the galleries at Chavín de Huantar (courtesy Pestana). Figure 62 (right). The Tello Obelisk from Chavín de Huantar (after Lumbreras 1970:82).

label him the "Irritated God," if one wishes to give him a name.

Other galleries probably also once contained sculptures with cult significance, but few, unfortunately, have remained in place. In addition to the Lanzón, at least two other equally important sculptures have been found: the Raimondi Stela and the Tello Obelisk.

The Raimondi stone (Figure 60) was discovered many years ago and brought to Lima, but its form indicates that it must once have been attached to a wall. The carving resembles that on the Lanzón in depicting an erect, anthropomorphized feline with a large, rectangular head and outstretched arms, holding a kind of staff in each hand. Fingers and toes are clawed. The mouth has four curved projecting tusks and thick lips, the extremes of which are turned downward in contrast to those of the divinity shown on the Lanzón. The nose is barely perceptible and the eyes have upward-directed pupils. The hair is represented by serpents and two serpents emanate from each side of the belt (the "Smiling God" has only one at each side). Above the head is a long and complicated series of designs resembling a headdress with radiations. The lower ends of the staffs terminate in feline heads, while the upper portions are covered with a harmonious combination of volutes, eyes, noses, tusks, and serpent heads that forms an intricate pattern of great sensitivity. Rowe (1962:20) has called this person the "Staff God" and believes that it may have replaced the "Smiling God" when the new temple was constructed.

The Tello Obelisk (Figure 62) was discovered by Tello outside the Castillo precinct near the great plaza, which must have been constructed more recently than the temple in which the Lanzón is located. Rowe (1962:12) places this sculpture earlier than the Raimondi Stela and later than the Lanzón. The stone is long, rectangular in cross-section, slightly cut back at the upper end, and decorated over the entire surface with an extremely complicated pattern. The principal figure is not anthropomorphic and has several highly stylized reptilian characteristics. The face, shown in profile, has a U-shaped mouth with four tusks projecting downward from the upper lip. Ornaments hang from the ears; the nose is barely perceptible. Heads of felines, serpents, and tusks cover the neck. The body consists of a variety of elements. On the upper part, among the most distinct are an anthropomorphic figure, a bat-like creature, feline and serpent heads

associated with vegetal elements, and representations of flowers, plants, stems, and fruits. On the lower part of the body is an anthropomorphic figure with a radiating headdress, similar to symbols of the sun, and with very large tusks; it is shown in a flying position. In the genital region is the mouth of an anthropomorphic feline, from which issues a plant with multiple branches; each branch has eyes and terminates in claws. Among other recognizable elements is a *Spondylus* shell, the upper part of which resembles a serpent head. Alongside the body, near the neck, are a feline, a bird, and a fish, as well as serpents and other less readily identifiable designs. The two faces of the monolith contain very similar but not identical figures, leading Tello to infer that two aspects of the same deity are depicted, one male and the other female.

Other examples of Chavín stone carvings include small quadrangular or rectangular slabs (Figure 63), similar in form to the Raimondi Stela and depicting distinctive personages ranging from anthropomorphic beings to serpents, with the most common motifs being condors or falcons, felines, and idealized human figures. In most cases, treatment is essentially the same as that already described, although in a few cases the representations are more realistic and less burdened with ornamentation. These slabs must have been incorporated into walls, perhaps on the facade of the building.

Figure 63. Block engraved with a stylized bat design.

Figure 64. Tenoned heads from Chavín de Huantar showing position in the wall and diversity of anthropomorphic and zoomorphic treatment.

Figure 65. Bas-relief falcons from Chavín de Huantar.

Another type of sculpture consists of large heads that were attached to the exterior wall of the temple, and which are commonly known as "tenoned heads" (Figure 64). These heads are the only three-dimensional sculptures known from Chavín de Huantar, the typical technique being a two-dimensional treatment emphasizing planes. They appear in humanized, bird-like, and other animal forms, but the great majority have the curved tusks of a feline or serpent. The hair is sometimes transformed into snakes.

Cornices, columns, and (rarely) ceiling beams were also decorated. The cornice ornamentation is similar to that on the stelae, but the sculptured areas are smaller. One famous piece shows eight falcons, seven facing one direction and one the opposite direction (Figure 65). This stone, together

Figure 66. The principal pyramid at Chavín de Huantar.

Figure 67. Portico with cylindrical columns at the entry to the principal pyramid at Chavín de Huantar.

with others recently discovered that contain six more falcons matching the single "contrary" one on the first stone, formed the lintel of a lovely portico on the largest pyramid (Figure 66). This lintel rested on two cylindrical columns, each bearing the ornate image of a gigantic and very ferocious falcon (Figures 67, 69). Other columns and lintels with feline images, known only from fragments, were placed at the entry to the stone staircases that provided access to the various platforms in the great ceremonial center. Viewed as a whole, the representations engraved on the stones of Chavín de Huantar suggest the existence of a complicated cult based principally on the feline, with serpents and birds as secondary elements.

Area of Chavín Influence

The importance of Chavín de Huantar does not lie in its antiquity, since it was not the earliest ceremonial center in the Central Andes, but in its religious sophistication and profound influence. The most complex world images of the time were apparently synthesized here and disseminated over a large area. Both processes were probably facilitated by its location at the junction of trails from the coast, the highland, and the forest—distinct regions whose integration was a basic factor in stimulating Central Andean cultural development.

Chavinoid structures have been found in several other parts of the Central Andes (Figure 54). In the North highlands, the most typical site is La Copa (also known as Kuntur Wasi), located in the Cajamarca zone. A temple of possible pyramidal form has been discovered here, along with characteristic Chavín sculptures and three-dimensional statues of felinized human beings, which have not been found at Chavín de Huantar (Figure 68). The temple located on a hilltop above the modern village of San Pablo, consists of three superimposed platforms constructed with irregular stones. It is probable that a complex of ceremonial structures formerly

Figure 68. Carved stone head from Kuntur Wasi (MNAA).

Figure 69. Rolled-out falcon design on one of the cylindrical columns at Chavín de Huantar.

Figure 70. Structures at Pacopampa in the North highlands.

existed on the summit. Pacopampa, east of Caja-marca, is another ceremonial center with super-imposed terraces, columns, and megalithic walls comparable to those at Chavín (Figure 70). It may be earlier than Chavín de Huantar.

The most important coastal centers are located in the valleys of Nepeña and Casma, while in more populous valleys, such as Chicama, only structures of secondary importance are known. This situation seems likely to reflect hierarchical considerations, since each Chavinoid ceremonial center appears to have served a relatively extensive region, which on the coast probably consisted of one or two entire valleys. The state of archeological investigation may also be a factor, however, since few coastal Peruvian valleys have been intensively surveyed (Figure 71). For example, a lovely temple, known as "Huaca de los Reyes" and decorated with Chavinoid motifs, has recently been discovered in the Moche Valley by Luis Watanabe and Michael Moseley (pers. comm.).

The temple of Cerro Blanco in the center of the Nepeña Valley is a solid platform of conical adobes and stones about 15 meters high, on the summit of which several compartments with ornamented walls were constructed. The decoration emphasizes typi-cal Chavín felines, in this case modeled in clay and painted. The temple of Punkurí, in the same valley,

consists of a platform of lower elevation (about 2.4 meters), also built of conical adobes. Its most notable feature is a clay sculpture of a rather realis-tic feline with Chavinoid characteristics.

There are several ceremonial centers in the Casma Valley. The most important is Moqeke, a solid pyramid some 30 meters high, built of stones and conical adobes and covered with clay. When it was cleared by Tello, a number of niches were revealed that contained clay sculptures representing anthropomorphic creatures, unfortunately incom-plete. They had been painted in several colors, in-cluding red, blue, white, black, and emerald green. Between the niches was a complex representation of unidentifiable composition in which only four personages were distinguishable; they were standing or seated, wearing fringed costumes, and holding serpents or something similar in their hands. Two small niches contained sculptured human heads. Other niches (and probably also the sculptures) must have been relatively large. Existing dimen-sions are about 4 meters wide and 2 meters deep; height is unknown. Another ceremonial center in the Casma Valley is Pallka. It, too, is a stepped pyramid constructed of stone and measures 25 meters high; the base is 105 by 222 meters. It has produced the best examples of Chavín pottery from the valley.

Figure 71. Chavín-style sculptures executed in clay at the site of Huaca de los Reyes in the Moche Valley (courtesy M. E. Moseley and Luis Watanabe).

Another ceremonial center in the Casma Valley has been a focus of speculation because of its unusual nature. This is Cerro Sechín, a site undoubtedly related to Chavín, but resembling it in a way that suggests it may be of somewhat earlier date. It may even have been initiated during the Lower Formative, although it appears to have been used and remodeled in post-Chavín times also. The discovery of a stone engraved with the figure of a warrior led Tello to undertake a large excavation in one of the platforms that must have formed part of a pyramidal structure. This brought to light a considerable number of carved stones of irregular shape and varying size, and the position in which they were found indicated that large and small ones alternated in the sustaining wall of the platform. The small stones are usually rectangular or quadrangular, while the large ones tend to be rectangular with an irregularly shaped top. The figures are not executed in the style of the Chavín stelae (Figure 72). Entire human beings in different postures cover the larger stones and appear to represent war-

a

b

c

Figure 72. Engravings at Cerro Sechín in the Casma Valley. *a–b*. Human figures on stone blocks forming the west wall. *c*. Fish carved in a plastered wall and painted (courtesy Lorenzo Samaniego).

riors. The small stones (and also some of the large ones) depict trophy heads, human heads or parts of human bodies. The complex as a whole seems to focus on aspects of warfare or rites involving dismemberment of human beings; almost all parts of the body—legs, arms, bones, eyes, etc.—are shown, along with warriors and what appear to be two banners, which were placed like columns at the central access to the temple. One of the interior walls behind the platform bears a naturalistic figure of a feline, reminiscent of the sculptured representation at Punkurí and the incised one from the temple at Chavín de Huantar.

The southern limit of Chavín influence is the Ayacucho region. The Chupas pyramid, discovered by José Casafranca, is an artificial mound of large stones secured by a sustaining wall of the type employed in several coastal pyramids. At Wichqana, also in Ayacucho Province, there is another ceremonial structure (Figure 73), apparently in the form of a U, constructed of stones alternating in size like those at Sechín but smaller and lacking engravings. Skulls of decapitated women were associated and exhibit the fronto-occipital or tabular erecta deformation typical of the Chavín period.

These ceremonial centers attest to the importance of religion during the Middle Formative Period. They reflect the development of cult forms along with the increased prominence of the priestly caste, which subsequently played a notable role in the social, economic, and political structure. It is

Figure 73. Portion of a ceremonial enclosure at Wichqana during excavation.

possible that by this time the priesthood had already become influential and that in addition to religious duties, priestly functions may have involved control of certain kinds of labor related to irrigation, cultivation, and other activities. The position of priests as full-time specialists would also have entitled them to certain privileges.

Chavinoid Ceramics

A significant aspect of the Chavín cult was the emphasis placed on the artistic and technological expression of religious elements. This tendency is especially pronounced in ceramics and Chavinoid pottery is distinguished by extraordinary workmanship. Plastic techniques of decoration received primary emphasis and only exceptionally was a color like red or silvery-black (graphite) employed. Contrasts were obtained either by covering portions of the surface with incision, stamping, or some other textural embellishment or by modeling. The pottery from the interior galleries at Chavín has been classified into two phases, which have been called "Rocas" and "Ofrendas" (Lumbreras and Amat 1965–1966). The Rocas phase, generally considered as "classic" Chavín, is characterized by a well elaborated but somewhat coarse pottery (Figure 74), whereas Ofrendas ware is fine and graceful. Recent excavations at Chavín indicate that Ofrendas is earlier than Rocas, contrary to what was previously believed.

Ofrendas, the highland counterpart of Cupisnique, is represented by a larger number of pottery types and greater elaboration within each type than exists in subsequent phases. The three most diagnostic are (1) Wacheqsa, (2) a polished gray type, and (3) a fine black type. Wacheqsa is a red ware with silvery-black (graphite) paint, which corresponds generally to Transitional Cupisnique (Larco Hoyle 1941, 1945b). The paint was applied to cover zones, which were frequently bounded by narrow incisions made when the paste was dry. The polished gray and fine black types are characteristically Chavín in treatment, in the sense that (as in the stone medium) decoration was accomplished by variations in relief, produced either by incision or modeling (Figure 75). Stamps were not used, but rocker stamping was a common method of producing textural contrasts between decorated areas (Figure 76). The motifs are the same as those on stone, with predominance of bird and feline representations. The most common vessel forms are

Figure 74. Chavín pottery bowl of the Rocas style (MUSM).

straight-sided bowls with flat or slightly rounded bottoms and bottles with straight spouts. The stirrup spout is typical only of the Wacheqsa type (Figure 77). Another style, known as "Raku" (Figure 78), exhibits extraordinarily close affinities to Cupisnique. In the chronology at Chavín, the stirrup spout is a late feature, indicating introduction from another area, which may have been the Cupisnique region of the coast.

Rocas pottery occurs in three principal varieties: (1) a red type decorated with broad incisions painted with graphite, generally associated with large thick-walled vessels more than 50 centimeters in diameter; (2) a fine, well-polished, black type with stamped designs in the form of stylized felines, circles, dots, etc., sometimes filled with pigment, and associated with straight-walled bowls having thickened beveled rims, ollas with an interiorly thickened (comma-shaped) rim, and rarely with bottle; and (3) a polished gray or black type decorated in a variety of techniques, including incision, stamped rings (often concentric), and prominent relief representations of felines and other animals; the characteristic vessel is a bottle with a small, broad, stirrup spout terminating in a flange rim, which sometimes extends a centimeter beyond the adjacent wall. A plain band bordered by incisions usually occurs on the interior (underside) of the stirrup. During the Rocas phase, most of the bottles were apparently decorated with relief figures; plain bottles have thick straight spouts that also terminate in a flange rim that is beveled toward the exterior.

Outside of Chavín de Huantar, the best described pottery is that known as "Cupisnique" or "coastal Chavín," whose center of distribution is the Chicama Valley on the North coast. The most common vessels are flat-based, globular-bodied jars with stirrup spouts (Figure 79), but a variety of modeled figures sometimes substituted for the globular body (Figure 80). Typical stylized Chavín representations occur along with highly naturalistic depictions (Figure 81). In Chicama, the Cupisnique artists modeled aquatic and terrestrial animals, as well as houses and other cultural elements. In addition to stirrup-spout jars, a great variety of plate, bowl, vase, jar, and other vessel forms was produced, with or without decoration. The excellent quality of the workmanship indicates both great technological control and notable esthetic perception.

It is obvious that the Ofrendas and Cupisnique potters belonged to different populations, although they may have been contemporary and consequently able to copy each other's forms and motifs (Figure 82); the same kind of relationship must have existed between the potters of the Rocas phase and those from Chongoyape, since these two ceramic complexes also have much in common. Rocas appears to follow Ofrendas in the highlands, and Chongoyape should consequently be later than Cupisnique on the coast. Since Chongoyape is a valley north of Chicama, this temporal correlation can be interpreted as evidence of successive periods of expansion of Chavín influence.

At a time intermediate between the Ofrendas and Rocas phases, the potters of Cajamarca, who were the builders of the temple of La Copa (Kuntur Wasi), developed an art that does not equal Cupisnique but nevertheless exhibits a notable elaboration in plastic ornamentation. The Cajamarcans, like the peoples of Chicama and Chavín, followed the basic pattern of vessel shape, design, and technique diagnostic of the period. The presence of many local features, however, implies a freedom of morphological expression that probably reflects a certain degree of independence between regional social groups.

During their dissemination, Chavín elements met with varying kinds of receptions. At Kotosh, their intrusion had little effect on the local ceramic tradition and is reflected principally in a complex of finer ceremonial pottery, closely related to the Rocas phase at Chavín but with a few Ofrendas elements. In the Casma Valley and also in Huarmey, by contrast, the pattern was closely similar to that at Chavín.

Farther to the south, on the Central coast, Early Ancón-Supe pottery also exhibits strong individuality, perhaps as a consequence of influence from the vigorous preexisting ceramic tradition. Nevertheless,

the Ofrendas-Rocas sequence is repeated with considerable fidelity, in spite of the fact that Central coast Chavín pottery is very austere and lacks even incipient modeling. The preferred decorative technique was stamping, along with incision for the delimitation of zones.

Middle Formative complexes are just beginning to be recognized in the Central highlands. Chavín elements have been reported, particularly at the site of Chupas south of Ayacucho. The southern limit of Chavinoid influence seems to be between the departments of Ayacucho and Ica, where a largely independent local complex emerged. In the coastal valley of Ica, not only the pottery but the entire cultural assemblage appears to be independent of Chavín. For this reason, its inclusion by Tello in his "Chavín stratum" has been rejected by many specialists. More recent investigators have verified Tello's hypothesis, however, by demonstrating a long history of development of the Paracas style from undisputably Chavín antecedents. Rowe (1962) has even presented stages correlated with the lithic art from Chavín de Huantar.

Paracas pottery possesses an important vessel shape foreign to other Chavinoid complexes; namely, the double-spout and bridge handle. This may have been a local pre-Chavín invention or it may reflect influences from Tutishcainyo in the eastern lowlands. Aside from this vessel form, the most distinctive feature is emphasis on polychrome decoration. In its initial form, however, Paracas pottery contains a number of diagnostic Chavinoid elements, among them globular, stirrup-spouted jars, broad incision to delimit decorated zones, and designs copied with considerable fidelity from Chavín art (Figure 83). With the passage of time, a series of alterations occurs that culminates in a very different style. In motif, there is a trend toward realism in which symbolic elements are converted into increasingly more accurate representations of natural forms. Menzel, Rowe, and Dawson (1964) have divided the evolution of Ica ceramics into ten phases, of which the first eight probably fall into the Middle Formative (Figures 84, 85) and the two latest into the Upper Formative. Phases I and II are closely related to pottery complexes of the Central and North coasts, including Cupisnique, and are represented at the earliest level of the Cerrillos site, excavated by Wallace (1962). Paracas Phases VI, VII, and VIII belong to the period that Wallace calls "Isla," which corresponds to the Chupas style of Ayacucho.

Figure 75. Chavín pottery vessels of the Ofrendas style with low relief and broad-line incised decoration (MUSM).

Figure 76. Chavín pottery vessels of the Ofrendas style decorated with zoned rocker stamping (MUSM).

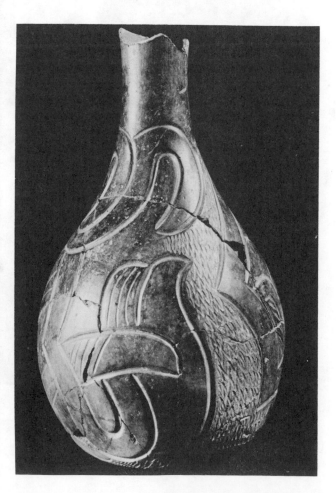

Figure 77. Stirrup-spout vessels of the Wacheqsa style of Chavín pottery (MUSM).

Figure 78. Stirrup-spout vessel of the Raku style of Chavín pottery (MUSM).

Figure 79. Stirrup-spout vessels of the Cupisnique style, coastal Chavín (a–b, MRLH. c, Museo Amano).

Figure 80 (*left and above*). Stirrup-spout vessels of the Cupisnique style, coastal Chavín (MRLH and Museo Amano).

Figure 81 (*below*). Jar in the form of a human head, Cupisnique
style, coastal Chavín (MRLH).

Figure 82. Stirrup-spout vessels of transitional Cupisnique style, reminiscent of Wacheqsa from Chavín de Huantar (MRLH).

Left
Figure 83. Stirrup-spout vessel of the earliest phase of the Ocucaje style from the South coast (collection of Cecilia C. de Blume).

Figure 84. Incised and painted bowl of the Ocucaje style, Phase 5 (MUSM).

Figure 85. Incised and painted jar of the Ocucaje style, Phase 8 (MUSM).

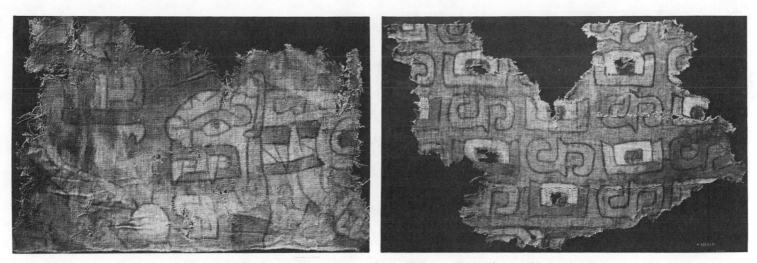

Figure 86. Chavín textiles with painted designs from the Ica Valley on the South coast (Museo Amano).

Other Arts and Crafts

Paracas culture is also remarkable for its textile industry. Loom-woven fabrics were common from the earliest phase and gauze began to be popular. Brocade, which involves insertion of additional wefts to produce a decorative effect, was also employed. Tapestry is believed to have been known. Initially, decoration appears to have been limited to painting on plain cloth (Figure 86), a notable contrast to the needlework that characterizes later Paracas weaving. The possibility that embroidery may have existed from a very early time cannot yet be eliminated, however, both because of the small size of the existing sample and also because this technique became so prominent in later Paracas phases.

The existence of textiles not only implies that the Chavín population dressed in cloth garments, but also indicates that clothing had a decorative aspect. Unfortunately, examples are still too few for description of the items of dress, although analysis of the sculptures from Chavín and other centers reveals the use of a kind of long shirt with a fringed lower edge, as well as belts and head-dresses. Loin-cloths must also have been typical. A textile that may be part of a mantle with a Chavín design has been found in Supe, as well as a head-dress ornamented with feathers.

The textiles provide the clearest evidence of Chavín cult influence on the South coast. One of the fabrics from Callango in the Ica Valley depicts an anthropomorphic deity similar to that shown on the Raimondi Stela; namely, a felinized figure holding a staff in each hand, with complex ornamentation consisting of serpents, claws, tusks, etc. Another piece of cloth displays typical felinic symbols combined in patterns of rhythmic regularity.

One notably divergent trait is metal working. Gold was the most widely used metal, and must have been obtained from superficial deposits or by sifting soil dredged from the rivers. On the North coast, particularly at Chongoyape where increasing numbers of objects are being encountered, gold was hammered into sheets that were decorated by the repoussé technique (Figure 87). Although

Figure 87.
Feline head in gold
(courtesy A. Guillén).

chronological data are tenuous, it appears that small quantities of copper and silver were employed in the Paracas region in addition to gold. If so, metal working was more advanced on the South coast than in the north, a conclusion that agrees with the information from Bolivia that copper was utilized during the Wankarani culture, dated at 1200 B.C. (see p. 57).

Figure 88. Zoomorphic stone mortars from the Gallery of the Offerings at Chavín de Huantar (MUSM).

The presence of metals provides insight into the elaboration of personal adornment, since many of the objects consist of ear, nose, and finger rings, chest ornaments, and bracelets. Jewelry was also made from lapis lázuli, turquoise, marine shell, wood, and other materials. The anthropomorphic representations at Moqeke, which have their faces decorated with paint of several colors, suggest that painting was another method of personal embellishment. Seals or stamps found at Cupisnique could have been used for producing designs on the skin.

Music may have been more highly developed than is evident at present. Few instruments are known, and the most important of these is a trumpet formed from a marine conch that is rare in Peruvian waters, implying its derivation by commerce from farther north in South America.

The tool kit was varied and even strictly functional artifacts tended to be ornamented. Mortars (Figure 88) in the form of a feline or a falcon and manos resembling serpent or feline heads have been found at Chavín de Huantar and in the Chicama Valley. Even undecorated examples are highly polished and symmetrical and often have a flange around the upper part. Well-made stone vessels were also produced.

Clubs were often embellished in an artistic manner by elaborating the striations into beautiful ornaments. They were employed principally in warfare, but also for hunting. Clubs, slings, and spear-throwers were the common weapons. The lance, an ancient instrument, served for warfare and hunting.

Burial Practices

Magical beliefs concerning death led to the production of many art objects, and Chavín tombs are thus a primary source of archeological evidence. They were not necessarily constructed with special care; many are simple pits that contain flexed or extended skeletons. Some, however, such as those of Cupisnique, were lined with stones. Secondary interments are suggested by skeletons showing traces of red paint. Offerings placed with the dead vary greatly from place to place.

Study of the skeletal remains has revealed that cranial deformation continued to be practiced. The fronto-occipital or tabular erecta type is characteristic (Figure 89).

Figure 89. Skull with tabular erecta deformation excavated at Wichqana, near Ayacucho.

The Upper Formative

During the final centuries before the Christian era, a strongly regional orientation began to develop both in areas influenced by Chavín and in areas that had remained unaffected. Without totally abandoning earlier traditional forms, each zone began to exhibit incipient manifestations of what appear to be autonomous cultural complexes. The Upper Formative is the period of emphasis on individuality and gradual loss of uniformity; it is the initial phase of regional cultural diversification. This diversification was not fully realized until later, however, and the Upper Formative complexes possess widespread similarities even though a strong cultural integration did not exist. A good example is the so-called "White-on-Red" stylistic horizon, a technique of pottery decoration that links widely separated regions. Since a similar degree of unity is not evident in other aspects of culture, some kind of selection must have operated on the elements transmitted by commercial activities, which appear to have intensified after the Middle Formative.

The Upper Formative has been characterized as "experimental" (Bennett and Bird 1949), a label that is appropriate, not only because of the regional cultural experimentation that existed, but also because it may be the last period during which it was still possible to formulate alternative solutions to problems raised by the new subsistence economy. During this interval, the agrarian structure of Andean society was defined and all or nearly all of the cultigens known in the Andes were fully domesticated. The most notable accomplishments were probably advances in agricultural techniques, especially in irrigation and perhaps the initiation of fertilization, which was later employed on a large scale. Hunting and fishing were not abandoned, but assumed an increasingly subsidiary importance relative to agriculture. Greater emphasis on agriculture was accompanied by a tendency for villages to concentrate in areas suitable for cultivation. The considerable increase in the size of population centers implies a notable demographic growth throughout the Central Andes.

Distribution of Sites

On the North coast, the Salinar and Puerto Moorin cultures (Figure 90) provide excellent examples of the changes operating in settlement pattern. In the Virú Valley, locus of the Puerto Moorin culture, two principal kinds of communities have been encountered: (1) a dispersed pattern of small houses reminiscent of the preceding Chavinoid Late Guañape period, and (2) irregularly agglutinated villages. The latter consist of about 25 houses or rooms, each forming an independent entity (there are no multi-roomed houses), distributed without symmetry, plan, or order. The occupation area covered by this kind of village is smaller than that of the dispersed type, but the number of rooms or living units is the same or larger. A single unit is approximately equal in size to a house in earlier villages. The floors are stone, but the walls are of conical or tooth-shaped adobes (Willey 1953:345). Another type of settlement associated with this period in the Virú Valley is a "Rectangular Enclosure Compound" (Willey 1953:66), which consists of an aggregation of stone-walled rooms or compartments surrounded by a rectangular wall. One measures about 20 by 30 meters, and contains 15 small, irregularly distributed rooms.

Several pottery vessels of the Puerto Moorin or Salinar period show houses with a shed roof. One has walls with stepped openings and a roof supported by three double beams resting on a central column and a large vertical beam. There are only three walls, one side being left open. Another building is circular but otherwise similar in construction.

Few new buildings for community use have been encountered and it is possible that those constructed during the preceding period continued in use. Willey (1953:66) mentions 14 isolated, rectangular, pyramidal mounds with early Puerto Moorin occupations. They were constructed of dirt and stone, of conical adobes covered with rocks, or of large adobes. Some contain floors of former buildings. Public structures connected with warfare are definitely associated with this period in the Virú Valley and one type, which has been termed a "Fortified Hilltop," contains both pyramidal mounds and living units (Figure 91). Although this type of redoubt is not common, one has as many houses as a normal village and could have sheltered several hundred persons.

Farther to the south, few studies have been made of Late Formative settlements. Existing evidence,

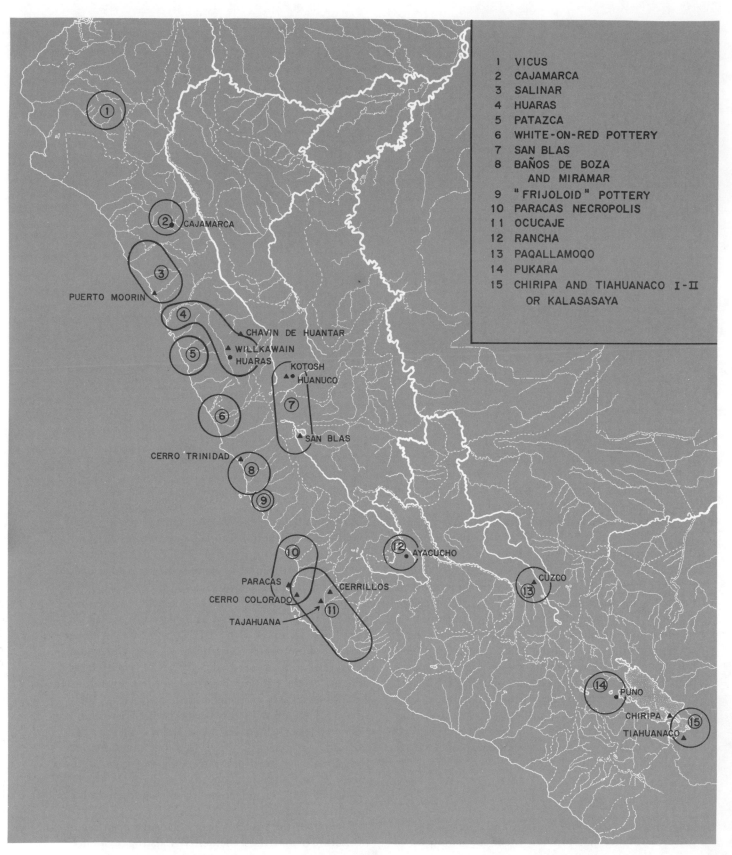

Figure 90. Location of the principal sites of the Upper Formative Period (▲ archeological site; ● modern town).

however, indicates the emergence of regional variations. In the valley of Casma, which was one of the richest in Chavinoid ceremonial centers, changes are exemplified by a strange spiral-shaped building known as "Chankillo." Although Chankillo is generally considered to be a fortress, largely because of its peculiar appearance and its location on the summit of a hill, all indications are that it is a ceremonial structure. Three concentric walls of angular, cut stone surround two low circular towers and an adjacent square room. The flat sides of the stones face outward, giving the walls an even surface. Several lintels of algarrobo wood have been salvaged from entrances. Associated with the structure are 13 peculiar stones of unknown function.

Several Upper Formative settlements are known on the Central coast. A typical site in the Chancay Valley is Baños de Boza, which contains a small, almost pyramidal building made of hemispherical adobes. Surrounding it is a compact group of small habitations of the same type of construction.

On the South coast, the geographical limit of Chavín influence during the Middle Formative, the best known site is Paracas. Semisubterranean houses have been reported, as well as true villages (Engel 1966c). Two large pyramids in the Chincha Valley, known as Huaca Alvarado and Huaca Soto, were constructed of very small adobes shaped like river cobbles and maize grains (Figure 92). The former were employed for fill and the latter for wall construction. The Huaca Alvarado contains compartments resembling houses.

In the Ica Valley, Phase IX is marked by an abrupt concentration of the population into a few large habitation centers (Menzel, Rowe, and Dawson 1964), whereas numerous, small, scattered hamlets along the margins of the valley had prevailed earlier. Two large settlements discovered by Rowe and his collaborators are Tajahuana, located almost in the center of the valley, and Media Luna, in the oasis of Callango. Media Luna is a complex of concentrated habitations about a kilometer long, incorporating 15 small mounds that probably represent temples and other kinds of public buildings. There are no fortifications at the site. Tajahuana is slightly smaller and contains remnants of the floors of small rectangular houses, along with a number of mounds about the same size as those at Media Luna. Tajahuana is a fortified settlement, however, with multiple walls. During Phase X, which was still part of the Formative Period, settlements were again small and very numerous, suggesting a redistribution of the population rather than a decline in numbers (Rowe 1963).

A complex of structures of probable ceremonial function has been reported at the site of Cerrillos in Ica. The "maize grain" type of adobes was used and the surfaces of walls and floors were plastered. Rooms and terraces were remodeled several times. The Isla phase, to which this complex belongs, probably represents a transitional stage from Chavín influence to independent regional forms and may be Middle rather than Late Formative (Wallace 1962:305). In the Nazca Valley, Strong

Figure 91. Site V-80, a fortified village of the early Puerto Moorin (Salinar) Period in the Virú Valley (after Willey 1953, fig. 18).

Figure 92. "Maize grain" adobes used for construction of the Huaca Soto, a Paracas period structure in the Chincha Valley (courtesy Dwight Wallace).

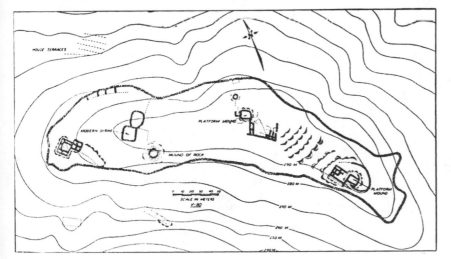

(1957) located Late Formative habitation sites with houses built of wooden posts.

In the highlands, the Rancha culture of Ayacucho underwent a development similar to that in the Ica Valley, to judge from the presence of early settlements of considerable extension. Farther to the north, in the Chavín area and in the Callejón de Huaylas, subterranean or semisubterranean houses occur.

South of the area of Chavín influence, development appears to have proceeded along lines initiated during the Lower Formative, although this is still somewhat speculative. In settlements of the Pukara culture, which follows Qaluyu in the Titicaca highlands and dates from the last century before Christ, public buildings and dwellings with adobe walls and stone floors continued to be erected on mounds. At the type site, three large structures of probable ceremonial function occupy a terrace, with habitations constructed nearby. A contemporary, slightly smaller settlement at Qaluyu is unusual in that the mound as a whole has the form of a lacustrine fish, which may have been intentional (Rowe 1963:7).

The Chiripa complex, which has been defined in the eastern part of the Titicaca Basin, may also belong to this period. The Chiripa site contains 14 rectangular houses around a central patio (Figure 93). The walls, which remain intact to a height of about a meter, were constructed of rectangular adobes. The dividing walls were double and their interior was used for storage. Entries were rectangular. Adobes painted green, white, and red have been found near the houses.

No habitations dating from Phase 1 have been found at Tiahuanaco; however, as at Chiripa, fragments of burned adobe have been encountered that are painted on one surface with designs similar to those on the polychrome pottery. A ceramic whistle described by Ponce Sanginés (1961) has the form of a house with a steeply gabled roof and a decorated facade.

In general, the Upper Formative is marked by a significant increase in the number of population centers, implying a notable demographic growth throughout the Central Andes that was undoubtedly made possible by refinements in agriculture and possibly also in animal domestication. The area influenced by Chavín is characterized by continuation of pyramid construction, a greater tendency toward concentrated settlement, and the erection of structures for defense; in each region, however, local expression is different. In the north, a decline in cult significance and an increase in secularity are clearly reflected in the decreased emphasis on construction of large temples and the diminution of religious motifs in arts and crafts, especially pottery.

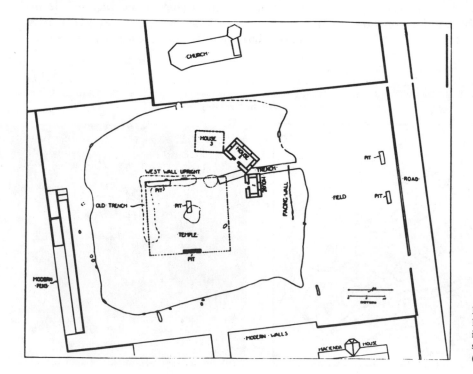

Figure 93.
Plan of the Chiripa site in the South highlands showing structures and excavations (after Bennett 1936, fig. 14).

Figure 94. Salinar-style jars with spout and strap handle (MRLH).

Figure 95. Bowl of the Huarás White-on-Red style from Chavín de Huantar (MUSM).

The White-on-Red Horizon

As previously noted, Late Formative pottery displays a sufficient degree of homogeneity over a large part of the Andean area to lead many archeologists to recognize the existence of a White-on-Red stylistic horizon. Salinar, Patasca, Huarás, San Blas, Baños de Boza, and possibly some southern complexes employed this decorative technique.

The description of Salinar pottery is based on vessels excavated from 228 tombs in a cemetery on the Jaguary hacienda in the Chicama Valley (Larco Hoyle 1945a). Technological competence is implied by the quality of execution and improved control in firing, which produced a pale color. A mold was sometimes employed. Decoration was by incision and painting, with white and red the most frequent colors. A slip was not used. Designs tend to be based on triangles, stepped lines, and other geometric elements. The principal vessel shapes are stirrup-spouted jars, bottles with cylindrical spout and strap handle (Figure 94), and jars with double spout and bridge handle. Modeled and mold-made forms include representations of human beings, felines, monkeys, rats, burrowing owls, and other animals. Sexual scenes are frequent, but exhibit few "aberrations" in comparison with the pottery of later periods. The related Puerto Morrin style from the Virú Valley is less attractive and modeling is less common, but it otherwise differs little from Salinar.

In the Casma Valley, the Late Formative pottery is called "Patasca" and is characterized by decoration in zones filled with white lines and dots, as well as by polished red and black types. Other techniques include impression, incision, and punctation. The most common motif consists of triangles radiating around the base of the vessel neck.

The climax area of white-on-red decoration is Chavín and the Callejón de Huaylas, where the pottery is known as "Huarás" as a result of Bennett's (1944) pioneer work at Willkawaín, near the modern city of Huarás. Designs emphasizing triangles, bands, and punctations were executed in cream-colored paint on a red surface (Figure 95). Vessel shapes differ from those of Salinar and have a massive quality very similar to that of Chavín bowls. The diagnostic form is a flat-bottomed bowl with slightly outslanting walls. Several Chavinoid types are associated.

A complex termed "San Blas" and showing certain resemblances to Huarás extends from Huánuco to Lake Junín. The predominant pottery is black monochrome decorated by stamping with a circular instrument that produced rings and S-shaped marks. This technique, which is obviously related to the Chavín tradition, is associated with white-on-red pottery both at the type site on the shore of Lake Junín and in Huánuco. In Huánuco, it occurs in post-Chavín structures, while in Junín it comes from refuse in an abandoned salt mine.

On the Central coast, white-on-red pottery was first identified at the sites of Cerro Trinidad and Baños de Boza in the Chancay Valley, and later at Huaca de la Florida in the Rímac Valley and at Ancón. The Chancay variant is known as "Baños de Boza" and the Ancón one as "Miramar." Baños de Boza painted designs employ dots, triangles, lines, bands, and circles, all carelessly drawn. Some vessels have large areas covered with white, which contrast with the adjacent red surface. Negative

painting occurs rarely, as does polished black surface treatment. Plates, bowls, bottles, and peculiar turtle-shaped vessels are characteristic, as well as double-spouted jars with bridge handles and modeled representations of birds. The Miramar variety places greater emphasis on a distinctive complex of elements ancestral to the subsequent regional complex (Playa Grande) than on those diagnostic of the white-on-red horizon. Miramar pottery employs various other colors for decoration, in addition to the frequent use of white-on-red (Lanning 1963a).

Two white-on-red complexes have been encountered in the Titicaca region, south of the limit of Chavín influence. Neither is closely related to those previously described. Paqallamoqo, a type consistently associated with Chanapata, is characterized by the use of a cream paint on a polished red surface and may be relatively late. The most fre-

Figure 96. Geometric decoration on bowls of the Chiripa style (after Bennett 1936, fig. 27).

Figure 97. Painted and modeled pottery of the Chiripa style (after Bennett 1936, fig. 28).

quent design elements are geometric, such as crosses, crosshatch, or circles; but biomorphic figures also occur, among them a highly simplified llama. Open vessel shapes predominate, especially shallow plates with decoration on the interior. The other complex, Chiripa, which occurs east of Lake Titicaca, may belong to this period but is possibly earlier. Motifs are geometrical and feature steps or serrations executed in a thick yellowish paint on a relatively dense background. Designs were occasionally outlined by fine incisions and modeled felines were often appliqued to the surface. The typical vessel shape is an open bowl with a flat bottom, straight vertical sides, and a thick rim (Figure 96). Trumpet-like tubes have been found, which may have been used for creating drafts to revive fires (Figure 97). In spite of the fact that cream-on-red is part of the complex, Chiripa pottery is so distinctive that it should not be incorporated into the White-on-Red Horizon, even as a marginal variant.

Other Ceramic Complexes

During the Upper Formative, types of pottery that are quite different from those so far described existed in several regions. Cajamarca I, in the North highlands, is known from only a few specimens,

but appears to have emphasized a white background and simple designs executed with relatively fine lines. The Rancha (Ayacucho) type from the Central highlands is a monochrome ware decorated by incision or application of a thin red paint. It preserves strong Chavinoid elements, but is more closely related to Paracas Necrópolis. Other noteworthy "isolated" groups are three southern complexes that share a number of distinctive decorative features, including the use of polychrome painting. They are Paracas, Pukara, and Kalasasaya (Ponce Sanginés 1971).

Pottery initially referred to as "Paracas Cavernas" and "Paracas Necrópolis" was discovered by Tello (1960) at a site near the Bay of Pisco, a region that today is desert. The finds came from very extensive cemeteries containing rich funerary offerings. Subsequently, Cavernas pottery has been encountered in almost all of the southern coastal valleys between Chicama and Nazca.

In the Ica Valley, the Paracas tradition has been broken into a long sequence of phases, eight of which belong to the Middle Formative (p. 72). The two final phases (IX and X) constitute a local development influenced by nearby valleys to the north (perhaps Cañete, Chincha, and Pisco), and which Tello called "Necrópolis" (Figure 98). Phase

Figure 98. Pottery vessels of the Paracas Necrópolis style from the South coast. (*left*) Modeled and incised jar (MUSM). (*right*) Bowl with negative painting.

ix and part of Phase x also continue the Cavernas ceramic tradition. Generally speaking, two decorative techniques coexisted during the Upper Formative on the South coast, one polychrome and the other monochrome. The polychrome pottery stems from the ancient Chavinoid tradition, although the designs and their method of execution became increasingly divergent with the passage of time. Motifs tend to become beautifully naturalistic and simplified and although painting continues to be applied after firing, large zones replace the profusion of elements typical earlier. Monochrome pottery is best known in the Necrópolis variant; it is usually cream or orangish and vessel shapes resemble gourds.

Pukara, which followed Qaluyu in the South highlands, is another ceramic complex with no relationship to the White-on-Red Horizon, but which instead shares certain elements with the later phases of Paracas that imply contacts between the two cultures. This inference is strengthened by the fact that both Pukara and Paracas ix to x have been dated between 100 B.C. and A.D. 100, making them also contemporary with Kalasasaya.

Pukara pottery is a harmonious combination of realistic and stylized motifs taken from nature (Figure 99). Its development may have been a long one, since two major classes or phases can be distinguished, one emphasizing designs closely imitating natural forms and the other featuring abstract or symbolic elements reminiscent of the Tiahuanaco style that developed on the opposite side of Lake Titicaca. Vessels representing the first phase are ornamented with scenes of deer hunting and compositions combining different kinds of animals, especially ducks and llamas; human figures are less common and geometric motifs are rare. Interestingly, treatment is closely similar to that characteristic of Ocucaje (Paracas) pottery of Phases ix and x. The decorative technique is also similar, the motifs being delimited by incisions. Paint was applied before firing and tends to be thick; the colors are black and red for design areas and white for filling of incisions. White was also occasionally employed for covering parts of the surface, as were gray and yellow. Certain features, such as the rigid and solid nature of the vessels, appear derived from the Qaluyu tradition of the Lower Formative, but some bowls and jars are sufficiently gracile to suggest Paracas influence.

The pottery of second Pukara phase is considerably different, although the same colors continue to be employed. Designs are far removed from reality and often have a nightmare-like quality. Felines with human or bird-like features, weird fishes, and rays projecting from assorted heads may represent supernatural beings. A frequent element is a feline with the face shown in front view and the body in profile. The head is usually modeled and appliqued

Figure 99. Pottery of the Pukara style with zoned incised and relief decoration (courtesy A. Guillén).

to the otherwise smooth surface of the vessel. The most common shape is an open bowl with concave walls and a high pedestal base. Faces are shown with the eyes divided perpendicularly into equal halves, one half painted white and the other black. The mouth sometimes has triangular canines, giving a pseudo-Chavinoid effect that is actually a reflection of Tiahuanacoid influence.

This type of Pukara pottery, in fact, looks so much like Classic Tiahuanaco ceramics that a close relationship must have existed between the two populations. Although many archeologists are inclined to place Pukara earlier than Tiahuanaco, what is known of Tiahuanaco history favors it as the ancestor and suggests that it began to influence Pukara during the first ceramic phase, causing the changes in the conceptual framework of the artists that are reflected in the ceramic evolution. Although there are good grounds for including Pukara in the Upper Formative, there is also reason to believe that it did not become extinct until around A.D. 800, when the whole altiplano came under Tiahuanaco domination.

The earliest pottery at Tiahuanaco, known as Kalasasaya, is predominantly plain (Figure 100), but painting and modeling occur. The paint is usually red or yellow, but black and white were also used. Designs are bordered by incised lines (Figure 101). Stepped figures provide a link with the earlier Chiripa tradition and also with Qaluyu, whereas representations of felines are reminiscent of those on Paracas or Ocucaje pottery of Phases IX or X. A carbon-14 date of 239 ± 130 B.C. makes Tiahuanaco slightly earlier than both Pukara and Paracas IX and X. What little information exists on Tiahuanaco II suggests that it has much in common with Pukara.

Figure 100. Undecorated pottery of the Tiahuanaco I style (courtesy Carlos Ponce Sanginés).

Figure 101. Tiahuanaco I style pottery decorated with zoned painting (courtesy Carlos Ponce Sanginés).

It is evident that Chiripa, Pukara, and Kalasasaya (Tiahuanaco I and II) belong to a regional cultural tradition. If Paracas is added, its area extends from Titicaca in the highlands to Ica on the coast. An important unifying element is a feline image, in which the body is shown in profile and the face in front view, as though it represented a very important personage. This position occurs only in this zone, and Menzel, Rowe, and Dawson (1964) indicate that it is a local Paracas element, distinct from the Chavín feline tradition.

Other Arts and Crafts

Among the archeological remains known from this period, the most fascinating are certainly the Paracas textiles. The refinement, esthetic quality, and degree of patience and skill that the finest examples imply cannot be fully appreciated by those of us accustomed to machine-made products. Weaving did not advance significantly during the Paracas Cavernas phase, but later on beautiful polychrome tapestry and embroidered designs were produced, along with gauze and double cloth. Background colors were usually white and brown, although light blue, yellow, and black were also employed. Tapestry was used only for small pieces, such as bands and small short ponchos. Cavernas textile designs feature interlaced animals with triangular heads and serrated bodies, suggestive of snakes or fishes, as well as feline and human representations. These motifs, particularly the interlaced ones, resemble Lima and Recuay designs, and the significance of this similarity should be more intensively investigated.

Necrópolis textiles, which correspond in general to Paracas x and Nazca I, are exquisite, particularly because of the use of embroidery as a basic decorative technique (Figure 102). Artistic expression reached its apex in the production of large mantles entirely covered with intermixed motifs that form harmonious components of a transverse pattern. Some of the Necrópolis tapestries have a type of geometric decoration reminiscent of Cavernas, but the most highly developed embroidery utilized extremely complex and variable nongeometric motifs, including felines of several kinds, humanized felines, two-headed worms or snakes, birds, foxes, and mice. Human beings with spear-throwers are common and often accompanied by trophy heads. The figures are generally distributed in vertical or horizontal rows on a dark, rectangular panel. They are small, evenly spaced, and often alternating in position, so that the heads of adjacent figures face in opposite directions. Up to nine different figures may appear on a single mantle, although repetition of one basic motif is far more typical. The pieces made at Paracas represent a great variety of articles of dress, among them simple loin cloths and sleeveless shirts, which sometimes have fringes in place of sleeves. There are also small ponchos, belts, and the famous mantles.

Although the Paracas textiles are well known and many pieces remain in a state of perfect preservation, little information is available on the textile industry during the Upper Formative in other parts of Peru. The Salinar population possessed loincloths and perhaps turban-like headdresses; the cloth is plain and represented by only a few fragments. Similar evidence has come from the Central coast.

Metallurgy also advanced notably during the Upper Formative, when silver, gold, copper, and possibly certain alloys became known throughout the Central Andes. This technology appears to have developed in the Peruvian-Bolivian altiplano. Alloys of copper and gold were produced in Salinar, where the earliest soldering has been reported. This alloy has been encountered in association with Baños de Boza pottery and must also have been known in Paracas, although pure copper, silver, and laminated gold were more characteristic, as they are in Tiahuanaco I. Copper was used in Chiripa.

Metal working reached its technological climax during this period, although bronze was not produced until later. Smelting must have been done in clay ovens using charcoal and a forced draft, produced with the aid of special trumpet-shaped pottery artifacts or tubes of some other material; another method may have been to place the fire where it was accessible to strong natural air currents. It has been suggested that the principle of alloying may have been an accidental discovery resulting from use of the same ovens for smelting of different metals.

Of the many techniques employed for the production of objects, the "lost wax" process was certainly one of the most frequent. This begins with modeling the desired figure in a mixture of fine clay and carbon, and then coating it with wax. The model is retouched to improve its quality and then covered with clay, leaving a perforation through which liquid metal could be introduced. The hot metal melts and replaces the wax, assuming its

Figure 102. Textiles of the Paracas Necrópolis style. (*above*) Portion of a large mantle. (*below*) Detail of weaving.

form. Such a mold obviously can be used only once. Both open and closed reusable molds were also employed. Cutting, repoussé, and incision were used for decoration or for the finishing of objects. The knowledge of plating was finally acquired and applied most frequently to copper. From this time onward, metal was an important material for the manufacture of tools and ornaments, as well as certain kinds of ritual objects.

Stone working advanced appreciably in some parts of the highlands. Sculptures closely resembling those of the later Recuay culture have been found associated with Huarás pottery, but the significance of this similarity has not been evaluated. In Pukara, by contrast, the association between stone sculptures and pottery is well established, and the sculptures like the pottery can be classified in terms of their resemblances to Tiahuanaco. In general, Pukara sculpture falls into two main groups: statues and stelae. The statues represent human beings and one handsome example about a meter tall may be a deity. The presence of a trophy head in his hand has led to his designation as "The Executioner." The geometric style is clearly related to the classical sculptures from Tiahuanaco, but other sculptures are less geometrical. Animals, human beings, or complicated panels with stepped, serrated, or rhomboid elements occur on stelae. The only realistic sculpture known from Peru is from Pukara (Kidder 1943, pl. V:1–3). It is the figure of a man wearing shorts that reveal his legs, which are separated. Unfortunately, the head is broken off.

Considerable attention was paid to art in general and many beautiful objects of turquoise, lapis lázuli, wood, shell, or other materials were produced for personal ornament, among them necklaces, bracelets, and rings. Painting does not appear to have advanced significantly, in contrast to music. At Paracas, panpipes and flutes possessing up to five notes have been found, and pottery drums resembling the bongo drums of Afro-American musicians are associated with Phase x.

Treatment of the Dead

In spite of the notable reduction in importance of the Chavinoid cult, the fact that Andean society in general did not abandon its religious character during the Upper Formative is readily evident from the emphasis placed on the cult of the dead. In Salinar, bodies were interred in elliptical tombs with the legs extended and slightly crossed. The hands were usually placed by the sides, but sometimes the left one rested on the pelvis. Tombs containing two individuals have been found. Typical burial goods consisted of pottery, textiles, collars, bracelets, and sometimes small sheets of gold near the mouth. In Baños de Boza, shallow graves dug in sand contain flexed skeletons, sometimes covered with stones.

Paracas tombs are noteworthy in being cut from soft rock to a considerable depth below the ground surface. At Cerro Colorado, contiguous tubes provide access to funerary chambers. The entrance or vestibule of each tomb is a cylindrical stone wall about 1.0–1.5 meters in diameter and about 2.0 meters high. Cavities in the walls of the passage probably served as steps, while those in the chamber were used as receptacles for the funerary bundles. Each tomb contained niches for 30 to 40 individuals, and when a larger number were buried, the overflow was placed in the access passageway. In the same zone where these chambers occur are the famous necropolises, which are very large enclosures in which bodies were piled.

Another interesting Paracas practice is mummification, which Tello (1929:134ff) described in the following way:

The manner in which the body was prepared for wrapping was very unusual. After extraction of the viscera and a major part of the muscles, the corpse was given special treatment to induce mummification. The head was sometimes severed from the body in order to permit removal of the lungs and heart and the abdomen was also cut longitudinally or transversally to take out the intestines and other viscera. Sometimes incisions were made in the extremities to tear out the muscles. Subsequently, the corpse was submitted to a mummification process involving use of fire and perhaps various chemical substances, to judge from the smoked and even carbonized appearance of certain parts of the body, and by the saline efflorescences resulting from substances applied. Next, the body was reduced to minimal volume by pressure on the extremities and the vertebral column. When not cut off, the head was forced down against the abdomen; the tightly flexed lower extremities were crossed over the neck and the arms were placed across the chest. This peculiar, ball-like position was maintained by firm bindings and spaces were filled with small pieces of rope, producing a rounded or ovoid bundle that was placed in a basket. These mummies were then wrapped in several layers of very rich woven and embroidered mantles, along with gold and stone ornaments. The unwrapping of several large bundles has permitted reconstruction of the process usually followed. Typically, small pieces of clothing were wedged along the sides of the body; the mummy and the basket were then wrapped in two or more pieces of coarse cloth, sometimes measuring 20 meters long by 4 meters wide and formed by joining two sections, each 20 meters long and 2 meters wide. Following this, other layers were added, often alternating plain cloth with embroidered mantles and small pieces of wearing apparel. The wrapping was done in such a manner that the final bundle had the form of a cone, at the apex of which was placed an artificial head.

Stone-lined tombs have been found beneath house floors at Chiripa, while Tiahuanaco 1 burials were in circular pits. In the latter culture, grave goods do not appear to have been numerous, since in some cases only a few sodalite (feldspar) beads have been associated.

Examination of the human remains has shown that not only cranial deformation but also trepanation was practiced, implying notable advance in surgery that must have been paralleled by equivalent progress in other therapeutic techniques. The trepanations at Paracas are the most numerous and best known. According to Tello (1929:144), nearly 40 percent of the burials from Cerro Colorado showed evidence of cranial operations. Methods employed were incision, scraping, and drilling. The first consisted in making four cuts to define a quadrangle or rectangle, which was then removed. The scraping technique resulted in gradual wearing away of the bone, while the third method was employed to outline a circular area that was subsequently extracted. Tello (1929:144) also stated:

Trepanations executed by scraping and circular incisions [perforations] are common and sometimes so extensive as to involve almost half of the cranium. The excellent state of preservation of the bones and especially the quantity and variety of objects utilized in these operations that accompany the body provide a large amount of information. . . . So far, the depressed, pulverized, and radiating types of cranial fractures that were the primary reason for such operations elsewhere in the Andean region have not been observed. Often, the operation consisted simply in the careful removal of the external surface by scraping, leaving the inner layer of the bone intact. . . . The majority of the subjects survived the operation and the tissues regenerated.

The existence of incipient medical practices in Salinar is implied by a pottery vessel showing an individual reclining on the back of another, a position suggesting a curing activity.

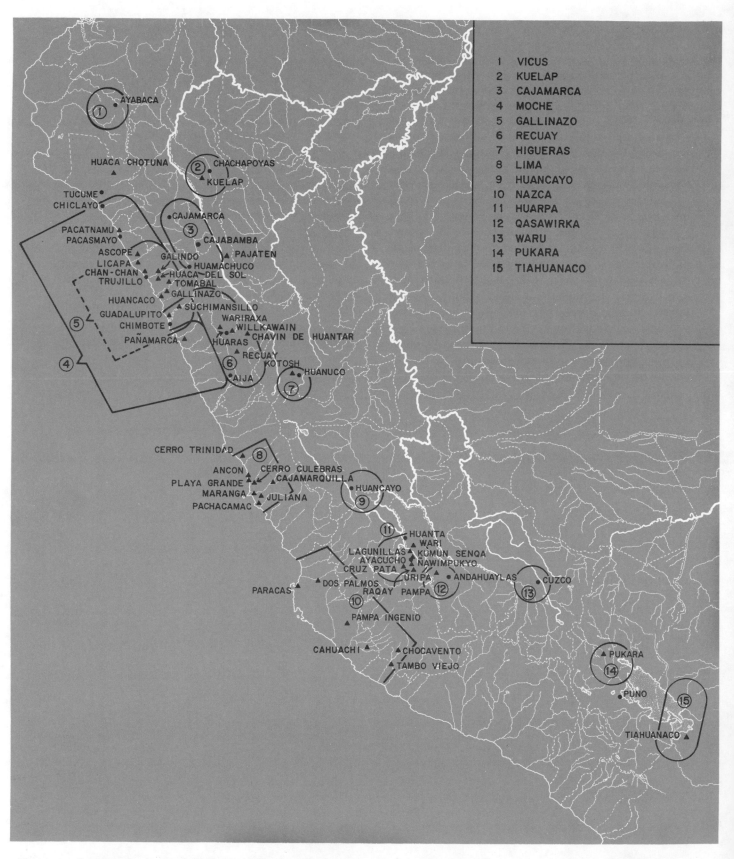

Figure 103. Location of cultures of the Regional Developmental Period and some of the principal sites (▲ archeological site; ● modern town).

THE REGIONAL DEVELOPMENTAL PERIOD

100 B.C.–A.D. 700

The Upper Formative experimental stage terminated in strong regional differentiation, which reached its climax about A.D. 300. On the North coast, the Moche culture crystallized in the valleys of Chicama and Moche (Figure 103). A little to the south, in the Virú Valley, the Gallinazo culture developed; in the Santa Valley, the Recuay culture encompassed both the highland and coastal portions, while in a large basin in the nearby highlands, the Cajamarca culture flowered. In Huánuco, a ceramic complex related to Gallinazo and Recuay has been called Higueras. The Central coast was the locus of the Lima culture and the South coast of the Nazca culture. In the Central highlands, Ayacucho was dominated by the Huarpa culture and the Waru culture emerged in Cuzco. Near Lake Titicaca, the famous Tiahuanaco culture reached its climax. Other regional manifestations undoubtedly remain to be discovered since only recently the first traces of the highly developed Vicus culture were found in the Piura region in the Far North and the blurred outlines of a Huancayo culture have begun to emerge in the Mantaro Basin of the Central highlands. This regionalism in cultural development reflects the special environmental characteristics of the Andean valleys and basins. On the coast, adjacent valleys were incorporated into regional entities, whose extent is generally a function of the proximity of the rivers. In the highlands, by contrast, cultural units more often correspond to drainage areas, such as Cajamarca, Marañón, Callejón de Huaylas, Mantaro, Huarpa, Urubamba, and Titicaca.

The notable artistic development attained by some of these regional nuclei has caused many observers to consider this a climax stage in Central Andean cultural development and this viewpoint is reflected on the terms "classic" and "florescent." Bennett and Bird (1949) labeled it the "Period of the Master Craftsmen." The Moche, Lima, Nazca, and Tiahuanaco cultures in particular achieved a level of creativity in ceramics, textiles, sculpture, and other media that probably represents the pinnacle of prehistoric Peruvian art. These achievements imply the emergence of craft specialists, who were differentiated from the peasants in the community and who were incorporated into the urban form of life that becomes clearly defined during this stage.

The cultural descriptions that follow are of unequal completeness because of the unevenness of the present state of knowledge. The Moche culture is so well known that its description could be expanded to fill several volumes; at the opposite extreme are the cultures of the highland basins, some of which are represented only by a few fragmentary remains.

95

The Gallinazo Culture (300 B.C.–A.D. 300)

Gallinazo has nearly always been described as an Upper Formative culture and, in fact, its earliest manifestations appear to be related to the last vestiges of the Salinar culture. When Bennett (1939) excavated in the Virú Valley in 1936, however, he concluded Gallinazo was later than Moche, an idea that was supported by Kroeber (1944). Its correct chronological position in Chicama and Virú was finally established, thanks to the work of Larco Hoyle and excavations undertaken by Strong and Evans during the Virú Project. In both valleys, it follows Salinar and Puerto Moorin and precedes Moche. It soon disappears in Chicama, being replaced by the Moche culture around the beginning of the Christian era; in Virú, by contrast, it represents a regional development that remained in existence until Moche expansion and domination around A.D. 300. Larco Hoyle (1945b, 1946) called the culture "Virú," correctly believing that its principal center of development lay in the narrow valley with this name.

There has been much speculation about the origin of the Gallinazo culture, not because the culture itself is particularly distinctive, but because the pottery features a decorative technique known as "negative," "lost color," or "resist painting," which has no local antecedents. Because of the complex nature of the technique, it is generally believed unlikely that it was invented several times, and its appearance consequently implies diffusion. Its earliest known occurrence in the Central Andes is at the Lower Formative site of Hacha on the South coast, the region where the negative painting tradition developed throughout the Formative Period. Elsewhere in the Central Andes, it equates with the Upper Formative and only in a few North coastal and highland valleys does it persist far into the Christian era. In Ecuador and Colombia, by contrast, its history was apparently more extensive and its origin cannot be resolved without reviewing the evidence from the northern Andes. What is certain is that in the Virú Valley, and on the North coast in general, the tradition was introduced from elsewhere.

Gallinazo has been divided into chronological phases based primarily on differences in building techniques. The earliest structures were built of large or small adobes. These were followed by constructions using several types of adobes, among the most important being spherical, tooth-shaped, and semi-spherical. The sequence ends with mold-made adobes in the shape of a parallelepiped with a rectangular base. The molds were of cane, which left grooves on the surface that are a diagnostic Gallinazo feature. Adobes made in smooth molds are the latest type.

Initially, Gallinazo elements are strongly mixed with Salinar traits and during Phase I many characteristics are pure Salinar. The diagnostic innovation is the appearance of the negative technique on pottery. Phases II and III are more distinctive.

SETTLEMENT PATTERN. During Phases I and II, most of the Virú population was concentrated in the lower part of the valley, but density was somewhat greater than in earlier times. During Phase III, a climax in population size was reached that provides a reliable measure of the success of the Gallinazo subsistence economy.

The general village pattern was agglutinative, the houses in some cases exhibiting a degree of regularity in arrangement around small plazas, but more often having an arbitrary and irregular distribution. Villages were nearly always associated with mounds, which were either artificially constructed in pyramidal form or the result of accumulation of refuse and rubbish from structures intentionally torn down. During Phase III, there is a very strong tendency toward concentration around the so-called "Gallinazo Group" in the northern part of the lower valley, a settlement that had begun to take shape during the preceding periods. It has been estimated that the Group contains around 30,000 rooms dating from Phase III in an area not over 5 kilometers square (Willey 1953).

The size of the sites varies considerably. Some have few rooms and occupy an overall area only about 15 meters in diameter. At the opposite extreme is the Gallinazo site itself. There is a general increase in the relative size of population centers from Phase I to Phase III, and a correlation can be observed between size and arrangement. The irregular settlements have between 30 and 100 rooms or houses, while the regular ones are much smaller and have only about 20 rooms combined with corridors and distributed symmetrically around a central plaza or chamber. Small villages surrounded by

Figure 104. The Castillo de Tomaval, a fortified Gallinazo site in the Virú Valley (courtesy Clifford Evans).

a rectangular wall occur, although much less frequently. There are also semi-isolated "mansions" similar to those of the Moche. These rectangular, stone-floored houses measure about 14 by 9 meters. They were constructed 100 to 200 meters from the villages and may have been residences of important individuals.

In addition to these buildings, which do not have a public aspect, there were pyramids, which must originally have been erected for religious purposes although they also contain dwelling places (Figure 104). Willey (1953) has suggested that some may have had politico-religious roles, and that the Gallinazo site may have been a kind of capital. This possibility is especially strong during Phase III. It should be noted, however, that it was an administrative and community center rather than a true city, the latter being a development that reached the North coast only at a later period. Other kinds of mounds apparently served as fortresses or defensive bulwarks, since they are protected by encircling fortification walls.

During all phases, houses were small and rectangular; some are only 1.25 meters square, while others measure 3 by 4 meters. The concept of windows and doors seems not to have existed until Phase III, when clearly defined entrances, including doors, are shown on pottery representations of Gallinazo houses. One pottery model consists of a platform with a single wall and two posts at the front to support the inclined roof (Figure 105); another has three walls leaving one side open. The roof is often gabeled. Other houses are completely enclosed and access is through a door, which is usually off center.

One of the most notable features of Gallinazo culture is decoration of the buildings. A wall at the Gallinazo site bears an incised design consisting of pentagonal heads on bodies formed by serrated bands, suggesting the interlaced serpents characteristic of Recuay, Paracas, Nazca, and Lima textiles. A similar design in low relief has been found in Chicama Valley at the Gallinazo site of Huaca Licapa (Figure 106). A more common technique of embellishment was a type of mosaic created by the arrangement of the adobes or by excision of portions of the clay to produce bands of geometric figures. This form of ornamentation is infrequent

Figure 105. Pottery vessel depicting an individual in a simple house (courtesy A. Guillén).

Figure 106. Wall with relief and painted decoration at the Huaca Licapa, a Gallinazo site in the Chicama Valley.

in the Central Andes and Bennett (1950) believed that the closest parallels were with Kuelap structures in the Utcubamba region, where similar effects were obtained in stone. Unfortunately, the chronological position of the latter buildings is unknown, but they seem related—morphologically at least—to recent finds in the zone of Pajatén.

SUBSISTENCE. The economy was based on intensive agriculture made possible by an advanced system of irrigation, which is clearly revealed by the remains in the Virú Valley. The canals were comparable in size to those of Moche and the increased productivity they allowed must have been responsible for the explosive population growth during Phase III. It appears that all cultivatable land in the valley was in use during this epoch. Naturally, neither fishing nor hunting was abandoned, but both declined to secondary importance.

SOCIAL ORGANIZATION. Little is known of the nonmaterial aspects of Gallinazo culture. Representations on pottery imply, however, that the feline cult introduced by Chavín survived to some degree here as it did in Moche culture. Some scenes show a condor eating a human being and this may also have cult significance.

ARTS AND CRAFTS. The best known pottery is that with negative painting, but numerous associated styles lack painted decoration. The most important ware is Castillo, which along with the negative type is diagnostic of the Gallinazo culture.

Castillo incised employs crude incision, punctation, or dentation. The paste is usually fired reddish orange and the surface is slightly polished or, more accurately, smoothed. Designs are limited to incised lines, areas of punctates, and punctates com-

Figure 107. Gallinazo-style vessel with negative-painted decoration (MRLH).

bined with lines. Castillo Modeled is much richer in forms and motifs, and emphasizes relief produced by applique, adornos, or modeling. Jar necks often have faces, in which the nose is modeled, the eyes are applique buttons, the ears are low relief, and the mouth is a broad incised line. Other faces were produced totally by incision. Adornos take the form of heads of felines, birds, monkeys, or human beings. The bird is a prominent element in Gallinazo art. During Phase III, Moche influence is discernible, especially in the increased sense of portraiture exhibited by the faces on jar necks.

Gallinazo Negative, as the name implies, is decorated by the negative technique, although modeling may be associated (Figure 107). The contrasting colors are black on a light orange surface. Designs are simple combinations of straight or undulating lines, circles, triangles, steps, spirals, and rings. Rare motifs suggesting felines probably date from Phase III and reflect influences from Recuay ceramics. Two other types, Carmelo Negative and Callejón Negative, also exhibit highland influences. The most common vessel shapes are plates (sometimes with an annular base), jars with tall straight or flaring necks, toasters, stirrup-spout bottles, bottles with a straight spout connected by a tubular handle to the body, jars with a spout and tubular bridge handle connecting with a modeled figure, double vessels with connecting bridge, and effigies. Pottery was also used for spindle whorls, figurines, trumpets, panpipes, polishers, and other objects.

Little is known of Gallinazo stone-working technology; all that has been found are polishing stones, manos, hammerstones, and other undiagnostic kinds of utensils.

Metallurgy advanced, but less than among the Moche. Objects of copper have been found, the majority worked only by hammering, and also a little gold and silver. Very thin disks, rectangular pendants, and objects with relief decoration occur.

BURIAL PRACTICES. The cult of the dead was important, as it was in all other Andean cultures. Few tombs of Phase I are known, but those of Phase II were simple circular or elongated pits containing direct interments, with the bodies usually extended but sometimes flexed. These burials are associated with earth mounds. During Phase III, grave pits were excavated in abandoned village sites and the bodies were extended, seated, or flexed. Generally, few offerings were provided. In the Callejón de Huaylas, Larco Hoyle (n.d.) found stone coffins similar to those of the Recuay culture.

The Moche Culture (A.D. 100–800)

Moche is a valley on the North coast, south of the city of Trujillo. Together with the Chicama Valley, it was the center of development of a great culture originally called "Proto-Chimú." Subsequently, it became known as "Mochica," which is still the most often employed term. "Early Chimú" is favored by those who view it as the earliest expression of the historically documented Chimú culture. The most prevalent designation, Mochica, has the defect that it is also the name of a language spoken by inhabitants of the North coast at the time of arrival of the Spaniards. To eliminate possible ambiguity, many archeologists prefer the name "Moche," taken from one of the valleys where the culture occurs, a practice followed in the naming of other cultures such as Nazca, Lima, etc.

Although information has existed for more than a century, the first systematic work was that of Uhle (1913) in the Moche Valley. Many others have followed, attracted in large part by the ceremonial pottery, which provides a remarkably extensive catalog of daily life. At the University of California, where Uhle deposited his Peruvian materials, Alfred L. Kroeber and his students analyzed the Moche collections and established a relative chronology that confirmed Uhle's hypothesis that Moche was pre-Tiahuanacoid and pre-Chimú. The most significant subsequent studies are those by Rafael Larco Hoyle (1938–1939, 1945c), who made finer subdivisions in Moche pottery and suggested a more precise chronology, which recent discoveries have supported. Kutscher (1950), Horkheimer (1961), Strong and Evans (1952), and other archeologists have also devoted themselves to various aspects of this culture.

SETTLEMENT PATTERN. Pyramids and ceremonial centers are common in all the valleys that came under Moche rule. One of the best known and certainly among the most beautiful is Pañamarca in the Nepeña Valley, composed of a group of very large platforms that terminate on the south in a stepped pyramid (Figure 108). The complex as a whole covers about 200 by 150 meters at the base and the pyramid is about 40 meters square. The interior walls were decorated with frescos, one of which shows part of the process of sacrifice of prisoners (Figure 109). The ceremonial center of Mocollope in the Chicama Valley contains several pyramidal mounds. Pyramids were usually rectangular, although conical ones also occur. All Moche structures of this kind were built of adobe. Some contain dwellings and functioned simultaneously as administrative and religious centers. In the Virú Valley, the old Gallinazo ceremonial centers were adapted with slight modifications, such as the addition of rooms. This type of structure is often depicted on pottery and usually has a house on the summit; a few examples, however, have a throne instead. Stepped pyramids are shown, as well as a spiral-shaped one. Access to the summit was facilitated by zig-zag ramps, staircases, or steps along one corner.

Many of the priests probably lived in the rooms on the pyramids, but isolated houses resembling unfortified "castles" may have been an alternative place of residence. In the Virú Valley alone there are at least five such structures, all quite large. If they were owned by families, they must have been very powerful ones. Most houses were more or less concentrated in agglutinated villages, perhaps partly for protection against attack and certainly to facilitate communal activities. While most appear to be unplanned, a few exhibit a tendency toward a kind of regularity in the arrangement of the houses. Some constitute true redoubts, protected by a rectangular adobe wall. Most houses were also adobe, although a few stone ones occur in the Virú Valley, especially in the upper part. The houses of the common people must have been simple, perhaps no more than four posts with a roof of woven reeds. Most dwellings shown on the pottery are rectangular and have a gabled roof, possibly a vestige of ancient highland influence. In general, both the villages and the semi-isolated houses are associated in some way with the ceremonial centers distributed throughout the valleys (Figure 110).

The most notable architectural achievements are Huaca del Sol and Huaca de la Luna in the Moche Valley. Huaca del Sol is an immense stepped pyramid that must once have reached a height of about 50 meters (Figure 111). It has been estimated that some 50 million small rectangular adobes were required for its construction, which was accomplished in numerous stages, each involving addition

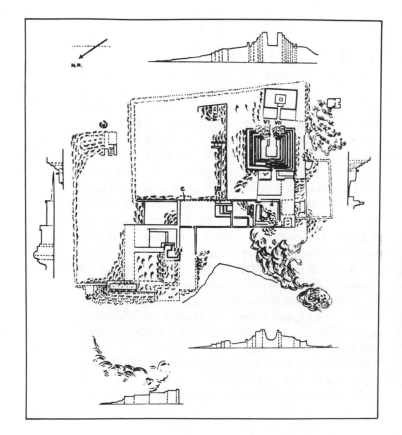

Figure 108. Plan of the ceremonial center of Pañamarca, a Moche period site in the Nepeña Valley (courtesy Schaedel and Bonavia).

Figure 109. Mural on a wall at Pañamarca showing captives and individuals of different social rank.

Figure 110. The Huaca Chotuna in Lambaycque Valley, attributed to the Moche culture (courtesy A. Guillén).

Figure 111. The Huaca del Sol in the Moche Valley (courtesy Clifford Evans).

of walls formed of columns of adobe bricks. The pyramid rests on a platform 228 meters long by 136 meters wide, composed of five terraces. Ascent is by a ramp 90 meters long and 6 meters wide. The pyramid, which also consists of five superimposed platforms, occupies the whole southern part of the summit.

Huaca de la Luna, about 500 meters away, is smaller, with a base 80 by 60 meters and a height of only 21 meters. One side is nearly vertical, while the other three sides rise via six stepped terraces. While few traces of structures survive on the summit of Huaca del Sol, large rooms remain on Huaca de la Luna and many have walls ornamented with lovely frescos. Outstanding among them is "the rebellion of the artifacts," which shows pottery vessels and other objects in attitudes of war and defiance. Other frescoes are exclusively decorative and many colors were employed in their execution.

In addition to religious and civil construction, fortifications are common in Moche territory and some contain walls nearly a kilometer long. Roads were also well maintained and some appear to have been bordered by walls.

SUBSISTENCE. Moche subsistence was based on farming, supplemented by hunting, fishing, and gathering, and by trade. Agricultural technology had advanced markedly during the Late Formative and new forms of social organization now permitted its potential to be realized. Complex irrigation systems were constructed, often involving canals several kilometers long. The reservoir of San José, with a capacity of several hundred cubic meters, is an outstanding example of Moche engineering; another is the famous channel of La Cumbre, which extends for more than 110 kilometers. The Ascope aqueduct in Chicama Valley, constructed of solid adobe and more than a kilometer long, is also an accomplishment of this time. Another notable advance was the use of animal fertilizer, the "guano of the islands" that became so important to world agriculture during the 19th century. To obtain this valued material, the Moche sometimes traveled hundreds of kilometers south to the Chincha Islands. Although these lie off that part of the shore occupied by the contemporary Nazca culture, the latter apparently did not recognize the properties of this fertilizer. The principal farming implements were digging sticks and hoes.

Many plants were cultivated and the diet must have been quite varied; among the cultigens were maize, common beans, lima beans, peanuts, sweet potatoes, white potatoes, sweet manioc, chili peppers, llacón, achira, gourds, and cucumbers. The most widely used fruits included chirimoya, guanábana, pacae, tumbo, granadilla, lúcuma, ciruela del fraile, papaya, and pineapple. It is not known whether coca was raised or obtained by exchange, but it was certainly used for medicinal and other purposes. Coca chewing is depicted on pottery and (as today) was taken with lime kept in a gourd, from which it was removed with a small stick. Chicha, an alcoholic beverage, was produced from maize.

Hunting remained a necessity, since the plant diet had to be balanced by consumption of a certain amount of meat. Deer appear to have been hunted as a sport of the elite, however, to judge from the elaborate costumes of the hunters depicted on the pottery (Figure 112). Dogs drove the victim into widely spread nets, where it was killed by atlatl darts or clubs. Seals were hunted as much for their hides as for their meat; they were caught on the beaches and beaten to death.

Meat was also obtained from domesticated animals, among which the duck is most often represented in pottery. The guinea pig (*Cavia cobaya*) and the llama were also utilized. Although the latter is a highland animal, it appears able to adapt to coastal conditions. Horkheimer (1961) has even suggested that a coastal variety of llama may have

Figure 112. Deer hunting scene painted on a Moche vessel.

existed, but this seems unlikely. In addition to these animals, dogs (*Canis familiaris*), parrots, and monkeys were kept as pets.

Fishing was done by hook and line or with nets from watercraft known as *caballitos de totora* (reed ponies), which are still used in the Huanchaco region near Trujillo. They are composed of bundles of totora reeds and float beautifully in the water. Larger craft were propelled by three or more persons equipped with paddles.

Other food resources included shellfish, shrimp, crabs, doves, roots. Certain terrestrial mollusks were prized.

SOCIAL ORGANIZATION. At some as yet undefined point in Moche history, the society began to assume a strongly hierarchical character. There are several indications of a high degree of social differentiation. Some pottery vessels bear hunting scenes in which richly attired "lords" are surrounded by numerous "beaters" with dogs, while others depict elaborately dressed personages being carried on litters. Individuals performing menial tasks generally are nude or wear only a loincloth or shorts. The fact that these servants may really have been slaves is suggested not only by scenes in which they form a line followed by individuals brandishing whips, but

also by burials from the guano islands, which were accompanied by curious sculptures, often of wood, representing nude men with a rope around their neck and their hands tied behind their back. Images of "convicts" similarly restrained are common in Moche pottery. Such people may have constructed the gigantic temples, which must have consumed so much time and labor.

Arts and crafts may have been differentiated by sex, but religious objects were certainly made by specialists. Generally speaking, women appear to have had low status and we know little of the role of children.

Status differences were clearly indicated by dress. Men in general wore a loincloth and a short sleeveless shirt beneath a tunic, which ended above the knee and was fastened around the waist by a colorful woven belt. More important persons completed their costume by adding a large mantle. Legs and feet were usually bare. The head was always covered and a great variety of headgear existed. Most common was a turban consisting of fine multicolored bands wound around a small cap and held in place by a strip of cloth that passed over the top and was tied under the chin (Figure 113). The back of the neck was generally covered by a cloth that

Figure 113. Modeled and painted vessels typical of the Moche style (MRLH).

fell over the shoulders, resembling the neck coverings used by the French Foreign Legion. Another typical headdress, which was certainly restricted to important persons, was made from the skin of an animal, whose head protruded at the front (Figure 114). Hats were sometimes decorated with feathers or small pieces of metal. The helmet worn by soldiers was conical and had a T-shaped ornament at the apex.

The costume was completed with a great variety of ornamentation, ranging from painting of the skin to jewelry worn on all parts of the body. The face and extremities were painted and a kind of tatooing appears also to have been employed. The nose, ears, and lips were adorned with ornaments of varying form. Earrings were generally cylindrical bars terminating in disks up to 15 centimeters in diameter, which covered most of the face; alternatively, pendants were suspended from the lobe by a ring. Nose ornaments were usually in the shape of a disk or crescent. The neck was nearly always adorned with large collars of stone beads or precious metal. On the arms, and especially the forearms, bracelets were worn, and leg ornaments also existed. Another method of enhancing appearance was cranial deformation. Most of this finery was restricted to men. The costumes of women were very simple, usually consisting of a loose tunic reaching to the knee and few ornaments. Individuals of lowest status apparently went nude.

Conquest of foreign territories is only possible for a society that is well organized, and especially militarily organized, and this appears to have been the case with Moche. The size and importance of the ceremonial centers argues in favor of a basically theocratic structure, and their construction required many hands and a rigid system of control over this labor. At its peak, Moche dominion was exercised over most of the North coast. Some authorities believe that the state was divided into independent principalities, one to each valley, and that these also may have been socially stratified.

Detailed analysis of the war scenes on pottery vessels reveals that some conflicts occurred between populations wearing similar costumes, while others were with people who must have been considered as "savages" since they are shown without any clothing; they appear to be associated with the highlands (Figure 115). Many prisoners were sacrificed to the gods in the temples, and it has been suggested that the clashes between towns in the same coastal valley may have been motivated by

the need for prisoners suitable for sacrifice. The ritual appears to have been carried out by cutting the victim's throat and offering the blood or the body to a celestial deity, perhaps the moon.

Religion, which provided the impetus for many of these practices, must have exerted strong socioeconomic control through its role in agriculture. In spite of the idea held by Larco Hoyle and others that there was a tendency toward monotheism among the Moche, the evidence seems to indicate that, although there may have been one or two principal gods, the pantheon was large. The majority of the deities possess several feline characteristics; prominent canines and ear ornaments in the form of serpent heads are particularly important attributes. Within the complex range of forms represented on pottery is a group of demonic animals with human traits that may represent lesser divinities. They include richly dressed and armed foxes, jaguars, crabs, fishes, owls, and other birds. Frogs are associated with food plants, and maize and beans have human attributes. The figure of Ai-apaec, however, stands out. He nearly always has snakes forming part of his belt; occasionally he is shown fighting a monster and always as the victor. He is associated with what appears to be a conception of "heaven": two scenes sometimes separated by a two-headed serpent. The personages in the upper part are demons or gods, while those below are musicians, lords, or slaves. Rain falls from the body of the serpent; above it are stars. A lunar god, which may have been the moon itself ("Si" in the Mochica language), is also represented on Moche pottery and Ai-apaec may have been related to this divinity.

We know nothing of the Moche concept of the afterlife, except for a few scenes on pottery showing cadavers dancing to the accompaniment of musical instruments, such as drums, flutes, and sticks with jingles. The belief in a better life for those who died in battle may have been an important incentive for the soldiers.

A by-product of warfare and an indication of advances in anatomical and physiological knowledge, is the development of brain surgery, undoubtedly to treat the severe concussions produced by blows with clubs. Trephined skulls exhibit healing indicative of successful operations. Treatment of dental maladies advanced to the extent of replacement of missing parts and tooth extraction. Such accomplishments imply the existence of specialists in curing.

Figure 114. Modeled and painted vessels typical of the Moche style (MRLH).

Figure 115. Scene from a Moche pottery vessel, apparently depicting the exchange of prisoners.

ARTS AND CRAFTS. The most outstanding feature of Moche culture is the pottery, which is a perpetual source of fascination because of its esthetic variety and excellence. Great plastic sensitivity is combined with a certain rigidity, reflecting the fact that although the potter had considerable freedom of formal expression, he exercised his art within strictly determined parameters. The shapes utilized were few and the colors available were also limited. The preferred form was a spherical bottle with a flat bottom and a stirrup spout. Another common form was a bell-shaped basin. Less typical are bottles with a simple spout and several kinds of ollas, cups, and toasters.

Decoration was by painting and modeling. On modeled surfaces, painting was employed primarily as a means of enhancing contrasts between light and shadow. The entire exterior was generally covered with a cream color, on which brownish red paint was applied. Rare pieces are decorated with white on a red background; a few are totally black. When a vessel was decorated by painting alone, the artist did not attempt perspective. Figures are always in profile, although the eyes and chest are shown in front view. Kutscher (1954:45) has distinguished two design styles: (1) linear, which emphasizes outlines, and (2) silhouette, which is not only done with a broader brush, but also has the spaces more completely filled. When painting is on an even surface, the themes are scenic. The artist was concerned primarily with composition and more influenced by the theme than the form, even when the delicacy of the lines would have permitted experimentation.

Modeled decoration is truly sculptural and the figures of animals, humans, plants, or mountains were sensitively treated (Figure 116). Often they seem to be portraits that attempt to record the circumstances of the moment. All kinds of expressions are illustrated, like a series of snapshots depicting variations in character and temperament.

In addition to contributing to ethnography and providing insight into the psychology of the artisans, Moche pottery also serves to mark the passage of time. Larco Hoyle (1948) has recognized five chronological phases. Phase I is distinguished principally by vessel forms and decorative treatment reminiscent of the contemporary Gallinazo style (called "Virú" by Larco). These resemblances are especially evident in the presence of double receptacles with spout and bridge handle and certain typical Gallinazo motifs. Vessels are small, with a

Figure 116. Moche vessel in the form of a deer (MRLH).

solid appearance, and the stirrup spouts terminate in a strongly everted rim like Chavín (or more correctly, Cupisnique) examples; walls are thick and there is a tendency toward flattened shapes (Figure 117). Decoration is executed with broad lines in geometric patterns that tend to cover the entire surface. Exceptional vessels have negative painting. Fine incisions, done when the paste was hard, were often used to delimit the designs. Both this phase and the following one are poorly represented in the Trujillo area, but are better defined in Piura Valley of the Far North coast, in the complex known as "Vicus." Phase II is characterized by diminished flatness and increased height and delicacy of the stirrup spout, as well as gradual disappearance of the external thickening of the rim (Figure 118). Geometric decoration tends to persist, but the lines are finer.

Figure 117
Vessels of Moche I style
(MRLH).

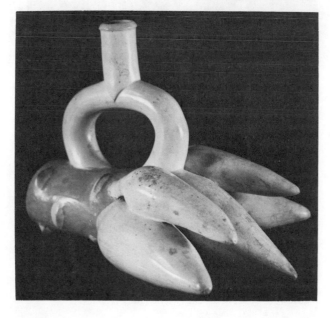

Figure 118. Vessels of Moche II style (MRLH).

Phase III represents the maximum purity of the Moche style (Figure 119). Vessels are typically slightly larger than during Moche II and stirrup spouts are taller, more delicate, and somewhat elliptical in form; the spout itself is short and slightly flaring. Phases III and IV are the "classic period" of the portrait vessel. Geometric decoration begins to be replaced by designs that depict for the first time scenes of real or mythical life.

Phase IV is the time of the great territorial expansion. Vessels become still larger and stirrup spouts assume a rounded or mildly trapezoidal form. The orifices are tubular, straight, and have slightly beveled rims (Figure 120). Other shapes resemble those of Moche III, but decorative motifs proliferate, particularly painted ones. Individuals shown on portrait vessels have turbans incorporating representations of animals. Scenes become more typical subjects for modeling than individual figures. Warfare and motifs related thereto are the theme of many painted and modeled scenes.

Phase V is the last and dates around the 8th century. In Larco Hoyle's (1948:35) opinion, it is marked by artistic decadence in which "the virile sculptural art was replaced by a pictorial linear style, lacking vigor and character"; he attributes this "decadence" to sexual perversion that began during Moche IV. The artist leaves no empty space in his eagerness to cover all the surfaces with his brush and motifs lose their identity beneath exuberant ornamental detail (Figure 121). Spouts, handles, everything is decorated, and occasional examples depict hideous creatures, the product of who knows what kinds of nightmares. Vessels become smaller, but stirrup spouts increase in size; the tube becomes slightly more slender, the stirrup becomes more trapezoidal, and the spout tends towards conical form.

Figure 119. Vessel of Moche III style (MRLH).

Figure 120. Vessel of Moche IV style (MRLH).

Figure 121. Vessels of Moche v style (MRLH).

Figure 122. Wooden staffs with decorated heads from a Moche tomb in the Virú Valley (MNAA, courtesy Clifford Evans).

Figure 123: Upper part of a wooden staff from the tomb of a warrior-priest in the Virú Valley (courtesy A. Guillén).

Technological progress is also evident in metallurgy. Gold, silver, copper, and various alloys were worked, along with lead and possibly mercury (Horkheimer 1961). Hot and cold soldering were employed. Ores were apparently obtained by trade with highland populations.

Wood, bone, shell, and other materials were utilized for ornaments and utensils (Figure 122). Furniture, strictly speaking, did not exist, but stools or benches and litters provided a degree of comfort.

The textiles used to create the elaborate costumes were woven by women, who accomplished all the tasks from spinning to weaving. Many fabrics were covered by multicolored feathers obtained from rare birds.

The art of warfare may have advanced somewhat, but the bow and arrow were not known. The most important weapon was the war club or mace; slings and spears propelled by spearthrowers were also employed.

Larco Hoyle, the notable student of the cultures of the North coast, believed that no culture could have achieved so advanced a religious and political organization without a system of writing. He attempted to demonstrate that designs on lima beans shown on pottery were really ideograms. Larco Hoyle (1943) also discovered that these beans were kept in small bags and transported by runners, comparable to the later well known Inca couriers. Whether or not he was right may never be proved because if such a system ever existed, it had been totally forgotten by the time the Spaniards arrived; furthermore, it has not yet been shown that the series of symbols correspond to ideas, or more specifically, to words.

BURIAL PRACTICES. Burials were accompanied by offerings, and in special cases these included sacrificed humans or llamas. The great majority of the bodies were interred in extended position. In Moche, mausoleums were constructed with adobes whereas in Pacatnamú, cylindrical coffins were placed in funerary caverns. The high rank and importance of Moche priests is exemplified by a grave excavated at Huaca de la Cruz in Virú Valley

(Strong and Evans 1952:150 ff). The deceased, an old man who had lost all his teeth before death, lay on his back in a rectangular coffin made of canes bound together with cords. The viscera had been removed and some attempt may have been made at mummification because although the bones were totally decomposed when the tomb was opened, the skin was better preserved. The body was covered with a fine cloth and the face was concealed beneath a copper mask. A once fabulous collar, composed of hundreds of turquoise beads, had by the time of excavation been reduced to a formless mass. At the right side of the old man was a child about 8 to 10 years old, who had been sacrificed. Above them were three staffs, one a warrior's mace, another topped by an owl, and the third headed by the figure of an old man with protruding canines, a belt terminating in serpent heads, and a headdress with the head of a feline; at his right is the figure of a boy (Figures 122, 123). From Chavín times onward, figures that appear to be deities wear belts ending in snake heads and have feline canines. The correspondence between the small sculpture and the arrangement of the burial is surely significant; one may depict the god, while the other may have been his high priest.

Scattered about in the coffin were 28 pottery vessels, multicolored feathers, textiles, small baskets, gourd containers, and many headdresses. One, a fox effigy, was beside an oblong jar of Phase IV style on which was represented the figure of a warrior-priest wearing a turban ornamented with a similar effigy. These were not the only offerings, however. Further excavation revealed the body of a man with arms and legs extended, who had been wrapped in a coarse cotton mantle. He was strong and muscular, about 1.7 meters tall, and 40 to 45 years old at death. His head lay on one gourd and was covered by a similar one; a flat piece of copper was found near his mouth and another was inside it. This person may have been the "guardian slave" of the old man. Near him were two sacrificed llamas, both headless. Below and to the right of the coffin were the bodies of two women, also sacrificed. Both were wrapped in coarse mantles similar to that surrounding the "guardian"; their heads were so strongly bent downward that in one case considerable force must have been required, which was undoubtedly applied after death. One was about 35 years old and had a blue and brown band around her neck, as though she had been strangled. She was seated facing the old man, with her back to the wall of the tomb. The other woman had a vessel near her hand.

Who were these people? They must have been basically the ones found by the Spaniards when they conquered Peru. Nevertheless, sculptural representations show what look like marked racial variations. Some types are strongly mongoloid, others negroid or even caucasoid. Although a well-known characteristic of Andean peoples is the absence of a heavy beard, some Moche sculptures are images of old men with long beards. Skeletal remains, however, do not exhibit racial differences.

The Recuay Culture (?–A.D. 800)

Although existing information indicates Recuay to be one of the most important cultural complexes in the Central Andean zone, whose influence can be detected from Piura (Vicus pottery) to the Callejón de Huaylas and the Santa Valley as well as on the Central coast, it is impossible as yet to specify its locus of development. The purest expression occurs in the Callejón de Huaylas and Bennett (1944), Tello (1929), and Kroeber (1944) all considered this region to have been the primary center. Larco Hoyle (n.d.), however, presented the hypothesis of a coastal origin involving the Gallinazo (or Virú) culture, which he viewed as the focus of radiation of the negative tradition. This possibility has been refuted by more recent evidence that both Gallinazo and Recuay received the negative technique from elsewhere.

The culture takes its name from the modern town of Recuay, located in the upper part of the Santa Valley near the inception of the Callejón de Huaylas, between the Cordillera Blanca and the Cordillera Negra. Various other names have been used, among them Huaylas, Callejón, and Santa. The latter was preferred by Larco Hoyle because of his view that the culture originated on the coast. Since the term "Santa" applies to the entire river drainage, including coast and highlands, it would be more appropriate. Unfortunately, however, it was employed by Tello to designate features corresponding to later periods in the region and thus is susceptible to misinterpretation.

The area of Recuay culture corresponds closely to the basin of the Río Santa. In contrast to the Moche, Nazca, or Tiahuanaco cultures, it cannot be categorized as coastal or highland since it occurs in both contexts. Its expansion seems to reflect the diffusion of certain elements to other centers by indirect means, perhaps through commerce.

SETTLEMENT PATTERN. Both in the highlands and on the coast, Recuay is best known from burials and little information exists on residences or buildings that might have fulfilled ceremonial functions. Three types of houses are known from the Callejón. One is composed of two adjacent gallery-like rooms roofed with large slabs and covered with earth. The rooms are connected and one has an exit to the outside. Another type of house of similar construction has four rooms. The third type is subterranean and usually consists of one room, but in one case had three; shape is always elongated and the entrance is through the roof. Coastal settlements have not been described, but they may have followed the Gallinazo pattern since contacts between the two cultures are evident beginning in Gallinazo III.

SOCIAL ORGANIZATION. Stone sculptures and pottery vessels provide a basis for general inferences about some of the characteristics of the nonmaterial culture. It is evident, for example, that Recuay society placed strong emphasis on warfare and that it was the basis of a cult. The most important supernatural forces may have been symbolized by the serpent, the feline, and the condor. The frequency with which human heads are depicted is an indication that this type of trophy played an important role in warfare. Whether this practice reflected a desire to incorporate the spiritual qualities of the vanquished, or increased the social status of the possessor, or was believed to have a favorable affect on agricultural productivity, or had some other significance is unknown. Unnatural creatures, among them two-headed animals and toothed monsters, must have had a magico-religious significance that also remains unknown.

Other scenes modeled on the vessels show activities that should be verifiable with additional fieldwork. One depicting a man surrounded by five women may portray either the practice of polygyny or a priest surrounded by his assistants in the cult. Scenes of men with musical instruments and of "dancing" figures exhibit details, such as differences in the relative size of the individuals, that may reflect rank distinctions and the presence of social stratification comparable to that of the Moche. One scene in which a corpse is being eaten by condors may represent either punishment or sacrifice. This same scene, it will be recalled, occurs on Gallinazo ceramics.

ARTS AND CRAFTS. The Recuay pottery style is distinctive and the best-known aspect of the culture, thanks to specimens undoubtedly obtained from burials. Although the paste is normally white, it is occasionally red and some incompletely oxidized examples are gray or black. When not fired white, the surface was frequently covered with a dark cream-colored slip. The principal forms are bowls (some with an annular base), toasters, spoons of various sizes, annular-based cups, tripod ollas, oblong jars with a narrow neck and broad everted rim, bottles with modeled heads joined by a bridge handle to a spout, double vessels, short-necked jars with a modeled figure on the upper part, stirrup-spout jars, effigy vessels, and finally, bugles.

Generally speaking, there are three major techniques of decoration: negative painting, positive painting, and modeling. All three are often associated on the same vsesel (Figure 124). Modeled figures usually occur on the upper part and consist either of single objects, animals, or human beings, or of scenes (Figure 125). Among zoomorphic representations, the condor, the heron, the owl, the jaguar (Figure 126), and the armadillo are most common. Trophy heads, a prominent feature of stone carvings, also appear on the pottery, either alone or in the possession of a head hunter. Depictions of houses are rare, but Tello (1929) mentions that they occur. Some vessels resemble pyramids, from which the existence of this type of structure has been inferred. No actual site has been identified, but some of the pyramids in the Callejón de Huaylas, such as Wariraxa, may belong to this period.

Painted decoration includes two- and three-color (black, white, and red) negative, red-on-white, and black, white, and red positive techniques. Three-color negative was produced by applying red to

Figure 124. Recuay-style pottery found near Huarás
(Museo Regional de Huarás, courtesy Hernán Amat).

Figure 125. Recuay-style pottery showing a variety of activities (courtesy A. Guillén).

Figure 126. Pottery vessel of the Recuay style from the site of Chavín de Huantar (MUSM).

a

b

Figure 127. Recuay jars with the "dragon" motif characteristic of this style (*a.* Museo Regional de Huarás. *b.* MUSM).

areas previously treated by smoking, creating a contrast between light and dark. Geometric figures and animals predominate and among the latter the feline, the condor, and the serpent are most often depicted. The feline is always shown jumping or running. A two-headed serpent-like creature with a triangular head and a feline or "dragon" with bared teeth are diagnostic motifs (Figure 127). Entwined heads are also popular and their presence may indicate a relationship with the earliest phases of the Lima culture, or perhaps with Paracas.

Stone sculpture, another typical element of Recuay culture, has been found throughout the Callejón and at Aija, on the west side of the Cordillera Negra (Figure 128). Schaedel (1948) made a stylistic analysis of the lithic art and suggested at least three chronological periods, of which the earliest is pre-Recuay and certainly associated with the white-on-red pottery of the Upper Formative. The principal Recuay styles have been named "Aija" and "Huarás"; the third style, Huantar, is less important.

The Aija style is represented by two principal kinds of statues: warriors and women. Standardization of treatment is clearly evident in the 27 examples studied by Schaedel, 16 of which were warriors and 11 women. The statues show the complete human figure and have an irregular prismatic form. They are about a meter tall and there is a strong tendency for the head to be disproportionately large, in some instances occupying half of the total height. The face has projecting features, while the extremities are less prominent. There is always an elaborate headdress decorated with incised designs. An interesting detail is the position of the feet, which are turned inward so that the toes abut at the center. The warrior type generally has a trophy head on his back and another is sometimes grasped in his hand; at his right is a club and at his left a shield. The ears usually have a large ornament and the headdress is decorated with incised feline figures. Representations of birds, hands, and feet sometimes appear on both body and headdress. Spiders are also among body designs. Separation between the head and body is not emphasized and the neck is no more than a simple groove; the head is narrower than the body. The statues of women are always slightly smaller and their facial features are less accentuated; the specialized warrior traits, such as the quadrangular shield and the trophy heads, are never associated.

Below and facing page
Figure 128. Recuay stone sculpture (Museo Regional de Huarás).

The Huarás style is less homogeneous, and Schaedel subdivided it into varieties A to H. A much simpler type of human figure is depicted, which has an ovoid form. Shape predominates; incised decoration is absent and sculptural treatment is sufficient only to produce the desired effect without achieving true three dimensionality. Variety A is the most localized geographically and is represented by a human figure with crossed arms and legs. Varieties B and C share with the Aija warrior and woman the possession of incised feline designs and warrior characteristics, such as the shield, the trophy head, and the club. Varieties C and D resemble the Huantar style, both consisting of relief figures executed on stone slabs. Stelae are abundant in the Callejón and generally depict human beings and felines. Tenoned heads also occur (Figure 129).

Evidence from burials both in the highlands and on the coast indicates that copper was widely used for personal ornament, as well as for some kinds of utensils; silver has also been found on the coast.

BURIAL PRACTICES. Highland tombs resemble the subterranean houses. Those investigated at Willkawaín consist of subterranean galleries entered through the ceiling via a tube somewhat over a meter long and about 65 centimeters wide. This tube was blocked by a stone where it emerges from the roof of the gallery. The chamber is about a meter high, a meter wide, and some seven meters long. The roof was a row of roughly worked stone slabs and the walls were of similar slabs placed against the sides of the excavation. The floor is clay. Offerings were few and the majority were in fragments when found, perhaps having been broken by earlier intruders.

On the coast, Larco Hoyle (n.d.) excavated several graves containing adults and children in the cemetery of Suchimansillo. The bodies were flexed and seated with their arms at their sides. Offerings again were few and had been placed above and beside the body. The individuals were covered with textiles and provided with collars and other ornaments of turquoise, lapis lazuli, and mother of pearl.

Figure 129. Tenoned heads of the Recuay culture (Museo Regional de Huarás).

The Lima Culture (A.D. 200–800)

The valley in which Lima, the capital of Peru, is located was originally known as "Rímac" (which in Quechua means "he who talks") and the river continues to bear this name. Max Uhle, one of the first to undertake archeological studies in the area, called the earliest pottery "Proto-Lima." Subsequent work in the Chancay, Chillón, Rímac, and Lurín valleys has increased the amount of information sufficiently to permit establishment of a ceramic chronology and a general reconstruction of cultural development.

The Lima culture has two principal components. The earliest was discovered in the Chancay Valley by Uhle, who labeled it "Interlocking" because this treatment was an outstanding feature of the pottery designs. This term was retained by Kroeber (1926), who analyzed the Uhle collections from Chancay; by Willey (1943), who excavated at Cerro Trinidad de Chancay; and by Strong and Corbett (1943), who encountered the same style during excavations at the Temple of the Sun at Pachacamac in the Lurín Valley, south of Lima. In 1953, however, a group of archeologists agreed to substitute the designation "Playa Grande," taken from a site of this name south of the Ancón beach resort, where the complex has also been found.

The second and more recent component, originally described on the basis of collections from the cemeteries of Nievería in the Rímac Valley, has been given a variety of names: Pachacamac, Proto-Lima, Nievería, Cajamarquilla, Early Lima, and Maranga. The latter is the most recent and most frequently used and will be adopted for this discussion. The first systematic classifications of this material were made by Gayton and d'Harcourt (Gayton 1927); there have been subsequent studies, but most of the results are too discoordinated to add much to our understanding of the culture. The work of Kroeber (1926a) and Jijón y Caamaño (1949) at Maranga, together with that of Stumer (1953), is the most important contribution of recent years.

Playa Grande and Maranga are not strongly differentiated either in pottery style or in associated objects, and represent successive phases of a single culture. Although many archeologists have treated them as totally independent, including Playa Grande in the Upper Formative and Maranga in the period of Wari influence, the chronological position of the Lima culture lies between these two extremes, along with Moche, Recuay, and other regional cultures.

This contemporaneity is demonstrable because of the importance of commerce. Far-flung relations are illustrated by the discovery in a tomb of a fragment of sodalite, a rare semiprecious blue stone so far known only in Bolivia, although there are indications that deposits may also exist in the North highlands. Permanent communication with other parts of the Central Andes is also implied by the evidence of influence on Lima pottery by nearly all the contemporary cultures: Moche, Nazca, Recuay, and Ayacucho. The strongest impact came from the Nazca and Ayacucho cultures, while the earliest relationships are those with Recuay. Consequently, although the Lima culture is distinctive, it cannot be understood without recognition of its relations with many other coastal and highland cultures, to whose influences it was highly receptive.

SETTLEMENT PATTERN. Little is known about settlement pattern. In Chancay, houses were built either of hemispherical, hand-made adobes, of large adobes, or of irregular stones. Some villages were agglutinated and probably irregular (Willey 1953: 406). At Maranga, however, small rooms with walls of hand-made rectangular adobes were arranged in rows (Jijón y Caamaño 1949). No large settlements are assignable to this culture and known habitation sites have not been studied. Hamlets have been observed near ceremonial centers (Patterson 1966).

Lima pottery is frequently associated with pyramidal structures, which probably fulfilled ceremonial as well as dwelling functions. The pyramid of Maranga in the Rímac Valley exhibits certain structural similarities to buildings in the Moche Valley on the North coast. Construction began with walls of small adobes, to which other walls were added until a solid and massive pyramid was produced. Painted mural decorations, another Moche characteristic, have been found at most of the Lima pyramids (Figure 130). At the well-known site of Cerro Trinidad, located in the Chancay Valley, Uhle discovered a wall 23 meters long by 1.6 meters high, made of loaf-shaped adobes and painted in four colors with the interlaced fish design typical on the pottery. The wall was associated with a small

Figure 130. Mural paintings of the Lima style. (*top*) From Cerro Culebras. (*bottom*) From Pachacamac.

pyramid or platform. A beautiful building in the Chillón Valley, called "Cerro Culebras," also has a pyramidal form. On the upper part, accessible by small stairways, are polychrome murals of the typical Playa Grande style featuring animals with interlaced serrated bodies (Figure 130 *above*). One of the frescoes contains the hexagonal-shaped head of a feline (Stumer 1954a).

The best-known buildings are in the Rímac and Lurín valleys. Three sites in the Rímac Valley have been assigned to this period: Maranga, Juliana, and Huaca Trujillo; the latter two, however, may be later, particularly Huaca Trujillo, which appears to represent the Wari period. Maranga is a cluster of three pyramids and smaller structures located near the present Ciudad Universitaria of the Universidad de San Marcos in Lima. The principal pyramid, oriented north-south, covers an area about 270 by 100 meters and is 15 meters high. It has been estimated that a million tons of hand-made, paral-

lelepiped adobes went into the construction of the three pyramids (Kroeber 1954:15–16).

Pachacamac in the Lurín Valley certainly constitutes one of the most notable centers of the Lima culture. At the present time, the Pachacamac buildings appear as large hills at the base and sides of the great Inca Temple of the Sun. The Lima pyramid is unusual in having at its base a stepped adoratory or shrine, the walls of which bear paintings retouched during various epochs. The dominant figure is again the fish. This adoratory appears to have remained in use until Spanish contact. These great pyramids, like all others of the Lima culture, were constructed of small hand-made, rectangular, parallelepiped adobes.

SUBSISTENCE. Information on the economy is also sparse. Several canals terminating at the base of the pyramids of Maranga and Juliana imply that irrigation underwent a notable development. This undoubtedly increased agricultural production and stimulated demographic growth, which provided manpower for the erection of the large pyramids.

The discovery at Maranga of remains of deer (*Odocoileus peruvianus*) and of spear-throwers is evidence that subsistence remained partly based on hunting. Fishing was not abandoned either, and it is possible that the population at Playa Grande lived primarily from the products of the sea. Patterson and Lanning (1964) have suggested that terraces were constructed for the purpose of drying fish and perhaps preparing them for a distant market, since the constant availability made preservation for local consumption unnecessary.

ARTS AND CRAFTS. The diagnostic and best-known aspect of Lima culture is the ceramic style. Playa Grande pottery, which must have developed out of the Miramar complex of the Upper Formative, is characterized by distinctive painted designs consisting of interlaced fishes or serpents with triangular heads and band-shaped bodies, one or both margins of which are often serrated (Figure 131 *left*). The most common colors are red, white, and black. Along with these patterns, which are in the majority, are zigzag bands and rows of circles or disks. Negative painting also occurs, usually in the form of simple lines, dots, or volutes applied to open bowls; interlaced elements are rare. Vessel walls are thick and surfaces are poorly polished. Predominant forms include turtle-shaped jars (otherwise known as "mammiform"), large straight-sided vases, small bowls with low walls, and jars with expanded necks. Decoration was applied to

Figure 131. Lima-style jars. (*left*) Huaca Pan de Azucar (Museo de Puruchuco). (*right*) Chorrillos (Instituto Nacional de Cultura).

the neck and the body of the vessel (Figure 131 *right*). The area of distribution of the Playa Grande ceramic style extends from the Chancay Valley to the Lurín Valley, and the best examples have come from the sites of Cerro Trinidad in Chancay, Cerro Culebras in the Chillón Valley, Playa Grande at Ancón, and Pachacamac in the Lurín Valley. Everywhere except at Playa Grande, it is associated with pyramids.

Maranga pottery is poorly defined, but incorporates at least two major substyles. One is associated with the Maranga pyramids, while the other exhibits certain relationships with later pottery, possibly of Wari affiliation, and is often referred to by the name of "Nievería." Gayton (1927) who classified the material excavated by Uhle from the Nievería cemetery, recognized four classes, which she designated as A, B, C, and D. The first two are the most important and may reflect chronological differences, although this remains to be established. The first of the major substyles is characterized by a red ware with black and white decoration resembling the pottery of Playa Grande but with less complex designs and new vessel shapes (Figure 132).

Figure 132. Maranga-style vessel of the Lima culture, in the form of a fisherman.

The principal decorative motifs are very simple interlaced elements and patterns radiating around the small necks of spherical jars. Negative painting does not occur. The ware is thick and somewhat coarse, with a dull surface much like that of Playa Grande.

The second and final substyle features a relatively thin, fine, brilliantly polished, orangish ware with painted decoration in which gray was sometimes employed in addition to red, white, and black. Vessel shapes are distinct and bottles with a slightly conical or expanded spout and a tubular handle extending from the middle of the spout to the upper part of the spherical body become common. This kind of pottery is contemporary with the Wari invasion.

The area of distribution of the pottery, and perhaps also of the culture, decreases during this final period and becomes largely confined to the Lurín and Rímac valleys. Ceramics that may be related occur in Cañete and pottery from Mala, south of Lima, may after further examination also prove to be assignable to the Lima culture. In the Chancay and Chillón valleys, and apparently also at Ancón, the Playa Grande style continued to develop until the arrival of Tiahuanacoid influences.

The textiles exhibit a certain degree of technological advance. Tapestry patterns were produced with multicolored wefts, most commonly white, red, yellow, blue, green, and gray, as well as black. Painting was a common method of decoration. Brocade is rare. The designs generally consist of interlaced fish resembling those on the pottery, and of crosses, a variety of stepped elements, and other geometric forms. Fish are shown individually as well as interlaced.

Little is known of the status of metallurgy, but copper was certainly used, although few fragments have been encountered.

BURIAL PRACTICES. As in other societies of this period, there was a form of cult of the dead and although the burials are less meticulous than in other regions, they were always accompanied by offerings, possibly including human sacrifices.

Burials were typically made directly in the earth. The bodies were normally extended, laid on a kind of bed of canes or branches bound together with cords, and covered with cotton or wool cloth. Nearly all were oriented north-south. Most of the burials excavated by Kroeber were in pairs, which must have had some significance in terms of the death rites. Graves at Playa Grande and Maranga contained few pottery offerings, sometimes only undecorated utilitarian vessels.

In his excavations at Maranga, Kroeber (1926a: 339–340) found an unusual grave containing remains of three adults. The principal individual lay on its back on a cane litter and was complete. The one on top of it, however, had been decapitated and both the head and arms were missing. The cranium and long bones of a third individual were scattered around the feet of the other two. While the fragmentary remains may represent a disturbed earlier interment, the decapitated person was clearly sacrificed when the principal individual was buried.

In some of the tombs, strange types of artifacts have been found. One is a rag doll sometimes tied to a small cane bed, which must have had some ceremonial relationship to the deceased. Another offering is a kind of cross known as a *guaipe*, consisting of two canes covered with strips of cloth or cords. The tombs also abound in twined baskets.

The Nazca Culture (A.D. 100–800)

The Nazca culture is one of the most famous in the entire world principally because of its polychrome pottery, which has attracted attention both because of its technological fineness and the exciting symbolism of its motifs. Its area of distribution includes the valleys of Chincha, Pisco, Ica, Nazca, and Acarí.

Although Nazca pottery has long existed in the museums in Peru and other countries, its importance began to be appreciated only at the dawn of this century. Again, it was Uhle (1920) who called attention to its antiquity and its significance. His excavations permitted him to recognize Nazca as one of his "protean" cultures, prior to the spread of

Tiahuanacoid influence. Subsequently, Tello, Yacovleff, Kroeber, and others confirmed Uhle's evaluation. The first systematic classification in the interest of historical reconstruction was made in 1927 by Gayton and Kroeber on the basis of the Uhle collections from the Nazca Valley, which consisted exclusively of pottery taken from tombs. They initially divided Nazca into four stylistic and chronological phases: A, X, B, and Y. Kroeber (1956) later reduced these to three by changing Y to C and eliminating X. The categories and their sequence were based on analysis of the interplay of groups of forms and motifs. This method was subsequently elaborated by others at the University of California, with the result that nine phases have been distinguished (Menzel 1971). The only systematic excavations with stratigraphic control are those by Strong (1957), who obtained a sequence that largely confirmed the postulations of Uhle and Kroeber.

Because of the complex nature of Nazca pottery, most studies have been oriented toward its stylistic definition and other aspects of the culture have been badly neglected. In general, however, it can be said that both the pottery and the culture as a whole are divisible into four major periods or phases: (I) Transitional from Paracas to Nazca, labeled "Proto-Nazca" by Strong; (II) Component A of Gayton and Kroeber, Strong's "Early and Middle Nazca," and what Rowe and his collaborators call "Monumental Nazca" (Phases 2, 3, and 4); (III) Component B of Gayton and Kroeber, Late Nazca of Strong, and Proliferous Nazca (Phases 5 and 6) of Rowe; and (IV) Nazca Y or C of Kroeber, Huaca del Loro of Strong, and Disjunctive Nazca (Phases 7, 8, and 9) of Rowe and Dawson.

To facilitate description of the culture, we will employ the Roman numerals I, II, III, and IV to refer to the phases, and will not become involved in the details of the subphases into which each is divided unless this becomes necessary.

SETTLEMENT PATTERN. Studies of settlement pattern and architecture are few, but Rowe (1963) and Strong (1957) have provided important observations. During his excavations in the extensive site of Cahuachi in the Nazca Valley, Strong encountered several Phase I buildings with walls made of small conical and loaf-shaped adobes. Dwellings, however, appear to have been constructed of "quincha" (canes bound together and covered with mud).

A large habitation site on the edge of the Hacienda Cordero Alto in the Ica Valley was occupied during Phase I and the beginning of Phase II (Rowe 1963). During Phase II, the inhabitants apparently moved to Cerro Soldado on the opposite side of the valley, where they remained until the early part of Phase III. Cerro Soldado is composed of small stone-walled houses scattered on an extensive rocky slope along the Río Ica. A shrine occupied the summit of one of the spurs of the hill.

Another Phase II site is Dos Palmos in the Pisco Valley. When photographed from the air in 1931 by the Shippee-Johnson Expedition, it covered about 500 by 300 meters (Figure 133). Except for five small scattered plazas, the settlement was composed of small, rectangular, contiguous rooms (Rowe 1963:10-11).

The site of Cahuachi in the Nazca Valley was also occupied during this time and was apparently abandoned thereafter. Strong (1957) believed that it served as a kind of capital for an incipient state that may have been created by conquest and which incorporated several other valleys. Construction combined adobe with quicha. Solid walls were built of long conical adobes, which were laid horizontally with the base outward to produce a flat exterior surface. Posts introduced into these walls served as the framework for the quincha and also must have supported the roof. Because of the perishable nature of the habitations, neither their total extension nor their number can be reconstructed, but they appear to have covered a considerable area.

During Phase II, several public buildings were erected at Cahuachi for ceremonial and administrative purposes (Figure 134). Most prominent is the Great Temple, a stepped pyramid 20 meters high constructed by facing and capping a natural rise with walls composed of elongated, wedge-shaped adobes. Around the base are adobe-walled rooms and plazas, the largest measuring about 45 by 75 meters (Strong 1957:31). The Great Temple is one of the few large structures from this period and from the Nazca culture in general. The existence of several other architectural complexes composed of smaller pyramids and plazas nearby places Cahuachi close to, if not within, the category of a city.

Several habitation sites dating to this phase have also been identified in the Acarí Valley. Tambo Viejo, the largest, is about a kilometer long and half a kilometer wide. It contains small rectangular rooms with field-stone foundations, several mounds that may have had religious or other public functions, and plazas. Tambo Viejo is surrounded by

Figure 133. Aerial view of the Dos Palmos site, Pisco Valley (courtesy the Shippee-Johnson Expedition).

fortification walls of stone and adobe and corresponds solely to Phase II, during which it was abandoned. Contemporary settlements in the upper part of the valley may have been occupied largely by farmers. Examples include Chocavento, smaller than Tambo Viejo but also fortified; Amato and Huarto, both smaller than Chocavento. Rowe (1963:11–12) has suggested that this florescence was stimulated by Nazca invasion and that its brevity implies that the resulting "empire" endured only a few generations. As already noted, Strong (1957) proposed that Cahuachi may have been the capital of such a state.

Little is known of the population centers and architecture of Phase III, but a decrease in concentration is attested by the abandonment of large sites such as Cahuachi, Dos Palmos, and Tambo Viejo. The only more or less extensive center still inhabited at the beginning of Phase III was Cerro Soldado

in the Ica Valley. This decentralization may reflect growing Nazca militarism, possibly initiated at Cahuachi about the middle of Phase II.

Phase III is distinguished by an unusual type of religious center near Cahuachi, known as "La Estaquería." This consists of a square, stepped, adobe-walled platform adjacent to 12 rows of tall algarroba-wood posts placed 20 to a row and about 2 meters apart, forming a rectangle. The upper end of each post was cut and the great majority were notched. Strong (1957:34) encountered only 47 posts in 1952 and today fewer remain. The manner in which the upper end is finished suggests they might have supported a roof. A similar but smaller "temple" occurs in the lower Nazca Valley.

During Phase IV, relatively populous centers reappeared. On the Pampa de Tinguiña in the Ica Valley, habitation remains corresponding to the first part of the phase extend over almost 600

Figure 134. Plan of the site of
Cahuachi in the Nazca Valley
(after Strong 1957, fig. 4).

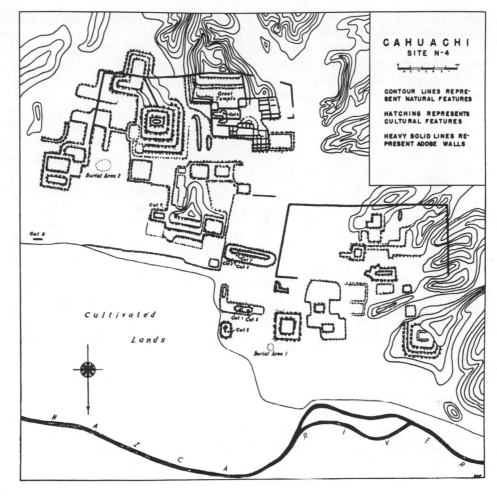

meters and this is probably only about half of what
existed before part of the site was destroyed by
floodwaters. Buildings with field-stone foundations,
small mounds, and a plaza survive. An impressive
palace constructed with adobes was demolished in
1959 (Rowe 1963:11).

Slightly later, a ceremonial center known as
Huaca del Loro was founded on the Río Tunga,
one of the tributaries of the Río Nazca. It consists
of a small circular temple at the south edge of a
complex of large compounds (Strong 1957:36–38).
The temple has thick stone and rubble walls, plastered and painted red. A staircase leads to the only
entrance, which faces south. Around the base are
several inclined ramps. The temple interior contained animal remains and unsculptured monoliths
perhaps used in sacrifices. North and east of the
circular building are remnants of spacious adobe-
walled compartments. Beyond these were numerous
tombs, many with elaborately painted adobe walls.

Nazca settlements have also been reported on the
Paracas peninsula south of the Pisco Valley (Engel
1957a).

SUBSISTENCE. Emphasis on hunting appears to
have increased during Phase III and fishing was
never neglected. Nevertheless, agriculture was the
principal activity and the entire social, political,
and economic system must have revolved around it.

Some form of ritual relating to agriculture may
underlie the creation of the large complexes of
designs on Pampa Ingenio in the Nazca Valley, and
which remain an enigma in spite of intensive investigation (Reiche 1949, Kosok and Reiche 1949).
They occur over an area of some 500 square kilometers in desert covered with dark reddish gravel
and were produced by removal of the patinated
surface stones to reveal the underlying yellowish
white layer. Strange triangular and trapezoidal
paths are associated with straight lines kilometers
long, whimsical zigzag figures, and gigantic repre-

sentations of animals and plants (Figure 135). One bird is some 120 meters long and a spider measures nearly 50 meters. While all the figures are clearly visible from the air, they are hard to recognize on the ground because of their large size and because the lines tend to merge into a confusing maze of paths.

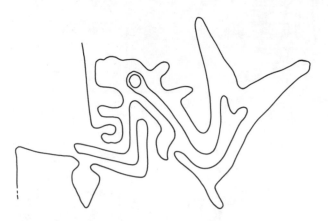

Figure 135. Figure of uncertain significance on the South coast desert.

This immense "zodiac" dates principally from Nazca III in the opinion of Strong (1957), and this estimate is supported by a carbon-14 date of A.D. 550 obtained from a post encountered in one of the paths. Kosok and Reiche (1949) contend that each of the lines, as well as 12 rounded or squared spirals, is equated with the motion of stars, while the animals are interpreted to represent stellar constellations. The figure of the monkey symbolizes the Big Dipper, whose history and movements must have been utilized by astrologers to predict events in the immediate future concerning the water supply, drought, etc.

This is not a farfetched hypothesis since astrology everywhere originated during the early stages of agriculture, when the correlation was noted between the motions of the stars and the times and intensities of availability of water. The constellations do not always make their appearance at the same hour and there is a day in each year, or in each period of years, when they reappear or disappear during daylight; the point on the horizon where this takes place, however, is fixed. These motions are periodic and thus can serve as time markers or indicators of approaching changes in weather. Even today, the Andean farmers can read in the stars the time for harvesting and the time for planting.

When the lowering of the water is awaited with anxiety and the flood arrives almost without warning, as is the case on the South Peruvian coast, the inhabitants must seek all possible means of "controlling" the water supply. A group of specialists, perhaps priests, must have dedicated themselves exclusively to the "calendar." The dolphin, the fish, the parrot, and the spider possibly represented specific epochs. The constellation of the monkey apparently announced the summer solstice, just as the sign of Cancer does in the Western system, which originated in the ancient civilizations of Mesopotamia.

SOCIAL ORGANIZATION. Those who took care of these figures, as well as the priests who lived in the temples, undoubtedly occupied a social position above that of other persons. There is no evidence of slavery comparable to that among the Moche, who needed large numbers of laborers for the construction of massive buildings. A few representations on pottery and the nature of the tombs indicate, however, that social stratification not only existed but was relatively rigid. Nazca society appears initially to have been essentially religious in character, but this emphasis declined little by little and was replaced by a militaristic form during Phase III. Phase IV was a period of decadence.

The patterns of interment must have been related to the religious system, on which great emphasis was apparently placed, but about which we actually know very little. The feline played an important role in the ideology, and its anthropomorphic attributes must reflect ideas about its qualities and powers. Other animal figures possessing human characteristics, such as the porpoise and the falcon, apparently also had magico-religious significance. Gold diadems, nose rings, circular earrings, and other ornaments are almost always associated with such creatures, as they are with burials of important persons. Trophy heads must also have been an integral part of the complicated theocratic-military structure, since they are represented in all possible media. In pottery, they are shown with eyes closed and lips fastened with thorns, like other depictions of the dead.

Differences between male and female costumes were described by Tello (1931) on the basis of a curious pottery piece from Phase III, which shows either a family scene or a group of priests. The central person is playing a panpipe and, according to Tello's interpretation, he is preceded by two sons, guarded by four dogs, and followed by two

Figure 136. Pottery vessel of the Nazca I style.

tinued to be made and the textiles are almost identical to those from the Necrópolis. Strong labeled the typical Nazca pottery "Cahuachi Polychrome Incised" to emphasize the fact that the painted designs are delimited by very fine incisions. The principal colors are red, white, black, buff, orange, brown, and gray. Surface burnishing, which appeared in minor frequency at the conclusion of Paracas, occurs on vessels with a dull black interior. Designs were drawn with a blunt instrument when the paste was dry, producing lustrous lines that contrast with the unpolished surface. Modeling is frequent.

Phase II is characterized principally by sober and refined naturalistic pottery (Figure 137). Decoration was applied to bottles with double-spout and bridge handle, bowls with curved walls, straight-sided and round-bottomed plates, and shallow bowls with outsloping S-shaped walls. Designs are multicolored and outlined with black lines on a red-slipped surface; about eight colors were employed. The pigments are of mineral origin and consequently durable. Animals and plants are executed with such realism that their identification is always possible. Among the plants depicted are chili, jíquima, pacae, lima bean, and maize; animals include the jaguar, deer, fox, llama, rat, monkey, frog, serpent, lizard, spider, pelican, sea gull, condor, falcon, humming bird, fish, and porpoise. A feline with human attributes, without projecting canines but with a mustache, is very common. Of all the designs, it is the least realistic and it probably represents a deity. Decorated areas are not highly ornamented and consist almost exclusively of the central motif alone, leaving much of the surface unadorned and creating a feeling of sobriety.

Phase III pottery, incorporates a large number of modifications that could be interpreted as implying external influences (Figure 138). Roark (1965), however, who studied the transition from Phase II to Phase III, concluded that changes took place only in the formal aspect of the style. The proliferation of embellishments produces a tendency toward abstraction and "mythification" of figures earlier given more naturalistic treatment. Although the primary decorative motifs remained essentially the same, their identity was often obscured by ornamental volutes and painting was applied increasingly to a white surface. Some representations retained a degree of realism, among them figures of warriors and farmers. The frequency of trophy head depictions is interpreted by Roark (1965) as an indication of

women with parrots on their shoulders (the last one may be a daughter). The man wears a headdress resembling one found in a tomb at Chaviña (see p. 133) and the two small individuals in front of him have similar turbans, while the women are bare headed. The man carries a small dog in his left arm and is dressed in a shirt and shorts; the boys are similarly dressed and have ornaments suspended from their lower lips. The women wear long tunics and carry burdens on their backs. The one immediately following the man has panpipes in both hands, while the other carries a vessel with a double-spout and bridge handle. This piece also suggests status differences between the sexes, with the women occupying an inferior position.

ARTS AND CRAFTS. The pottery of Phase I retains so many Paracas elements that Menzel, Rowe, and Dawson (1964) consider the separation between the Paracas and Nazca cultures to be arbitrary. The most perceptible alterations are substitution of pre-fired painting for the fugitive, post-fired or "cloisonné" technique, along with some new decorative motifs and changes in vessel shape (Figure 136). Monochrome pottery of Necrópolis type con-

Figure 137. Pottery vessels of the Nazca II or Nazca A style (MUSM).

Facing page and above
Figure 138. Pottery vessels of the Nazca III or Nazca B style (MUSM).

Below
Figure 139. Vessels of the Nazca IV or Nazca Y style, related to pottery from Ayacucho (MUSM).

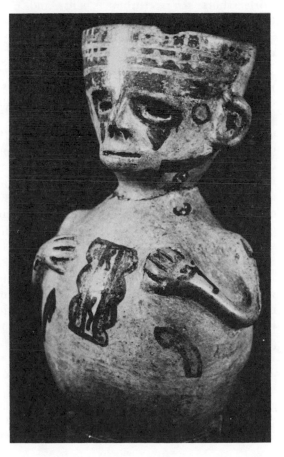

growing militarism. Vessels tend to be more angular and taller; tubular vases with slightly S-curved walls are typical.

During Phase IV, pottery underwent a pronounced decline in quality. The surface changed from white to red and decorative motifs are degenerations of those of Phase III, frequently reduced to an abstract interplay of volutes (Figure 139). There was an increase in the number of vessel shapes, the most important being bottles sometimes bearing a modeled or painted face on the neck, flattened jars with diverging double-spout and bridge handle, flat-bottomed vases of diverse forms, and ollas with small handles on the upper part. Double vessels with crude representations of male-female sexual relations also occur. The impact of contacts with distant regions is most notable during this time, especially with Ayacucho and Lima.

Textiles were cotton or wool, and polychrome designs were produced principally by tapestry (Figure 140) and brocade techniques. Crochet and embroidery also were common. Plain cloth was sometimes painted with patterns resembling those on the pottery. Articles of dress included sleeveless shirts, short skirts, turbans, belts, and mantles; leather sandals and cloth or leather bags for carrying coca were also common. Feathers were often employed for ornament.

Although Nazca technology has been described primarily in terms of ceramics, metals such as gold and copper were used. Stoneworking was uncommon and typically of poor quality, although Tello described a stone vessel of Phase I that was finely ornamented with designs similar to those on Necrópolis textiles. Aside from pottery and weaving, interest appears to have been directed mainly toward practical activities. Outstanding in this category are irrigation canals, some of them underground, which transported water from distant sources and attest to a level of engineering achievement seldom exceeded.

Music, which may have been part of religious ritual as well as secular festivities, was an important component of Nazca culture. The instruments were generally highly ornamented and included panpipes of pottery or cane, pottery drums (Figure 141), trumpet-shaped horns, and rattles.

BURIAL PRACTICES. Burials of Phase II at Cahuachi are typically circular pits excavated in the ground and unlined; some were covered with lashed canes and contained offerings of pottery and food (Strong 1957). The bodies were flexed and all faced

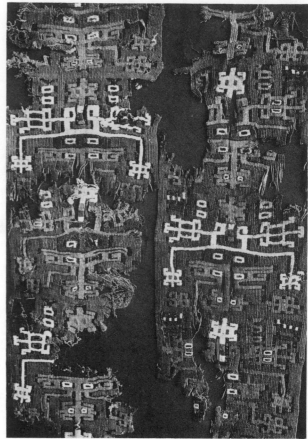

Figure 140. Nazca textile of Period IV done in the tapestry (kelim) technique (Museo Amano).

Figure 141. Drum of pottery from the Nazca culture (MUSM).

132 / *Regional Developmental Period*

south, toward the Great Temple. Four individuals showed cranial deformation of the fronto-occipital type. No adobe tombs containing gold ornaments of the kind frequently encountered by treasure hunters were found at Cahuachi and only a few copper fragments were found at Acarí, in spite of the richness of the other offerings.

A tomb associated with pottery of Phase II, encountered by Pezzia (1962:75) in the Ica Valley, contained a body inside a circular funerary bundle. The relative rarity of this method of interment, to judge from its lack of representation among burials excavated at Cahuachi, suggests the individual was of higher rank.

A group of seven burial cists from Chaviña at the mouth of the Río Acarí provides clearer evidence of social stratification during Phase III (Lothrop and Mahler 1957). They were adjacent, rectangular chambers (about 1.1 by 0.8 meters) with plastered adobe-brick walls. The roofs consisted of several parallel poles or reeds bound together and then covered with cobbles. Arrangement was in the form of a truncated T, with two rows of three cists forming the cross-bar and the seventh, the short "stem." The central cist in the top (south) row contained an individual of considerable importance, judging by the unusual style of his headdress. The one flanking it on the west contained two adults, one of them female and the other of undetermined sex, along with the head of a mouse. The body of the mouse was in the cist on the east,

which also produced the decapitated body of a man whose head had been replaced by a calabash provided with a turban, and an urn containing an infant. The cist in front of the latter one held the bodies of two children, which the presence of spear throwers suggests may have been male. The remaining cists had been previously looted. A great number of offerings had been placed in the cists, the most common being very beautiful pottery vessels of Period III, textiles, pyro-engraved gourds, spindles, beads, spear throwers, and pottery figurines representing obese females. Lothrop and Mahler (1957:44) conclude that this burial complex "represents an individual of importance who was interred with his retainers of both sexes and various ages," a practice also documented in the Virú Valley on the North coast (see pp. 110–111).

Many burials were excavated by Strong in a Phase III cemetery at Cahuachi, which is contemporary with the Chaviña cists. The only surface indications were remains of posts that may have once served as markers. The graves were circular or oval; diameter varied between 60 and 160 centimeters and depth from 0.35 to 2.60 meters. Only four were lined with conical adobes. Most were covered with canes and, as at Chaviña, children had been placed in broken utilitarian vessels. The bodies of adults were flexed and faced south; several skulls exhibited cranial deformation. Two trophy heads were also found. None of these burials was as rich as that described earlier.

The Huarpa Culture (?–A.D. 700)

The Huarpa culture in the Ayacucho zone is currently under investigation and relatively little is known about it, although Tello deduced its existence in 1931 on the basis of large pottery ladles of "archaic" appearance and crude vessels with three handles and a conical base (Lumbreras 1960b:194) found principally at the sites of Tanta Orqo and Auki Willka, in the center of the Ayacucho-Huanta Basin.

In 1946, Rowe, Collier, and Willey (1950) made a small surface collection from the site of Wari, which they studied in conjunction with another surface collection obtained earlier by Lila O'Neale (Kroeber, 1944:49). Among the fragments of pottery

were several with black-on-white decoration, which were designated as "Huarpa," but not incorporated into the local chronology. Subsequently, Bennett (1953) excavated at Wari and other sites around Ayacucho and developed a sequence in which the "Huarpa Series," characterized by two and three color decoration, represented the final Wari period, following the "Tiahuanacoid" styles. More recently, Menzel (1964) and Lumbreras (1960b) demonstrated independently that Huarpa is an earlier style than Wari, and contemporary with Nazca, Moche, Tiahuanaco, and other Regional Developmental cultures. Their data also confirm that Huarpa is a regional culture of a complex nature.

In 1971, Rosa Mendoza F., Marcela Ríos R., and a group of students conducted fieldwork in cooperation with the Ayacucho Archaeological-Botanical Project directed by MacNeish, and publication of these results will substantially increase the amount of available information.

The name "Huarpa" is taken from a southern tributary of the Río Mantaro, which drains a basin more than 100 kilometers long by over 50 kilometers wide. This basin is occupied by two modern cities, Huanta and Ayacucho, and supports a considerable population today.

SETTLEMENT PATTERN. Present information suggests that the archeological culture was limited to the Huarpa Basin and that sites were located between 2600 and 3600 meters elevation. There are indications in the form of a few accidental finds of pottery vessels that it may extend eastward toward the border of the forest via the Río Apurímac, but this zone has not been systematically explored.

The Huarpa settlement pattern has a rural character. The population must have been large since 300 of the approximately 500 sites recorded in the region are of Huarpa origin. Except for Ñawimpukyo, which was a city, all are villages or households (Figure 142). At Lagunillas, in the central part of the basin, the population lived in rocky areas, incorporating the outcrops into the walls of their houses. Where outcrops did not occur, dwell-

Figure 142. Wall of a Huarpa house at Ñawimpukyo, Ayacucho Valley, showing the type of stone construction.

ings were constructed in areas of low potential agricultural productivity. The most populous sector, on the summit of the largest hill, contained some 50 dispersed households. Although dry farming is still carried on in this region, it is no longer inhabited.

Ñawimpukyo, on a hilltop overlooking the modern town of Ayacucho, is called "Ranra-ranra" ("quarry") by the modern residents. Ñawimpukyo means "spring" and there are springs nearby that justify this name. The architecture differs from that at other Huarpa sites. Whereas rural houses are irregular, although with a tendency toward circular or elliptical form, and were constructed on crags or other kinds of terrain unsuitable for cultivation, this type of house occurs only on the perifery of Ñawimpukyo or in the vicinity of the terraces. Other groups of buildings exhibit a different type of construction that gives them an elite aspect. The walls were built by a technique very similar to that of the best-constructed terrace walls, consisting in the placement of large rocks vertically in rows and filling the intervening space with very small stones. A decorative effect was achieved by the selection of trianguloid stones for the vertical members. This uniformity of technique indicates that both kinds of structures—the buildings of Ñawimpukyo and the terraces—were community projects executed under the same type of supervision. This has suggested the hypothesis that Ñawimpukyo was the capital of a Huarpa regional state and that the public buildings and houses of an urban elite reflect a power structure related to control of the water resources and the advanced agricultural technology.

Three sectors in Ñawimpukyo appear to be composed of public buildings or dwellings of the elite. All face north. The central group consists of platforms and probably was a ceremonial precinct, while the lateral ones appear to contain granneries, administrative buildings with patios, and large plazas, along with dwellings. The largest residential areas surround these groups and are located principally in rocky places. Planning is implied by the orderly arrangement and by the existence of canals for distribution of water throughout the town. The site occupies a strategic location both in terms of control of the permanent water sources in the basin and of defense, most of the Ayacucho region being visible from the summit of the hill.

There may have been another city similar to Ñawimpukyo in the lower part of the basin, in the Huanta zone. This region has not yet been explored fully, but certain cultural differences are apparent that may reflect some kind of division, perhaps of a political nature.

SUBSISTENCE. An outstanding feature of Huarpa culture is its advanced agricultural technology. Ayacucho is one of the most arid highland zones and much of the region consists of ravines and irregular surfaces that leave little land suitable for cultivation. Extensive portions are semi-deserts covered with spiny plants that can survive with minimal moisture. Rain falls during only three months each year and the remaining nine months are characterized by drought of such intensity that the few streams cease to flow and the soil turns to powder. Although these environmental conditions make the Ayacucho region unfavorable for modern agriculture, techniques for the conservation of resources not only permitted cultivation of the steepest slopes and the driest zones during Huarpa times, but were so successful that five times more land was agriculturally productive than today. The reasons for this difference lie in the Huarpa elaboration of hydraulic technology and methods of soil preparation, and in their rational use and distribution of the small quantity of water available.

Given the fact that one of the primary problems is the irregular morphology of the terrain, with steep slopes subject to erosion and loss of soil into the ravines where it is swept away by the rivers, one solution is to offset this process by construction of terraces following the contours of the hillsides. Huarpa terraces or "andenes" consist of carefully built containing walls of varying composition resembling those constructed many centuries later around Cuzco by the Incas. Their spacing was determined by the angle of the slope, so that some are only 1.5 meters wide while those on more gradual inclines are 10 meters or more in width.

Around Lagunillas (Pacaicasa), in the central part of the basin, terraces remain preserved over several kilometers of hillsides, testifying to the organization of the peasantry into a labor force that serviced them and also benefited from their existence. About 100 terraces extend from the summit to the valley bottom; not a centimeter of useable surface was overlooked (Figure 143). Since the site lacks water, it is probable that cultivation was seasonal, as it is in most of the basin today. That is, the terraces were used for one crop a year, which was planted to take advantage of the rainy season. Lower down in the valley, on the other hand, agriculture could be practiced the year around, with two or three annual harvests. Traces of irrigation canals imply the existence of reservoirs or cisterns to catch rainwater.

Although not well represented at Lagunillas, one of the most notable aspects of Huarpa culture was the construction of canals and dams. The site of Quicapata (Hill of Chalk), south of the city of Ayacucho on the border between the upper and middle parts of the basin, incorporates a remarkable system of canals and reservoirs associated with terraces, which cover the hillsides. A permanent natural spring fed a chain of reservoirs located at different levels, from which canals distributed the water over the cultivated area in a uniform manner. This site was inhabited beginning in the Rancha period of the Upper Formative.

At the site of Raqay Pampa, in Chupas, a canal brought water to a village of a few houses located on the agricultural terraces. From the main canal, which crossed from south to north, there issued lateral canals that in turn separated into smaller channels for irrigation of the terraces. Excavation of a number of canals in different places has shown them to be constructed with great care and lined with an impermeable plaster. Some are 1.6 meters wide and several kilometers long.

Evidence of hunting is provided by small, triangular, obsidian projectile points and there is clear evidence that domesticated guinea pigs and llamas were both abundant.

Figure 143. Terrace wall at Lagunillas, Ayacucho Valley, showing the combination of natural outcrops with smaller stones.

ARTS AND CRAFTS. The most distinctive trait, and in fact the only one mentioned in the literature as yet, is the pottery, which has been treated as a single style representing a single chronological phase. Although the principal decorative technique (red and black painting on a white-slipped surface) maintains a surprising degree of uniformity, and designs generally tend to be linear and geometric, careful analysis permits recognition of four chronological phases, designated as A, B, C, and D. The earliest is associated with pottery of the Rancha type, which belongs to the Upper Formative, while the latest dates near the beginning of the Wari period.

Huarpa Phase A is dominated ceramically by two types: Huarpa Fine and Caja. The pottery is thin-walled and the predominant forms are open bowls with an S-shaped profile, a rounded base, and occasionally with projecting handles extending from the rim to the body; rims are tapering and often beveled toward the exterior. Decoration is applied to the exterior in vertical or horizontal red or black stripes, while tongue-like bands cover the upper part of the rim interior. The most characteristic motif is three horizontal bands on the upper half of the vessel, the middle one undulating and the other two straight. One of the few nongeometric elements is a human face, which occurs either on bowls or large, oblong, conical-based jars. The eyes are painted rectangles; the mouth may be either a line or a rectangle, and the nose is often modeled. The face is frequently painted with lines running in different directions (Figure 144).

Caja ware, derived from Rancha, is light orange, fine grained, and compact, with temper rarely visible. Vessel shapes are similar to Huarpa ones, but painting is done with brown lines on the natural surface. The most common motif is an undulating line on the interior of bowls with slightly beveled rims.

In Phase B, the dominant pottery types are Huarpa B and Kumun Senqa. Huarpa B ware is not as fine as Huarpa A, but possesses a greater variety of forms (Figure 145); outstanding are tall cups with slightly convex walls and rounded bases.

Pottery vessels of the Huarpa style (MHRA): Figure 144 (*top*) Phase A; Figure 145 (*two center vessels*) Phase B. Figure 146. Musical instrument of the Huarpa Black-on-White style (MHRA).

One of the most diagnostic features is a change in the three-banded motif; whereas in Phase A all three bands were the same color, generally black, the straight bands are now black and the intervening undulating one is red. The Kumun Senqa type began in Phase A, but attained its maximum popularity during Phase B. It is a monochrome pottery with dark-red slip. A special function is implied by its limitation to ollas and large amphoras with short, thickened, everted necks.

During Phase C, the dominant types are Huarpa Black on White and Cruz Pata. The former persists with variations until Phase D and subsequently becomes integrated into styles associated with the earliest phases of Wari. It is a thick pottery with a thick, white, unpolished slip. Decoration is geometric and composed of wide and narrow lines. A characteristic treatment is a broad band around the rim and extending one or two centimeters down the interior, combined with vertical and horizontal bands and lines forming checkerboard or striped patterns (Figure 146). Curvilinear motifs, such as spirals, are very rare. A "tricolor" variant, created by the addition of purplish red bands or areas occurs occasionally, particularly in the Huanta zone. The color is the same as the slip used in Kumun Senqa and Cruz Pata types. The most common vessel shape is a large V-shaped urn with a flat base, straight walls, and a greatly thickened rim, sometimes beveled. Other vessel shapes resemble those of Kumun Senqa pottery, especially the large conical-based amphoras.

Cruz Pata is a fine pottery associated with the Huarpa A and B types, and possesses similar vessel shapes and decorative motifs, although the combinations are different. Decoration consists of various combinations of painting: black, red, orange, and gray on a white slip; black, white, orange, and gray on a red slip; and the same colors on an unslipped surface. Motifs are less geometric than in earlier phases and there is a tendency toward curvilinear designs; one consisting of a circle with radiating, "corkscrew" lines gives the effect of a spider or octopus. Peculiar human figures with rectangles or simple lines for eyes are reminiscent of certain Nazca IV motifs. The bowl with the S-shaped profile continues to evolve, but in this type it has a flat base; later, tall vessels with lateral strap handles and smaller dimensions become characteristic (Figure 147).

Phase D is dominated by the Okros A and Cruz Pata ceramic styles, and Huarpa Black on White is

Figure 147. Pottery of the Cruz Pata style. (*above*) Conchapata, Ayacucho (MUSCH). (*below*) Huancavelica (MHRA).

retained with some alterations. In its earliest form, the Okros style is closely related to Cruz Pata both in vessel shape and decoration. The exterior is white slipped and large areas are painted black. New motifs are introduced, however, as well as a peculiar brilliant orange slip, initially used mainly on the interior of bowls and vases but later applied to the entire surface, making it a diagnostic feature. Decoration is much more complex than in the Huarpa style and many motifs resemble surrealistic, unidentifiable plants and animals. One of the most typical figures is an octopus with two bodies and six or eight volute-shaped appendages suggesting legs or tentacles: radial patterns in general are very common (Figure 148). Correlations between Cruz Pata and Nazca IV designs now become unmistakable. Typical vessel shapes include flat-based bowls with diverging walls, spherical neckless bowls, and jars with globular bodies, flat bases, and narrow necks, sometimes in the form of a human face with a handle at the back. The eyes resemble those on Huarpa pottery, especially the incised variant, and have prominent eyelashes.

Technological advances are also discernible in other aspects of culture. Copper probably had been known since the Upper Formative, and was used for pins, needles, and other small artifacts. Little is known about agricultural tools and domestic utensils. In the latter category, a pottery spoon manufactured in a variety of sizes and shapes is one of

the most diagnostic elements. Also characteristic are L-shaped objects of a slaty stone, which appear to have served as hoes and also as knives and axes.

BURIAL PRACTICES. The few burials that have been excavated are all direct interments. Offerings of pottery occur in some cases, while others have no offerings. When pottery is associated, the vessels were placed near the head and there are usually two (Figure 149). Some burials appear to be secondary and there are reports of urn burials, although none of these has been systematically excavated.

A tomb of Huarpa Phase C, containing Cruz Pata pottery, was discovered by construction workers in a cemetery in the eastern portion of the immense site of Conchopata, where the Ayacucho airport now lies. It was boot-shaped, with a tubular entrance at one edge, and had been excavated in the rock. The body was extended and at its side were copper pins with large, flat, paddle or fan-shaped "heads" and two vessels similar in form to those of Nazca III, except that they had a flat bottom and a vertical strap handle at the waist. An earlier grave, probably from Phase B, contained a flexed body lying on its back. From Phase D, only one tomb is known; the body was flexed. The most interesting feature is the discovery of burials of rats, reminiscent of the situation at Chaviña (Nazca III) except that at Conchopata none were associated with human beings.

Figure 148. Pottery vessel of the Okros style from Conchopata, Ayacucho Valley (MUSCH).

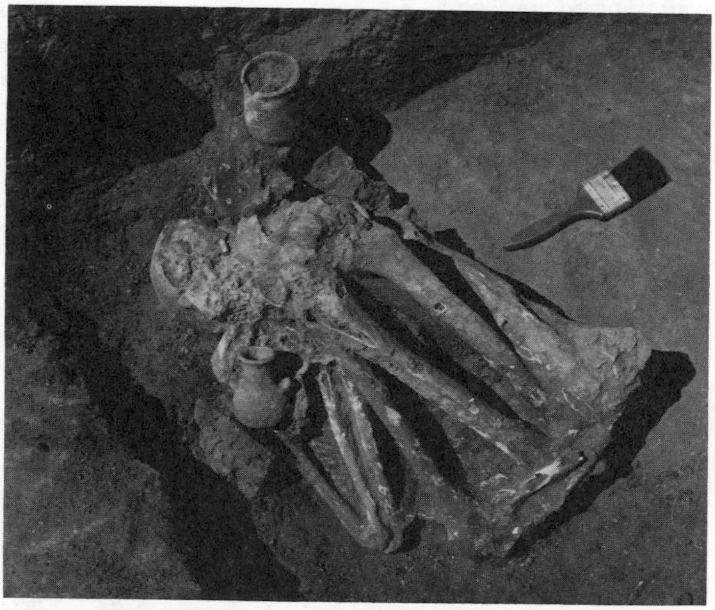

Figure 149. Huarpa burial of Period B found in Chupas, Ayacucho (MNAA).

The Tiahuanaco Culture (A.D. 100–1200)

The ruins of Tiahuanaco lie near the eastern margin of Lake Titicaca, at an altitude of about 4000 meters on the Peruvian-Bolivian altiplano. At this elevation, trees cannot grow and wild grass is the only form of vegetation over a major part of the immense plain. The monotony of the landscape is broken by carved stones and mounds, which for centuries have testified to the former existence of an active society of farmers and herders.

In the Americas, no other culture has evoked as much fantasy as Tiahuanaco, perhaps because it was the first pre-Inca civilization known, or because of the monumentality of its remains or the intensity of its impact over the Andean region as a whole. Arturo Posnansky believed that Tiahuanaco was the cradle of American culture, with an antiquity of at least 14,000 years. More qualified investigators than he have viewed the site as the capital of an ancient "Megalithic Empire," and Uhle considered it the center of dispersion of a culture later designated as Tiahuanacoid. Until a few years ago, the hypothesis of a Tiahuanaco expansion throughout the Central Andes was accepted by most Peruvianists and some still support it. The following discussion will attempt to separate fiction from fact.

The earliest references to Tiahuanaco date back to the Spanish chroniclers, who speak of bearded, white builders who preceded the Inca. Many travelers have written about the ruins, admiring their magnitude and the skill of the stone cutting. The first systematic description, however, did not appear until the end of the nineteenth century, when Stübel and Uhle (1892) published a volume based on notes taken by Stübel. Uhle visited the site two years later.

The first serious archeological excavations were conducted by Bennett in 1932. These eliminated the idea of "Megalithic Tiahuanaco" as a single cultural epoch and demonstrated the existence of three phases, which were designated Early, Classic, and Decadent (Bennett, 1934). This sequence has been expanded by Ponce Sanginés (1961), who has added two phases, both preceding Bennett's Early Tiahuanaco and representing the Upper Formative (page 89). Phases III and IV (Bennett's Early and Classic, respectively) belong to the Regional Developmental Period, while Phase V (Decadent) corresponds to Expansive Tiahuanaco (page 151), when elements of this culture were widely dispersed over the southern Andean area and played a role similar to the Wari expansion, although its character was apparently different.

During the three post-Formative phases, the center of the Tiahuanaco culture was on the altiplano, and during Phases III and IV activities were apparently concentrated in this region although there are indications of expansion to the north and possibly also the south that need further investigation. Phase V was a period of dispersal into the valleys and over the highlands and coasts to the east, west, and south. Few sites corresponding to the Regional Developmental Period are known, but the sporadic discoveries of tombs, sculptures, and fragments of pottery indicate that most of the Department of La Paz was occupied. Closer relations with the area west of Lake Titicaca during Phase IV are implied by changes in the Pukara culture (pp. 88–89).

SETTLEMENT PATTERN. The Tiahuanaco site north of the modern town of the same name contains six architectural complexes, of which the largest and most important is Kalasasaya in the center of the ruins. To the east is the "Semisubterranean Temple" and on the west are the enclosures of Putuni, Laka Kollu, and Q'eri Kala. Farther toward the west, in the direction of the lake, is the cemetery. An immense natural hill known as Akapana lies to the south. It has been considered the remnant of a pyramid and idealized reconstructions have been made of its ancient form. Only fragmentary worked-stone walls survive, however, making it risky to postulate anything regarding the buildings that may have been associated. Perhaps it was a temple similar to that at Cahuachi, where the natural shape of the hill was exploited for the foundation. Most of the buildings that have been examined probably served a ceremonial function. No dwellings are known, although some people certainly lived at Tiahuanaco. Investigations by Ponce Sanginés (1964) have shown that the temples were constructed during Phase III. During Phase IV—the so-called "Classic"—only a few structural changes were made, but the addition of new sculptures may indicate increased complexity in ritual.

The Semisubterranean Temple, which was completed excavated by Ponce Sanginés (1964:44–61), is a large, open, sunken patio, about 1.7 meters deep, 28.5 meters long, and 26.0 meters wide. The walls consist of several courses of rectangular sandstone blocks interrupted at irregular intervals by pillars. The west wall has 15 vertical members, while the others have 14, 11, and 9; they differ in height, width, and thickness. No mortar was used and the exposed surfaces were only superficially polished. A few of the pillars appear to have been decorated with high relief sculpture and there are also traces of a painted coating. More obtrusive are the anthropomorphic heads that project at intervals between the blocks forming the second and third rows, into which they were inserted by means of tenons (Figure 150). The technique of attachment, but nothing else, is reminiscent of the ornamental heads at Chavín. The material is very soft volcanic tuff and the carving is stylized. The temple was entered by six steps near the center of the south wall, opposite Akapana. Small channels run parallel to the walls.

A stela 2.5 meters high, found by Bennett in his 1932 excavations, is assigned by Ponce Sanginés (1964:61–63) to the same phase as the temple. The front has a human figure with a crescent surrounding the mouth that has been identified as a beard or a nose ring. The arms are low relief; the right hand is raised and the left one rests on the abdomen. Beneath are two felines. On the sides are snakes and animals that may be foxes. The sculpture on the rear is poorly preserved.

During Phase IV, the temple was slightly modified by the addition of a gigantic reddish anthropomorphic pillar, known as the Bennett Stela, after its discoverer. It is 7.3 meters tall and has a rectangular cross-section. When found, it was lying beside the small Phase III stela described above. The pedestal is 1.8 meters high and must have been set in the floor at the center of the temple. The carving and costume are typical: a large quadrangular headdress with a broad band across the forehead, a suggestion of a collar, arms in low relief, a raised band forming a wide belt, and legs separated by a shallow groove. One hand holds a kero-like vessel and the other an object resembling a *Strombus* shell. The surface of the pillar is covered with incised designs composed of anthropomorphized felines, birds (falcons?), human-like beings, fish, and geometric frets.

A beautiful and delicately ornamented receptacle of Phase IV encountered by Ponce Sanginés (1964) must have been utilized in conjunction with the

Figure 150. Tenoned heads in the wall of a subterranean temple at Tiahuanaco.

Figure 151. Colossal head of the Tiahuanaco IV style carved from stone.

Figure 152. A staircase in the Kalasasaya sector of Tiahuanaco.

gigantic statue and another less elaborately ornamented one found by Bennett in 1932. The receptacle is a massive low cylinder decorated on one side by a circular mark, inside of which are radiating semitrapezoidal heads bearing crowns with three points, each terminating in what appears to be a human head. These are surrounded by a row of fish heads. The rim has an ornamental band composed of eight deities with rectanguloid heads, from which radiate the heads of fishes. They hold a staff in each hand and wear a tunic with a belt also terminating in fish (or perhaps serpent) heads. These figures are similar to the one on the Gateway of the Sun at Kalasasaya and on the Raimondi Stela at Chavín.

The great enclosure of Kalasasaya, west of the Temple, was also probably constructed during Phase III according to Ponce Sanginés (1964:68). It is a large platform accessible by six steps on the east side (Figure 152). The retaining walls employ the same construction technique as those of the Temple (that is, vertical stones separated by horizontal blocks), but lack the ornamental heads. The large pillars are irregular in form, but more equally spaced than those in the Temple walls. At the base of the south wall are several water-catchment basins and canals, which probably served a ceremonial function. In the eastern half of Kalasasaya is a rectangular patio with a beautiful statue in the center, known as the Ponce Monolith in honor of its discoverer. It resembles the giant Bennett Monolith, but is only 3 meters tall. The surface is covered with a series of designs of magico-religious significance.

Some of the other anthropomorphic sculptures (Figure 151) dating from Phase IV may once have occupied the western part of the great enclosure. The most notable feature of this sector, however, is the "Gateway of the Sun," a slab about 3 meters high carved in the form of a doorway located at the extreme northwest, near a hill. Its fame derives from a beautifully executed frieze on the upper

Figure 153.
The Gateway of the Sun
at Tiahuanaco, dated in Phase IV.
(after Kelemen 1944, pl. 46).

part, corresponding to the lintel (Figure 153). At the center is a person with a staff in each hand, a radiating headdress, and clothing similar to that worn by the figures on the band ornamenting the cylindrical receptacle found in the Temple. At each side are three rows of "angels" with bird (falcon or condor) or human countenances facing toward the center, in a running or perhaps kneeling position. The central figure became a popular motif throughout the area of Tiahuanaco influence and appears on pottery and textiles, as well as stone.

Farther toward the west is the Putuni enclosure, composed of four wings surrounding a patio. A series of drains or covered canals constructed of dressed stone has been found there. The lower one measures one meter wide and is 3 meters below the surface. North of Putani are two Phase IV structures: the Laka Kollu mound and the Q'eri Kala enclosure, also a rectangular building with four wings arranged around a large open patio. The floors were dressed and polished stone and the walls were adobe. Each wing contained contiguous habitations, some of them interconnecting. The corners were well-finished pillars.

Changes in construction can be summarized as follows: roughly hewn stones employed during Phase III were finished and polished on the exposed surfaces during Phase IV. The latter phase also saw the introduction of thin adobes for double-wall construction and of mural painting (Ponce Sanginés 1961). Even more striking improvement took place in stone carving during Phase IV (Figure 154).

SUBSISTENCE. Tiahuanaco economy was based predominantly on the cultivation of potatoes, quinoa, cañiwa, coca, and mashwa—all plants adapted to cold climate and high elevation. Products raised in valleys adjacent to the altiplano may also have been consumed. Although herding was a more important activity, hunting contributed significantly to the food supply, along with fishing in the lake. Hunting was done with bow and arrow, to judge from the many very small, fine, stemmed points chipped from quartz or obsidian that have been found at the Tiahuanaco site.

SOCIAL ORGANIZATION. Little attention has been paid to the reconstruction of Tiahuanaco social organization. It is obvious, however, that religion played a major role in the culture, since there is no other way to explain the great luxury of the capital. Religious ideas must have been disseminated as a by-product of commerce during Phase IV. It is difficult to form an idea about the nature of the cult in spite of the existence of numerous representations in pottery and stone. The figure holding the batons represented on the Gateway of the Sun may represent one of the principal gods during Phase IV, along with the human being depicted in various ways on statues and on pottery.

Skull deformation of the tabular oblique type was practiced by the Tiahuanacans, either for esthetic or religious reasons. Trophy heads must have played an important cult role, since they are depicted frequently in all media. Receptacles made from human skulls, dating from Phase IV, may also reflect ritual practices.

ARTS AND CRAFTS. Phase III pottery is of poor quality and very homogenous in form and decoration (Figure 155). Painted and incised patterns were usually applied to the interior of everted necks and consist of complex representations of felines, birds, and fish, all of which have three annular appendages on the head. The rendition is never naturalistic and seems to be a stylization of designs employed during Tiahuanaco I and especially II. The most popular vessel shape was a shallow jar with a flat bottom, slightly constricted neck, and

Figure 154. Monolith carved in Classic Tiahuanaco style from Khonkho Wankani, Bolivia.

Figure 155. Pottery vessels of Tiahuanaco III style (Museo de Tiahuanaco).

broad flaring rim. Associated are spherical bottles with long, slightly flaring necks and bowls with straight, parallel sides and undulating rims. The latter were sometimes ornamented by a modeled feline head. Bowls and plates were uncommon.

During Phase IV, the "Classic" period, pottery is fine and varied (Figure 156). Decoration is painted and incised, as in Tiahuanaco III, but differs in that Phase III designs were applied directly on the natural buff surface and somewhat crudely executed, whereas during Phase IV they are on a well-polished and usually red-slipped surface. The motifs were outlined with black or white lines and are figurative or geometric, with the figures tending toward angularity. Modeling is frequent and exhibits a preference for human heads, some of which are magnificent portraits. Painted decoration is rarely combined with incision; the latter was generally reserved for vessels blackened by reduced firing. Polychrome motifs, which employ up to six colors, give preference to stepped designs, felines, serpents, fish, decapitated bodies, head-hunters, and falcons.

Left
Figure 156. Pottery vessels of Tiahuanaco IV style (Museo de Tiahuanaco).

Below
Figure 157. Pottery vessels of Tiahuanaco V style (*left,* courtesy A. Guillén. *right,* Museo de Tiahuanaco).

Some motifs resemble those on stone sculpture, but only the quadrangular head from the Gateway of the Sun was widely employed (Ponce Sanginés 1948). The principal vessel forms are the so-called "kero," which continues into Phase v (Figure 157), and a relatively tall, flat-based, hour-glass shaped container. A variant that is less constricted and provided with vertical handles or has an undulating rim and the head of a feline is known as a "fumigator." Most examples have a pedestal that comprises almost a third of the height. Other forms include bottles, bowls, plates, and ollas. Ovoid jars with tall flaring necks are also common.

A curious artifact is a kind of pottery lamp, consisting of cylindrical chambers for oil. Pottery disks, either specially made or adapted from sherds, may have been used in a game or in some sort of ritual.

Another notable aspect of Tiahuanaco technology is metallurgy. It was here, apparently, that alloying of copper with tin to produce bronze was discovered. By Phase iv, this technique was already well developed. In other parts of the world, bronze working was accompanied by such notable cultural advances that a "Bronze Age" has been recognized. In the Andes, however, it had little impact and diffused only in association with a few other Tiahuanaco traits, about which more will be said later (pp. 155ff.). Gold was also known and worked in sheets. During Phase iv, metal was used in architecture, in the form of copper clamps to unite large stones. Stones clamps also occur.

BURIAL PRACTICES. Only one tomb has been found; it dates from Phase iii and contained an individual accompanied by a dog.

Little-Known Cultures (A.D. 100–800)

Contemporary with Moche, Nazca, Lima, Tiahuanaco, Huarpa, and Recuay, other Regional cultures developed in the Central Andes about which much less is known. Evidence of new complexes comes to light whenever an archeologist moves outside the boundaries of known cultures. Only a brief synthesis will be attempted here, in the hope that it will encourage efforts to secure more detailed information. Discussion will proceed from south to north.

North of Lake Titicaca, a complex known as Pukara is represented by well-elaborated pottery. In the Cuzco region, the monumental Inca buildings have concealed the remains of the earlier cultures by distracting attention from the less conspicuous settlements of preceding groups. The Cuzqueños themselves have a saying that whoever comes to Cuzco is converted into a "Machupicchologist" on seeing the extravagant beauty of that imperial town. The Lower Formative occupation of Cuzco, Chanapata, was followed by the relatively simple Waru culture. Waru is known only from its pottery and even here the data are deficient. One type probably assignable to this complex has been called "Carmenca" (Rowe 1944, fig. 16:3–8) and consists of open bowls painted with simple red-on-white designs composed of straight or undulating lines and dots. Modeled representations of figures, possibly human, also occur.

Associated with this relatively fine pottery is another red-slipped or unslipped type with crudely modeled or incised decoration.

Northwest of Cuzco, in Andahuaylas, Rowe discovered a ceramic complex that he called "Qasawirka" and which he believed to be Formative. Subsequent investigations have shown, however, that it belongs to the Regional Developmental (Grossman, pers. comm.). It is associated with towns of moderate size and the use of copper. Farther north, in the Mantaro Valley, Kroeber (1944:98) noted a well-developed black-on-red pottery type (Figure 158), which he called "Huancayo," and which bears cursive and geometric decoration related to the Caja style of the Huarpa culture. More recently, Matos Mendieta (pers. comm.) has shown that this pottery dates from the Regional Developmental Period and is represented at several population centers, some of considerable size.

More information is available concerning the occupation of the upper Marañón and the upper Huallaga, in the Department of Huánuco. At the site of Kotosh, the Japanese expedition found pottery closely related to Gallinazo ceramics from the North coast and to pottery of the Callejón de Huaylas. This complex, named "Higueras," includes a red type with incised and modeled decoration

Figure 158. Pottery vessel of the Huancayo style (courtesy Ramiro Matos Mendieta).

Below
Figure 159. Pottery vessels of the Higueras style from Kotosh (courtesy Seiichi Izumi).

(Figure 159) and a negative-painted type. It is uncertain as yet whether it should be assigned to the Regional Developmental Period or to the Upper Formative. At Tantamayo, farther to the north and west, some peculiar buildings that have usually been considered very late are associated with a red pottery somewhat resembling Higueras. Flornoy (1955–1956), who has studied the structures, has been unable as yet to establish their age or their position in the cultural sequence. The walls are stone set in clay. There are houses with up to 7 floors, which is unusual in the Andean area. All have windows and intercommunicate on the interior by means of stone steps projecting from the walls. Buildings in villages on hilltops south of Tantamayo are also several stories high and have corbelled-arch roofs. Nothing is known of the cultural context of these structures or of those at Chauchaq, near the ancient lithic sites of Lauricocha.

West of the Marañón, in the Sierra de Cajamarca, is the Cajamarca culture, known since Tello's time and studied more recently by the Reichlens (1949). The best reported feature is the pottery, which has been divided into five phases. Phase V corresponds to the Inca period, Phases III and IV to Tiahuanacoid influence, and Phase I probably falls into the Upper Formative, although too little is known about it to be certain. Phase II is thus the one corresponding to the Regional Developmental, although Phase III is, from the ceramic standpoint, the most distinctive regional manifestation. The principal characteristic of Cajamarca pottery is the use of a white (kaolin) paste, which generally serves as the foundation for designs painted in red, black, and occasionally orange (Figure 160). Motifs tend toward cursive and consist of volutes, spirals, or simple curves drawn with fine lines, creating a "floral" effect that reached its maximum elaboration during Phase III. In Phase II, cursive motifs are much simpler and accompanied by linear and circular elements.

Neither the area of expansion of this culture nor its center of development is precisely known; it may lie in Cajamarca or farther to the south. It attained great popularity in Cajabamba and Huamachuco during Phase III, when the Huamachuco zone was preeminent in the region (McCown 1945). A culture intermediate between Recuay and Gallinazo, with negative-painted pottery, appears to have preceded the Cajamarca occupation.

Investigations by the Reichlens in the Utcubamba zone north of Cajamarca have resulted in the identification of three cultures: Kuelap, Chipurik, and Ravash (Reichlen and Reichlen 1950). Horkheimer (1959) attempted to place these in chronological sequence using the Reichlens' data, supplemented by his own observations. The earliest appears to be Kuelap (Kuelape), which perhaps corresponds to the Regional Developmental Period. Chipurik is distantly related to Cajamarca and may also belong to this period. Ravash has characteristics that suggest it may be a "rebirth" of Kuelap.

The Kuelap culture takes its name from a well-known ruin in the Department of Amazonas that exhibits similarities in mosaic architectural ornament to that on Gallinazo buildings (page 97). The Kuelap population preferred to live on hilltops and no sites occur in the warmer valley bottoms. Both Kuelap and Chipurik constructions include circular buildings of stone. Large quantities

Figure 160. Pottery vessels of the Cajamarca III style (MUSM).

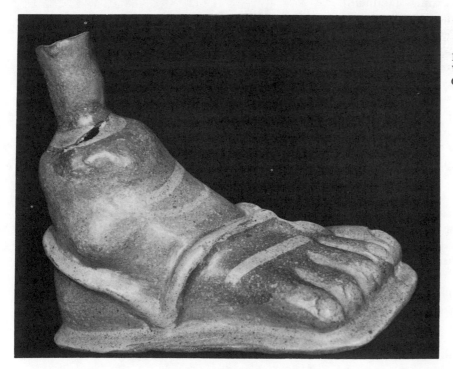

Figure 161. Pottery vessels of the Vicus style (collection of M. A. Garrido Molo).

of llama meat were consumed, possibly from domesticated animals; cotton, coca, and gourds were cultivated. Hunting was done with spear throwers.

Kuelap dead were buried in niches, whereas the Chipurik practiced mummification and buried their dead in caves along with strange funerary figures. Chipurik costume consisted of a cotton shirt and a woolen coat; ornaments included feathers and body painting. Trephining was practiced. The flute and copper were known.

Kuelap pottery is very crude and decoration is primarily by applique, modeling, and incision. The most common motif is an undulating applique band bearing incised decoration. Vessels with two adjacent horizontal handles are similar to those of Tiahuanaco I. Reichlen and Horkheimer believe that Kuelap pottery was influenced by Cajamarca III (modeled).

Chipurik pottery, by contrast, was painted and motifs consist mainly of spirals executed in a cursive manner resembling the Cajamarca style. There is also an unusual red-on-black type reminiscent of the Black Decorated of Wari culture. Connections between Chipurik and that portion of the Cajamarca sequence equating with Tiahuanacoid influence may be an indication that these groups are relatively early. This zone as a whole exhibits closer relationships with the little-known northern Andean area than with the Central Andes, however, making chronological correlations tenuous without more detailed investigation.

Considerable publicity has recently been given to the ruins of Pajatén, near Pataz, a mountainous environment similar to the Kuelap habitat. These ruins consist of circular buildings with walls also decorated by the mosaic technique, except that Pajatén exhibits greater elaboration and a larger number of ornamental motifs than Kuelap structures. Information supplied by Bonavia (1968) and Félix Caycho indicates that the ruins were occupied during Inca times and pottery of the Cuzqueño style has been found at Pajatén. Much additional study is needed, however, since this appears to be a new culture area, distinct from the Central and North Andean ones.

The same comment applies to the Piura zone on the Far North coast, where the rich Vicus cemetery is located. Vicus pottery has been found principally by treasure seekers, but several tombs were excavated on behalf of the Peruvian Government by Carlos Guzmán L. de G. (pers. comm.) with the assistance of José Casafranca. An entrance about 80 centimeters below the surface and a quadrangular shaft about 70 centimeters across provide access to a chamber 4 to 5 meters in depth. Some tombs contain offerings of metal, usually copper, but sometimes gold and silver. The chamber and shaft were filled with sand.

Vicus pottery must have a long history, since it exhibits affinities to Chavín, Recuay, Gallinazo, Moche, Salinar, Guangala (of Ecuador), and other complexes (Figure 161). Larco Hoyle (1965) published a preliminary analysis of Vicus ceramics, in which he proposed a sequence extending from the Middle Formative to the Spanish conquest. This is another culture, or cultures, that urgently needs study, particularly in view of its potential for clarifying relationships between the sequences of the Central Andes and those to the north, especially in Ecuador.

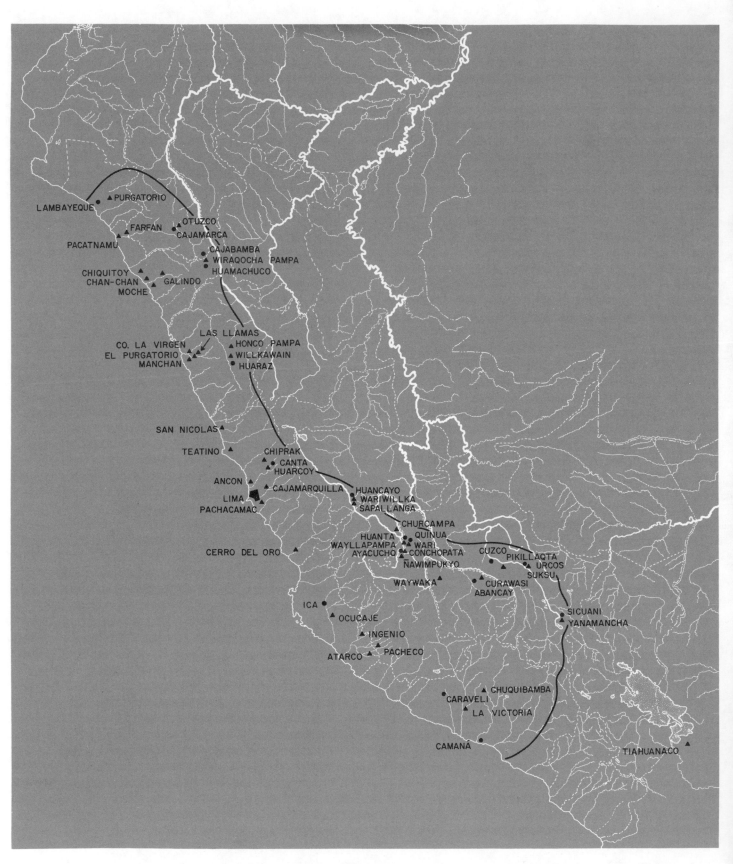

Figure 162. Boundaries of the Wari Empire and location of some of the principal sites (▲ archeological site; ● modern town).

THE WARI EMPIRE

A.D. 700-1100

When Uhle established the first cultural sequence in the Central Andes, based principally on his work at Pachacamac and Moche, he recognized that a culture with Tiahuanacoid characteristics had been superimposed over all of the Regional cultures, suggesting an expansion from the Peru-Bolivia altiplano. Although this hypothesis received general acceptance by Americanists, Uhle (1920) felt that stylistic differences between objects from the coast and the altiplano were so great that the relationship must have been a nebulous one. To reflect this situation, he referred to the coastal styles as "Epigonal."

Subsequent investigations have clarified the characteristics of both the highland and coastal complexes. Based on evidence from Nazca, Lima, and Moche, Kroeber and other archeologists designated the coastal manifestation as "Tiahuanacoid." While the existence of a relationship with Tiahuanaco could not be denied, its nature was still uncertain and this term could be interpreted as meaning "derived from," "similar to," "Tiahuanaco-like" or even "non-Tiahuanaco." Some historians were more audacious and supported the idea of a Tiahuanaco empire—the Aymara Empire, as it was called. Tiahuanacoid features were also found in the Peruvian highlands, for example in the Callejón de Huaylas. Bennett (1934), who excavated at Tiahuanaco, visualized a Peruvian Tiahuanaco horizon. These interpretations were based on the assumption that the Peruvian manifestations were of Bolivian derivation and that the relationship must have been a direct one.

During the 1940s, it became evident to archeologists that the Tiahuanacoid manifestations both on the coast and in some parts of the highlands had interrupted the earlier Regional traditions, causing their collapse and introducing new settlement patterns of an urban nature. Since urbanism did not yet exist on the altiplano, the idea of an invasion eminating from Tiahuanaco could no longer be accepted. The imposition of homogeneous new patterns over this large area implied the existence of a source that not only possessed the same style of pottery, but also cities like those that made their appearance along with the pottery on the coast.

Since Tello's visit to Ayacucho in 1931, the ruins of Wari have been known to contain pottery and stone statues similar to those at Tiahuanaco (Figure 162). Amateur archeologists in Ayacucho, among them Pío Max Medina and Benedicto Flores (Lumbreras 1960a), had also noticed these Tiahuanacoid elements and had mentioned them in short articles in nonprofessional journals. In 1931, Lila O'Neale visited the site with Tello and made a surface collection, which was later described by Kroeber (1944). Rowe, Collier, and Willey (1950) also published a brief comment based on a few hours examination of the site. The principal importance of these publications was their demonstration of the existence of strong relationships with both Nazca and Tiahuanaco.

Larco Hoyle had visited the Central highlands prior to 1948 and in his synthesis of the North coast published in that year, he presented the hypothesis that the center of distribution of Tiahuanacoid pottery was Wari. He consequently gave the name "Northern Wari A" to the complex he believed to be the result of an initial invasion from Ayacucho. This position was supported by Bennett (1953) on the basis of excavations at the Wari site. Relationships both to the Tiahuanaco site and to the "Peruvian Tiahuanaco" styles, as well as the urban character of Wari, indicated that it was the center of distribution. Conquest was envisioned as the mechanism of dissemination (Lumbreras 1960a), until Menzel (1958) suggested that a proselytizing religious doctrine was involved. Subsequently, Menzel (1964) also favored the idea of conquest, without abandoning the position that the basic stimulus was religious. Menzel's work, which is an excellent taxonomic contribution, provides conclusive evidence for the conquest hypothesis. She accepts the idea of a Central Andean empire, tentatively proposed by earlier authors, the capital of which must have been Wari.

The great quantity of pottery fragments on the surface has permitted a general reconstruction of the chronology of the Wari site, and also of the history of the culture and the process of development of the expansive state.

At the close of the Huarpa period, the populations of Ñawimpukyo and other administrative centers moved northward to Conchopata and Wari, with the result that these cities grew with remarkable rapidity. Simultaneously, there was increased communication with Tiahuanaco, where by this time religion had pervaded the entire culture. Statues and pottery both emphasized representations of mythical anthropomorphic beings. Keros were ornamented with rectangular heads resembling that of the central individual on the Gateway of the Sun, done in relief and painted in several colors, and secondary personages on the Gateway also appear on pottery.

In the Central Andes, the custom of pilgrimages to distant ceremonial centers began at an early time and was never lost. The Spanish reported that the prestige of the temple at Pachacamac, near Lima, was so great that many visitors came from other parts of Peru to bring tribute. The people of the Ayacucho region may have behaved this way toward Tiahuanaco, whose imposing ceremonial center seems to have achieved considerable pan-Andean renown. If so, this would explain why the only Tiahuanaco elements that occur in the Ayacucho area are copies from stone sculptures, which were the principal ritual objects. This emphasis is

characteristic of the Conchopata ceramic style, named after a site where it was found by Tello in 1942. This pottery apparently had ceremonial significance since vessels have so far been found almost exclusively in pits, where they were interred after having been intentionally broken. The only exceptions are a few fragments encountered in one of the refuse accumulations in Conchopata, but this was near the "potter's house" and contained large quantities of broken pottery of many types, generally discarded because of defects. Although the Conchopata style faithfully reproduces classic Tiahuanaco motifs, it is easily distinguished from pottery made at Tiahuanaco. The few vessels known are urns or large open basins some 60 centimeters tall, with thick flat rims, which resemble in execution the thick Huarpa pottery.

During this period, the Ayacucho region was also in close communication with Nazca and slight indications of relations with the Central coast exist in the form of influences on the pottery of Cerro del Oro from Cañete and the latest phase of Lima. The Conchopata style is associated with various other local complexes, some derived from Huarpa and others (such as Chakipampa; Figure 163) related to Nazca (Phases VIII and IX). The pottery varies in each region and none of these "derivatives" attained the excellence of Conchopata, nor did they absorb any Tiahuanacoid motifs.

By the time that Tiahuanacan traits had become firmly established in the Ayacucho area, Ayacuchan pottery began to be strongly influenced by another tradition known as Wari. The consequence was emergence of a new and vigorous Tiahuanacoid style called "Robles Moqo," which is closely similar in form and decoration but superior in surface finish to vessels from Tiahuanaco (Figure 164). Conchopata and Robles Moqo pottery are diagnostic of Wari period 1, which has been divided into Phases A and B. The occurrence of Phase B pottery on the coast from Chancay to Nazca (and possibly Acarí) and in the highlands as far north as Huarás in the Callejón de Huaylas (Menzel 1964) indicates that Wari expansion began during this period.

The most important Phase B style is Robles Moqo, which contains three types, two painted and one in which painting is combined with modeling. Robles Moqo Thick occurs principally at Wari and at Pacheco in the Nazca Valley (Figure 165), and appears to have fulfilled a function comparable to that of the Conchopata urns. At Pacheco, fragments have been found in adobe chambers especially con-

Figure 163. Pottery vessel of the Chakipampa style.

Figure 164. Pottery of the Robles Moqo style, diagnostic of Wari I (MNAA).

Figure 165. Fine pottery of the earliest phases of Wari at Pacheco on the South coast (Nazca). (MNAA).

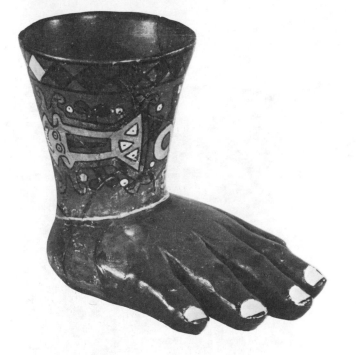

Figure 166. Wari fine pottery vessel from the South coast (MNAA).

structed for their interment. The vessels are as
large as those of Conchopata, but decoration is
more regionalized and employs many elements not
present at Tiahuanaco. Among these are maize,
other varieties of plants and flowers, and distorted
variations of Tiahuanacan motifs. Some urns from
Nazca depict the divinity on the Gateway of the
Sun, while immense keros imitate Tiahuanaco IV
forms and motifs, including the prominent rectangular head. Robles Moqo Thin vessels have almost
the same motifs as the thick type, but are thin-
walled and of "normal" size (Menzel 1964). Modeling is a new feature and is characteristic of specimens that do have Tiahuanacoid painted decoration
(Figure 166). Forms are not of Nazca or Huarpa
derivation, but related instead to typical Tiahuanaco
ones. Innovations include tall tubular jars.

During Phase B, people from Wari or another
settlement of the same culture appear to have gone
to the altiplano with offerings of gold, since a representation of maize executed in characteristic
Robles Moqo style has been found in the Tiahuanaco area. In his excavations at Pariti in Bolivia,
Bennett (1936) found a burial containing various
bone and gold objects of a style also more closely
related to Wari than to Tiahuanaco, but no other
traces of Wari were encountered. Impressions
brought home by such travelers could explain the
amplification of Tiahuanacan influences on Wari.

In addition to possessing a much finer variety of
Nazcoid pottery, derived principally from Nazca
IX, Phase B of Wari I is characterized by Ayacucho
Polychrome (Bennett 1953). Motifs are more rectilinear and volutes are more regular in form, becoming nearly circular (Figure 167). This ceramic
style achieved the widest dissemination, spreading
as far as Huarás in the North highlands. The
Huarpa ceramic tradition apparently terminated at
this time.

Wari II was a period of refinement of the Tiahuanacoid style in Ayacucho and the emergence of
a distinctive result. The pottery types corresponding to this period are those generally designated as
"Coastal Tiahuanaco." Three stylistic variants
have been distinguished by Menzel (1964), who
called them "Viñaque," "Atarco" (Nazca), and
"Pachacamac" (Central coast). A fourth and slightly
later variety has been termed "Curawasi" by Wallace (pers. comm.). All four derive from Robles
Moqo. A probable fifth variety, identified by Neira
and Lumbreras in the Arequipa region, has been
named "Qosqopa."

Figure 167. Wari-style pottery (a, collection of Galvez Durand,
Huancayo. b, MNAA. c, MHRA).

Figure 168. Pottery vessels of the "Coastal Tiahuanaco"
Atarco style (courtesy A. Guillén).

Right
Figure 169. Wari-style vessel from the Central coast (MNAA).

The Viñaque style is the most important and equates in general with Bennett's Wari Fine Polychrome. It is characterized by small vessels with an S-shaped profile, manufactured from fine paste and decorated with anthropomorphic, zoomorphic, and fitomorphic elements executed in a manner somewhat reminiscent of both Tiahuanaco and Nazca. Bowls with straight parallel sides, double-bodied vessels connected by a tube, and jars with faces on the neck also occur. All have highly polished surfaces and polychrome painting. The preferred motif was a square head wearing a crown with three appendages, one usually a feather and the others falcon heads. Representations of falcons, felines, and serpents are common, and are treated in the Tiahuanacan manner. Human skulls, plants, and geometric designs also occur, the latter emphasizing bands of chevrons and crossed lines.

The Atarco style (Figure 168) developed primarily on the South coast. The preferred vessel was a bottle with two diverging spouts connected by a bridge handle. Decoration is more varied than on Viñaque pottery and there is greater emphasis on Nazcoid motifs. The most diagnostic element is a running feline represented in profile.

The Pachacamac variety retains strong influences from the earlier Lima style, in particular a globular bottle with a long conical spout joined to the body by a handle (Figure 169). Painted decoration is relatively uniform and a good deal of modeling was employed. The diagnostic motif is a feline or a falcon with a feline body, which has a segmented band around the neck from which issues a row of plumes. The region of development of the Pachacamac variety is principally the Central and North coast.

The Curawasi variety, whose area of distribution is the zone of Cuzco and Abancay, emphasizes geometric feather designs. The typical vessel shape is a kero with slightly diverging, straight walls. One side usually bears a face with eyes that are almond-shaped rather than the two-part circles that are a Tiahuanaco feature retained in Viñaque and the other regional styles. This variety is associated with a type called Black Decorated, which is typically smoked or reduced, producing a dark gray color, and is painted in rectilinear and curvilinear designs in brilliant red, giving the impression of negative painting (Figure 170).

In the North highlands, Cajamarca III ceramics were incorporated into Wari II. Another local style, which is restricted according to present evidence to the Central highlands, has a light-colored kaolin paste painted in fine black, violet, red, and brown (and rarely, gray) geometric patterns featuring steps and naturalistic motifs that are slightly reminiscent of Nazca II designs, although unrelated to them.

The Qosqopa variety occurs in the valleys of Sihuas, Ocoña, and Caravelí in the southern part of the Central Andes and probably dates from Wari III. It is characterized by more careless workmanship and by motifs derived directly from Viñaque.

Figure 170. Wari Black Decorated vessels (*left and center*, MUSH. *right*, Galvez Durand Collection).

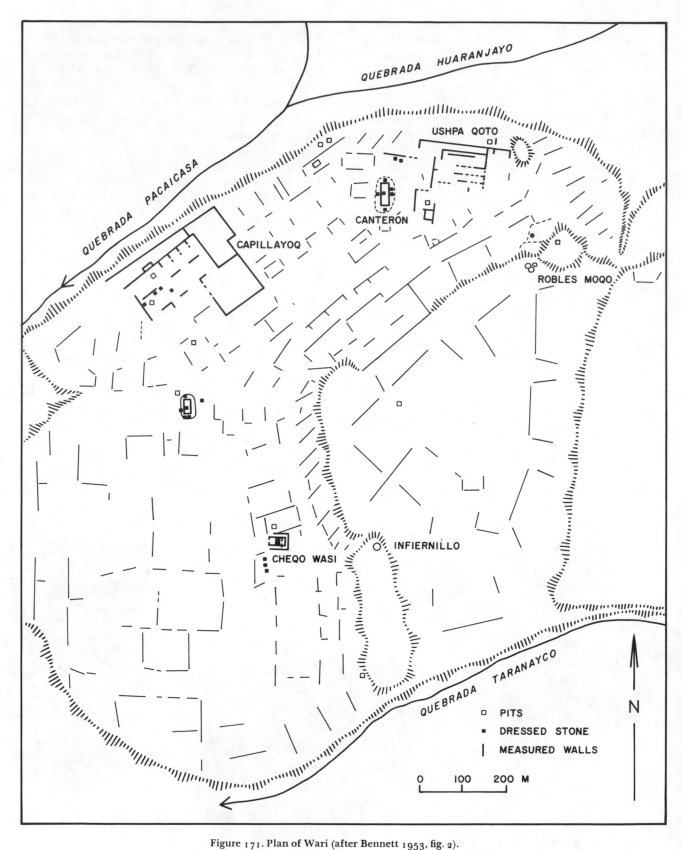

QUEBRADA HUARANJAYO

QUEBRADA PACAICASA

USHPA QOTO

CANTERÓN

CAPILLAYOQ

ROBLES MOQO

INFIERNILLO

CHEQO WASI

QUEBRADA TARANAYCO

□ PITS
■ DRESSED STONE
| MEASURED WALLS

0   100   200 M

N

Figure 171. Plan of Wari (after Bennett 1953, fig. 2).

The Wari Culture

SETTLEMENT PATTERN. Wari was known as Viñaque when Cieza de León visited it in 1550. By then, it was already a very ancient ruined city, which according to tradition had been founded by bearded men in pre-Inca times. Many amateur archeologists searched unsuccessfully for these ruins during the 19th century, and in 1894 carved stone statues were finally discovered on a plateau of volcanic origin about 25 kilometers north of the modern city of Ayacucho. The remains consist of various groups of rectangular buildings constructed of field stone and surrounded by walls hundreds of meters long and between 6 and 12 meters high. Most of the site is under cultivation and excavation has been minimal. The best preserved sectors are Ushpa Qoto, Capillayoq, and Canterón. Other important sectors appear to be Qawarikuna and Cheqo Wasi (Figure 171).

Ushpa Qoto occupies a sloping area of about 300 by 500 meters in the northern part of the city. It is bounded on the north by an immense wall, on the east by Robles Moqo hill, on the south by the Canterón sector, and on the west by a ravine called Ocopa. Buildings of considerable size and containing up to three stories surround a large rectangular plaza and there are some semicircular buildings around a small plaza about 30 meters in diameter. Houses are rectangular and must have been divided into rooms by partitions of perishable construction. In the entire sector, only four or five windows and a few entries have been identified. The latter are rectangular with vertical jambs; no lintels have been found. A few small and scattered niches have stone lintels. The walls are faced with small, angular field stones set in clay, with the flatter surface generally facing outward, and the intervening portion is often filled with rubble and clay. Some walls have cornice-like rows of stones protruding at different elevations, which may have served as house-roof supports or perhaps to anchor the thick plaster that appears once to have covered the surface (Figure 172). Excavations in one of the large, walled

Figure 172. Wall at Wari with projecting rows of stones that may have served as roof supports.

Figure 173.
A wall in the Capillayoq
sector of Wari.

Figure 174.
Stone slab structures in the
Cheqo Wasi sector of Wari.

compounds revealed agglutinated rooms around a kind of semicircular patio. A large pottery workshop and storehouse containing molds, supplies of prepared clay, and other equipment was encountered in another place. This suggests that the city may have been divided into precincts inhabited by occupational specialists.

A notable feature of the Ushpa Qoto sector is a complicated system of subterranean channels, some of them associated with hewn stones or petroglyphs. One of the channels is a little more than a meter below the present surface and runs beneath a massive wall in the eastern part. It has a rectangular cross-section about 50 centimeters wide by 30 centimeters high and was lined with fine clay. The roof was constructed of elongated stones laid horizontally. Very fine, clean sand was found inside. A little more than 10 meters were examined and it extended farther in both directions.

The Capillayoq sector, one of the most beautiful complexes in Wari, is about one kilometer southwest of Ushpa Qoto. The principal building is a triangular structure about 200 meters long, in the center of which is a large trapezoidal platform about 10 meters high. It gives the impression of being a ceremonial precinct and is surrounded by rectangular buildings containing many stone-walled rooms (Figure 173). At the end of the triangle is a square enclosure known as the "Chapel," the walls of which contain numerous small niches 10 to 15 centimeters wide. The walls are double and the one on the western boundary has sections more than 3 meters thick; it runs along the edge of the plateau, above the Ocopa ravine. Circular terraces and worked stones are associated with the Capillayoq structures. A stone ornamented with a series of parallel grooves and an unfinished human head were found near the remains of a strange pyramidal building, which had on the summit a row of closely spaced, worked stones bearing designs and small cavities on their western faces. This side had a staircase.

About a kilometer south of Capillayoq is a complex known as Cheqo Wasi, which consists of three box-like buildings about 50 meters apart. They are constructed of worked stone and must originally have been subterranean. Some of the walls are composed of a single large slab and the roofs are generally also constructed of slabs (Figure 174). Courses of stone occur only in one part. The structure on the highest elevation contains three floors. The lower level consists of two cubical chambers whose only communication with the exterior is by some perfectly circular openings under 10 centimeters in diameter. The second floor, which is roofed by two slabs, is a rectangle with an entrance at one side. All that remains of the third floor is an incomplete feature that may have been either an entry or a niche. Each storey is about 1.8 meters high and approximately the same width. The lowest chamber is nearly 4 meters long. The other two associated complexes are lower and smaller. Remains of galleries and aqueducts have been observed alongside the main structure.

In a rocky area east of Cheqo Wasi is a cave known as "Infiernillo," from which clay for pottery making was apparently obtained. Above the cave are many petroglyphs (Figure 175) and small holes cut in the stone. Near the summit is a large circular cistern a little over 10 meters deep.

Figure 175. Petroglyph from Wari.

Between these complexes are numerous more poorly preserved structures; in fact, the largest concentration of buildings seems to have been between Cheqo Wasi and Ushpa Qoto. The basic plan consisted of thick-walled rectangular enclosures containing streets, plazas, platforms, compounds, and other kinds of features, which were in turn surrounded by higher and thicker walls that delimited areas or districts. There are a few circular buildings, one of which was about 8 meters in diameter and showed remnants of stone "locks" (rings and pegs) set into the walls by the same method used to attach the stone heads at Tiahuanaco (although similar heads occur in Wari, none has as yet been found in place). An interesting architectural detail, represented in a structure of irregularly shaped stones, is the use of thick ropes made of vegetal fibers to join two walls at the corner. This is not a normal feature, however, and may date from one of the early stages of occupation in the city.

In addition to Wari, there were 10 settlements in the region between Ayacucho and Huanta, and a small population probably still occupied the extensive site of Conchopata during this period. The towns follow a regular plan of rectangular houses, streets, and plazas, and are generally located on hillsides near water sources. They cover an area averaging 300 by 100 meters. The most significant are Tunasniyoq (Figure 176) and Santo Domingo near Ayacucho; La Compañía opposite Wari; La Vega and Allqo Machay near Huanta.

The roads of ancient Peru are impressive engineering feats, and the construction of so extensive and complicated a system in the short span of the Inca Empire would be difficult even with modern technology. Consequently, it appears that the first steps must have been taken in Wari times and there is documentary evidence that the so-called "Chinchaysuyu trunk lines" are pre-Inca. Regal (1936) cites a passage in the chronicle of Lopez de Gómara, who says of one of these main lines that "Guainacapa lengthened and restored it, but did not construct it as some have said; it is an ancient work and could not have been completed in his lifetime." Regal (1936:7) also reports that a Kipu Kamayoq ("Keeper of the Quipu") informed Vaca de Castro that the Inka Pacha Kuteq "ordered the repair of the highways and rest houses throughout the land and commanded new ones to be built. . . ."

The routes followed by some of the prehispanic roads also suggest they date from Wari times. Two branches originate in the Huanta region, near Wari. Both lead to Huancayo via towns like Wari Willka and Churkampa, which were constructed during the Wari period. Many other roads lead directly to Wari centers, among them Willkawaín in Huarás, Wiraqocha Pampa in Huamachuco, and San Nicolás in Supe. Finally, there is another reference by Regal (1936:45–46) to the war between the Chankas and the Incas, in which he indicates that the route known as the "Inca highway" was used, implying that it existed prior to the Inca Empire. This road

Figure 176. Excavated dwellings at the Wari town of Tunasniyoq, near Ayacucho.

may have led from Wari to Pikillaqta, which was one of the most important Wari administrative and habitational centers in that region.

SUBSISTENCE. Wari lies in the midst of a zone of limited resources, where agriculture depends mainly on the rain that falls during three months of the year. Wari itself occupies a site totally devoid of water, which explains the care that was taken in the construction of canals for its provision. References at the beginning of this century mention channels cut in the rock to bring water from lakes more than 10 kilometers distant. The modern hacienda of Waka Urara is supplied by an aqueduct originating near Quinua, some 4 kilometers from Wari. These sources could not have satisfied the requirements of a population as large as appears to have inhabited the city.

The economy of the Wari people was based primarily on agriculture. Hunting and herding were also important, however, to judge from the numerous triangular projectile points and corral-like enclosures at the site. Excavations have produced large quantities of animal bones. Nevertheless, local resources may have been insufficient to supply the capital with food, even if the valley of Huanta several kilometers to the northwest, where permanent agriculture was possible, was part of the sustaining area. The population, especially during Wari II, was extremely large. It thus seems likely that demographic pressure underlay the religious zeal for conquest of other territories by the Wari population.

SOCIAL ORGANIZATION. Little is known of Wari sociopolitical organization, but its military achievements would have required strong mechanisms of social control and efficient economic support. The existence of a centralized government implies some kind of social ranking and a nobility that must have held control. It seems probable that the Chimú and the Inca adopted aspects of this system, which may have resembled that of the Sinchis of Cuzco. Examination of the Wari pattern of dispersal shows that it foreshadowed in many details the Inca distribution and, more importantly, initiated a new era in Andean cultural development. The elaboration of all kinds of technology to a high level implies the existence of urban specialists, who were probably directly under the supervision of the rulers.

In so complex a society, commerce must have played an important role. One indication is the presence of very hard green turquoise, which was employed for ornaments and religious articles. This stone is not known from the Ayacucho region and

may have been brought from as far as Bolivia. Small turquoise figurines are among the most beautiful examples of Wari art.

Religion was both a powerful instrument of control and a pretext for conquest. The principal divinity was that depicted on the Gateway of the Sun at Tiahuanaco. Other supernatural beings included the feline, the falcon, and the serpent. Representations of the gods were almost always stylized, although a few exceptional examples tend toward realism. The anthropomorphic divinities have feline aspects, such as triangular canines, or falconoid elements and weeping eyes. Serpents are less common. Human heads, which occur in the form of trophies or of skulls, are undoubtedly expressions of a cult.

ARTS AND CRAFTS. Wari sculpture dates from Phase B and is closely related to that of Tiahuanaco; it exhibits sufficiently distinctive features, however, for it to be considered a separate style. With the exception of a few isolated examples from a habitation center in the Huancavelica region that Tello (1942:683) called Hatun Wayllay, all statues are from the site of Wari. They were carved from an ashy gray volcanic tuff, which contrasts strongly in color with their surroundings. Of the eleven that are known, one is a feline and all the others are human beings (Figure 177). The sculptures are three-dimensional and give the impression of portraiture but the technique of carving emphasizes planes, which produces a two-dimensional feeling. In contrast to the Classic Tiahuanaco statues, there is no supplementary decoration and only the personage involved is represented. The monolith carved in the form of a feline exhibits a degree of naturalism unusual in the Andes. The animal is seated, with its tail undulating, its mouth open, and its eyes almond-shaped. It is one of the few Wari pieces that displays rounded contours.

The human figures are generally richly attired and have an elaborate trapezoidal headdress with four points—a typical Tiahuanacoid feature—or a hat apparently covered with feathers. There are ten examples, five in the hacienda house of Waka Urara to the north of Wari, one in Quinua, another in the town of Pacaycasa, two at the Wayllapampa hacienda, and one in Ayacucho. Two of the pieces at Waka Urara are almost identical; they are men with long costumes apparently covered with a mantle, and are the tallest known, attaining a height of almost 1.6 meters. Another carving at Waka Urara is a fountain in the form of a man whose circular mouth must have served as an exit for the water.

Figure 177.
Stone statues of the Wari style
(Hacienda Waka Urara, Ayacucho).

Two other sculptures represent the decapitated bodies of very simply dressed persons, one wearing a plain tunic and the other a tunic with prominent horizontal bands.

The smallest of the statues is in the village of Pacaycasa and depicts a personage holding what appears to be a trophy head in one hand. The statue at Quinua is most similar to those from Tiahuanaco, particularly because of the rigidity of its angles and its quadrangular, columnar form. One of the statues at the Wayllapampa hacienda has thick braids and a long tunic-like dress that is covered by an ample cape. The other is a seated figure, but arms and legs have been broken off. A similar statue is in the Museo Regional de Ayacucho.

The statues are homogeneous stylistically, although they differ in costume and headdress. The eyes are almond-shaped and the pupil is almost always defined by fine incisions; the nose is flat and trapezoidal; the chin is slightly protruding; the arms are usually at the sides, and have well-carved hands and fingernails. The feet do not have toes, but several depict the Achilles tendon. All have a quadrangular pedestal 10–15 centimeters high.

BURIAL PRACTICES. Little is known of the cult of the dead. Most of the burials encountered in the highlands so far probably represent individuals of low social status, since they were interred in rock shelters and provided with only a few offerings of pottery and occasionally of copper. A tomb at Wari Willka, near Huancayo, however, consisted of a stone box containing very fine pottery and gold objects. On the coast, by contrast, true mausoleums containing very rich trappings have been found.

The "Tiahuanacoid" Expansion

Wari expansion began during Phase I and between A.D. 600–700 its effects were felt principally on the coast between the valleys of Nazca and Chancay and possibly as far north as Huarmey. In the highlands, influence penetrated to the Callejón de Huaylas, where Okros and a related type of pottery became very popular. Local ceramic styles and settlement types were not disrupted by these innovations. The great conquests of Wari II, by contrast, subjugated almost the entire Central Andes from Lambayeque and Cajamarca in the north to Camaná and Sicuani in the south, including the Moche, Cajamarca, Recuay, Lima, and Nazca territories. The effect of these Wari II conquests was a despotic regime, in which the conquerors imposed their domination by force, destroying any way of life different from theirs. Control was strongly centralized, although some cultural differences remained because of natural regional variation. By the end of Wari II, however, certain regional administrative and ceremonial centers achieved sufficient importance to exercise significant power. The eminence of Pachacamac is indicated by glottochronological studies, which suggest that it was one of the centers of dispersal of the Quechua language during this time (Torero 1971).

Wari expansion and political domination had a strong impact on Andean culture, which is reflected not only in new economic, settlement, and technological patterns, but also in new kinds of ideology, notably the emergence of a proselytizing religion, a centralized and despotic political organization, and an eagerness for conquest initiated by powerful and wealthy classes in the city.

SETTLEMENT PATTERN. One of the most notable alterations was in settlement pattern, manifested particularly by the advent of urbanization and the secularization of religious centers. Each valley had at least one large habitation area and several smaller ones, which may have been dependent villages. General architectural characteristics include the introduction of large planned settlements composed of houses, plazas, and streets surrounded by very high walls provided with few entries and no windows; the walls were constructed of irregular stones and clay.

These changes seem most pronounced on the North coast, perhaps because the archeology is best known there. Although the Virú Valley was not one of the more important coastal valleys, it underwent a series of modifications tending toward planned settlements and the abandonment of villages and ceremonial centers (Willey 1953). The population was large but did not surpass that during Gallinazo III. The use of stone for construction of a large number of structures might be interpreted as an indication of the arrival of people possessing a different cultural tradition, but the persistence of old patterns in other aspects of the culture, especially nonceremonial types of pottery, argues against this view. Furthermore, stone construction existed in earlier periods, although it was rare. There are 79 habitation sites corresponding to the period of Tiahuanacoid influence, or Wari as it is now called. At least 26 agglutinated villages of the Gallinazo and Moche tradition remained inhabited, but some increased in size to 100 or more rooms. The rooms tend to be oblong rather than rectangular as a consequence of the unevenness of the terrain. Rectangular compounds also continued in use. Nine have been discovered, some measuring only 22 by 17 meters and others about 52 by 38 meters. In the former group, small to middle-sized rooms are distributed without any apparent plan; by contrast, the larger compounds have patios, corridors, and symmetrically arranged rooms. Semi-isolated houses also persist; 17 have been found and they too are much larger than in earlier times, some by as much as 20 meters. In addition, there is one site with totally new characteristics, which Willey (1953:238) terms a "Great Rectangular Enclosure Compound." It is surrounded by massive adobe walls and contains structures twice as large as those at other sites. Internal compartments are rare, as at Wari, but the few that exist are of the same size as in other houses in the valley. The function of these buildings must have been principally administrative. The ancient pyramid-towns and pyramidal temples were almost entirely abandoned; those that remained in use functioned primarily as burial places. The militaristic nature of the period is reflected in defensive constructions, including a wall 1800 meters long in the Niño ravine.

In the economic sector, there was great emphasis on the conservation and distribution of water to permit maximum utilization of the cultivable land, which extended almost to the beach. The irrigation system apparently made possible a rational distribution of water via complicated systems of ditches. During this time, also, a highway seems to have been constructed across the valley.

On other parts of the North coast, changes must have been much more drastic than in the small valley of Virú, but unfortunately insufficient studies have been made to permit detailed description. In the Moche Valley, although the important ceremonial centers of the Sun and the Moon declined in importance, urban settlements with stone-walled houses and rectangular compounds appeared in the nearby zone of Galindo. The great Chimú city of Chan-chan must have been founded during this period. It has immense rectangular enclosures, some 400 by 200 meters, surrounded by tapia walls as high as those at Wari. In the Chicama Valley, north of Chan-chan, the sites of Chicamita and Chiquitoy follow the regular plan of other Wari constructions, although they are smaller.

The northernmost of the known great urban centers is Pacatnamú, which is located on a plateau near Pacasmayo. It overlies a Moche settlement, to which the pyramids and other buildings constructed of semi-cylindrical adobes probably belong. Later structures with thick walls of packed mud or tapia are undoubtedly assignable to the Wari invasion.

Another valley that exhibits notable changes in traditional patterns indicative of Wari influence is Casma, south of the Moche area. Thompson (1964a: 93) mentions the site of Manchán, a planned town with tapia walls, which dates from late Wari II. Previously, Tello (1956) drew plans of Las Llamas and El Purgatorio, two sites of typical Wari construction, which he assigned to the Santa culture (equivalent to Wari in date) or the subsequent Casma culture. El Purgatorio and Pampa de las Llamas are undoubtedly part of a single urban complex, in which the latter structure could have served a purely ceremonial function. Nearby is the temple of Chavín de Moqeke. Las Llamas, at the base of the Cerro San Francisco, consists of a system of quadrangular plazas surrounded by small rooms. This complex is connected by a straight road to El Purgatorio, which is composed of habitation structures.

In the Supe Valley, farther to the south, the site of Chimú Capac also has a series of square platforms at different levels, arranged around a great plaza. Fragments of Wari pottery have been found here. San Nicolás, a large Wari cemetery, is probably associated.

On the Central coast, where the Wari occupation began during Phase I, the city that may have been founded first is Cajamarquilla in the Rímac Valley (Figure 178). Wari dominance gradually increased in this region and by Phase II the center of power had shifted to Pachacamac in the Lurín Valley.

Cajamarquilla is on a broad plain on the north

Figure 178. Views of the city of Cajamarquilla in the Rímac Valley, Central Coast.

side of the Río Rímac. According to Villar Córdova (1935), it contains three principal sections or "barrios," the eastern one being the best preserved. The numerous plazas surrounded by tapia walls are typical of coastal architecture of the Wari period, as are the groups of houses and narrow streets. The houses are rectangular and their walls are plastered. There is only one entrance per house, on the street side. All openings are small and narrow. Cylindrical storage pits about 1.0 meter in diameter and 1.8 meters deep have been found in the floors of some houses.

The city of Pachacamac had been occupied since the beginning of the Lima culture or before and it is impossible to differentiate as yet between the portions that correspond to Wari and those of later date. The influence of the Tiahuanacoid tradition was so strong that a cult related to Wari seems to have continued in existence even during the Inca epoch. Only a few years ago, an elongated, cylindrical, wooden post carved with figures possessing attributes of Wari divinities was discovered. The upper part depicts a man who holds a bola in his hand and wears a large chest ornament. The remainder of the post bears representations of two-headed serpents, felines, and a figure reminiscent of the "angels" on the Gateway of the Sun. Beautiful examples of Tiahuanacoid art were retrieved by Uhle from a large Wari cemetery at Pachacamac.

There appear to have been no important changes in settlement pattern on the South coast, although Wari habitation sites have not been sufficiently studied to be certain. Remnants of structures at Pacheco, south of the Río Nazca, cover an area about 300 meters square (Menzel 1968:76). Better known than settlements are the cemeteries of the Wari period, such as those at Atarco, Ocucaje, and Ingenio in the Nazca and Ica valleys.

In the highlands south of Wari, large towns have been reported. An example is Pikillaqta, which is an elaborated copy of Wari. In addition, there were small population centers, such as Waywaka on a hill near Andahuaylas; Yanamancha near Sicuani, and Suksu in Urcos. Recently, the University of Cuzco sponsored excavations under the direction of Chávez Ballón at the large habitation and ceremonial center of San Pedro de Cacha, where the pottery was identified as pure Wari II. The cemeteries of Batan Urqo, near Cuzco, and Curawasi have also produced Wari ceramics in abundance.

The most important site is Pikillaqta ("Town of the Fleas" or "Small Town"), which is composed of a residential district and a system of storehouses, both of equal extension. The ruins are about a kilometer in width and length, widening slightly at the center, and are better preserved than those at Wari. Excavations by the University of Cuzco under the direction of William Sanders revealed pottery possibly corresponding to the early part of Wari II. The city was divided into sectors or "barrios" surrounded by walls up to 10 meters high. The residential zone contains remnants of straight, long, and narrow streets and several large plazas surrounded by long narrow houses with very high walls. Appearance and construction, including the presence of false cornices, resembles that at Wari. As in most buildings of Wari origin, entries are notably scarce. Canals have been discovered, including a large one that apparently brought water from the heights of Lucre. In contrast to Wari, which grew somewhat spontaneously, Pikillaqta resembles other provincial urban centers in being totally planned. The result is a remarkable degree of regularity. The storage sector, which contains several dozen enclosures for grain and other kinds of products that may have come to Pikillaqta as part of the regional tribute, has only one entry and one exit.

Cuzco was the southern limit of Wari expansion in the highlands and the distribution of Wari pottery and architecture terminates in the vicinity of Sicuani; interestingly, no traces of the movement of travelers from Tiahuanaco to Ayacucho have been encountered, although they must have passed through the area.

In the North highlands, although Wari conquered the Cajamarca culture, the pottery of the latter continued to enjoy great prestige and was not only utilized in Wari but distributed to many other regions, among them Moche. The provincial capital may have been the magnificently planned urban center of Wiraqocha Pampa, near Huamachuco, since it follows the typical Wari pattern in every detail, including the technique of construction of the walls which, as at Pikillaqta, are of angular stones set in clay. The city is quadrangular (Figure 179), measuring 580 meters east to west and 565 meters north to south (McCown 1945:267ff). There appear to be only two entrances to the great enclosure, one at the north and the other at the south, connected by a road about 5 meters wide. West of this street are a few houses, large compounds surrounding a large quadrangle, and several small compartments, the majority in the southern part of the area. Toward the east, by contrast, structures are very numerous and surround a large plaza, which is exactly in the

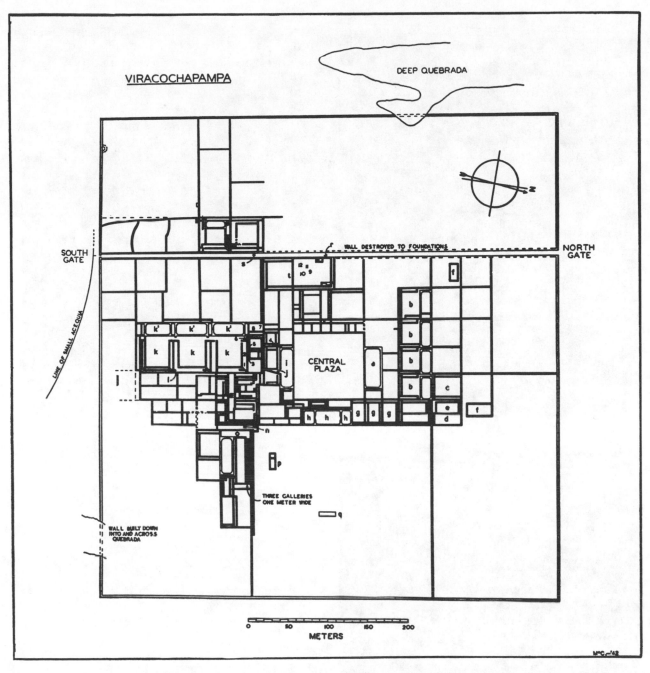

VIRACOCHAPAMPA

DEEP QUEBRADA

WALL DESTROYED TO FOUNDATIONS

SOUTH
GATE

NORTH
GATE

LINE OF WALL ACEQUIA

CENTRAL
PLAZA

THREE GALLERIES
ONE METER WIDE

WALL BUILT DOWN
INTO AND ACROSS
QUEBRADA

0   50   100   150   200
METERS

Figure 179. Plan of the site of Wiraqocha Pampa near Huamachuco in the North highlands (after McCown 1945, fig. 13).

center of the site. On the north side of this central plaza is a building of ordinary dimensions but very thick walls that may have been the principal administrative structure. There are niches in its north wall. It is surrounded by smaller buildings, which are most numerous toward the north and east. On the south side is another similar building and the zone in general contains a large number of structures arranged according to a complicated plan.

There are no windows or entrances and communication occurred via open areas or narrow passages. As at Wari and Pikillaqta, there are "false cornices" in the form of rows of stones projecting from the walls; the latter attain a height of about 6 meters.

In the Huamachuco region, another center that may have been important during this period is Marka Wamachuku, but its occupation was much more extensive during Inca times.

Figure 180. Views of Willkawaín, near Huarás in the
Callejón de Huaylas.

A large urban center in another part of the Cajamarca Valley is now almost totally obscured by earth and vegetation. It contains reservoirs of worked stone similar to those at Wari and an administrative center, which is readily visible because the region is under cultivation (which is affecting the site noticeably). At an immense cemetery known as "Las Ventanitas de Otuzco," pottery of Cajamarca III and IV (Tiahuanacoid) abounds and many sherds with pure Wari-style decoration have been collected.

Farther south, in the Callejón de Huaylas, populations must also have been large to judge from the number of sites. The settlement pattern is distinct from that of preceding periods and stepped pyramids of probable ceremonial function become a prominent feature. Subterranean galleries are also common. The best known site is Willkawaín (Figure 180), near the modern city of Huarás (Bennett 1944:15–17). It is dominated by a three-story structure erected on a partly artificial and partly natural platform and associated with terraces and habitations. The walls are stones set in clay and the ceilings of the first and second levels (which constitute the floors of the rooms above) are large slabs. A single entrance on each floor provides access to seven interconnecting rooms. Those at the center are long narrow galleries. A 43-centimeter-wide shaft in the north wall has openings on each floor for ventilation. The roof, which has a maximum height of 9.25 meters, is a dome created by sloping the slabs of the upper story ceiling and covering them with dirt and stones. Projecting flat stones form eaves that protect a continuous niche 55 centimeters wide, beneath which tenoned puma heads were formerly inserted into the wall at regular intervals.

In the Akillpo region, not far below the zone of perpetual snow, a city of this period is known as "Honco Pampa." The habitation sector has plazas and streets like those of other Wari towns. In the "ceremonial" sector are some eight temple structures of the Willkawaín type (Vescelius and Amat, pers. comm.). Other large sites in the Central highlands are Huarcoy and Chiprak in the Canta region. Wari Willka near Huancayo must also have contained a considerable population (Figure 181).

ARTS AND CRAFTS. Although Wari influenced other types of crafts, changes are most evident in pottery. Detailed studies made in the Virú Valley show a sudden break in continuity in the ceremonial types. Moche forms were replaced by Tia-

Figure 181. Details of a large enclosure excavated at Wari Willka, near Huancayo.

a

b

c

Figure 182. Wari-influenced pottery from the North coast. *a*, An unusual Wari-Moche vessel (Museo Amano). *b*, Jar with Wari-style polychrome painting (MRLH). *c*, Vessel of Wari-Lambayeque style (MRLH).

Figure 183. Vessels of the Santa style from the North coast (courtesy A. Guillén).

huanacoid ones, polychrome painting displaced bichrome, and stiff multicolored designs showing Wari divinities were substituted for three-dimensional modeling and scenic painting (Figure 182). To this assemblage was added Cajamarca Cursive, which is associated in Wari burials with the Pachacamac and Viñaque varieties of Tiahuanacoid pottery. Modifications in domestic wares, by contrast, were slow and gradual (Collier 1955). The color of the plain pottery changed from red to black and molds replaced modeling, less because of Wari intervention than as a consequence of local trends in the relative popularity of already known techniques. During Moche times, use of the mold was limited to very complicated vessels, usually ceremonial in function, whereas from Wari onward molds were employed for mass production of domestic pottery. This expanded application is obviously related to the altered nature of the economy imposed by the conquering regime. The continuity of domestic styles led Collier (1955:137) to infer that the abrupt alterations in Moche social and religious patterns did not result from major displacements or replace-

ments of people. It is unfortunate that the preoccupation of archeologists with decorated pottery makes it impossible to extend this type of analysis to other parts of the Central Andes.

On the North coast, a distinctive local ceramic style did not emerge until after the termination of Wari hegemony. This style, called Santa or Huaylas Yunga (Coastal Huaylas) by Tello and later designated as Northern Huari B by Larco Hoyle (Figure 183), was distributed between the valleys of Lambayeque in the north and Huarmey in the south. A black ware began to differentiate from the domestic pottery and to assume ceremonial functions. As time passed, it became increasingly popular and culminated in the highly elaborated, mold-made, black Chimú style.

On the Central coast, ceramic history probably followed a course similar to that in the north, but this cannot be demonstrated until the domestic pottery has been systematically studied. As already noted, the Central coast achieved special prominence during this time and its pottery was widely distributed along with that of Wari. Although changes in the ceremonial pottery were less abrupt than on the North coast, the dominant style (known as Pachacamac) is distinct from those characteristic of the preceding Lima culture. In the valley of Ica, the Wari-influenced variety has been called Ica-Pachacamac (Menzel 1964:71). Many of the earlier Lima patterns were perpetuated in the contemporary Nievería style, a very fine orange ware with polychrome and sculptured decoration of novel appearance that was limited to the valleys of Chillón, Rímac, and Lurín. Another notable component of Central coast pottery is the Teatino style, characterized by an opaque red color and decoration based primarily on incision. Some motifs are reminiscent of the Formative pottery from Ancón, while others are imitations of Tiahuanacoid designs (Bonavia 1963). Teatino, which persisted into post-Wari times, is restricted to the Chillón and Chancay valleys, and at Ancón it is associated with the Pachacamac, Viñaque, and Huamanga varieties of Wari II pottery. On the Central coast in general, traits implanted during the Wari invasion were gradually transformed until they crystallized in types called "Epigonal" and "Three-color Geometric," which paved the way for the emergence of a later regional variety known as Chancay.

Notable changes are also evident in the polychrome pottery of the South coast, where the Atarco style, which combines strong Tiahuanacoid ingredients with Nazcoid elements, replaced the indigenous tradition (represented principally by Nazca IX). Round-based vessels and other typical Nazca shapes appear not to have died out, however, since the Epigonal or Pinilla ceramic style that emerged after Wari II is characterized by a partial return to Nazcoid forms.

The South highlands have been little studied and what is known of Waru pottery is inadequate to define the nature of the changes precipitated by the Wari invasion. Certain elements of the later Killke pottery imply a strong Tiahuanacoid impact, although some earlier decorative patterns were retained, among them linear designs and the tendency to bichrome on a light-colored surface. The ceramic style known as "Lucre" also developed as a consequence of the Wari invasion; it is a tricolor Epigonal variety emphasizing red and black, reminiscent in some respects of the Nazcoid version of Wari. Lucre may be a regional pottery type contemporaneous with Wari II, and comparable to Teatino or Nievería on the Central coast.

In the Cuzco region, the persistence of remnants of Wari influence or contacts with Tiahuanaco is suggested by an aryballo and a vase ornamented with conventionalized Tiahuanacoid motifs found at the Inca fortress of Sacsahuaman. These motifs do not correspond to any of the known Wari or Tiahuanaco styles, however.

Cemeteries in the Chuquibamba highlands north of Arequipa have produced evidence of another regional ceramic complex exhibiting Wari affiliations, principally with the Viñaque style. This pottery, known as "Qosqopa," develops into the Chuquibamba style (black on red). Absence of knowledge concerning earlier manifestations in the zone makes it impossible to discuss the specific nature of the Wari impact.

In the Northern highlands, ceramic evolution in the Callejón de Huaylas gradually led to a style reminiscent of Santa, which exerted an influence over the whole northern part of the Central Andes. Negative painting was replaced by polychrome, but many Recuay designs and vessel shapes persisted for a long time.

By the time that Wari influence reached the Cajamarca area, farther to the north, the cursive style of Cajamarca III had already attained considerable prestige (Reichlen and Reichlen 1949) and was widely traded. The principal center of production must have been between Huamachuco and Cajamarca, and vessels have been found in Moche, Huancayo, and Wari. Cajamarca III pottery has dark red or brown painted designs on a white background. Vessels are often thin and delicate, and sometimes so well fired that they approach the hardness of porcelain. The motifs may be animal figures, but are based on volutes and spirals that give them a distinctive appearance and which has led to the designation of the style as "Cursive." It has been divided into "Classic" and "Floral" variants, differentiated by the exuberance of the designs. Associated with Cajamarca III fine pottery is a coarse monochrome decorated by applique and incision. Spoons and open plates with annular bases were made of the fine ware, while ollas or jars are more typical coarse monochrome forms. Tripods are common.

As Wari domination became more intense, the Cajamarca style gradually absorbed certain Wari elements. Among the most important is the feline representation diagnostic of Cajamarca IV, along with greater emphasis on the utilization of light red and of bands bordered by fine lines. Cajamarca IV may represent either a ceremonial style contemporary with Wari or a later stage, when Wari pottery was no longer being made in the region.

These alterations in ceramic styles throughout the Central Andes involve not only adoption of Wari techniques of decoration, but also the acceptance of religious elements derived from the Tiahuanacoid tradition. The changes occurred more abruptly in some places than in others, but the general result was to replace local styles with an "international" style (Figure 184). When Wari domina-

tion terminated, certain introduced elements were retained and gradually modified in individual ways that brought into existence new local ceramic complexes, such as the coastal Epigonal styles. At Wari, this process led to the emergence of the Huamanga series, within which two groups are important: one derived from the Huarpa tradition and the other from Wari. The latter includes two local styles with very limited distribution during Wari III: Black and White on Red with stepped designs, and Cursive.

Figure 184. Wari-influenced pottery from various regions. *a*, Huaura style (MNAA, courtesy A. Guillén). *b*, Tiahuanacoid vessel from Sacsahuaman near Cuzco (courtesy A. Guillén). *c–d*, Qosqopa style from the Chuquibamba region north of Arequipa (MUA, courtesy Máximo Neira).

Although weaving is one of the most outstanding aspects of Wari technology, the perishability of textiles prevents collection of a sufficient number of samples to judge the extent of the changes that may have been produced by Tiahuanacoid influence. The major innovation was adoption of tapestry as the principal method of decoration, although the technique itself has been known since the Formative Period. Beautiful fabrics were also produced by brocade, double cloth, painting, twining, and featherwork. Designs were polychrome, with dark brown, light brown, blue, red, and orange being the preferred colors. Weaving illustrates better than any other kind of handicraft the extent to which religious elements affected art. Textile designs replicate the classic patterns of Tiahuanacan sculpture with greater fidelity and frequency than do those on pottery. Particularly prominent are the "angels" that surround the central figure of the Gateway of the Sun at Tiahuanaco and the Tiahuanacoid designs seen on Atarco and Viñaque ceramics of Wari II. The fact that these motifs are perfectly compatible with the structure of tapestry has led Muelle to suggest that the geometric character of Tiahuanacan art may imply its derivation from the textile medium (Figure 185).

An important characteristic of this period was the appearance of bronze, which must have had its origins in Tiahuanaco. Although it represents an advance in metallurgical technology, it did not have the repercussions that are associated with the introduction of bronze in other parts of the world. It never became a primary metal or replaced copper for general use. Gold and silver continued to be employed in large quantities, especially for ceremonial purposes.

Figure 185. Textiles of the Tiahuanacoid style (courtesy E. Versteylen).

A glimpse of the wealth and pomp that must have existed during Wari times is provided by the numerous small ornaments made from a variety of materials, among the most prominent being turquoise and bone. Miniature felines, birds, or human beings were carved from shell or bone and often incrusted with obsidian, wood, or turquoise. Both jewelry and objects of probable ceremonial significance are abundant and their extreme fineness of workmanship implies the expenditure of considerable time and patience on the part of the makers.

Small stone figurines have been found at Wari, Pikillaqta, Pachacamac, Ica, and other places. These amulets or idols sometimes resemble Wari sculptures, although the styles of clothing and headdress are highly variable. Length occasionally exceeds 3 centimeters, but the majority are smaller. A burial encountered many years ago at Pikillaqta contained a large number of these figurines, but no other elements of Wari culture. Many have been collected at Wari, where they are sometimes found on the surface of the ground. The abundance of ritual objects contrasts with the paucity of ceremonial structures, giving the impression that Wari religion was an unusual mixture of mysticism and secularity. The priests and military governors must have formed a homogeneous category, somewhat reminiscent of the situation in Inca society described by the European chroniclers.

BURIAL PRACTICES. Treatment of the dead, although little known, provides additional insight into the unusual nature of Wari ideology. A considerable number of tombs has been found on the coast, although many have not been described. On the South coast, rectangular subterranean chambers with rounded corners were constructed of rectangular adobes and roofed with beams and clay. Orientation was east-west, with the entrance toward the west. The body was seated and flexed, with the knees against the chest, and usually wrapped in textiles. The resulting bundle was provided with an artificial head of cloth and ornamented with gold objects and feathers. This kind of tomb has also been reported on the Central coast, but seems to be rare farther north. Most of the burials known from the North coast have a careless appearance and few offerings, suggesting that they represent lower-class individuals. In the highlands, interments from the Curawasi region are accompanied by offerings indicative of high rank. One contained 85 pottery vessels (70 of them miniatures) and 2 figurines. A burial found at Batan Urqo contained several gold objects.

Notable among the interments during both Wari I and II are those containing only broken ceremonial pottery. The ones at Conchopata and Pacheco were described earlier (pp. 152, 155). Similar caches have been found near La Victoria in the Ocoña Valley, except that here the vessels were complete. The archeologist Toribio Mejía Xesspe, who arrived after the discovery of ceremonial vessels up to 1.5 meters tall, was able to excavate several more in modern corrals that occupied a flat area in the center of the village. They had been placed in pits and covered with feather mantles.

CONCLUSION. In spite of the paucity of existing information, it is evident that the Wari conquest of the Central Andes served as a strong vehicle for economic, social, and cultural transformation through the medium of a centralized and despotic state regime, a proselytizing ecumenical religion, and a pronounced socio-economic stratification in which Wari formed the apex, and the least prestigeous towns the base. Technology, science, and the arts underwent marked changes in a number of respects, although the process was not catastrophic in nature. Urbanism and militarism began with Wari and gradually affected all the Central Andean societies.

A conquest state initiates a process of bilateral acculturation through which the conquerors adopt customs of the areas they incorporate and the conquered tend to accept new ingredients that are compatible with their pre-conquest culture. The blending may be insufficient, however, to eliminate the aversion of a local population to domination by foreign masters. This seems to have been true of Wari, since the conquered provinces appear to have seized the first opportunity to destroy the power that held them in submission and to regain their freedom.

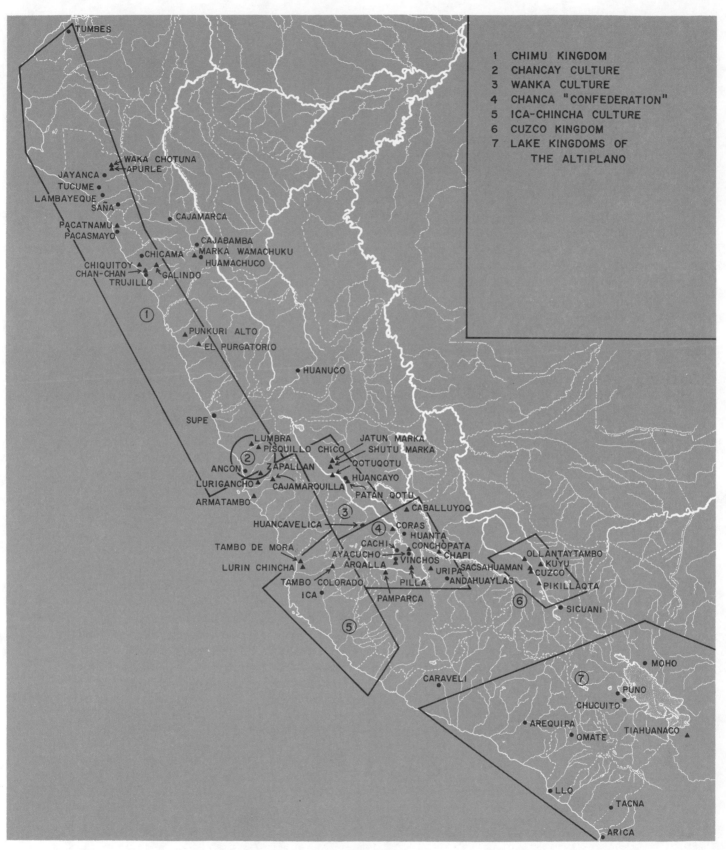

Figure 186. Location of the Regional States and some of the principal sites (▲ archeological site; ● modern town).

THE REGIONAL STATES

A.D. 1100–1470

The decline of the Wari Empire disrupted the unity that had been imposed on the Central Andes and permitted the resurgence of local or regional political organizations. This process is partly documented by traditions concerning founders of the nations extant in the 16th century, so that for the first time archeological problems can be approached with the aid of data from history and ethnology.

When the Spaniards arrived in Peru in 1532 and imprisoned the Inca emperor Atawallpa, they encountered a state organized under the hegemony of the Cuzqueños, about which they received numerous conflicting historical explanations. While providing this information, the natives sometimes digressed to speak of nations that had been conquered by the Inca and had been incorporated into the great Empire of Tawantinsuyu. Most chroniclers paid little attention to the "unofficial" statements concerning the various regions subdued by the Inca and only a few documents contain specific references to pre-existing cultures. According to the "official" version, prior to Inca dominance all of Peru was occupied by scattered, unorganized, and unimportant tribes, living close to nature and predisposed to servitude. They were contemptuously referred to as "chaotic" and the Cuzqueños were pictured as civilizers, who introduced order throughout the Andes.

This image of pre-Inca Peru was completely erroneous except in the Northern and Southern highlands, where agricultural societies had remained at a rudimentary level, at best reaching a degree of development comparable to that achieved in other parts of the Central Andes immediately prior to the Wari conquest. But the "barbarians" and "savages" neighboring the Incas were certainly mislabeled, since in most cases they had already developed a social organization based on cities and towns, although they did not achieve large-scale political integrations.

Archeological evidence clearly demonstrates the high level of development reached by many towns and the cultural unity that sometimes prevailed over extensive areas (Figure 186). At present, however, the Chimú Kingdom is the sole regional state on the coast for which historical confirmation exists. In the highlands, the only developed or incipient state was that of Cuzco. There are unconfirmed reports of at least two kingdoms on the Central coast: Cuis Manco, which included the valleys of Chancay, Chillón, Rímac, and Lurín, and Choke Manco, which extended from Chilca to Cañete. The archeological Chancay culture corresponds in general to the domain of Cuis Manco, except that the Lurín Valley relates more closely to a poorly known culture that extends over the Choke Manco area, and which might be called "Chilca." It is closely related to Chancay. Such correlations tend to confirm the historical validity of these kingdoms or chiefdoms, but final affirmation must await future investigation. As a consequence, the Central coast can be discussed only from the standpoint of archeological evidence, leaving sociopolitical considerations to the time when the data are more complete.

The chroniclers refer frequently to the "Lord of Chincha," who is believed to have ruled over the valleys of Chincha, Pisco, Ica, and Nazca on the South coast. The existence of such a political entity has not been verified archeologically, however, and although many cultural elements are common to these four valleys, there are also distinctions between them. Furthermore, cultural similarity is not necessarily correlated with political unity. At present, the possibility that independent states occurred in each valley cannot be eliminated, nor can the existence of more extensive kingdoms be proved. Consequently, the South coast also must be described solely in archeological terms.

Some references pertaining to the highlands speak of kingdoms, confederations, chiefdoms, nations, and states, but other sources suggest that the groups conquered by the Inca were principally territorial rather than political or cultural entities. In the North highlands, a small kingdom apparently existed in the Cajamarca region. It was allied with the Chimú at the time of the Inca conquest, but historical references concerning its organization or nature are minimal and the names of only a few of the rulers are known. Cajabamba and Huamachuco, which are south of Cajamarca, may have been included in this kingdom, although the "province of Huamachuco" is sometimes mentioned separately. The extensive site of Marka Wamachuku is an example of the important kind of centers that may date from this period, and which were reused by the Inca. Since Chimú influence penetrated as far as the Utcubamba region, this whole northern highland zone will be considered here as affiliated with the Chimú Kingdom.

Other important political centers existed in the zones of Huánuco and the Callejón de Huaylas, but they can only be dealt with in a very superficial manner because of the paucity of data concerning them.

The Mantaro region may either have been divided into local chiefdoms or unified under a single state. Archeological remains permit recognition of three cultures in the Central highlands at this time: one in the Mantaro Valley, defined initially by Mantaro pottery and later by the Patan Qotu style; the second in the valleys of Huanta and Urubamba (Acobamba), associated with Coras pottery; and the third in the valleys of Pampas and Ayacucho, including the Apurímac region, correlated with Arqalla pottery. These three manifestations have certain features in common, but also exhibit important differences. One may correspond to the Wanka and the others to the Chanka, but evidence as yet is insufficient to confirm this correlation. Pending the acquisition of more specific information, the Central highlands will be discussed in terms of the Chanka confederation, which was of great importance in the formation of the Inca Empire.

In the extreme south of the Central Andes, remnants of Tiahuanaco gave birth to kingdoms and chiefdoms about which more is known. At least two stages can be recognized. The first followed the fall of the Wari Empire and was characterized by the emergence of a number of petty states, whose names have survived in oral traditions. The second, which was protohistoric, began toward the end of the 14th or beginning of the 15th century under the leadership of new dynasties that fought first for the Inca and later for the Spanish, and thus impinge on the historical period.

The Kingdom of Chimú

Chimú, Chimo or Chimor, is the ancient name for the valley of Moche or Trujillo, at the extreme northwest of which are the remains of Chan-chan, a grandiose city that was the capital of a kingdom or small empire. Rowe (1948) has made a serious attempt to reconstruct the details of this kingdom based on the study of several extremely significant 17th century documents, such as those by Carrera (1939), Calancha (1938), certain chapters in a work written in 1586 by Cabello Balboa (1951), and an anonymous history written in 1604 (Vargas Ugarte 1942), and much of what follows is based on his work.

According to these documents, the Chimú Kingdom extended from Tumbes southward to the Río Chillón. Its southern limit must have been reached shortly prior to the Inca conquest, because cultural differences and other kinds of evidence suggest that the Chancay and Chillón valleys were not firmly integrated into Chimú culture. The southern limit is most clearly defined in the vicinity of Supe. In the highlands, Chimú influences can be discerned as far east as the Utcubamba Valley, and although the Cajamarca and Huamachuco regions may have been associated only by political alliance, their cultural affiliation is obvious.

Archeologically, the origin of the Chimú culture can be traced from the dissolution of the Wari Empire and the resulting depopulation of the North coast, which permitted revival of earlier Moche elements. Although the legends concerning the historical origins of the kingdom and its governing dynasties speak of the arrival of culture bearers from elsewhere, this is not verifiable in the archeological sequences. Rather, the evidence suggests a gradual amalgamation between Wari and Moche ingredients, crystallizing ultimately in a distinctive style.

Traditions concerning Lambayeque Valley speak of a hero named Ñam-lap, who founded a dynasty that ruled the area prior to its conquest by the Chimú. According to the legend, Ñam-lap came from a place far to the south in a fleet of balsa rafts, along with his wife Ceterni (or Sotenic), a harem, a group of courtiers, and a greenstone idol called "Yam-pallec"; the latter was an image of Ñam-lap and was his representative and bore his name (Rowe 1948:37). The courtiers who accompanied Ñam-lap were Pituzofi (Blower of the Shell Trumpet), Niñacola (Master of the Litter and Throne), Niñagintue (Royal Chancellor), Fonga (Preparer of the Way), Occhocalo (Royal Cook), Xam-muchec (Steward of the Face Paint), Ollopcopoc (Master of the Bath) and Llapchullulli (Provider of Feathered Cloth). The culture hero established himself at Chot, where he founded a sanctuary that Rowe (1948:38) believes may survive as the pyramid now called "Huaca Chotuna." When Ñam-lap died, he acquired wings and flew away.

Ñam-lap was succeeded by a son named Cium, who constructed a palace and married Zolzdoñi (also known as Ciernumcacum). His other sons colonized adjacent valleys: Nor went to Cinto, Cala to Túcume, and a fourth to Collique. Llapchillulli, one of the courtiers who had arrived with Ñam-lap, established himself in Jayanca. The dynasty initiated by Ñam-lap included the following series of rulers (Rostworowski de Diez Canseco 1961:52): (1) Ñam-lap or Ñaymlap, (2) Cium or Suim, (3) Escuñain, (4) Macuy, (5) Cunti-pallec, (6) Allascunti, (7) Nofan-nech, 8) Mulumuslan, (9) Llamecoll, (10) Llanipat-cum, (11) Acunta, and (12) Fempallec.

The last representative of the dynasty, Fem-pallec, fell under the spell of a beautiful woman, who seduced him for the purpose of removing the altar of Ñam-paxillaec or Nam-pallec) at Chot. Her effrontery brought a deluge lasting 30 days and a year of sterility and hunger; in retribution, the priests tied her hands together and threw her into the sea. After the dynasty ended, many years of obscurity passed before the Chimú conquest and the establishment of a new dynasty, which was composed of (1) Pongmassa, (12) Palles-massa, (3) Oxa, and (4) Llempisan (1407?).

Although it is not certain that all the names refer to real persons, the first dynasty may have lasted for more than a century, during which the valley was a local independent chiefdom. Pong-massa, Pallesmassa, and Oxa precede the Inca conquest, which occurred during the rule of Llem-pisan. The Inca did not replace the local chiefs and may have respected all of the privileges to which they had been entitled. The names recorded during the period of Inca domination are (5) Chullem-pisan, (6) Cipromarca, (7) Fallem-pisan or Efquen-pisan, (8) Xecfuin-pisan (1531).

The Spanish conquest took place during the reign of Xecfuin-pisan. By that time, at least three epochs had existed according to traditional history: (1) a period of local rule under the dynasty of Ñam-lap; (2) a period of subordination to the Chimú Kingdom under a new dynasty, and (3) a period of subordination to the Inca Empire, during which the Chimú dynasty continued to provide local administration.

After the Spanish conquest was well consolidated, the ruler of Lambayeque was Pedro Cusco Chumbi, who, as his name indicates, had become a Christian.

Other records have survived in Trujillo, the center of the Chimú Kingdom, although the list of rulers is less complete than that from Lambayeque. This history begins with the arrival of Taycanamo, a culture hero who also came on a balsa raft. He wore cotton clothing and carried magical yellow powders, which he used in ceremonies (this may have been gold, a metal much prized by the Chimú). His origin is not specified and may be identifiable with the Wari conquest, although he was reputed to have been sent by a great lord who dwelt beyond the seas. He spent a year constructing a palace and learning the local language, after which he was accepted as the ruler of the valley. The dynasty he founded endured until Spanish colonization.

On his death, Taycanamo was succeeded by his son Guacri-caur, who conquered the lower part of the Moche Valley. He in turn was followed around the middle of the 14th century by his son Ñançen-pinco, who not only subjugated the upper valley, but took control of the coast between Saña and Santa. Seven rulers intervened before the time of the great Minchan-çaman, who completed the expansion of the kingdom by extending its borders to Tumbes in the north and to Carabayllo in the south.

Although the Chimú established a reputation as conquerers, especially after the reign of Ñançen-pinco, they were frequently required to combat enemies to the south and north. Their inability to dominate Lima completely may imply the existence of a strong army in that region; it is also possible, however, that their expansion was interrupted by the Inca conquest, which came like a great wave from the south.

Allied to the Chimú were the Cajamarcans, whose ruler Cusmancu sought assistance from the Chimú ruler Minchan-çaman to hold off the armies of the Inca. In the Utcubamba Valley toward the east, Chimú influence was nearly as important as it was in Cajamarca and this may be the area from which gold and feathers of forest birds were obtained. In the Huamachuco region, part of the Wari town of Wiraqocha Pampa must have remained inhabited, but the great city of Marka Wamachuku surpassed it in importance and perhaps achieved the status that it possessed during the Inca period. The ruler, Tauricuxi, must have lived there. While the nature of the social organization of the valley during this period is unclear, Chimú influence is evident, especially in the pottery.

Around the third decade of the 15th century, the first news of the Inca expansion in the Central Peruvian highlands reached the Chimú, and the alliances with highland groups east of the valleys of Trujillo and Lambayeque may have been initiated at this time. During this period, Cuzco and the growing empire were ruled by Pacha Kuteq Inka Yupanki ("he who restores the earth"), who sent his younger brother, Capac Yupanki, to conquer the Central highlands as far north as the Río Yanamayo. The army was headed for the Callejón de Huaylas when its progress was halted by the desertion of a large contingent of Chanka, who fled eastward toward the forest. Part of the remaining forces pursued the Chanka unsuccessfully and Capac Yupanki decided to send his entire army after them. In so doing, he crossed the Río Yanamayo and penetrated the Cajamarca region without authorization of the Inca emperor.

Having gone this far, Capac Yupanki decided to conquer the small kingdom, believing that this might placate the Inca's wrath at his having allowed the Chanka to desert. The Cajamarca ruler Cusmancu sought aid from the great Minchan-çaman and received it; the battle was hard fought, but the Cuzqueños finally won and Cusmancu was killed. Capac Yupanki returned to Cuzco with the news of the victory, but instead of being honored, he was tried for disobedience and lack of caution and put to death by order of Pacha Kuteq. Subsequently, the Inca sent his son and heir Tupac Capac (Tupac Inka Yupanki) to the region, first having insured the capitulation of the kingdoms of Cajamarca and Chimú by totally subduing all of the intermediate region. This accomplished, the expedition continued to Cajamarca to complete its subjection, and then sent groups to occupy the various North coastal valleys, conquering Moche via Huamachuco. The resistance offered by Minchan-çaman was unsuccessful and, after the fall of the Great Chimú, the Inca advanced easily to Ecuador.

The Chimú king—called Chimú Capac by the Inca—was taken to Cuzco, where he was maintained with full honors; his son Chumun-caur replaced him in the government, but his function was reduced to carrying out the interests of the Empire of Tawantinsuyu. Later, the Chimú Kingdom was eliminated and its ruler became just one more Alaec in the valley of Moche. After their submission to Cuzco, the residents of the North coast were obliged to send gold, silver, clothing, and maidens annually to the Inca capital in the highlands, thousands of kilometers to the south. Apparently, not all of the Chimú complied readily because the Inca system of mitimaes (population transfers) was extensively applied to the region. The governers, however, were transformed into docile representatives of the empire by showering them with privileges and exempting them from the tribute necessary to keep the coffers of the imperialists constantly filled.

Although the highlands south of Cajamarca and Huamachuco are extremely rich in archeological remains, it is impossible to discuss their status because of insufficient investigation. In the Callejón de Huaylas, Bennett (1944) was unable to find a culture assignable to this period and the Wari tradition may have continued here until the Inca epoch. There are many sites in Huánuco, on the banks of both the Marañón and the Huallaga, but their chronological position and cultural affiliation remain to be determined.

SETTLEMENT PATTERN. The great urban centers characteristic of the area occupied by the Chimú culture indicate that the city fulfilled an important function in economic, social, and political affairs. There was a hierarchy of settlements of differing size and importance. The capital possessed the greatest prestige because of its size and the centralization of services there; immediately below it were the cities that served the capital directly, such as the provincial capitals, where the governors lived. Centers subject to the provincial cities occupied the third level, and at the bottom were the small towns and rural villages.

The Chimú capital was Chan-chan, and nearly every valley in the empire had at least one urban center, sometimes rivaling the capital in size. The most important were Chiquitoy and Chicamita in the Chicama Valley and Pacatnamú in Jequetepeque. One of the largest cities was Apurlé in Motupe. In Saña Valley, only the town of Cerro Corbacho is known; Pátapo and Saltur in Lambayeque are relatively small, as are the Chimú centers in Virú and Chao, south of Moche. There is a large town in Nepeña called "Punkurí Alto" and one in Casma referred to as "El Purgatorio." The southernmost known city is Chimo Capac in Supe. Each of these urban centers was supplemented by towns of lesser importance. In the central part of the valley dominated by Chan-chan, for example, was Galindo, and the addition of its area to that of Chan-chan indicates that the Moche Valley sustained an enormous population during Chimú times.

Although Chan-chan must have been founded during the Wari conquest, its principal development occurred during the Chimú period. It covers some 20 kilometers, making it one of the largest cities of pre-Spanish Peru, and is divided into 10 walled sectors or "barrios," separated by very straight, narrow streets and planned plazas (Figure 187). The sectors are rectangular and each contains houses, terraces, reservoirs, parks, roads, and public buildings. Walls were constructed of tapia and adobe bricks, and usually decrease in width with increasing height. Some exceed nine meters in elevation and are more than three meters thick at the base. The capital must have been a very attractive place to live. Although today it is a desert of dust and adobes with marshes toward the west, traces of many reservoirs remain, and their water must have sustained vegetation that has since disappeared. The walls of the palaces and probably the temples were beautifully decorated with relief friezes carved in clay, some composed of geometric designs and others depicting complicated mythical figures that probably related to a cult (Figure 188). One part, known as "Huaca del Dragón," has a scene that may represent the heavens; it is dominated by the Moche two-headed serpent, associated with a complex of dragon-like elements derived from the Wari feline (Figure 189). The Uhle sector, named after the early expert on Andean archeology, also has well-preserved friezes with birds, fishes, and plants arranged in parallel, diagonal rows. Investigations by Francisco Iriarte and Jorge Zegarra, and more recently by a team of archeologists from Harvard University directed by Michael Moseley and Carol Mackey, have revealed many other handsomely ornamented buildings (Figure 190).

Apurlé or Apurlec, the second largest Chimú city, is located south of Motupe on the road to Jayanca. The perimeter of the ruins is about two kilometers. There are many streets, the majority narrow and very regular; buildings are adobe and tapia, as at Chan-chan, and walls are sometimes covered with a yellowish plaster. Among the specialized structures are storehouses and small pyramidal temples.

The city of Pátapo in Lambayeque is neither as beautiful nor as large as the preceding two, but it must have contained a sizable population. Platforms erected on natural hills are surrounded by a group of enclosures of typical Chimú arrangement. There are a few stone structures, but these may date from the Inca occupation.

El Purgatorio in Casma consists of a complex of pyramids and walled enclosures on three sides of a natural elevation. The remaining side is occupied by the cemetery. Following the pattern initiated by Wari, the city has few portals of access.

Thanks to the study made by Willey (1953), we know that in the Virú Valley changes in residence construction following the Chimú conquest were minor. In this valley, which apparently was of little importance in Chimú political, economic, and social organization, irregular agglutinated villages persisted and more regular arrangements disappeared. Rectangular enclosures with rooms around a central patio continued in use and one of them may have served as an administrative center.

Figure 187. Air view of the Rivero and Tschudi compounds at Chan-chan, capital of the Chimú Kingdom (courtesy M.E. Moseley).

Figure 188. (*below and facing page*). Decorative treatment of the plastered walls in the Tschudi compound at Chan-chan.

Figure 189. Plaster frieze at the Huaca del Dragón near Chan-chan.

Figure 190. Wooden figure in a niche at the principal entrance to the Rivero compound in Chan-chan (courtesy M.E. Moseley).

It is noteworthy that the population increase in the Moche Valley appears to have been accompanied by a marked demographic decline in the other valleys; this trend is best documented in Virú and Casma (Willey 1953:394; Thompson 1964:97).

SOCIAL ORGANIZATION. There is little information on the character of Chimú government, the rules of succession, or the nature of the social hierarchy. Leadership may have passed from brother to brother and from father to son. The title designating local chiefs was "Alaec," while "Ci-quic" ("Great lord") may have been a title of the king. The Piura region, inhabited by the Tallán, was ruled by women, a practice probably dating from pre-Chimú times. They were referred to by the Spaniards as "cocoons" because their clothing covered their bodies from neck to feet (Rostworowski de Diez Canseco 1961). These female chiefs changed spouses frequently and were all-powerful. The existence of a kind of incipient feudal organization is implied by petitions from the chiefs of Piura and Monsefú late in the Colonial Period, in which they requested restitution of lands on the ground that "during pagan times, all land was under the jurisdiction of the chief, who held it as his own, leasing it to the Indians, who retained part of the harvest for their own use" (Rostworowski de Diez Canesco 1961:8). The system may also have provided for personal services, since in 1768 the chief of Monsefú requested as part of the rights corresponding to his rank the assignment to him of men "older than 50 years, boys, and old women free of suspicion" for household tasks, agricultural labor, etc. (Rostworowski de Diez Canesco 1961:9). The existence of local variations indicates that the Chimú rulers permitted continuation of many of the practices indigenous to each valley and probably did not replace former governments everywhere. In Lambayeque and a few other regions, however, a new dynasty was imposed by the conquerors.

As a consequence of a state structure based on conquest and undoubtedly despotic in character, a well-defined social stratification emerged. At the summit were the Great Lord Ci-quic and the chief Alaec. Beneath them was a group of courtiers known as "pixllca" or gentlemen, who must have been city dwellers with some degree of prestige and economic position. The lowest stratum consisted of the "paraeng" and the "yana," terms that have been translated as "vassal" and "domestic servant" respectively, although their roles were probably more closely equivalent to peasants and slaves. Although

the categories of "gentlemen" and "vassals" may reflect an attempt to describe the local social system in terms of familiar European categories, the existence of a legend in which kings and nobles are derived from two stars and common people from two planets suggests that there was a marked separation between the two groups and little or no mobility between them.

Little is known about family life. Polygyny existed among the upper class, to judge from the reference to the harem of Ñam-lap, who however had a favorite wife, Ceterni. A family was composed of father ("ef"), mother ("eng"), son and/or daughter ("eiz"). The term for husband was "ñang" and for wife, "mecherraec." A man was called "ñofaen." Other kinship terms included "cocaed" (older sister or aunt when ego was male), "ñier" (older brother or uncle when ego was female), "uxllur" (brother, younger sister, nephew, niece when ego was male), and "chang" (sister, younger brother, niece or nephew, when ego was female). Affinal relationship was recognized by the terms "yquiss" (father, mother or brother of the spouse, when ego was male) and "pon" (sister-in-law, whether ego was male or female) (Rowe 1948:48). Adultery was punished by throwing the culprit from a cliff.

The growing demand for goods in quantity is reflected in the emergence of household industries and of specialists, whose skill is particularly evident in the quality of workmanship in metal and textiles. All types of objects, including simple domestic utensils, were mass produced. This must have stimulated the development of markets and a commercial system, probably based on barter since nothing resembling money appears to have existed.

Forms of land ownership were intimately linked to the sociopolitical structure and large tracts appear to have sometimes been the private property of powerful alaecs. Much land possibly also belonged to the Ci-quic and his family. As already noted, the chief of Piura spoke of land holdings in a manner suggestive of a feudal system of ownership.

Religion serves as an excellent mechanism of social control because behavior is subject to supernatural rewards and punishments. The beginnings of law and justice appear in the extensive regulations that are associated with the developing church structure. Among the Chimú, disrespect to the temples and disobedience to civil laws were both punished by burying the culprit alive. Sacrifices were made to Si (the Moon) and to Patá (Orion) to gain their assistance in finding a robber; when he was caught, he, as well as his father and brothers, were handed to the victim for execution.

Chimú religion centered around a series of supernatural forces that could to some extent be influenced or manipulated by priests, curers, and sorcerers. The gods made themselves visible to the faithful and their aid could be elicited by abstinence from certain foods, among them salt and pepper, and by refraining from sexual relations (Rowe 1948). Several kinds of birds, such as the owl, were viewed as omens.

The principal divinity according to Larco Hoyle (1938–1939) was Ai-apaec, derived from the Moche cult mentioned earlier (page 104). Rowe (1948:50), however, believes that "ai-apaec" is simply the nominal form of the verb "to make" and means only "creator." If so, Ai-apaec might be comparable to the Inca god Wira Qocha (Viracocha), an invisible all-powerful deity from which all else originated.

Although there are no documentary references to Ai-apaec, some do exist for the goddess Si (the Moon), who was the supreme deity, omnipresent, and responsible for the weather and agricultural productivity. Since the arrival of the rains and the motions of the sea are linked with the Moon, the food supply depended upon Si. She was believed to be much more powerful than the Sun because she was visible both night and day, and eclipses were interpreted as battles between the two gods. A lunar eclipse was considered a misfortune, whereas a solar eclipse was a joyful occasion (Rowe 1948:50). There are references to a temple called "Si-an," dedicated to the goddess Si, which probably is the Huaca Singan in the Jequetepeque Valley and may be the structure known today as "Huaca del Dragón."

The Sun, a secondary deity, was linked to magic stones known as "Alec-pong," which were simultaneously his daughters and representatives of the ancestors of the people. Some constellations were venerated, especially Pata (Orion's Belt), which depicted the act of justice, and Fur (the Pleiades), which marked the beginning of the year and was the patroness of agriculture. The Sea was another important divinity and offerings of maize flour were made to it to insure an abundance of fish (Rowe 1948:50).

There was a clear distinction between curers and sorcerers. The former were supported by the State and conducted their professional activities with the aid of herbs, while sorcerers were either scorned or feared. Calancha (1938) speaks of gatherings of male and female sorcerers, in which cannibalism and sexual orgies took place. (On the North coast of Peru, and especially in the Moche Valley, sorcerers continue to exist and many peasants still seek their services.)

ARTS AND CRAFTS. Chimú pottery is easily recognized by its black color and metallic sheen, produced through a combination of smoking and burnishing, and by its predominantly angular form (Figure 191). Both ceremonial and domestic vessels were mold made. Polychrome pottery (black, white, and red) painted with geometric designs continued in use on the North coast for a long time after the end of Wari domination, but was ultimately replaced by relief decoration, three-dimensional representations of figures on the upper part of vessels (Figure 192), or modeling of the entire piece. Oxydized red pottery also disappeared except in a few of the northern valleys, where it continued to be manufactured for domestic purposes. Wari shapes remained popular, especially vessels with two conical spouts connected by a bridge handle and jars with a face on the neck. There was a resurgence in popularity of the stirrup spout, which was rare in the central part of the Chimú area during Wari times but persisted in the Lambayeque region.

Although pottery attained a notable artistic development, the most outstanding form of Chimú craftsmanship was metal working, especially gold (Figure 193). Greater and better use was made of precious metals than at any earlier or later time, and a tremendous diversity of forms was created in spite of the limited technical resources available. Even after the Inca conquest, Chimú goldsmiths were accorded high prestige and, in addition to the rich booty that they gathered from the North coastal valleys, the Cuzqueños took Chimú metal workers to the capital at Cuzco.

Gold and silver ceremonial vessels were fashioned in a great variety of forms, ranging from vases with engraved human faces to complicated, delicate bottles with double spout and bridge handle. Representations of animals or human beings were either solid or hollow in construction. Laminated pieces were decorated by repoussé and hammering, and some examples bear scenes of men and animals surrounded by plants. The "tumi," a semi-lunar knife with a handle sometimes in the shape of a mythological being, was one of the most common instruments made of precious metal. Cups, bowls, plates, bangles, pins, and miniature replicas of all kinds of animals were produced. Personal ornaments, such as masks, earrings, and lip ornaments are also common. Art, which in earlier times was

Figure 191. Black pottery vessels of the Chimú style (MRLH).

Figure 192. Pottery vessel of the Lambayeque style.

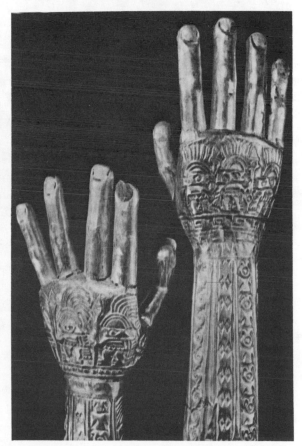

Figure 193. Gold hands of Chimú style from Lambayeque
(Museo Mujica Gallo).

in the hands of the potters, appears to have been transferred to the goldsmiths. Even today, in spite of the decades of looting of archeological monuments, exquisite objects of gold and silver continue to be found on the North coast.

Other forms of technology did not advance appreciably, although weavers produced cloth beautifully decorated with feathers. Tapestry, gauze, and brocade were the dominant techniques (Figure 194), and painting was the most common form of decoration. Stone working was insignificant. In contrast to earlier times, when all or the major part of the artistic activity was inspired by religion, Chimú creations were for secular purposes.

BURIAL PRACTICES. The burial pattern generally continued that established during Wari times in most of the region. The dead were interred with ritual offerings and food. Cemeteries were close to the settlements, in lands reserved for this purpose. The tombs reflect the nature of Chimú society, the wealthy being placed in chambers along with rich funerary accoutrements, while the poor were given simple burials and provided with the few utilitarian objects required in the afterlife. The bodies were flexed and usually placed in a seated position, but sometimes laid on one side; rarely, they were extended.

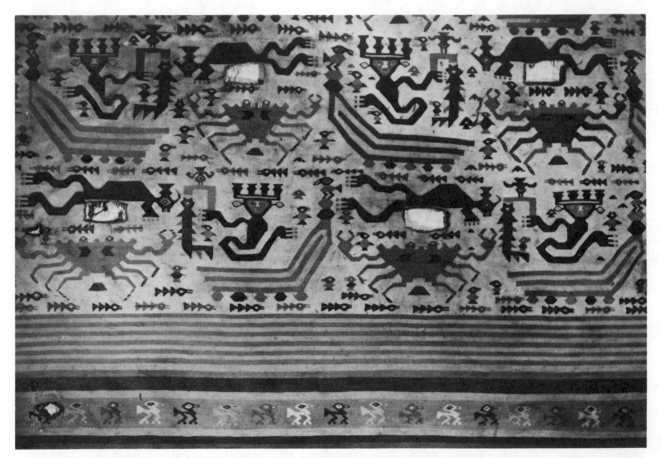

Figure 194. Textile exhibiting Chimú influence, encountered in the Rímac Valley (MUSM, courtesy E. Versteylen).

The Chancay Culture

There are vague indications of possible intervalley political organizations on the Central coast. The chronicler Bernabé Cobo speaks of a "nation" that had expanded over the valleys of Lurín and Rímac as far as Carabayllo at the time of the Inca conquest. In post-Spanish times, Tauri Chumbi was governor of Pachacamac and Tauri Chusca, of Lima. The valley of Mala, farther to the south, was ruled by a lord named "Chuqui-mancu" (Choke Manco).

Archeological evidence supports the existence of a fairly homogeneous culture, known as Chancay, in the valleys of Chancay and Chillón, with influences extending from Huaura to Rímac. Farther south, little fieldwork has been done, but existing data indicate a more or less uniform pattern of culture with local variations, which was strongly affected by developments on the South coast. Especially notable is the close relationship between the contemporary complexes in Cañete and Chincha.

SETTLEMENT PATTERN. In the Chancay Valley, the most typical urban center is Pisquillo Chico, located inland on the south side of the river. It is composed of a ceremonial sector containing a few rooms and various pyramidal mounds connected via ramps with a rectangular plaza, a habitation sector with structures of stone and clay, and a cemetery. The ceremonial sector has produced caches of offerings. Buildings were constructed either of clay, adobe, or field stones imbedded in clay. The corners were not bonded, with the result that they tend to separate. Entries were rectangular, niches were rare, and wall surfaces were undecorated. On the slope of a nearby hill is a rectangular enclosure with interior compartments, which may have been the principal administrative center, following the pattern on the North coast.

Lumbra, another complex of buildings, is associated with extensive engineering works in the form of terraces, reservoirs, and canals. A semi-isolated administration building with clay walls resembles the one at Pisquillo Chico. The ceremonial sector has a large temple at the center and several smaller temples constructed of clay and stones. Streets and plazas in the residential area are bordered by carelessly built houses. The presence of Teatino pottery indicates that this town was founded during the Wari Period.

In the Chillón Valley, the poorly preserved site of Zapallán appears also to have been another very extensive town. Buildings of clay and adobe were divided into rooms and patios: a large cemetery has been virtually destroyed by illegal treasure seekers.

Although the Rímac Valley contains numerous monuments and is readily accessible, dating is still poorly defined. Stumer (1954a) speaks of a mixed occupation, in which Chancay appears as an imported culture while the local one is known as Huancho. The habitation centers, however, correspond in a general way to those of Chancay, with variations attributable to influence from the Lima culture, which did not penetrate as far as the northern valleys of the Central coast during its final periods. Cajamarquilla, which flourished throughout the Wari epoch, appears to have been partially or completely abandoned with Wari decadence, and the revival of interest in ceremonial structures is apparent in the new settlements that replaced it. The sites of Mango Marca, Lurigancho, Huaycán, Armatambo, and Caraponga belong to this period, although the majority persisted without significant modification during the Inca times. Chancay pottery has also been found at Encalada, El Pino, and Vásquez (Stumer 1954a).

ARTS AND CRAFTS. The Chancay culture was originally identified on the basis of pottery vessels obtained from extensive cemeteries near Ancón and in the Chancay Valley. The workmanship is rather crude and the most popular variety has designs executed with blackish paint on a whitish slip. The surface is almost never smooth because of the gritty nature of the clay. Vessel shapes are varied, but the most common forms are oblong jars with a narrow neck bearing a modeled and painted human face; jars with a narrow neck, incurved rim, and handles extending from the neck to the body; tall pedestal-based vases resembling "floreros"; vases with straight, outsloping walls; annular-based plates, and small semi-spherical bowls. Decoration is generally by painting and motifs are usually geometric, but animals, people, and even plants occasionally appear. Modeling was employed to produce small applique figures. Zoomorphic vessels also occur, particularly birds and llamas. Female figures with outstretched arms are common and the majority have eyes embellished with a line that extends beyond both sides.

The development of this ceramic style began with

post-Wari independence and the emergence of a series of regional variants known as Huaura (or Epigonal). Huaura designs, painted in black-and-white on red, retained some of the formal aspects of the earlier Tiahuanacoid patterns but altered their content. Three-color Geometric, which followed, is characterized by the total elimination of Tiahuanacoid influence and its replacement with abstract black-and-red-on-white decoration. This, in turn, gave rise to the distinctive Chancay Black on White (Figure 195). The Teatino style, associated with the Wari occupation on the Central coast, persisted with very slight modification almost until the epoch of predominance of black-on-white painting. The Lauri style in the Chancay Valley, distin-

guished principally by decoration impressed with a cane or blunt instrument on an unpainted red surface, may constitute the domestic Chancay ware. The nearly universal use of molds for both simple and complicated forms (Figure 196) and the production of large quantities of objects are indications that, as among the Chimú, pottery manufacture had attained an industrial level.

Cloth was also mass produced and its high quality implies some degree of specialization (Figure 197). Chancay tombs are notable for their textiles, particularly the gauzes, which were a specialty of this culture and which exhibit great artistry and technical skill. Other techniques include brocade, openwork, and painting on plain weave.

The skillful decoration of gourds by pyroengraving is also worthy of mention; many beautiful examples exist, some embellished with mother-of-pearl incrustations.

Another important activity was trade, which connected the zone with the North and South coasts, the highlands, and possibly even the tropical forest. Many examples of pottery imported from Ica have been encountered at Ancón and Zapallán (Río Chillón), as well as copies of diagnostic Chimú forms. Some special ornaments incorporate feathers of birds found only in the tropical forest region.

BURIAL PRACTICES. One of the most notable aspects of Chancay culture is the nature and size of the cemeteries, as well as the great quantity of funerary offerings that were deposited with the dead. The distinctive types of graves certainly reflect the economically based social stratification. Variation extends from beautifully constructed chambers containing a profusion of offerings to simple burials consisting only of a body wrapped in plain cloth and provided with a few objects.

The mausoleums of the upper class are either circular with adobe walls or rectangular. The most luxurious type is rectangular or quadrangular, two or three meters deep and about the same in lateral dimensions, with well-finished clay walls and a roof of canes and poles. In some instances, there is a stairway leading down from the surface. The high status of the occupant is indicated by the presence

Above and facing page
Figure 195. Pottery vessels of the Chancay Black-on-White style (MUSM).

Right
Figure 196. Mold-made vessel of the terminal Chancay style (courtesy A. Guillén).

Figure 197. Chancay textiles (*below*, courtesy E. Versteylen).

not only of dozens of pottery vessels and textiles, but also of silver offerings. A more common but less sumptuous type of tomb has adobe walls defining a smaller rectangle and contains few offerings. Graves of poor people are shallower. An intermediate variety is a circular or rectangular pit cut into the earth. Most tombs at Ancón contain two bodies and one case has been noted in which there were three. Cranial deformation of the oblique or fronto-occipital type is typical.

The bodies are generally seated, flexed, and wrapped in cloth; some have a false head similar to that found on Wari burial bundles from the South and Central coasts. Lothrop and Mahler (1957) have described the tomb of an apparently important woman, whose arms were tatooed and who was accompanied by two sacrificed dogs, silver objects, a large quantity of pottery (especially figurines), a rich assortment of textiles, and some peculiar rag dolls. She was seated on a basket.

The Ica-Chincha Culture

The existence of a more or less homogeneous culture extending over several valleys on the South coast has been recognized for several decades (Uhle 1914, 1924a, 1924b). Recent studies by the University of California at Berkeley have permitted definition of regional variations in the form of the Chincha, Ica, Poroma, and Acarí pottery styles. Although they share elements that imply continuous inter-valley communication and in reality constitute a single culture, each of these ceramic complexes has its own history. Ica appears to have been the most important cultural center, although the Chincha Valley may have had greater political significance.

The Inca conquest of the South coast occurred during the rule of Pacha Kuteq. Most chroniclers are of the opinion that little effort was required and that the people of Chincha and Ica submitted peaceably. If these coastal valleys had been interconnected by a centralized political regime directed from Chincha, the conquest of the latter would have been sufficient to achieve dominance over the whole South coast. This unification cannot be considered proved, however, since although Cabello Balboa speaks of political connections between the valleys of Mala, Cañete, and Chincha, other sixteenth-century informants such as Castro and Ortega Morejón indicate that Ica, Chincha, and Cañete retained some degree of autonomy. The fact that the Inca efforts to strengthen their domination during the reign of Tupac Inca Yupanki met with considerable resistance also favors the interpretation that a similar response may have greeted the initial invasion.

SETTLEMENT PATTERN. The buildings that appear to have been of greatest importance are distributed over the extensive valley of Chincha. Among the more outstanding is the Tambo de Mora group on the west side. The principal feature, known as "La Centinela," is a clay-walled pyramid complex that incorporates several embankments along with patios, rooms, and streets. Other associated mounds include the impressive Tambo de Mora, which is nearly as large as La Centinela and has walls decorated with relief friezes in geometric motifs and stylizations of birds, similar to those at Chan-chan. The Tambo de Mora complex apparently served as the principal administrative center prior to the Inca conquest, and the Inca continued to utilize it for this purpose. The fact that roads lead from it in different directions is further evidence of centralized administration in pre-Inca times (Menzel 1959). Among other similar architectural complexes are Lurín Chincha and San Pedro. At San Pedro, located in the south part of the valley, there is another building called "La Centinela" (Figure 198) with proportions and characteristics implying an importance comparable to its namesake at Tambo de Mora.

The Cañete Valley to the north, which appears to have been intimately linked with Chincha, contains sites that follow the same pattern of pyramids associated with plazas, roads, and rooms. An example is the "fortress" of Ungará, which was later utilized by the Inca.

To date, no significant buildings or towns assignable to this period have been identified in the Pisco Valley, implying that it played a secondary role until the Inca epoch, when the city of Tambo Colorado was constructed there.

Although the Ica Valley was an important source of cultural influence, especially in ceramics, most of

Figure 198. La Centinela at the site of San Pedro in the Chincha Valley (courtesy Dwight Wallace).

the population was distributed in small hamlets scattered throughout the valley. The most notable site, Ica Vieja, in the Tacaraca region some 10 kilometers south of the modern city of Ica, consists of a complex of structures erected on mounds following the pattern employed in Chincha. It continued to be occupied following the Inca conquest, when it probably served as the regional administrative center.

The Nazca Valley also contains few important centers. The towns of Tambo de Calao and Paredones may have been founded during this period, although they are principally Inca installations. South of Nazca, evidence is scanty.

ARTS AND CRAFTS. Ceramics in general follow a uniform pattern and variations are important mainly as indicators of a certain degree of cultural independence between the valleys, at least in pottery making. The unifying characteristic is a polychrome style, in which white and black painting on a red surface is the most common technique. Decorative motifs are geometric, with a predominance of designs adapted from textiles and the substitution of stepped lines for curved or oblique ones. Conventionalized representations of birds and fish are also frequent, but may be difficult to recognize in the maze of angular forms. Pitchers with a narrow neck, everted rim, globular body, and rounded

Figure 199. Pottery vessels of the late Ica style (MUSM).

base are characteristic; jars and bowls with an angular shoulder and flange rim are also common. As on Nazca and Wari vessels, designs fill bands or areas bordered with black (Figure 199).

An important characteristic of Ica-Chincha culture was its strong emphasis on commerce. Pottery must have been an item of considerable prestige to judge from the fact that it has been found in sites on the Central coast and also in the Río Pampas region, near Ayacucho. The arrival of Inca influence brought minor stylistic changes, limited primarily to a few new forms, among them the "barrel" with an "arybaloid" neck (i.e., with a strongly everted rim) and small handles at the junction of the neck and body. Nazca and Wari weaving techniques continued, although the motifs assumed a distinctive appearance that is related to the designs on pottery (Figure 200). There are also certain similarities to Chimú motifs. Gold, silver, copper, and bronze were used for ornaments, tools, and weapons.

BURIAL PRACTICES. The cemeteries were relatively extensive and close to the settlements. Tombs generally consisted of rectangular chambers, in which the bodies were placed in a flexed position and provided with cloth, pottery, and other offerings of bone, wood, shell, and metal.

Figure 200. Textiles from Ica (courtesy E. Versteylen).

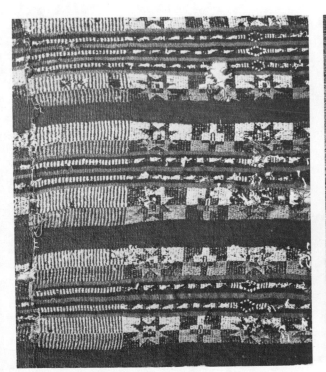

The Chanka "Confederation"

The centralized international organization that became the Inca Empire stemmed from the seige of Cuzco by its traditional enemies, the Chanka, who lived on the opposite side of the Río Apurímac. The defeat of the Chanka armies and the conquest of their territory northwest of Cuzco was the initial step in the great Inca expansion, which subsequently flowed over the length of the Andes.

The Cuzqueño traditions speak of semi-savage tribes that attacked Cuzco during the reign of the Inca Wira Qocha under the leadership of Astu Waraka, Tumay Waraka, and a commander known as Anku Ayllu. It is not known whether these warriors belonged to a single political organization or whether they represented a confederation of small groups that joined forces for warfare, nor is there concrete information on the territory they inhabited or whether all or a major portion of the "provinces" of the Central highlands belonged to the "Chanka alliance." The modern province of Andahuaylas is traditionally identified as Chanka territory, but historical references tend to define their area to include the extensive valley of the Río Pampas and the region west of the Apurímac, which was the nuclear zone of the Wari culture.

Archeological investigations undertaken by the universities of San Marcos in Lima and San Cristóbal de Huamanga in Ayacucho have made it possible to recognize a more or less homogenous culture over the Río Pampas Basin, extending from the headwaters to the junction with the Río Apurímac and westward as far as the confluence of the latter with the Mantaro (Figure 201). In the Mantaro region, which has been identified with the Wanka, a closely related culture has been discovered. Between the two zones is a regional variant called "Coras." Although a correlation between the archeological remains and the groups that fought against the Inca in the 15th century has not been conclusively demonstrated, this hypothesis will be provisionally accepted here.

THE PAMPAS BASIN. In the Pampas Basin, gradual abandonment of Wari customs occurred during the Huamanga period. Small villages replaced the large cities, planned arrangement was largely discontinued, and houses assumed asymmetrical forms tending toward rectangularity. The walls at Conchopata and Tunasniyoq were irregular and constructed of field stone. A new ceramic complex appeared, characterized by decoration in two or

Figure 201. Chanka pottery from the Ayacucho-Apurimac region (MUSCH).

three colors. Two varieties are distinctive: (1) carelessly executed cursive designs on a light background and (2) geometric motifs in black and white on a red background, especially a stepped figure outlined in white and filled with black or dark brown. Sloppily executed volutes represent survivals from the Ayacucho tradition. Surface treatment was typically poor, leaving a rough finish. The predominant vessel forms are spouted bottles resembling modern teapots, shallow plates, and spherical ollas with a flattened base.

Somewhat later, unsystematic arrangements of circular and rectangular structures, with the former predominating, began to appear on the hillsides. The associated pottery is typically plain and only minor survivals of elements from the preceding phase are discernible, among them simple patterns of dark brown lines on a cream slip. A new type appears, known as "Arqalla" and decorated with incision and applique (Lumbreras 1959).

When Inca influence began to penetrate the zone, the dominant settlement pattern was agglutinated villages composed of circular buildings located on the summits of the highest hills, and the diagnostic pottery was Arqalla. Arqalla (or Chanka) villages occur throughout the valley of the Río Pampas and its tributaries in such numbers as to imply a scattered but large population. Average size is 100 houses, although some are much more extensive; there is little trace of community facilities. Houses are irregularly arranged, with the entry generally toward the north. In settlements at higher elevations, exemplified by Pamparca and Qaqamarca, the walls are inclined slightly inward and doorways tend to be pointed at the top. Buildings at lower altitudes usually have circular stone walls under 1.5 meters high. Typical of the latter type are Arqalla, Pillucho, Caballuyoq (Bonavia 1964), and Cachi in the Department of Ayacucho.

One of the richest Arqalla cemeteries is at Chapi. The best complete ceramic vessels come from there and from Andahuaylas and Uripa. The pottery is generally plain with a rough finish, but occasionally it has a very thin red slip over the entire surface. Relief decoration in the form of applique nubbins or small anthropomorphic figures is associated with incision or circular stamping. Shallow plates and narrow-necked jars, sometimes ornamented with a crude face, are characteristic (Figure 202). Bases are conical or rounded on jars and flat on plates. Vessels have been found in the village of Pamparca that certainly were traded from Ica or Pisco.

Arqalla village sites contain large quantities of stone objects, among them mortars and circular clubheads or mauls. Adzes percussion-chipped from slate-like stone are also abundant and exhibit use-polish on both faces of the cutting edge. This type of artifact began with Huarpa, although the forms during that period were asymmetrical, whereas in Arqalla they are triangular or rectangular.

Burials are of two kinds: (1) circular mausoleums constructed with a corbelled vault of stone, and (2) graves excavated in the ground near the houses. The mausoleums, usually called "chullpas" by the local residents, contain multiple burials. Caves or rock shelters were also utilized, a custom that appears to have originated during the latter part of the Wari Empire, since similar finds have been made at Wari. Offerings consist of pottery, a few copper objects, and coarse textiles, which probably covered the bodies. Cranial deformation of the oblique, fronto-occipital, tubular form was practiced.

THE MANTARO BASIN. Farther to the north, in the Mantaro region, the decline of Wari was followed by emergence of a complex resembling Huamanga and known as Mantaro. It is characterized ceramically by predominance of a creamy white pottery reminiscent of Chancay, with geometric, black, painted designs featuring cursive elements.

Figure 202. Pottery vessel of the Arqalla type from Ayacucho.

Associated is a black, white, and red type that differs from Huamanga red ware only in a few motifs and forms. Jars with faces on the neck, globular bodies, and flat bases are characteristic (Figure 203).

The succeeding Patan Qotu style shares many aspects of settlement pattern and ceramics with Arqalla. Structures at Shutuy Marka in Jauja, Jatun Marka, and Qotuqotu have a circular plan, sometimes a corbelled-arch roof, and usually are better constructed than Arqalla ones. Pottery features linear black-and-white-on-red painting, applique nubbins, incision, and circular stamping. Axes or adzes resemble a ping-pong racket in form.

THE INTERMEDIATE ZONE. A culture called "Coras" with affinities to Arqalla and Patan Qotu has been recognized in the still poorly defined intermediate zone (Ramiro Matos Mendieta, pers. comm.). It is represented by rather large villages with circular houses in the Churcampa zone of Huancavelica. The pottery has a pale surface (Figure 204) and appears to be a continuation of the Huamanga Cursive tradition.

The Lake Kingdoms of the Altiplano (A.D. 1100–1450)

The decline of the Tiahuanaco culture permitted the emergence of a regional complex around the borders of Lake Titicaca, with local variations that may correspond to the political and/or ethnic units in existence when the zone was incorporated into the Inca Empire. One of the most outstanding of the shared traits was language. Aymara or Hak'e-aru ("language of people") was spoken throughout the area, while Uru and Pukina were used by local ethnic minorities. It is consequently possible to speak of "Aymara kingdoms and chiefdoms" centering on Lake Titicaca.

From the Titicaca altiplano, influences and also colonists passed over the western cordillera to occupy parts of the coast between Arequipa in Peru and Arica (and possibly Atacama) in Chile. The northern limit has not been well defined, but it may have approached Sicuani. In the south, the boundary was on the puna and salt flats of the Chile-Bolivia highlands, probably near Oruru. On the east, evidence extends into the lowlands ("yunga") of the Department of La Paz, Bolivia, and influences may have reached Cochabamba in the highlands. There is some information to indicate a southward penetration into the Humahuaca Valley in northwestern Argentina. This cultural distribution does not necessarily imply domination of the entire region; on the contrary, expansion of these kingdoms appears to have been motivated less by conquest than by the desire to exploit the resources of distinct environmental niches, following the principle of "verticality" proposed by Murra (1968:121–125, 1972:464–466).

Thanks to several sixteenth-century documents, we know that there were at least two powerful kingdoms west of Lake Titicaca: the Colla and the Lupaqa. Other ethnic groups that may also have been structured as independent kingdoms or chiefdoms are the Cana and Canchi south of Cuzco, the Collagua west of Puno, and the Pacaje south of Puno along the Río Desaguadero. This level was not reached, however, by the Umasuyo north and east of the lake, the Ubina in the Arequipa highlands, the Callaguaya of the eastern altiplano, the Uru on the northern margin of the lake, the Charca of southern Bolivia, and other local groups.

Since the written sources refer to the period after these political and/or ethnic groups had been incorporated into the Empire of Tawantinsuyu, their previous composition and territorial boundaries are poorly documented. It is only because the Incas often retained pre-existing political divisions and local patterns to facilitate incorporation of conquered areas into their own organization that the records tell us something about the earlier altiplano kingdoms.

Documentary information and archeological evidence both attest to the existence of a cultural unity that extended beyond language to include technology, settlement type, burial pattern (utilizing the famous chullpas or funerary towers), and other cultural features. There are many references to the Colla, whose capital was the town of Hatuncolla, northwest of the lake and north of the modern city of Puno. Information is even more abundant on the Lupaqa Kingdom (see especially Díez de San Miguel 1567), whose capital was at Chucuito, a few kilometers south of Puno on the shore of Lake Titicaca. The Lupaqa and Colla chiefs were addressed as "Mallcu," a term indicative of a position of power, and there was a traditional rivalry between these two kingdoms. Even during the Inca epoch, conflicts erupted over territorial control or simply for the pleasure of quarreling. The descendants of Zapana, who was the king of Hatuncolla, fought with those of Cari and Cusi, who ruled in Chucuito.

The archives relating to the Lupaqa (Murra 1968) permit a tentative reconstruction of the political organization and other aspects of the culture that are obscure archeologically, although it must be emphasized that the following description is subject to verification both by more detailed analysis of the documents and by further archeological investigation.

The Lupaqa economy was based primarily on cultivation of Andean tubers and herding of llamas and alpacas; the chronicles and other documents speak of tens of thousands of animals owned either by the community or by individuals. The nobility owned thousands of animals and had herdsmen in their service; some wealthy individuals possessed as many as 50,000 head. The Andean herds provided wool of varying quality for the production of cloth and also were exploited for meat, which was consumed either fresh or dried. The animals were kept on the extensive highland plains of the puna under the care of full-time herdsmen (Murra 1965:198–199).

Other kinds of food were obtained by gathering, fishing, hunting, and agriculture. The lake provided a variety of fish as well as plants; some of the latter were edible and others, such as totora (*Scirpus totora*), were used for roof construction and for making a type of watercraft known today as a "little reed horse." Although birds and deer were hunted extensively, agriculture was the mainstay of subsistence. The principal highland plants were potatoes (*Solanum tuberosum*) and quinoa (*Chenopodim quinoa*), which were supplemented by other kinds of tubers, such as oca (*Oxalis tuberosum*), mashwa (*Tropaelum tubersum*), and olluco (*Ullucus tuberosus*), and grains, among which cañiwa (*Chenopodium pallidicaule*) played a significant role. Domesticated guinea pigs (*Cavia porcellus*) were also eaten.

In spite of the variety and high nutritional value of these vegetal and animal products, the populace of the lake area required additional kinds of plants that could not be raised on the altiplano, either because of the excessive altitude (about 4000 meters above sea level) or because of the drastic fluctuations in daily temperature (which alternate between daytime heat and nightly frost). One of the most desired cultigens, maize (*Zea mays*), could be grown only in temperate valleys at a considerable distance from the political and economic centers on the margin of the lake. In some instances, barter was employed, but documentary and archeological evidence indicate that both maize and coca were more often obtained by direct exploitation of the appropriate environmental contexts. Thus, the Lupaqa provided themselves with maize by maintaining colonies in the coastal valleys, at distances of 40 to 50 days travel by caravan. Murra (1964b:428) says:

Those valleys that could not be reached on foot in a single day or through seasonal migration were colonized by groups (sometimes as small as a single household), who herded on the puna, gathered salt, cultivated pepper or coca leaves in the eastern lowlands and cotton or maize on the Pacific coast.

This system of "vertical control" operated by the exploitation of a series of discontinuous territories or "environmental archipelagos" rather than domination over large areas. The political jurisdiction exercised by a lake kingdom was limited to a small zone or enclave in a valley, the remainder of which was occupied by other colonies or controlled by the indigenous population. The cultural heterogeneity exhibited by the coastal valleys from Arequipa southward into northern Chile is a reflection of this system of verticality.

The same form of exploitation was employed in the eastern lowlands. In describing the inhabitants of the eastern portion of the altiplano, Vásquez de Espinosa (1942:614) states:

Next comes Sangaván, with the villages of Itata and Mocomoco, and farther E., the Pelechuco Valley, where the Indians of the Province of Omasuyo [on the altiplano near the lake] have their gardens and farms with fruit and delicacies, which they take out to their province. In it they raise some wheat and plenty of corn, which is the source of supply for most of the provinces of the Collao, since it is so abundant and rich.

The functioning of this kind of system depended upon development of a certain level of military, political, and economic organization. The governing structure was centralized in the capital, which in the case of the Lupaqa was Chucuito. Six additional urban centers, all near the lake, played roles similar to those of a "county seat." Their names were Acora, Llave, Juli, Pomata, Yunguyo, and Zepita.

Political organization was based on a duality of power, which reflected the division of each town into two groups known as moieties. Murra (1964:426–427) explains that

not only was there a Hanansaya ruler ("Alasaa" in Aymara) over the seven Lupaqa towns, who in this case was Cari, but there was also an Urinsaya ruler ("Maasaa" in Aymara) named Cusi. Both had similar privileges and access to qualitatively comparable resources. The Hanansaya leader had higher status, however, as well as a greater quantity of resources especially with respect to human energy than the leader of the Urinsaya group. [This was not universally true, however, since] Cusi had

at his disposal 17 herdsmen in comparison to the 10 that looked after the herds of Cari, of the Hanansaya moiety, [perhaps because the Urinsaya herds were larger. In addition,] Six of the seven towns were also divided into two parts, Hanansaya and Urinsaya, each with its own leader. These leaders enjoyed generally equal status and income, but there were differences in details. In Juli, the Urinsaya moiety was subdivided into two parts, with the result that this town had three social groupings (the third was called "Ayanca"), each with its own herds and lords.

The mechanism by which power was structured through this dual division is not yet clear. Each of the "kings" (Cari and Cusi) had under him a number of lords, each responsible for a "province." The Lupaqa kings also had two kinds of retainers: "mittani," who served temporarily, probably for one year, and "yana," who served for life. Cari had 60 mittani, consisting of 10 herders, 15 farmers, 10 domestic servants who supervised the storehouses, and 25 colonists. The latter were stationed in the coastal valley of Moquegua, where they raised crops and transported them to the capital. Ten yana had been given to Cari's ancestors by one of the provincial towns and were sent to live on the puna, where they worked as herders. By the time of Spanish contact they had increased to 50 or 60, including women and children (Murra 1966).

This description implies a social hierarchy with at least three classes. At the summit were the kings and local lords. Beneath them were the "Aymaras" and the artisans, among which silversmiths ("sunacoya") and potters ("copi") are most frequently mentioned. At the bottom were the yana and the Uru, an ethnic minority of lake fishermen who had been dominated by the Aymara. All the above categories were represented in each locality: one community, for example, contained 17 "hatha" (lineages or "ayllus"), of which 10 were Arymara, one a potter, one a silversmith, and 5 Uru. The yana are not mentioned because they were incorporated into their masters' lineages.

The archival information is of great potential value in interpreting the archeological evidence obtained both from the lakeside area and the extensive "periphery." Unfortunately, the spectacular ruins of Tiahuanaco have made it the focus of attention, with the result that other sites and regions have been neglected. One of the earliest reports was by Nordenskiold (1906), who undertook excavations along the Peru-Bolivia frontier between 1904 and 1905. During the 1930s, Bennett's (1934, 1936) investigations in various Bolivian sites led him to propose a period intermediate between Tiahuanaco and Inca, which he initially called "Chullpa," although he later preferred the designation "Collao," at least for the Puno region (Bennett 1948c:91). Several local amateurs, including J. M. Franco Inojosa, Emilio Vásquez, L. Llanos, and A. González have described habitation sites and cemeteries in the Puno region, but the only detailed publication is by M. Tschopik (1946) on investigations west of the lake. Ryden (1947) also worked at sites of the Regional States Period in various parts of Bolivia. During this time and previously, many travelers re-corded their admiration for the funerary towers, especially those at Sillustani west of Puno (Figures 205, 206). The most important work aside from that of Tschopik has been conducted by Ponce Sanginés (1957) in the Muñecas zone northeast of the altiplano. Recently, Neira (1967) explored the northern portion of the region.

The "colonial" areas have been studied only on the coast, and there is no information on the Cana, Canchi, Charca, Umasuyo, Pacaje, and other "Aymara" peoples, or on their neighbors. In the western highlands, only the Río Collca region,

Figure 205. Views of the site of Sillustani, Puno (courtesy Máximo Neira).

Figure 206.
Views of the site of
Kekerana near Moho in Puno
(courtesy Hermán Amat).

which equates with the Collagua, has been explored (Neira, pers. comm.). Although a little work has been done in the Arequipa Valley (Bernedo Málaga 1958), no systematic investigations have been made of sites of this period. The Pukina are said to have occupied the region, but this is clearly a linguistic rather than an ethnic identification. Kroeber (1944: 11), who described the pottery, called it "Churajón."

A considerable amount of exploration has been undertaken on the extreme south of the Peruvian coast, although the results unfortunately remain mostly unpublished. Vescelius worked there in the late 1950s, Ghersi Barrera (1956) excavated a cemetery at Chiribaya in Ilo, Flores (1969) has surveyed the Caplina (Tacna) Valley, and Linares Málaga (1961) conducted investigations in the Arequipa region. In northern Chile, work has been much more extensive. The earliest research was again by Uhle (1919), whose findings provided the basis for interpretations until Bird (1943, 1946) excavated on the Arica coast and refined Uhle's conclusions. Subsequent work by Schaedel (1957), Munizaga (1957), Dauelsberg (1960), and Núñez (1965) has increased the range of information substantially.

To facilitate presentation of the archeological information on the lake kingdoms, the following discussion will be divided into four parts: (1) the altiplano; (2) the Mollo and Churajón culture; (3) the coast; and (4) eastern Bolivia and northwestern Argentina. Three general cultural stages can be recognized throughout this portion of the southern Andes: (1) "pre-altiplano," (2) "Expansive Tiahuanaco," and finally (3) the "altiplano" or Regional States Period that concerns us here.

The Altiplano of Titicaca

After the demise of the Tiahuanaco ceremonial center, a seemingly uniform culture emerged. It is identified with two- and three-color painted pottery, which M. Tschopik (1946) classified into "Allita Amaya" and "Collao" styles. Their relationship is not well established, but they are likely to be contemporary. Allita Amaya pottery has been found only in burials and appears to be restricted to the Lupaqa region, whereas Collao ceramics come principally from habitation sites and occur primarily in the Colla territory. If these associations are confirmed, they will be useful in interpreting the nature of the two kingdoms and particularly their expansion, since Allita Amaya pottery is closely related to such complexes as Churajón, Mollo, and Chiribaya,

while Collao appears to be well represented only in restricted portions of a few valleys, among them the upper Caplina in Tacna (Flores 1969) and Azapa in Arica.

M. Tschopik (1946:51) also described another kind of pottery, which she called "Sillustani" and which may have originated in pre-Inca times. It is found principally in the area associated with the Colla Kingdom, with a few intrusions into Lupaqa territory, except for one type known as Sillustani Brown on Cream, which appears in sites in the Omasuyo area. Lumbreras and Amat (1968:88–89) have renamed the latter the "Kekerana" style, after the type site near Moho.

Information on Allita Amaya is restricted to a few burials (M. Tschopik 1946:19–20). The type site is about 3 kilometers from Chucuito, the Lupaqa capital, and consists of two collective tombs containing the remains of 19 and 20 individuals, respectively. Seventeen pottery vessels had been placed in one tomb and a dozen in the other. A third tomb was encountered at the site of Kachakacha, also in the Lupaqa area. It contained 16 skeletons and some 15 associated objects. Although the pottery is not crude, it is much inferior technologically and artistically to the earlier Tiahuanacoid wares. A minor proportion is decorated with fugitive black and white paint on a red surface of variable tone, and designs are geometric, with preference given to triangles arranged in rows and filled with crosshatch (Figure 207). The most common

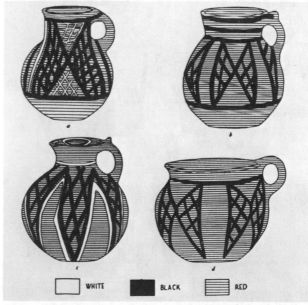

Figure 207. Pottery of the Allita Amaya style (after M. Tschopik 1946, fig. 20).

vessel shapes are jars with a flat base, globular body, and short, narrow neck, which sometimes has decoration on the rim interior. Flat-based bowls and vases with straight, outsloping walls also occur. Handles extending from the rim to the body are common; in some instances, they are confined to the neck or to the body.

More information is available on the Collao complex, which has been encountered at a large number of sites, among them Sillustani, Kojra, Cheqnarapi, Paroparo, Mercaymarca, and Qutimpo. Collao pottery originated much earlier but it continued to be made during Inca times so that all the sites where it occurs are not necessarily pre-Inca. An example may be Chucuito, which has a prominent Inca occupation. Although the chullpas or burial towers on the altiplano have been considered pre-Inca, existing information indicates that they are exclusively of Inca origin even when pottery of the Collao style is associated.

Final definition of the chullpa epoch and also of the villages associated with Collao pottery awaits future investigations, but a few characteristics can be mentioned. One of the most outstanding aspects of the settlements is fortification. Chejnarapi, for example, is located on a hill some 300 meters in elevation and is surrounded by up to four parallel walls that follow the contours of the slope. Kojra is also fortified. One of the largest communities is Mercaymarca, near the village of Moho; it contains remains of houses with 2.5 meter-high walls, plazas, terraces, and other structures.

Collao pottery is coarser than Allita Amaya. The paste is tempered with large, white, calcarious inclusions and the surface is poorly smoothed and somewhat gritty. Large vessels may have applique fillets ornamented with rows of punctation on the neck or incision on the upper exterior. Black-on-red painted designs were carelessly executed on jar necks and bodies, on the exterior of bowls, and the interior of plates (Figures 208, 209). Crude figurines occur.

It is probable that the various Sillustani pottery types will prove to have chronological significance

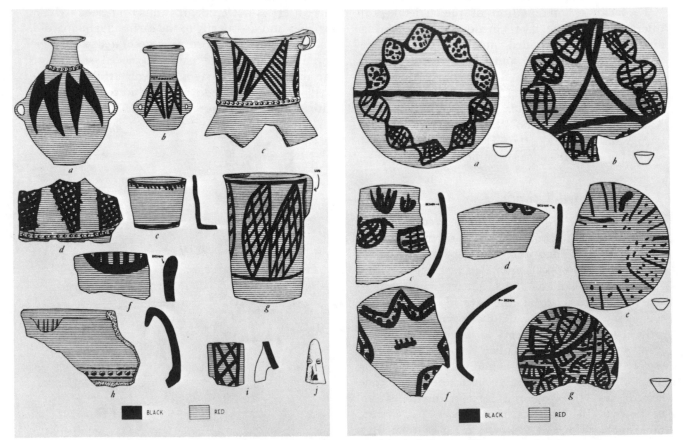

Figures 208 and 209. Pottery of the Collao style (after M. Tschopik 1946, figs. 8 and 9).

when more is known. Sillustani Brown on Cream (or Kekerana) is relatively fine and resembles Collao pottery in some features; it has a cream-colored paste and dark brown painted decoration. Sillustani Polychrome on White, which appears to be of Inca date (M. Tschopik 1946:25–26), is a fine ware with designs carefully drawn in dark brown and red on a white slip. Both Sillustani Black on Red and Sillustani Black and White on Red are probably also from the Inca Period and appear to be related to an Inca type called "Chucuito."

The Mollo and Churajón Culture

The Mollo culture is located in the Bolivian province of Muñecas northeast of the altiplano, in a valley that drains into the Amazon Basin. The Churajón culture, by contrast, is in the Arequipa Valley on the Pacific slope. Although several hundred kilometers apart, they are manifestations of a single complex that is intimately linked with the Allita Amaya pottery of the altiplano and the Chiribaya style from the south coastal valleys between Arequipa and Arica. This distribution suggests that Mollo and Churajón probably represent large colonies of the Lupaqa or other lake kingdoms.

Three altitudinal and ecological zones are represented in the lower part of the valley formed by the Ríos Paqchani and Llika, which is the locus of the Mollo culture (Ponce Sanginés 1957). Between 1550 and 2000 meters elevation, the climate is warm and dry, and natural vegetation consists of shrubs, cactus, and spiny legumes. This portion is rarely used for cultivation today. Between about 2200 and 3700 meters, the climate is temperate and trees occur. It is here that intensive maize agriculture is now conducted. Above 3700 meters, it is cold and the land is utilized principally for raising potatoes.

The whole valley appears to have been occupied by the makers of Mollo pottery, although the lower and middle portions were certainly more intensively exploited than the upper one. Structures include agricultural terraces, a well-organized system of irrigation canals constructed with small stone slabs, and remains of dwellings erected on platforms. Piñiqo, on the Río Paqchani at an elevation of about 1800 meters, is composed of closely spaced rectangular houses built on terraces. The walls were adobe and the floors, stone and clay. Burial in subterranean cists resembles the Allita Amaya practice, except that here each cist contained a single individual.

The pottery has been classified into two major categories: Mollo Plain and Mollo Painted. The typical forms include plates with flat bottoms and diverging sides, single or double bowls with or without handles (when double, the two bodies are joined by a bridge handle), and occasional bowls with "a miniature vessel of similar form attached in such a manner that it could serve as a handle" (Ponce Sanginés 1957:67). More or less cylindrical vases, slightly flaring toward the rim, "exhibit a kind of belt or relief on the exterior of the waist and a corresponding groove on the interior. Frequently, there is a button-like prominence near the rim" (ibid.). Globular ollas and jars also occur. All are characterized by a "projecting" type of flat base. Asymmetrical, "shoe-shaped" vessels were produced, as were spouted jars. The most typical variant of the latter type has an hour-glass-shaped body and a lateral spout handle consisting of a tube connected to the upper portion of the body by a bridge. It is sometimes ornamented on the anterior part by an anthropomorphic face with eyes, nose, and chin modeled in relief. Decoration is by dull black and thin yellowish white paint applied over various shades of red. The principal motifs are crosshatched diamonds and squares, either isolated or placed in horizontal or vertical bands; triangles of diverse shapes forming serrated figures; and straight lines or stripes. Curvilinear designs are rare, as are zoomorphic elements, which are simple and stylized. A few pieces with applique bands around the neck and nubbins on the handles resemble Collao ornamentation.

Churajón, east of Arequipa at an elevation of 3100 meters, is a labyrinth of walls surrounding habitations, patios, and plazas (Figure 210; Bernedo Málaga 1958:140). Bernedo Málaga (1958:141) and Valcárcel have interpreted it as an agricultural colony rather than a city, a view that is in accord with the documentary evidence. A nineteenth-century account by Juan Huaraca reports the tradition that "all these towns were governed by the high chief of Churajón. The last chief of this people was Sacrun, who was defeated by Indians originating from the Titicaca area. The battle took place in Ñawan, today called Ozuña" (Bernedo Málaga 1958:72). Like Mollo, Churajón culture occurs over nearly the whole valley, implying a large influx of people. The fact that Churajón pottery (Figure 211) is extremely similar in technology, morphology, and decoration to Mollo pottery indicates that the two groups must have a single origin. Furthermore, the existence of

Figure 210. Wall construction at the site of Churajón, Arequipa (courtesy Máximo Neira).

Figure 211. Pottery of the Churajón style (MUA, courtesy Máximo Neira).

Figure 212. Agricultural terraces at Mollebaya near Churajón, Arequipa (courtesy Máximo Neira).

environmental conditions resembling those in the Mollo area suggests that the people were fundamentally maize cultivators, an inference further supported by the presence of agricultural terraces (Figure 212) and complex irrigation networks comparable to those in the Churajón region. Bernedo Málaga (1958:124) says that "the irrigation works extend over an area of more than 200 kilometers from north to south, beginning near the city of Arequipa and continuing as far as the town of Quimistacas, near Omate, between the base of the maritime cordillera and the valley of Tambo." (The possibility cannot be denied, of course, that many of these canals were constructed later under Inca administration.).

Settlements in the Arequipa region are relatively extensive and very similar to those in the Mollo area and on the altiplano. One of the most notable is located at an elevation of 2400 meters, some 4 kilometers from the center of Arequipa near the modern town of Tingo. It covers an area about 2 kilometers long by 500 meters wide and is divided into two parts, which certainly equate with the Maasaa and Alasaa social subdivisions mentioned

earlier (p. 202). The part known as Casa Patak has been described by Bernedo Málaga (1958:147–148) as

surrounded by a large wall of uncut stones laid in two rows and joined with clay. The dwellings are rectangular or square, also of unworked stone, and lack interior partitions. . . . The second group consists of buildings and defensive walls constructed on the summit of the Cerro Huacuchara, a hill separated from Casa Patak by a ravine that bears the same name as the fortified city.

Another large population center, Pocsi or Huactalacta, is some 28 kilometers from Arequipa at an elevation of 3000 meters.

As was the case with the Mollo and Allita Amaya complexes, the dead were placed in subterranean cists, some of which contain two stories. This type was encountered at Tres Cruces near Tingo. Bernedo Málaga (1958:81) states that "associated with the skeletal remains of these primitive Andean inhabitants, I found knives and rudimentary weapons of quartz and obsidian, fragments of wooden harpoons, bows and arrows . . . [and] several well polished feldspar beads that must have been part of beautiful ornamental collars, copper pins (tupus). . . ."

Figure 213. Pottery vessels of the Chiribaya style (courtesy A. Guillén).

Although the pottery (Figure 213) and burials from Chiribaya in the lower Moquegua Valley closely resemble those of Churajón-Mollo, Chiribaya has no altiplano counterpart. It therefore probably represents a regional integration between altiplano and coastal cultural forms, rather than a colonial intrusion of highland origin.

The Coastal Cultures

Cultural evolution on the coast between Arequipa and Atacama (in Chile) followed a pattern totally different from that described so far. Until well into historic times, the level of development here did not exceed that prevalent to the north during the Archaic Period. While the Central Andes were dominated by urban societies like Moche, Nazca, and Tiahuanaco, this region remained marginal and primitive. Agriculture did not develop by the slow process of local domestication that appears to have operated to the north, but instead was introduced in a fully developed state to populations whose primary activity remained fishing and marine hunting. The persistence of the ancient way of life into post-Spanish times is documented by the chronicler Gerónimo de Bibar (cited by Hidalgo 1971:10), who states that "barbaric Indians lived along the shore of the sea, in bays or coves. They lived on fish . . . [and inhabited the region] . . . between Arica and the valley of Coquimbo, a distance of more than two hundred leagues." The presence of mature cultigens in this "pre-agricultural" context suggests that these shoreline fishermen obtained their agricultural produce by barter from "colonists" of highland origin. Since the fifth century A.D. at least, groups of advanced agriculturalists coexisted in the nearby valleys, where they exploited the coastal oases as part of the pattern of verticality developed on the altiplano.

The histories of these oasis farmers and maritime groups remain to be worked out in detail. In the past, they were considered consecutive parts of a unilinear sequence, but this viewpoint has been invalidated by the ethnohistorical evidence indicating that the local populations followed one line of development and the immigrant groups various other lines. The hypothesis of verticality implies that the zones exploited by the lakeside centers for subsistence products were multi-ethnic in composition, placing the archeological evidence in a new context. Complicating the situation is the fact that the altiplano groups settled on the coast south of Arequipa about the same time or shortly after the emergence of local agriculturalists, represented by the Arica culture in the northern region and the Atacama or San Pedro culture, with a characteristic black pottery, in the Atacama zone. It is the Arica culture that interests us here.

The Arica culture was defined by Bird (1943, 1946) on the basis of his own excavations and those of Uhle (1919) in Tacna and Arica. More recently, Dauelsberg (1960), Flores (1969), and other archeologists have provided additional information. Bird recognized two phases. Phase I had been called "Atacameña" by Uhle and the most diagnostic pottery is now known as "San Miguel" (Dauelsberg 1960). Phase II was called "Chincha-Atacameño" by Uhle and the typical pottery is now labeled "Gentilar." An intervening transitional phase is known as "Pocoma."

Typical vessel shapes of San Miguel pottery from Arica I are large jars with a globular body, conical base, narrow neck, and usually two lateral handles on the body; jars with a single handle; and slightly bell-shaped vessels. Decoration consists of geometric designs, usually curvilinear, painted in red and black on a dull, white-slipped surface. The most frequent elements are spirals and parallel or stepped lines (Figure 214). The Gentilar pottery of Arica II is finer and vessels are much smaller. Jars have a flattened, globular body, a flat base, and usually a single handle; there are also vases and bowls. The surface is covered with a bright red slip and designs are painted in black, white, and red (Figure 215). Curvilinear elements predominate and spirals are frequent, although their arrangement differs from that during Arica I. Zoomorphic and anthropomorphic motifs also occur (Munizaga 1957, fig. 2).

Other aspects of Arica I have been described by Mostny (1971:91) as follows:

Cemeteries contain cylindrical tombs, sometimes with niches or small lateral chambers. The flexed bodies were wrapped in large shirts and cloths, usually of dark color, and tied with cords or placed in totora reed nets; the head was covered with a small knitted skullcap or a headdress with a tuft of feathers . . . the women were provided with weaving implements and the men with fishing equipment, miniature bags, bows and arrows. Other offerings included sandals, baskets, mats, gourds, wooden spoons, and small boxes. . . . The carbon-14 dates for Arica place its florescence between A.D. 1050 and 1350.

Although small villages with structures of river cobbles and containing storage facilities occur, perishable dwellings such as must have existed at the

Figure 214. Pottery vessel of the Arica I or San Miguel style (Museo de Arica, courtesy P. Dauelsberg).

Figure 215. Pottery vessels of the Arica II or Gentilar style (Museo de Arica, courtesy P. Dauelsberg).

site of Guaylacan in the Lluta Valley were probably more common (Schaedel 1957:13–15).

More information is available on habitation sites of Arica II. Alto Ramírez, in the Azapa Valley on the north Chilean coast, is a settlement composed of subterranean houses, the majority of which were constructed of superimposed layers of mats. Cerro Moreno A, also in Azapa, contains numerous stone structures including circular houses with a doorway. Stone mortars are associated (Schaedel 1957:15–16).

Both phases of this local or regional culture appear to have coexisted with enclaves of altiplano groups and to have maintained some contact but not necessarily mixed with them. Mollo-Churajón and Collao types of pottery occur, along with varieties closely related to Chiribaya. Vessel shapes are basically the same as those of Allita Amaya and Mollo-Churajón. In both Tacna (Flores 1969) and Arica, the agricultural groups (and especially those of definite altiplano affiliation) tended to occupy the middle and upper portions of the valley.

The persistence of the altiplano tradition on the coast during Inca times is implied by the presence of groups possessing black-on-red pottery, perhaps affiliated with the Chucuito style of Puno, which Dauelsberg (1960) has called "Chilpe."

Eastern Bolivia and Northwestern Argentina

Pottery similar to the altiplano tricolor has been encountered in the interior of Bolivia and in northwestern Argentina, but more extensive investigations are required before the precise nature of these relationships can be ascertained. While Alfarcito Polychrome from the Quebrada de Humahuaca in Jujuy Province of northwest Argentina (Bennett 1948b) exhibits many similarities to Chiribaya, Mollo-Churajón, and Allita Amaya, the differences in surface finish and style are sufficiently great to suggest that it may have a separate origin from the tricolor ceramics of the altiplano. Another kind of pottery, known as "Hornillos" (Bennett 1948b), may be distantly related to Collao, to judge from the use of black-on-red decoration and certain coincidences in motif and vessel shape. Several pottery types from Cochabamba in the interior of Bolivia may also reflect direct or indirect relationships with the altiplano, but they are still too poorly defined for accurate assessment. Other better described complexes, such as Presto-puno, Huruquilla, and Mojocoya Tricolor, have little in common with any of the groups discussed so far in this chapter, although they appear to be contemporary with them.

Figure 216. Pottery of the Chuquibamba style (MUA, courtesy Máximo Neira).

West of the Titicaca altiplano and north of Arequipa, in the region associated with the Collagua, there is a well-defined black-on-red style that has been designated as "Chuquibamba" (Kroeber 1944:19). The Chuquibamba culture occupied the valleys of Sihaus, Majes, and the upper part of Ocoña as far as the Río Collca. The pottery is fine, lustrous, red-slipped, and painted with black or (rarely) white, linear designs. Motifs include highly stylized birds and animals, geometric figures emphasizing squares, and a kind of eight-pointed star; panels of crosshatched rhomboid elements similar to those of Mollo-Churajón pottery also occur, as well as rows of triangles forming "saw-teeth." Typical vessel shapes are narrow-necked jars and a great variety of round-bottomed bowls (Figure 216). More detailed analysis may reveal differences between the coastal and highland Chuquibamba pottery, but at present they cannot be distinguished. Associated are numerous flattened cobbles resembling tablets, on which were painted llamas, circles, eight-pointed stars, and other figures similar to those on Australian churingas. This kind of artifact is rare in Peru except in this culture.

During his explorations in Caravelí, Neira (pers. comm.) found many Chuquibamba habitation sites (Figure 217). Chirisco, on the slopes of Cerro Amargoso, contains large, low-walled corrals and many rudely built, circular structures 2 to 5 meters in diameter, with walls up to 2 meters high; subterranean tombs were found inside. There was no apparent pattern to the distribution of the buildings over the slope. Cortadera, some 400 meters south of Chirisco on the same hill, has more substantially constructed habitations, some of them contiguous and others separated by narrow streets, creating an irregular, agglutinated pattern. These two settlements may correspond to the Hanan and Urin moieties. The hill also contains numerous agricultural terraces. The site of Warka, also in the Caravelí zone, appears to have been very important; the ruins are similar to those at Amargoso. Chercana in the upper Ocoña, Wamantambo and Qosqopa in the upper Majes, and Markawra and Timirán in Sihuas are also representative of the Chuquibamba culture, which appears to have endured until the Inca epoch and possibly into Spanish times.

Figure 217. Ruins at Maca in Caylloma, Arequipa, associated with Chuquibamba-style pottery (courtesy Máximo Neira).

The Kingdom of Cuzco

The establishment of the Empire of Tawantinsuyu about the middle of the fifteenth century by the Cuzqueños inspired the proliferation of legends concerning its past that only systematic interdisciplinary investigation will be able to disentangle. In Cuzco, as in Lambayeque and Moche (see pp. 181–182), a culture hero reputedly arrived from elsewhere and taught civilization to the inhabitants of the valley. There are two traditional versions of the origin of the State. One speaks of a couple that emerged from Lake Titicaca on the southern altiplano and was ordered to Cuzco by the god Inti (the Sun), who was their father, to civilize that region. The man was Manco Capac, who initiated the first dynasty (known as Urin Cuzco) and whose memory was retained by his royal lineage, which bore the name of Chima Capac until the Spanish Conquest. The woman was Mama Oqllu. They founded Cuzco on the spot where a golden peg that had been given to Manco Capac by Inti fell magically to the ground. The Urin Cuzco dynasty was composed of the following kings: Manco Capac, Sinchi Roca, Lloke Uypanki, Mayta Capac, and Capac Yupanki. In spite of the conquests attributed to them and a series of events with which they are associated, all remain legendary figures like the founder and it may be more correct to view them, as some authorities do, as a symbolic expression of one aspect of Inca social organization than as a dynastic sequence with historical validity.

The other legend concerns four brothers of the Ayar family, who established themselves in the Cuzco Valley. Their names were Ayar Cachi, Ayar Manco, Ayar Auca, and Ayar Uchu, and they were accompanied by their wives, Mama Wako, Mama Oqllu, Mama Qora, and Mama Rawa. After many years, during which various supernatural events took place, only Manco remained and he became the founder of the dynasty. Once again, this tale may refer to social conflicts rather than to the activities of real individuals. Valcárcel for example, has interpreted the "Ayar" as competing clans, among which the "Manco" clan became dominant and instrumental in the formation of the new state, which later developed into the empire.

The second dynasty, known as Hanan Cuzco, was established by Inca Roca and endured until the Spanish Conquest. He was succeeded by Yawar Waqaq, who in turn was followed by Wira Qocha Inca. The successor of the latter, Pacha Kuteq Inca Yupanki, converted the Kingdom of Cuzco into the Empire of Tawantinsuyu ("Land of the Four Regions").

In the opinion of Zuidema (1962), neither of the dynasties has historical validity. He believes that they should be interpreted as reflections of the form of clan organization that existed in Cuzco and which became a distinctive feature of Inca society. This hypothesis is based on the following reasoning (Zuidema 1962:718–719):

> The Incas are reported to have come out of a mountain situated some distance from Cuzco. Proceeding from this mountain under the leadership of Manco Capac, the founder of their royal dynasty, they attacked and conquered Cuzco. Manco Capac was followed by a succession of ten kings. The two sons of the 11th and last king became involved in a civil war which facilitated the Spanish conquest of their kingdom, around 1530. For a short time the Spaniards continued the dynasty by the appointment of a series of puppet rulers. Some of the last descendants of the royal family fled to unconquered areas, although by 1572 the last of the independent kings had been captured and beheaded at Cuzco. The stories of the origin of the royal dynasty are probably largely mythical, as are many of the incidents and events concerning the succeeding kings. . . .
>
> One interesting point in this context is the degree of correlation between the history of the kings and the social organization of Cuzco. . . . The people of Cuzco were divided into two moieties called upper and lower Cuzco. The moieties were divided into royal and common clans. Each king was said to have founded his own clan which included all of his descendants with the exception of the son who ruled the Incas before the accession of the two brothers who became involved in a civil war. Strangely enough, in the social organization of Cuzco no mention is made of the clan of the 11th king. The five royal clans founded by the first five kings belonged to lower Cuzco and the five royal clans founded by the following five kings belonged to upper Cuzco. The remainder of the population was also divided into five common clans of lower Cuzco and five common clans of upper Cuzco.
>
> . . . It appears that the ten royal clans and ten common clans which comprised the two moities of Cuzco belong to a special type of social organization in which each of these groups fulfilled an essential role as a marriage class.

The existence of eleven rather than ten Incas might signify that Manco Capac was the founder of both dynasties, and that Sinchi Roca of the Urin (lower Cuzco) and Inca Roca of the Hanan (upper Cuzco) were both his descendants. This interpretation would also imply that Pacha Kuteq, the ninth Inca in the traditional dynasty, corresponds to Mayta Capac, the fourth ruler in the first dynasty, and may explain why many acts of the latter king resemble those attributed to Pacha Kuteq.

Valcárcel, Rowe, and other historians disagree with Zuidema and believe that the traditional history of Cuzco and the empire possesses some degree of authenticity. Rowe (1946:196) even accepts parts of the chronology proposed by Cabello Balboa. In the opinion of Rostworowski de Diez Canseco (1953), the initial rulers were the "sinchi" or elected military chiefs, who subsequently adopted the custom of giving the power to the son of the king. She equates the inception of the Hanan dynasty (Inca Roca) with the new custom of co-rule.

Archeological evidence indicates that prior to the appearance of the cultural elements that were disseminated over the Andes with the expansion of the Inca Empire, there developed in the Cuzco region a local or regional kingdom that still existed in the time of the Inca Wira Qocha. The frontiers coincided with those of the valley of Vilcanota, although confederations for military purposes may have existed with neighboring towns. A number of small villages, only rarely exceeding 200 meters in length, date from this period. Examples include Qencha-qencha in Cuzco and Kuyu near Pisac. The

Cuzco area began to be inhabited, to judge from evidence at Sacsahuaman and other sites. The large city of Pikillaqta, a major administrative center during the epoch of Wari domination, was abandoned and the inhabitants resettled in Lucre, at higher elevation. In a small village south of Pikillaqta, survivals of the Wari settlement pattern can be detected in the architecture and the internal distribution of dwellings. Little is known about this period, but it is possible that the architectural developments of the imperial epoch were beginning to take form.

The most diagnostic element of the pre-Inca stage of Cuzco is a ceramic style known as Killke, which is the product of fusion between Wari and earlier elements. There is a fine type and a coarse type; decoration is painted in black and red on a cream or an unslipped buff surface. Designs are typically linear and geometric, and representations of human faces occur on jar necks. The most common forms are vessels with more or less vertical sides, open bowls, and wide-mouthed jars. There is considerable resemblance to the forms of the later Cuzco style, better known as Classic Inca. Domestic pottery is simple and very crude; occasionally, it has decoration made by impression, as in Waru.

Metal objects are rare, while bone tools are frequent, along with slate knives that were probably inserted in a wooden handle. Burials were generally in caves; the bodies were placed in a seated, flexed position and covered with cloth.

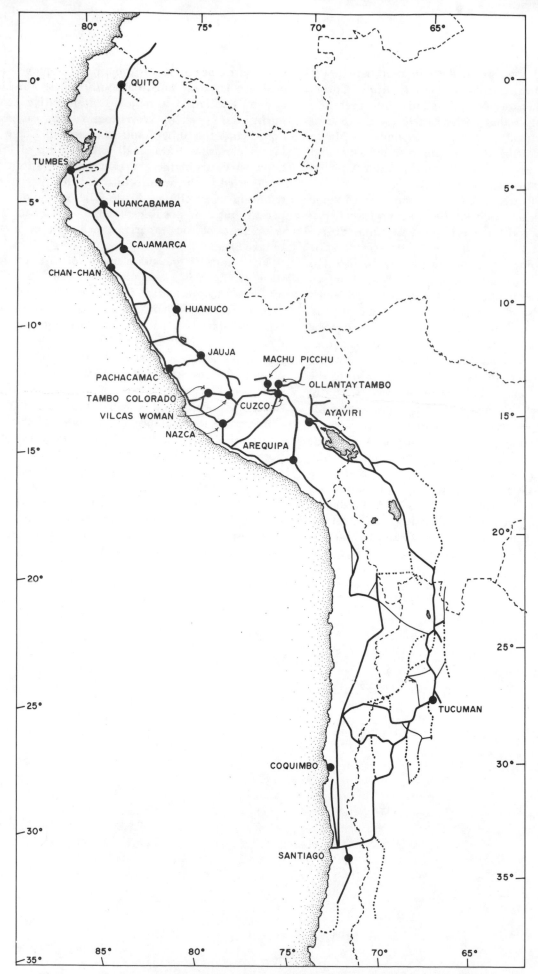

Figure 218. The Empire of Tawantinsuyu, showing the major roads and some of the principal
centers (after Erdmann 1963, Cieza de León 1959, von Hagen, 1955).

THE EMPIRE OF TAWANTINSUYU

A.D. 1430-1532

When the Spaniards arrived on the Peruvian coast in 1532, they came into contact with populations in the northern valleys that belonged to a great centralized political organization called "Tawantinsuyu" (Figure 218). Its capital was Cuzco, a city in the Southern highlands, and its supreme leader was an emperor called "Inca," son of the god Inti (the Sun) and descendent of legendary dynasties. At that moment the empire was undergoing a severe internal crisis provoked by a power struggle between two brothers, Waskar and Atawallpa, which culminated in the belated victory of Atawallpa, when he was already a prisoner of the Spaniards. It is important to keep in mind that Inca history prior to the Spanish conquest comes to us through the eyes of European chroniclers, whose interpretations of the Inca genealogy were influenced by familiarity with their own royal lines.

The history of the Inca Empire began with a military action that must have had remote antecedents: the battle between the Chanka and the Cuzqueños. The Chanka apparently intended to take over the neighboring regions inhabited by the Qichwa, who had long before chosen to affiliate with the rulers of Cuzco. The sources speak of conflicts between these groups from the time of Inca Roca, the founder of the Hanan dynasty of Cuzco.

During the reign of Inca Wira Qocha, and encouraged by certain weaknesses displayed by this sovereign, the Chanka decided to make a final seige of Cuzco. The city was thrown into great disorder and the Inca along with his heir, Urco, sought refuge in the region of Chita, leaving Cuzco in the hands of his principal generals and another of his sons, Cusi Yupanki. Cusi, his brother Roca, the generals Vicaquirao and Apu Mayta, and several members of the royal court undertook to defend the city. The Canchi and Cana came to the aid of the defenders, but other tribes that were summoned remained on the sidelines until victory was assured.

Cuzco was attacked by the Chanka under the leadership of Astu Waraka and Tumay Waraka: "They descended from the heights of Carmenca screaming and shouting; their faces were painted with black and red, their long hair was oiled and carefully braided, and they were brandishing lances" (Rostworowski de Diez Canseco 1953:90). Some sources state that the Chanka retreated in terror when they saw the strength of the Cuzqueños, but other evidence indicates that a bloody battle took place. The people of Cuzco, finally aided by the Colla, defeated the attackers and pursued them as far as their own territory. The final engagement took place near Ichubamba and was a decisive victory for the Cuzqueños, who conquered the Chanka realm and assimilated it by force. Prisoners were cruelly punished to demonstrate the strength and power of the victors. Cusi returned triumphantly to Cuzco, where he was recognized as the new ruler under the name of Pacha Kuteq Inca Yupanki. According to an arbitrary chronology provided by Cabello Balboa (1920), this event occurred toward the end of the third decade of the fifteenth century, that is between A.D. 1430 and 1440.

Immediately following the conquest of the Chanka, Pacha Kuteq set about consolidating his power in the Cuzco area. After conducting a campaign in the valleys of Urubamba and Vilcanota, he proceeded to the Qichwa region with which an alliance already existed, and continued south to subjugate the Vilca (Vilcas Waman) in the region of Río Pampas and Soras. An exploratory expedition sent to the South coast established control over the western portion of the sierra and the southern part of Cuzco Province. At that time, an alliance already existed between the Cuzqueños and several groups of the altiplano of Titicaca, such as the Colla. Later, Capac Yupanqi was sent to conquer the north, resulting in the nominal subjugation of Cajamarca and later of the Chimú Kingdom. Subsequently, Pacha Kuteq made his son Tupac Yupanki his military commander, while he dedicated himself to administration of the conquered regions and the remodeling of Cuzco, producing the fabulous city that existed on the arrival of the Spaniards. The campaigns undertaken during the joint reign of Tupac Yupanki and Pacha Kuteq extended the empire from the South coast almost to Quito, the modern capital of the Republic of Ecuador.

Pacha Kuteq was succeeded about 1470 by his son Tupac Inca Yupanki, who attempted to penetrate the forested portions of the province of Cuzco. After conquering the Wachipayre and the Masqo, his plans were changed by the unexpected uprising of the Lupaqa, Colla, Umasuyo, and Pacaje of the Titicaca Basin, which he had to suppress. In the process, he subjugated the latter two groups, which up to that time had been independent. This accomplished, the Inca utilized the newly acquired lands as a base for extending his conquests toward Bolivia, Chile, and northwestern Argentina. At its culmination, the empire incorporated almost the entire Andean area, from the Río Ancasmayu, near Pasto in southern Colombia, to the Río Maule in central Chile. On the east, the limit was the border of the forest, although permanent trade relations existed with the inhabitants of the adjacent Amazonian lowlands.

Tupac Inca Yupanki was followed about 1493 by Wayna Capac, who annexed the Gulf of Guayaquil and the Island of Puná. Before his death in Quito about 1527, this Inca apparently was informed of the existence of the Spaniards, who made several abortive voyages south from Panama before beginning the conquest of the Andean area. He was succeeded by a son, Waskar Inca, who was crowned in Cuzco on receipt of the news from Quito. The de-

ceased ruler had been accompanied in his military campaign by another son named Atawallpa, who took command in Quito. This dual government initiated five years of civil war, which terminated only when Francisco Pizarro and his men imprisoned Atawallpa in 1532 in the city of Cajamarca, just about the time that the word was received of the defeat and death of Waskar. The Spanish, acting according to their own form of "justice," sentenced the captive Inca to death.

SETTLEMENT PATTERN.   The capital of the empire was Cuzco, where the most fabulous treasures imaginable were to be found in such quantities that a legend developed of "El Dorado," a mysterious city almost completely covered with precious stones and metals. As the seat of administration, Cuzco was an orderly arrangement of streets and houses, provided with water and drainage systems. Here, the Inca and his court resided and from here the vast dependent territory was controlled.

The existence of houses with walls covered with gold and silver is not pure mythology. The temple of Qori Kancha ("building of gold"), where Wira Qocha, the Sun (Inti), the Moon (Killa), and the stars (Koyllur) were worshipped, was such a place. It occupied the spot where the Christian temple and convent of Santo Domingo are located today, and contained various sanctuaries, each dedicated to a different celestial deity. The exterior walls measured about 68 by 59 meters and a semicircular annex on the southwestern side projected to a height of more than 34 meters. An ornamental freize consisting of a sheet of gold almost a meter wide ran along the center of the exterior wall and the entrances were covered with thick gold plates. The interior walls were coated with the same metal. A large central patio is said to have contained a partly natural and partly artificial garden that was provided with water by channels sheathed in precious metals and issuing from a central octagonal fountain of stone completely encased in gold. Beneath the semicircular structure were plants made from gold and gems, among them stalks of maize with leaves and ears. Cieza de León (1959:147) gives a detailed description:

There was a garden in which the earth was lumps of fine gold, and it was cunningly planted with stalks of corn that were of gold—stalk, leaves, and ears. These were so well planted that no matter how hard the wind blew it could not uproot them. Aside from this, there were more than twenty sheep [i.e., llamas] of gold with their lambs, and the shepherds who guarded them, with their slings and staffs, all of this metal.

Many such objects were included in the fabulous treasure taken by the Cuzqueños to Cajamarca to provide the ransom required for the liberation of Atawallpa from his Spanish captors.

The principal sanctuary was dedicated to Inti, the Sun. All its walls were covered with gold and the idol on the altar was a thick gold slab. It was flanked by the mummies of former rulers, which were later burned by the Spaniards. The image of Killa (the Moon) was of silver and the mummies of the wives of the Incas appear to have been placed in this sanctuary. The other "chapels" were associated with cosmic divinities, among them certain constellations, Lightning, and the Rainbow. The wealth of the temple of Qori Kancha was so great that the list of booty sent as tribute to the Spanish king included more than 20 fully clothed, life-sized statues of women made of solid gold and silver, along with life-sized llamas, reptiles, spiders, shrimp, and other animals, all of precious metal.

Cuzco also contained other temples of lesser importance, along with palaces, public buildings, and residences for members of the court. Public buildings were made of finely hewn stone, finished with such precision that the joints matched perfectly and there was no need for mortar (Figure 219). In some walls, it is impossible to insert a pin into the cracks between the stones. Great technical skill and much manpower were required for the construction of these architectural monuments. The workers were common people who paid their tribute to the Inca in the form of labor, and who served under a system known as "mita"; the architects and engineers must have been specialists employed by the state.

The first task was to plan the building, and many stone models have been found that may have been used for this purpose. The second step must have been selection of the source of the stone and its cutting into the required shapes, a task that was accomplished with instruments of stone and bronze. Some quarries were nearby, while others were in distant regions. Wet sand was used for polishing by abrasion. The forms of the stones incorporated into the Cuzco walls reflect an underlying esthetic sensitivity, expressed in arrangements that vary from an even surface composed of rows of equal-sized stones to a technique known as "cellular polygonal," in which the stones with different numbers of sides were fitted together so precisely that they resemble the cells of an organic tissue. The outer face of a wall generally exhibits slight convexity because of the pillow-like contours of the stones.

The city of Cuzco was primarily the work of Pacha Kuteq, although some modifications were made by his successors. Few buildings exceeded one story. The variations in construction considered by some authorities to have chronological significance are the result of differences in the type of raw material and in the function of the buildings. Aside from the technique of stone fitting, the outstanding characteristic of the architectural style is the trapezoidal form of apertures, with the lintel narrower than the sill and resting on inward sloping jambs. In some instances, there is a second and smaller casing, producing a "double jamb." Many walls contain niches of the same form as the doors and windows. Not all Inca buildings were made of cut stone; many were constructed of irregular field stone and others of adobe, as in the case of the temple of Cacha south of Cuzco, attributed to the god Wira Qocha (Figure 220). The walls were seldom ornamented, and then only with small figures of serpents, llamas, or pumas carved principally on jambs and lintels.

Cuzco was not a typical Inca city, which is to say that it does not represent a style widely distributed over the Andes. It was the nucleus of the empire and its plan reflects its function—an administrative center inhabited primarily by nobles, priests, military officers, and their servants. Surrounding it were villages occupied by people called "mitmaq," who were brought from other parts of the empire. The most important of these "satellites" were Qarmenqa, Cayaucachi, Tococachi, and Colcampata, which had an estimated population of some 100,000 families.

Figure 219. Fitted stone, characteristic of Inca architecture.

Figure 220. The Temple of Wira Qocha in Cacha, south of Cuzco (courtesy Elías Mujica B.).

Figure 221. Portions of the fortress of Sacsahuaman outside Cuzco.

A group of buildings in the middle of the city has been interpreted as the residences of courtiers. Among the most impressive were those of the following dignitaries: Kiswar Kancha, who traced his lineage to the Inca Wira Qocha, and who lived where the basilica of the Cathedral in the Plaza de Armas of Cuzco stands today; Hatun Kancha, who was related to the Inca Yupanki; and Amaru Kancha, a descendant of Wayna Capac, whose residence was later incorporated into the original Jesuit church and convent of Cuzco, now part of the University of Cuzco. Colcampata, who belonged to the royal family of Manco Capac, resided in one of the suburbs. Other buildings served ceremonial functions, among them Aqlla Wasi, a large and very carefully constructed, walled compound where the "aqlla" or "chosen ones" lived. Yachay Wasi, "the house of learning," where the sons of the nobility received their instruction, was another beautifully constructed building. There were also prisons, among which Pardo (1957) mentions Sanqa Kancha and Wimpillai. The streets and plazas were apparently also identified by names; the most important plaza was Waqay Pata, where the principal ceremonies took place.

Houses in the suburbs were constructed of field stone and clay or of adobe. They were rectangular and had gabled, thatched roofs. The rooms were usually built against the outer wall leaving a central patio. Such structures were probably inhabited by an extended family. The suburban, satellite villages were unfortified and rarely planned, except when the inhabitants included officials of the state.

In a few instances, fortifications or "pukaras" were erected for defense. An example is Sacsahuaman, the great fortress located on a natural elevation north of the city of Cuzco. The northern zone is particularly impressive because it consists of a succession of platforms with zig-zag walls formed of gigantic boulders (Figure 221). On the highest part of the site, buildings of varying size surround the "tower of Muyuq Marka," a strange structure possibly used for rituals.

The zone of maximum population concentration was the city of Cuzco, but the surrounding region contains a large number of ruins. Many were executed with great esthetic feeling, such as Tampu Machay; shrines like Qenqo are also notable.

The Urubamba Valley—today called "the sacred valley"—also contains outstanding examples of Cuzqueño architecture. The city of Ollantaytambo, about 68 kilometers northeast of Cuzco, was con-structed on a sloping hillside and surrounded by a high wall. Other evidences of fortification occur in the form of walls built of such immense stones that they stimulated early European visitors to postulate their construction by giants prior to the appearance of the human race. There are two fortification walls, instead of three as at Sacsahuaman. Residences occupy the lower portion of the hill and many of the houses are still inhabited by local peasantry.

Another Inca city is the famous Machu Picchu, located on the summit of a steep mountain spur (Figure 222). It was undoubtedly planned and constructed as a unit, probably by the mita system, as Rowe (1946) has suggested. Many of the houses were built of rough stone and their walls were probably covered with a layer of clay plaster. This treatment may also have been applied to some of the buildings constructed of dressed stone.

As the Inca expanded their dominion by conquest, they established administrative centers in each newly annexed province, sometimes utilizing existing cities and sometimes founding new ones. Where urbanism was already advanced, as in the Chimú region, they generally preferred to continue using the local administrative centers, just as they retained the services of local government officials wherever they could be relied upon for the provincial administration. On the North coast, as a consequence, changes in settlement pattern during Inca rule were almost nonexistent and new ceremonial or administrative centers did not replace those previously constructed by the Chimú.

The almost total absence of change in material culture on the North coast (which is partly the result of the short period of time between assimilation of the Chimú Kingdom and the arrival of the Spaniards) illustrates one of the problems underlying the attempt to reconstruct sociopolitical conditions on the basis of archeological evidence. In this region, the presence of the Inca is attested only by a few fragments of pottery from restricted locations. Without the aid of oral traditions, these could be attributed to commercial contacts or some other exchange mechanism. Rowe (1948) has suggested that the Inca may have incorporated many Chimú features into their administrative system after the region was conquered by Yupanki. This seems possible and, if so, the prestige of the local government may be an additional factor in explaining why more intensive domination was not exercised over the North coast.

Figure 222. Views of Machu Picchu.

Figure 223 The Temple of the Sun at Pachacamac, with a pre-Inca structure in the left foreground (courtesy A. Guillén).

A similar pattern of consolidation was employed on the Central coast, although here the Inca often established new communities or added Cuzco components to earlier structures. They did this at Pachacamac, which attained great prestige as a ceremonial center. Among the Inca innovations was the Mamacuna, a stepped pyramid erected in homage to the Sun on a natural elevation occupied by earlier buildings and still known as the Temple of the Sun (Figure 223). A local temple dedicated to the god Pacha Kamaq ("he who embraces the entire earth"), and apparently traceable to a Tiahuacanoid origin, was also mentioned by the Spanish. Cieza de León (1959:334–336) described Pachacamac as it was at the time of the conquest:

This valley is pleasant and fertile, and there stood there one of the most sumptuous temples to be found in these regions. They say of it that, despite the fact that the Inca lords built many [temples], aside from those of Cuzco, and glorified and embellished them with riches, there was none to compare with this of Pachacamac, which was built upon a small, man-made hill of adobes and earth, and on its summit stood the temple which began at the foot, and had many gates, which, like the walls, were adorned with figures of wild animals. Inside, where the idol stood, were the priests who feigned great sanctimoniousness. And when they performed their sacrifices before the people, they kept their faces toward the door of the temple and their backs to the figure of the idol, with their eyes on the ground and all trembling and overcome, according to certain Indians still alive today, so that it could almost be compared to what one reads of the priests of Apollo when the [Greek] Gentiles sought their vain oracles. And they say more: that before the figure of this devil they sacrificed many animals, and human blood of persons they killed; and that on the occasion of their most solemn feasts they made utterances which were believed and held to be true. In the terraces and foundations of this temple great sums of gold and silver were buried. The priests were greatly venerated, and the lords and caciques obeyed them in many things that they ordered. And it is told that beside the temple there were many spacious lodgings for those who came there in pilgrimage, and no one was deemed worthy nor allowed to be buried in its vicinity except the lords or priests or pilgrims who came bearing gifts to the temple. When the great yearly feasts were celebrated, many people assembled, carrying on their diversions to the sound of the musical instruments they possessed. And as the Incas, powerful lords that they were, made themselves the masters of the kingdom and came to this valley of Pachacamac, and, as was their custom in all the lands they conquered, they ordered temples and shrines built to the sun. And when they saw the splendor of this temple, and how old it was, and the sway it held over all the people of the surrounding lands, and the devotion they paid it, holding that it would be very difficult to do away with this, they agreed with the native lords and the ministers of their god or devil that this temple of Pachacamac should remain with the authority and cult it possessed, provided they built another temple to the sun which should take precedence. And when the temple to the sun had been built, as the Incas ordered, they filled it with riches and put many virgins in it.

In the Lima Valley, by contrast, many sacred structures were completely remodeled by the Cuzqueños to make them more efficient seats of administrative and religious control. Several planned communities, of which Tamboinga (Inca Tampu) north of Lima is an example, were also constructed.

On the South coast, the Inca settlement pattern consisted of rectangular structures surrounding a rectangular or slightly trapezoidal plaza. Typically, there was a large quadrangular building at one side containing a complex of small rooms and patios, the walls of which had painted decoration or contained niches. Mural paintings replaced the relief decoration so common during the Inca-Chincha period. At La Centinela in the Tambo de Mora, where both techniques can be observed in different sectors, the painting (black and red on white) is in a building dating from the Inca reoccupation and superimposed on older structures. Less important buildings occupied two other sides of the plaza and the fourth side remained open. A low platform generally extended in front of the principal structure and platforms were sometimes also added to those at the sides. The largest building usually stood on the summit of a platform or natural hill. Construction was of adobe (Menzel 1959: 129). Like other Cuzqueño towns, those of the South coast were composed of groups of interconnected houses inside an enclosure that had a single exit.

One of the most impressive towns on the South coast is Tambo Colorado, located near the hacienda of Humay in the Pisco Valley (Figure 224). It is also the best-preserved coastal city for two reasons: (1) it was abandoned shortly after the Spanish conquest, and (2) it is remote from modern population concentrations. The two principal sectors are separated by a level, open, trapezoidal area. The northern one, adjacent to some hills, appears to have been the most important. It consists of a central walled enclosure with a single opening toward the south, in the middle of which is a quadrangular plaza surrounded by buildings of varying size that appear to have been living quarters. Opposite this, toward the south, is a complex of structures apparently associated with a ceremonial center. On the east and west are other buildings of lesser importance.

In the highlands, Inca buildings are easily recognized when they are constructed in the highly elaborated Cuzqueño style; namely, of worked stone joined without mortar. Many of the houses, however, were made of stones and mud. Not only do they exhibit few diagnostic Inca architectural features,

but they seldom produce Inca pottery, so that their chronological identification is often difficult. In fact, a large part of the non-official provincial population either continued to follow their old traditions or, as a consequence of the mitmaq system, altered them in various ways that are not distinctively Incaic. In an effort to clarify this situation, Murra (1962) and a group of collaborators have been attempting to reconstruct the provincial Incaic center near Huánuco utilizing documentary and archeological information.

Many structures and administrative communities built in Cuzqueño style have been reported from various portions of the Andean highlands, among the most noteworthy being Tumibamba in Ecuador and Cajamarca, Huánuco Viejo, Jauja, Vilcashuamán, and Huaytará in Peru. None are known from the southern Andes.

In Cajamarca, where the Inca Atawallpa was captured by the Spaniards in 1532, a city of considerable size must have existed to judge from the descriptions provided by the chroniclers who accompanied Francisco Pizarro. They speak of a large plaza surrounded by walls and houses. Today only a few minor ruins survive, one of which is known as the "ransom house," because local tradition identifies it as the place where the great treasure demanded for the release of Atawallpa was deposited. The ruins are within the limits of the Spanish town of Cajamarca.

Huánuco Viejo, one of the better preserved and more beautiful examples of Inca architecture, is located at an elevation of about 3700 meters at the base of a hill. In the center of the ruins is a rectangular platform, which is known as the "Usno" or Castle. Staircases lead to the summit and it is surrounded by walls constructed in the finest Cuzqueño workmanship. Two carved stones bear relief feline figures. Aside from this great platform, there are groups of rooms, room complexes, and patios inside rectangular enclosures, and a large plaza. One of the most striking features is a series of eight trapezoidal doorways, which follow a straight line that connects a complex of buildings.

Little remains of the settlement of Jauja, which achieved considerable renown at the time of the Spanish conquest. The community lies about 3 kilometers from the modern city of the same name and all that survives are a few walls of Cuzqueño style. Apparently the Inca residential pattern had little impact in the Mantaro Valley and the populace was permitted to continue occupation of old buildings

Figure 224. Views of the site of Tambo Colorado in the Pisco Valley (courtesy A. Guillén).

Above, right, and facing page
Figure 225. Structures at Vilcashuamán, Ayacucho.

like Wari Willka in Huancayo, which had been constructed in Wari times and functioned during the Inca epoch as a shrine or oracle.

One of the places most favored by the Inca was Vilcashuamán (Figure 225), perhaps because it was located in the territory of their ancient rivals, the Chanka. Great efforts were expended on the construction of the city and the chroniclers indicate that the Temple of the Sun was richly ornamented with gold and silver. A few vestiges of the old structures survive in spite of their use by the modern populations as a source of building stone. The most important are the Temple, the Usno, and the "palace," all constructed in classical Cuzqueño style around a large trapezoidal plaza. As in Cuzco itself, techniques of construction differ according to the type of stone or the function of the wall. Outstanding because of its uniqueness is a spiral pyramid with a quadranguloid cross-section, scaled by a staircase on the south side. On the upper platform is a large stone bench, which according to the chroniclers was formerly totally covered with sheets of gold.

Figure 226. The Inca citadel of Quebrada de la Vaca, Arequipa (courtesy Ramiro Matos Mendieta).

Figure 227. Depiction in pottery of the type of "foot-plow" used by the Inca to till the soil (MRLH).

Near Vilcas is another badly damaged town of Inca origin, known variously as Cal y Canto, Puma Qocha or Senqato, and which may once have been even more beautiful than Vilcas. It is on the margin of Lake Puma Qocha, which was converted into a reservoir by the construction of an immense wall that nearly surrounds it. According to Cieza de León (1959), one of the sons of an emperor was born here.

Huaytará, another Inca town constructed in Cuzco style, is in the province of Castrovirreyna, in Huancavelica, some 100 kilometers northeast of Ica. The surviving remnants consist of walls that formed part of an enclosure constructed for ceremonial and administrative purposes; a Christian temple has been built on top of them. Many other towns were remodeled or constructed by the Cuzqueños in various parts of Peru, among the most famous being Marka Wamachuku in the mountains of the Chimú region.

During the Inca Period, rectangular structures with stone and clay corbelled-arch roof construction appeared throughout the Andes. Whether the Incas learned this technique in the Titicaca Basin, the Ancash highlands, or some other region, they disseminated it everywhere with great success. Prior to the Inca conquest, such buildings, generally termed "chullpas," were not popular except possibly in the North highlands, and because of their dissimilarity to structures normally associated with the Inca, they used to be considered pre-Inca wherever they occurred. In the Central highlands, they are clearly associated with the Chanka; in the Mantaro region, they have been attributed to the Wanka, and in the altiplano they equate with the pre-Inca "Altiplanic Expansive" period. Inca remains are not invariably associated and in some instances, especially where the constructions are circular, Incaic elements have seldom been found. Nevertheless, chullpas nearly always occur in regions of very late occupation, which are closely affiliated to Inca culture either in ceramic features or in chronology. A town at "Quebrada de la Vaca," south of Chala, is undoubtedly Inca, although it shows no evidence of the Cuzco style except that most of the buildings are of the chullpa type (Figure 226). The most beautiful chullpa-type buildings in the Titicaca Basin are clearly Incaic, as are the well-known ruins of Sillustani. In Ayacucho, a distinction may exist between rectangular chullpas, which are associated with the Inca Period, and circular ones, which may be slightly earlier, although this cannot yet be proved. In the city of Chiprak in the mountains near Lima, which is totally Inca both in date and in artifact content, all of the buildings are variants of the chullpa type (Villar Córdova 1935). Several other similar settlements occur in this region.

It is obvious that the centralized Inca organization did not develop an exclusivistic and ethnocentric policy; rather, it employed as much as possible the preexisting facilities in conquered regions. In some instances, certain Inca patterns were imposed, perhaps more for strategic than for ideological reasons. Two new types of buildings were constructed everywhere, however: (1) "tampus" that served as supply stations and rest houses for travelers along the highways, especially official ones, and (2) storehouses for food and clothing, which could be withdrawn during periods of economic depression or for the support of the army in the field.

The highways played an outstanding role in the Inca economy, since they permitted rapid communication between cities and villages. The two trunk lines, one along the coast and the other through the highlands, connected the principal administrative centers and were linked at intervals (Figure 218). The coastal route ran from Tumbes to Arequipa, terminating near Santiago; the highland one led from Ancasmayu to Quito, and from there to Huancabamba, Cajamarca, Jauja, Vilcas, Cuzco, Ayaviri, Ghuquisaca, and Tucumán, with branches running to the coast and Santiago de Chile. The major transversal links were between Cuzco and Nazca, Cuzco and Arequipa, Jauja and Pachacamac, and Chanchan and Cajamarca. Some roads were more than five meters wide, straight, and provided with bridges of the suspension type constructed of vines and poles. Some rivers were crossed by means of small platforms suspended from ropes. In rugged terrain, rocks were removed or sustaining walls were constructed; on slopes, stairways were built. Large segments were paved with stone.

SUBSISTENCE. Since the economy of the empire was agriculturally based, regional production was very important and much emphasis was placed on good yields. All the products of the highlands and the coast were utilized and those grown only in the tropical forest were obtained by barter. The agricultural system was managed by a tight organization that permeated most of the state structure. To maximize agricultural production, terraces or "andenes" were constructed on steep slopes. Thick retaining walls held back the fill, producing a series of stepped platforms that were often provided with irrigation water. Many of the andenes, however, were utilized only during the rainy season. Other systems of land improvement, such as construction of dams and canals, were also employed to greatest advantage.

Labor in the fields was required of all men, except, of course, the Inca. The state, which meant the Emperor, owned all the land and the rest of the population was entitled only to its use. Only the ruler could give or distribute land. Each man received an allotment known as a "tupu" and each woman half an allotment, so that a family normally possessed one and a half tupus. Since nobles were allowed more than one wife, they could receive a larger amount of land. Agricultural workers were obliged to cultivate not only their family allotments, but also those assigned to the Emperor and the Sun God. The latter lands provided sufficient surplus food to support the entire administrative bureaucracy, the armies, and the priesthood. Very simple agriculture implements were employed, such as the "taqlla" and the "qorona," variations of a type of hoe or spade (Figure 227). The value of guano as fertilizer had been known for centuries; fish heads and the excrement of llamas and birds were also utilized. This activity counted toward payment of the tribute that the empire required from all inhabitants, as did participation in public works, mining, working on coca plantations, or other kinds of labor, including obligatory military service. Part of the agricultural system was supported by the "ayni," a system of mutual aid that gave a certain collectivistic character to Inca society. Another form of labor organization, which was not limited to agriculture, was the "minka," by means of which community projects were executed.

While herding did not have the same importance as agriculture, it was a major resource in the Inca economy and the system of state ownership was an integral factor here also, since large herds were the exclusive property of the Emperor. The domestic animals were the llama, the alpaca, the guinea pig, and the Muscovy duck. The dog was also domesticated and is reputed to have been eaten by the Wanka, with the result that they were referred to as "dog eaters."

Gathering, hunting, and fishing played secondary roles in most of the empire, although fishing was the principal activity in some coastal villages. Sport hunting or "cako" was sometimes practiced, in which the sling and a type of bola were utilized. It is said that the Inca ruler liked to eat fresh fish and that he ordered a supply brought to Cuzco from the coast, from which it arrived in good condition thanks to a system of "mail" very efficiently executed by the "chaski," who were specially trained as very fast runners and who frequently carried important official communications, either verbally or in the form of quipus. Whereas the Spaniards required 12 or 13 days to travel from Lima to Cuzco on horseback, the chaski made the trip in three days. They were said to be able to cover 240 kilometers in a day by employing a relay system in which messages were passed from one courier to another at established intervals.

Storage of food in the imperial storehouses was facilitated by complex methods of dehydration, which preserved normally perishable commodities for long periods. Meat ("charki"), potatoes ("cocopa" and "chuño"), and fish were treated in this way. It is interesting to note that many of these granaries were of the chullpa type, with a roof in the form of a corbelled arch. Exchange by barter occurred in town markets and there was also a system of periodic fairs in fixed locations that remains in existence today among the rural population of Peru.

SOCIAL ORGANIZATION. Effective control over this kind of situation, in which production originated in an increasing number of heterogeneous towns, could be maintained only by a well-organized political hierarchy. Large contingents of workers were continuously needed to fulfill the requirements of the state and since their registration could not be totally centralized in the capital, responsibilities were allocated according to a hierarchy. Its apex was the Inca himself and the bottom were the heads of families, who were called "pureq." The incorpo-

ration of all the pureq in the Inca government has led some people to infer that the system was basically democratic, especially since one of the pureq, who was called "Curaca," was elected annually to a popular assembly. Participation in the power structure is an illusion, however, since the Curaca's responsibility consisted simply of assuring the Cuzco officials that his "constituents" were fulfilling their obligations in production, consumption, and the rendering of tribute.

The pureq achieved this status by marriage, when he received the one and a half parcels of land to which he was entitled as the head of a family. He simultaneously acquired obligations to the state, which were liquidated by devoting to it a part of his time, as mentioned earlier. To simplify the record keeping, he was grouped with four other pureq, one of whom became responsible for the five families and was called "Pichqa Kamayoq" ("he who has five"). Two five-family units were grouped under a leader called "Chunka Kamayoq" ("responsible for ten"); in turn, five Chunka Kamayoq were united under an official called "Pichqa Chunka Kamayoq"; over him was a Pachaq Kamayoq, responsible for 100 pureq or families. The Pachaq or Curaca was the leader of an "ayllu" or communal group and was elected annually during the festival of Kamachikuq.

The Curacas served as intermediaries between the Imperial hierarchy and the populace. The officials to whom they reported belonged to the upper class of Cuzco or were appointed by the Inca. Five Curacas reported to a Pichqa Pachaq Kamayoq and two of the latter were under a Waranq Kamayoq (supervisor of 1000 pureq); these in turn were supervised by a Hunu Kamayoq, responsible for 10,000 families. The Hunu Kamayoq, who were governors of provinces, were grouped into fours under a military leader called "Wamani"; all the residents of a major region or "suyu" were directly under a chief known as "Suyuyuq Apu" ("Lord of the Suyu"). This gave the Empire its name; Tawantinsuyu or "Four Regions" was composed of Chinchay Suyu (the north), Anti Suyu (the east), Colla Suyu (the Titicaca highlands), and Kunti Suyu (the south). In addition to the Hunu Kamayoq or Imperial governor, it appears that each province had a high chief, known as "Toqrikuq," and a visiting inspector or Tukuy Rikuq ("he who sees all"). The Inca, lord and ruler of everything, governed with the aid of a supreme council, but his decisions and will could not be challenged. As soon as the heir to the throne was capable of assuming responsibility, he became co-ruler so that he was able to learn the art of governing.

The hierarchy was strictly functional and stemmed principally from the character of the tribute collected by the state. It also provided the Emperor with up-to-date information on the composition and number of his subjects, although the figures were not completely accurate since a pachaq did not always contain exactly 100 families. The accounts were kept with the aid of a "quipu" (Figure 228), a system of cords and knots that was interpretable only by specialists known as "Kipu Kamayoq." This device was also a means of recording events, to judge from references by the chron-iclers to the history "read" by the Kipu Kamayoq from the quipus. It has been suggested that a system of hieroglyphic writing superior to the quipu is preserved on textiles (de la Jara 1970); if so, its decipherment might greatly enrich our knowledge of the Andean world.

A natural consequence of this formalized hierarchy was a social stratification of little flexibility. The Cuzco nobility and the supreme governors were at the top, followed by the provincial nobility. Some of the latter derived their status from pre-Inca times, while others acquired it by a system known as "privilege," employed by the Inca to reward those who rendered outstanding service to the state. Members of the nobility were recognizable

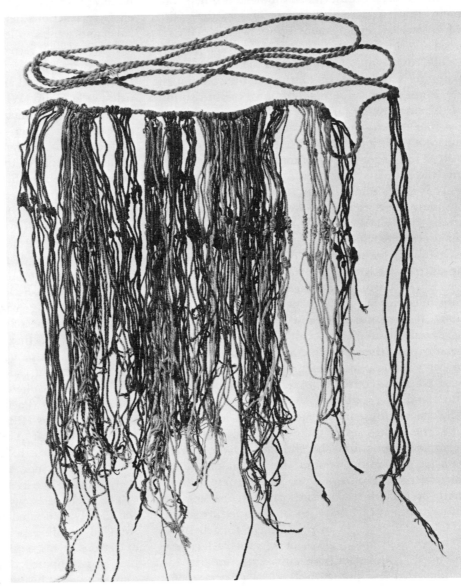

Figure 228. A quipu, used for keeping accounts (NMNH).

by dress, residence, and above all by the wearing of large ear ornaments, which deformed the lobe to such an extent that the Spaniards referred to them as "big ears." The headdress of the Inca included a distinctive feature called "mascaipacha," which consisted of a diadem of feathers from a very rare bird.

The family was organized on the base of the "ayllu," which was a community entity that often involved kinship ties. The nuclear family was composed of "yaya" (father), "mama" (mother), "wawa" (daughter), and "churi" (son). "Wawqe" and "pani" were the terms for brother and sister of a boy; "turi" and "ñaña" were the equivalent terms used by a girl. "Willka" meant grandfather; "qosa," husband, and "warmi," wife. All other relatives, except for the father's brothers and mother's brothers and their children were simply members of the ayllu, which was an endogamous entity with patrilineal descent.

The royal family was known as the "panaka" and polygyny was restricted to the nobility. Although the lower classes were monogamous, the institution of "sirvinakuy," a form of trial marriage, made it possible to have more than one wife or husband, but not simultaneously. The Emperor was permitted to have sexual relationships with his sisters, and the principal wife, or Coya, was a sister.

The distinction between men and women was clearcut in every aspect of life, from economic activity to family status. Differences in dress and personal ornament indicated the inferiority of women. A man wore a tunic and mantle, sandals, and a headdress. He generally carried a bag for coca, which was consumed sparingly; its distribution was controlled by the state, which owned the plantations. Women wore a simple long dress, consisting of a rectangular piece of cloth joined at the shoulders by pins; they also used a small shawl in which to carry things. Men enhanced their appearance with bracelets, cranial deformation, facial painting, rings, and other forms of embellishment, while the only ornament used by women was the shoulder pin.

At the village level, there were two other categories of populations in addition to the pureq; namely, the "mitmaq" and the "yanakuna." The mitmaq were groups of people transferred from their homeland to another part of the empire, either to serve as models to be followed by newly conquered peoples or as punishment for rebellion. The yanakuna were slaves or servants, who were relegated to this condition apparently for life, for reasons that are not entirely clear (Murra 1966).

This institution and certain others may have been taken over from the Chimú, among whom "yana" was the term for slaves. The Spaniards adopted the same name for their Indian slaves and it is still applied to serfs on highland haciendas in Peru.

Although the functioning of this system required firm management, it did not depend on abusive treatment. Justice concentrated on three basic prohibitions: thievery, idleness, and lying. These offenses were drastically punished, often with death. Other crimes included adultery and murder. Idleness was a crime against the state and those who neglected their work were severely punished; on the other hand, individuals who were unable to work because of illness, age, or some other legitimate reason received public assistance. The most effective sanctions derived from the divinity of the ruler and were applied through religious channels.

Inca religion recognized the existence of a supreme deity, named "Wira Qocha," who was the creator of the world and everything in it, and whose titles "Illa Tiqsi Wira Qocha Pacha Yachachiq" indicated his copious powers and knowledge. He appears to have been represented by an oval image. Mythology relates that he appeared in Tiahuanaco at the beginning of the world, creating man out of stone and naming him to give him life; he then created the sun, the earth, and the stars, along with animals and plants. He went to Cacha, about 100 kilometers south of Cuzco, where a temple was erected to him. Although some authorities believe him to be a recent deity, it is interesting to note that excavations in the zone of San Pedro de Cacha, where the temple is located, have revealed a dense occupation during Wari III. Inti (the Sun), second in importance in the pantheon, was a visible god and the father of the Inca. Other deities included Killa (the Moon), Illapa (Lightning), Choqe Chinchay (the constellation Orion), Chaska Koyllur (Venus), and other cosmic phenomena, among them the Rainbow. The Earth (Pacha Mama), the Water (Mama Qocha), and the Hills (Waka) were also endowed with supernatural qualities. Man, who inhabits the surface of the earth, emerges from its depths via caverns and springs; after death, he may go to join the gods that live in a distant place in the sky.

The high priest was called "Willka Umu" and was closely associated with the Inca. He lived surrounded by other priests and had a large number of persons at his service. Part of the religious complex was composed of the aqlla or "chosen," who were especially beautiful women obtained as part of the village tribute and who were kept secluded in places known as "aqlla wasi" until the Inca requested their service or they were presented to someone as a gift. The aqlla were trained by mamakuna ("the ladies"), particularly in the art of weaving, to which they devoted a major portion of their time. Such "storehouses" of women existed in most of the large Inca towns and their occupants were at the service of the Sun.

Part of the religious ritual consisted of sacrifice of animals or children, who were offered to the deity on certain festival days. These events were always related to the agricultural cycle, which was controlled by a special calendrical system under the supervision of priests known as "Inti Watana" ("those who control the sun"). It was recorded on wheel-like stones that were located in sacred places in the cities. The year was divided into twelve months, which were approximately the same as those of the western calendar. It began with Capac Raymi (December) and continued through Kamay, Hatun Poqoy, Paukar Waray, Ayriwa, Aymoray, Inti Raymi (June), Chawa Warkis, Yapakis, Situwa, Uma Raymi, and Aya Marka (November). Each month had 30 days, making a total of 360 days.

ARTS AND CRAFTS. One of the most interesting by-products of herding was the production of wool for the manufacture of textiles, and weaving assumed great importance in the social and economic context of the empire, being one of the most useful and desired forms of tribute (Murra 1962). Clothing was made of wool or cotton, and alpaca or vicuña were the most valuable fibers. Mantles were sometimes covered with feathers. Textile patterns were geometric and all of the techniques known in the Andes were employed, with tapestry being the most popular. Although Inca technological innovations were few, the fabrics were highly distinctive in artistic expression (Figure 229).

Pottery is a diagnostic Inca element because of its unusual forms and motifs. The most widely distributed styles were Cuzco, Qoripata, and Urcu-suyu. The former was the most popular and is characterized by emphasis on geometric designs on

Figure 229. A typical Inca textile (Museo Amano).

a red background. The two major varieties are known as A and B. Cuzco A is distinguished by the predominance of a "fern" motif, while Cuzco B decoration consists of black triangles or rhomboids, usually placed in horizontal rows. The most typical shape is the aryballo, a vessel with a very long and narrow neck terminating in an expanded rim, often with small ornamental pendant lugs; the body is rounded, and the bottom is conical or flattened (Figure 230). The Cuzqueño aryballo is distinctive in having a small modeled figure at the base of the neck, intermediate between the two vertical strap handles that always occur lower down on the body. Another common form is a shallow circular plate, which almost always has a vertical or horizontal handle on one side and an animal head or geometric ornament in the form of a double arch on the opposite margin (Figure 231). Also frequent are curved bowls with flat horizontal rims, chalices (covered receptacles on a pedestal base), toasters, and cups, the majority provided with horizontal strap handles.

With rare exceptions, the Cuzco styles employ only black, white, and red painting, in contrast to the Urcusuyu and Qoripata styles, which also utilized orange. The Cuzco and Qoripata variants were the most widely disseminated, while the Urcusuyu style appears to have been manufactured only in Cuzco and on the altiplano. Another variant has been labeled Huatanay (M. Tschopik 1946). In addition to these Cuzqueño styles, which occasionally employed naturalistic designs composed of insects, birds, and other life forms, new ceramic varieties appeared in the colonized regions during the period of the Inca conquest. This did not occur everywhere; for example, Inca influence on Chimú pottery was restricted to manufacture of a few aryballos. A distinctive style that appears to be associated with Cuzqueño pottery at Pachacamac emphasized vessels with faces on the neck and decoration by polychrome painting on a white slip. Ceramic modifications were not significant in Ica, but a few new forms and motifs can be detected in the variety known as "Tacaraca."

Figure 230. Inca aryballoids (courtesy A. Guillén).

Aside from pottery, the manufacture of a particular kind of wooden vessel known as a "kero" is an outstanding Inca feature (Figure 232). The form dates back to Tiahuanaco IV and continued in use during the nineteenth century, as is evident from examples bearing decoration commemorating independence from Spain. In addition to the skill in woodworking that they exhibit, the keros are magnificent sources of information because the exterior was painted with multicolored ritual, battle, and ceremonial scenes, some of which include the figure of the Inca.

BURIAL PRACTICES. Associated with religion was a cult of the dead, based on the belief in an afterworld to which all who died went. Consequently, burial was conducted according to specific rituals and the nobility were especially favored. In Cuzco, the Inca rulers were mummified and their bodies appear to have been preserved in the Qori Kancha temple rather than in tombs. Other people were generally buried in caves or rock shelters. Their graves were covered with field stones and clay after offerings of food, pottery, clothing, and other things had been placed with the body. Collective tombs have been found, which undoubtedly represent burials of common people. In Machu Picchu, tombs have been discovered associated with houses. Children were occasionally buried in pottery urns. In other parts of the Andes, interment usually followed ancient customs, although many graves contain objects of Inca style. The dead were a source of protection for the family; they were "mallki" or guardians to whom one appealed for certain kinds of favors.

The indigenous people who inhabited the Andes and who conquered them in their entirety did not die out with the arrival of the Spaniards. They persist today, working the land and maintaining the ayllu while patiently awaiting their redemption by an Indian messiah, whom they call "Inkarrí."

Figure 231. Inca vessel with the head of a llama (courtesy A. Guillén).

Figure 232. A wooden kero (courtesy A. Guillén).

LITERATURE CITED

Anderson, Edgar
1952. *Plants, Man and Life.* Boston: Little, Brown and Co.

Baessler, Arthur
1902–1903. *Ancient Peruvian Art.* 4 volumes. Berlin and New York.

Bandelier, Adolph F.
1905. The Aboriginal Ruins at Sillustani, Peru, *American Anthropologist*, 7:49–68.
1911. The Ruins at Tiahuanaco. *Proceedings of the American Antiquarian Society*, 21:218–265. Worcester.
1940. Los Indios y las Ruinas Aborígenes de Chachapoyas en el Norte del Perú. *Chaski*, 1(2):13–59. Lima.

Bennett, Wendell Clark
1934. Excavations at Tiahuanaco. *American Museum of Natural History Anthropological Papers*, 34 (part 3):359–494. New York.
1936. Excavations in Bolivia. *American Museum of Natural History Anthropological Papers*, 35 (part 4):329–507. New York.
1939. Archaeology of the North Coast of Peru. *American Museum of Natural History Anthropological Papers*, 37(part 1):1–153. New York.
1944. The North Highlands of Peru. Excavations in the Callejón de Huaylas and at Chavín de Huantar. *American Museum of Natural History Anthropological Papers*, 39(part 1):1–114. New York.
1946. The Archeology of the Central Andes. Pages 61–147 of part 2 of volume 2 in Julian H. Steward, editor, Handbook of South American Indians. *Bureau of American Ethnology Bulletin*, 143. Washington, D.C.
1948a. The Peruvian Co-tradition. *Society for American Archaeology Memoir*, 4:1–7.
1948b. (Editor). A Reappraisal of Peruvian Archaeology. *Society for American Archaeology Memoir*, 4.
1953. Excavations at Wari, Ayacucho, Peru. *Yale University Publications in Anthropology*, 49. New Haven.

Bennett, Wendell Clark, and Junius Bird
1949. Andean Culture History. *American Museum of Natural History Handbook Series*, 15. New York [1960, revised second edition.]

Bernedo Málaga, Leónidas
1958. *La Cultura Puquina.* Arequipa, Perú: Populibro.

Bird, Junius
1943. Excavations in Northern Chile. *American Museum of Natural History Anthropological Papers*, 38(part 4):173–318. New York.
1946. The Cultural Sequences of the North Chilean Coast. Pages 587–597 of part 3 of volume 2 in Julian H. Steward, editor, Handbook of South American Indians. *Bureau of American Ethnology Bulletin*, 143. Washington, D.C.
1948. Preceramic Cultures in Chicama and Virú. *Society for American Archaeology Memoir*, 4:21–28.
1963. Preceramic Art from Huaca Prieta, Chicama Valley. *Ñawpa Pacha*, 1:29–34. Institute of Andean Studies, Berkeley.
1969. A Comparison of South Chilean and Ecuadorian "Fishtail" Projectile Points. *The Kroeber Anthropological Society Papers*, 40:52–71. Berkeley.

Bonavia, Duccio
1963. Sobre el Estilo Teatino. *Revista del Museo Nacional*, 31(1962):43–94. Lima.
1964. Investigaciones en la Ceja de Selva de Ayacucho. *Museo Nacional de Antropología y Arqueología. Arqueológicas*, 6. Lima.
1968. Las Ruinas del Abiseo. Lima: Universidad Peruana de Ciencias y Tecnología.

Bosch-Gimpera, Pedro
1943. Posibles Conexiones entre las Culturas de Norteamérica y las del Viejo Mundo. Pages 339–344 in *El Norte de México y el Sur de Estados Unidos.* México, D.F.: Sociedad Mexicana de Antropología, Reuniones de Mesa Redonda.

Cabello Balboa, Miguel
1920. Historia del Perú Bajo la Dominación de los Incas. *Colección de Libros y Documentos Re-*

ferentes a la Historia del Perú, second series, volume 2. Lima.
1951. *Miscelánea Antártica* [1586]. Lima: Universidad Nacional Mayor de San Marcos.

Calancha, Antonio de
1938. Crónica Moralizada del Orden de San Agustín en el Perú, con Sucesos Ejemplares de Esta Monarquía, [1638–1653]. *Biblioteca de Cultura Peruana,* 4:15–140. Paris.

Cardich, Augusto
1958. Los Yacimientos de Lauricocha; Nuevas Interpretaciones de la Prehistoria Peruana. *Studia Praehistorica,* 1. Centro Argentino de Estudios Prehistóricos, Buenos Aires.
1964. Lauricocha, Fundamentos para una Prehistoria de los Andes Centrales. *Studia Praehistorica,* 3. Centro Argentino de Estudios Prehistóricos, Buenos Aires.

Carrera, Fernando de la
1939. Arte de la Lengua Yunga (1644). Radamés A. Altieri, editor, *Publicaciones Especiales del Instituto de Antropología,* 3. Universidad Nacional de Tucumán, Tucumán.

Carrión Cachot, Rebeca
1948. La Cultura Chavín; dos Nuevas Colonias: Kuntur Wasi y Ancón. *Revista del Museo Nacional* 2(1):99–172. Lima.

Childe, V. Gordon
1936. *Man Makes Himself.* London.

Choy, Emilio
1960. La Revolución Neolítica y los Orígenes de la Civilización Peruana. Pages 149–197 in *Antiguo Perú: Espacio y Tiempo.* Lima: Editorial Juan Mejía Baca.

Cieza de León, Pedro de
1959. *The Incas.* Translated by Harriet de Onis. Norman: University of Oklahoma Press.

Coe, Michael D.
1962. An Olmec Design on an Early Peruvian Vessel. *American Antiquity,* 27:579–580.

Collier, Donald
1955. Cultural Chronology and Change as Reflected in the Ceramics of the Virú Valley, Perú. *Fieldiana, Anthropology,* 43. Chicago Natural History Museum, Chicago.

Cutler, H. C., and T. W. Whitaker
1961. History and Distribution of the Cultivated Cucurbits in the Americas. *American Antiquity,* 26:469–485.

Dauelsberg, Percy, Jr.
1960. Contribución al Estudio de la Arqueología del Valle de Azapa. Pages 273–296 in *Antiguo Perú, Espacio y Tiempo.* Lima: Editorial Juan Mejía Baca.

de Candolle, Alphonse
1886. *Origine des Plantes Cultivées.* Paris.

d'Harcourt, Raoul
1922. Le Céramique de Cajamarquilla-Nievería. *Journal de la Société des Américanistes de Paris,* 14:107–118. Paris.

de la Jara, Victoria
1970. La Solución del Problema de la Escritura Peruana. *Revista del Museo de Arqueología de la Universidad de San Marcos,* 2:27–35. Lima.

Díez de San Miguel, Garci
1567. *Visita Hecha a la Provincia de Chucuito . . . Documentos Regionales para la Etnología y Etnohistoria Andina.* Lima: Casa de la Cultura [1964].

Dollfus, Olivier
1964. Préhistoire et Changements Climatiques Postwurmiens au Pérou. *Bulletin de l'Association Française pour l'Etude du Quaternaire,* 1:6–11. Paris.

1965. Effets des Fluctuations et des Accidents Climatiques sur l'Écologie Humaine du Pérou. *Journal de la Société des Américanistes,* 54:227–238. Paris.

Donnan, Christopher B.
1964. An Early House from Chilca, Peru. *American Antiquity,* 30 (part 1):137–144.

Engel, Frederic
1957a. Early Sites in the Pisco Valley of Peru: Tambo Colorado. *American Antiquity,* 23:34–45.
1957b. Sites et Etablissements sans Céramique de la Côte Peruvienne. *Journal de la Société des Américanistes,* 46:67–155. Paris.
1958. Algunos Datos con Referencia a los Sitios Precerámicos de la Costa Peruana. *Arqueológicas,* 3. Instituto de Investigaciones Antropológicas, Lima.
1960. Un Groupe Humain Datant de 5000 Ans à Paracas, Pérou. *Journal de la Société des Américanistes,* 49:7–30. Paris.
1963a. Notes Relatives à des Explorations Archéologiques à Paracas et sur la Côte Sud du Pérou. *Travaux de l'Institut Français d'Etudes Andines,* 9:1–72. Paris.
1963b. A Preceramic Settlement on the Central Coast of Peru: Asia, Unit 1. *Transactions of the American Philosophical Society,* 53(part 3):3–139. Philadelphia.
1964. El Precerámico sin Algodón en la Costa del Perú. *35 Congreso Internacional de Americanistas, Actas y Memorias,* 3:141–152. México.
1966a. *Geografía Humana Prehistórica y Agricultura Precolombina de la Quebrada de Chilca.* Lima: Universidad Agraria.
1966b. Le Complexe Précéramique d'El Paraiso (Pérou). *Journal de la Société des Américanistes,* 55(1):43–96. Paris.

1966c. *Paracas, Cien Siglos de Cultura Peruana*. Lima: Editorial Juan Mejía Baca.

1970. La Grotte du Mégathérium à Chilca et les Ecologies du Haut-Holocéne Peruvien. *Echanges et Communications: Mélanges Offerts à Claude Lévi-Strauss*, 1:413–435. Mouton. The Hague.

Erdmann, Leon S.
1963. Vialidad Imperial de los Incas. *Instituto de Estudios Americanistas, Serie Histórica*, 33. Universidad Nacional de Córdoba, Córdoba, Argentina.

Flores, Isabel
1969. Informe Preliminar sobre las Investigaciones Arqueológicas de Tacna. *Mesa Redonda de Ciencias Prehistóricas y Antropológicas*, 2:295–302. Lima.

Flornoy, Bertrand
1955–1956. Exploration Archéologique de l'Alto Marañon. *Travaux de l'Institut Français d'Etudes Andines*, 5:51–81. Paris-Lima.

Ford, James A.
1962. A Quantitative Method for Deriving Cultural Chronology. *Pan American Union Technical Manual*, Washington, D.C.

Ford, James, and Gordon R. Willey
1949. Surface Survey of the Virú Valley, Peru. *American Museum of Natural History, Anthropological Papers*, 43(part 1). New York.

Gayton, Anna H.
1927. The Uhle Collections from Nievería. *University of California Publications in American Archaeology and Ethnology*, 21(8):305–329. Berkeley.

Gayton, A. H. and A. L. Kroeber
1927. The Uhle Pottery Collections from Nazca. *University of California Publications in American Archaeology and Ethnology*, 24(1):1–46. Berkeley.

Ghersi Barrera, Humberto
1956. Informe Sobre las Excavaciones en Chiribaya. *Revista del Museo Nacional*, 35:89–119. Lima.

Hidalgo, Jorge
1971. *Las Culturas Protohistóricas del Norte de Chile*. Santiago: Universidad de Chile (mimeographed).

Horkheimer, Hans
1959. Algunas Consideraciones Acerca de la Arqueología del Valle del Utcubamba. *Actas del II Congreso Nacional de Historia del Perú*, 1:71–90. Lima.

1961. *La Cultura Mochica*. Lima: Compañía de Seguros y Reaseguros Peruano-Suiza.

Hutchinson, Thomas J.
1873. *Two Years in Peru, with Exploration of its Antiquities*. London.

Izumi, Seiichi, and Toshihiko Sono
1963. *Excavations at Kotosh, Peru, 1960: Andes 2*. Tokyo: Kadokawa Publishing Co.

Jijón y Caamaño, Jacinto
1949. *Maranga, Contribución al Conocimiento de los Aborígenes del Valle del Rímac, Perú*. Quito: La Prensa Católica.

Kalafatovich, Carlos
1956. *La Glaciacion Pleistocena en Urubamba*. Cuzco.

Kaplan, L., Thomas F. Lynch, and C. E. Smith, Jr.
1973. Early Cultivated Beans (*Phaseolus vulgaris*) from an Intermontane Peruvian Valley. *Science*, 179:76–77.

Kelemen, Pál
1944. *Medieval American Art*. New York: The Macmillan Co.

Kelley, David, and Duccio Bonavía
1963. New Evidence for Preceramic Maize on the Coast of Peru. *Ñawpa Pacha*, 1:39–41. Institute of Andean Studies, Berkeley.

Kidder II, Alfred
1943. Some Early Sites in the Northern Lake Titicaca Basin. *Papers of the Peabody Museum of American Archaeology and Ethnology*, 27(1). Cambridge, Mass.

1948. The Position of Pucara in Titicaca Basin Archaeology. *Society for American Archaeology Memoir*, 4:87–89.

Kosok, Paul, and Maria Reiche
1949. Ancient Drawings on the Desert of Peru. *Archaeology*, 2:206–215.

Krieger, Alex D.
1964. Early Man in the New World. Pages 23–81, in Jesse D. Jennings and Edward Norbeck, editors, *Prehistoric Man in the New World*. Chicago: University of Chicago Press.

Kroeber, Alfred L.
1926a. Culture Stratification in Peru. *American Anthropologist*, 28:311–351.

1926b. The Uhle Pottery Collections from Chancay. *University of California Publications in American Archaeology and Ethnology*, 21:265–304. Berkeley.

1944. Peruvian Archeology in 1942. *Viking Fund Publications in Anthropology*, 4. Wenner-Gren Foundation for Anthropological Research, New York.

1949. Art. Pages 411–492 of part 1 of volume 5 in Julian H. Steward, editor, Handbook of South American Indians. *Bureau of American Ethnology Bulletin*, 143. Washington, D.C.

1954. Proto-Lima, a Middle Period Culture of Peru. *Fieldiana, Anthropology*, 44(1). Chicago Natural History Museum, Chicago.

1956. Toward Definition of the Nazca Style. *Univer-*

sity of California Publications in American Archaeology and Ethnology, 43(4). Berkeley.

Kroeber, Alfred L., and William Duncan Strong
1924a. The Uhle Collections from Chincha. *University of California Publications in American Archaeology and Ethnology,* 21(1–2). Berkeley.
1924b. The Uhle Pottery Collections from Ica. *University of California Publications in American Archaeology and Ethnology,* 21(3). Berkeley.

Kutscher, Gerdt
1950. Iconographic Studies as an Aid in the Reconstruction of Early Chimu Civilization. *Transactions of the New York Academy of Sciences,* series 2, 12(6):194–203. New York.
1954. *Cerámica del Perú Septentrional; Figuras Ornamentales en Vasijas de los Chimúes Antiguos.* Berlin: Verlag Gebr. Mann.

Lanning, Edward P.
1963a. An Early Ceramic Style from Ancón, Central Coast of Perú. *Ñawpa Pacha,* 1:47–59. Institute of Andean Studies, Berkeley.
1963b. A Ceramic Sequence for the Piura and Chira Coast, North Peru. *University of California Publications in American Archaeology and Ethnology,* 46(2). Berkeley.
1963c. A Preagricultural Occupation on the Central Coast of Peru. *American Antiquity,* 28:360–371.
1967. *Peru Before the Incas.* Englewood Cliffs, New Jersey: Prentice-Hall, Inc.

Lanning, E. P., and T. C. Patterson
1967. Early Man in South America. *Scientific American,* 217(5):40–50. New York.

Larco Hoyle, Rafael
1938–1939. *Los Mochicas.* Lima.
1941. *Los Cupisniques.* Lima.
1943. La Escritura Mochica sobre Pallares. *Revista Geográfica Americana,* 20:1–36. Buenos Aires.
1944. *La Cultura Salinar.* Buenos Aires: Sociedad Geográfica Americana.
1945a. *La Cultura Virú.* Buenos Aires: Sociedad Geográfica Americana.
1945b. *Los Cupisniques.* Buenos Aires: Sociedad Geográfica Americana.
1945c. *Los Mochicas.* Buenos Aires: Sociedad Geográfica Americana.
1946. La Cultura Virú. *Revista Geográfica Américana,* 25:209–222. Buenos Aires.
1948. *Cronología Arqueológica del Norte del Perú.* Buenos Aires: Sociedad Geográfica Americana.
1965. *La Cerámica de Vicús.* Lima.
n.d. *La Cultura Santa.* Lima: Litografía Valverde.

Lathrap, Donald W.
1958. The Cultural Sequence at Yarinacocha, Eastern Peru. *American Antiquity,* 23:379–388.
1970. La Floresta Tropical y el Contexto Cultural de Chavín. Pages 235–261 in *100 Años de Arqueología del Perú.* Lima: Instituto de Estudios Peruanos.

Lathrap, Donald W., and Lawrence Roys
1963. The Archaeology of the Cave of the Owls in the Upper Montaña of Perú. *American Antiquity,* 29:27–38.

Le Paige, R. P. Gustavo
1963. Continuidad o Discontinuidad de la Cultura Atacameña. *Anales de la Universidad del Norte,* 2:7–25. Antofagasta.

Linares Málaga, Eloy
1961. Mapa Arqueológico del Departamento de Arequipa. *Boletín del Museo de la Universidad de Arequipa,* 1.

Lothrop, Samuel, and Joy Mahler
1957. A Chancay-style Grave at Zapallán, Perú. *Papers of the Peabody Museum of Archaeology and Ethnology,* 50(1). Cambridge, Mass.

Ludeña, Hugo
1970. San Humberto, un Sitio Formativo en el Valle del Chillón. (Informe Preliminar). *Revista del Museo de Arqueología de la Universidad de San Marcos,* 2. Lima.

Lumbreras, Luis G.
1959. Sobre los Chancas. *Actas del II Congreso Nacional de Historia del Perú,* 1:211–242. Lima.
1960a. Espacio y Cultura en los Andes. *Revista del Museo Nacional,* 21:177–200. Lima.
1960b. La Cultura de Wari, Ayacucho. *Etnología y Arqueología,* 1:130–226. Universidad Nacional Mayor de San Marcos, Lima.
1967. La Alimentación Vegetal en los Orígenes de la Civilización Andina. *Perú Indígena,* 11(26):254–273.
1970. *Los Templos de Chavín; Guía para el Visitante.* Lima: Publicación del Proyecto Chavín.

Lumbreras, Luis G., and Hernán Amat
1965–1966. Informe Preliminar sobre las Galerías Interiores de Chavín (Primera Temporada de Trabajos). *Revista del Museo Nacional,* 34:143–197. Lima.
1968. Secuencia Arqueológica del Altiplano Occidental del Titicaca. *37th International Congress of Americanists, Actas y Memorias,* 2:75–106. Buenos Aires.

Lynch, Thomas F.
1967 The Nature of the Central Andean Preceramic. *Occasional Papers of the Idaho State University Museum,* 21. Pocatello, Idaho.
1970. Transhumancia Estacional y Ocupación Precerámica en el Callejón de Huaylas. *Wayka,* 2:1–14. Programa Académico de Antropología, Universidad Nacional del Cuzco, Cuzco.

Lynch, Thomas F., and Kenneth A. R. Kennedy
1970. Early Human Cultural and Skeletal Remains from Guitarrero Cave, Northern Peru. *Science,* 169:1307–1310. Washington, D.C.

MacNeish, Richard S.
1969. *First Annual Report of the Ayacucho Archaeo-*

logical-Botanical Project. Andover, Mass.: Robert S. Peabody Foundation for Archaeology.

1971. Early Man in the Andes. *Scientific American,* 224(4):36–46.

MacNeish, R. S., A. Nelken-Terner, and A. García Cook
1970. *Second Annual Report of the Ayacucho Archaeological-Botanical Project.* Andover, Mass.: Robert S. Peabody Foundation for Archaeology.

Matos Mendieta, Ramiro
1959. Los Wanka, Datos Históricos y Arqueológicos. *Actas y Trabajos del II Congreso Nacional de Historia del Perú,* 1:87–210. Lima.
1970. El Período Formativo en la Sierra Central. *El Serrano,* 19:14–17. La Oroya, Peru.

McCown, Theodore
1945. Pre-Incaic Huamachuco: Survey and Excavations in the Northern Sierra of Peru. *University of California Publications in Archaeology and Ethnology,* 39(4). Berkeley.

Meggers, Betty J., and Clifford Evans
1969. Como Interpretar el Lenguaje de los Tiestos. Smithsonian Institution, Washington, D.C. (Multilithed).

Menzel, Dorothy
1958. Problemas en el Estudio del Horizonte Medio de la Arqueología Peruana. *Revista del Museo Regional de Ica,* 9(10):24–57.
1959. The Inca Occupation of the South Coast of Peru. *Southwestern Journal of Anthropology,* 15:125–142.
1964. Style and Time in the Middle Horizon. *Ñawpa Pacha,* 2:1–106. Institute of Andean Studies, Berkeley.
1968. New Data on the Huari Empire in Middle Horizon Epoch 2A. *Ñawpa Pacha,* 6:47–114. Institute of Andean Studies, Berkeley.
1971. Estudios Arqueológicos en los Valles de Ica, Pisco, Chincha y Cañete. *Arqueología y Sociedad,* 6. Universidad Nacional Mayor de San Marcos, Lima.

Menzel, Dorothy, John H. Rowe, and Lawrence E. Dawson
1964. The Paracas Pottery of Ica, A Study in Style and Time. *University of California Publications in American Archaeology and Ethnology,* 50. Berkeley.

Middendorf, E. W.
1893–1895. *Peru.* 3 volumes. Berlin.
1943. La Antigua Ciudad de Huadca. *Revista del Museo Nacional,* 12(1):81–96. Lima.

Moseley, Michael E., and Linda Barrett
1969. Change in Preceramic Twined Textiles from the Central Peruvian Coast. *American Antiquity,* 34:162–165.

Mostny, Grete
1971. *Prehistoria de Chile.* Santiago: Editorial Universitaria.

Muelle, Jorge C.
1935. Restos Hallados en una Tumba en Nievería. *Revista del Museo Nacional,* 4:135–152. Lima.
1936. Chalchalcha. *Revista del Museo Nacional,* 5(1): 65–88. Lima.
1937a. Filogenia de la Estela Raimondi. *Revista del Museo Nacional,* 6:135–150. Lima.
1937b. Los Valles de Trujillo. *Revista del Museo Nacional,* 6:3–24. Lima.

Munizaga, Carlos
1957. Secuencias Culturales de la Zona de Arica: Comparación Entre las Secuencias de Uhle y Bird. *Arqueología Chilena,* 2:77–122. Universidad de Chile, Santiago de Chile.

Murra, John
1962. An Archaeological "Restudy" of an Andean Ethnohistorical Account. *American Antiquity,* 28:1–4.
1964. Una Apreciación Etnológica de la Visita. Pages 421–444 in *Visita Hecha a la Provincia de Chucuito por Garci Diez de San Miguel en el Año 1567.* Lima: Ediciones de la Casa de Cultura del Perú.
1965. Herds and Herders in the Inca State. Pages 185–216 in *Man, Culture, and Animals.* Washington, D.C.: American Association for the Advancement of Science.
1966. New Data on Retainer and Servile Populations in Tawantinsuyu. *36th International Congress of Americanists, Actas y Memorias,* 2:35–45. Sevilla.
1968. The Aymara Kingdom in 1567. *Ethnohistory,* 15(2):115–151.
1972. El "Control Vertical" de un Máximo de Pisos Ecológicos en la Economía de las Sociedades Andinas. Pages 429–476 in Iñigo Ortiz de Zúñiga, *Visita de la Provincia de León de Huánuco (1562),* 2. Huánuco: Universidad Hermilio Valdizan.

Neira, Máximo
1967. Informe Preliminar de las Investigaciones Arqueológicas en el Departamento de Puno. *Anales del Instituto de Estudios Socio-Económicos,* 1:107–164. Puno: Universidad Técnica del Altiplano.

Nordenskiold, Erland
1906. Ethnographische und Archäologische Forschungen im Grenzgebiet zwischen Peru und Bolivia 1904–1905. *Zeitschrift für Ethnologie,* 38:80–99. Berlin.

Núñez, Lautaro
1965. Desarrollo Cultural Prehispánica del Norte de Chile. *Estudios Arqueológicos,* 1:37–115. Antofagasta.

Pardo, Luis
1957. *Historia y Arqueología del Cuzco.* Cusco.

Patterson, Thomas C.
1966. Early Cultural Remains on the Central Coast

of Peru. *Ñawpa Pacha*, 4:145–153. Institute of Andean Studies, Berkeley.

1971a. Central Peru: Its Population and Economy. *Archaeology*, 24:316–321.

1971b. The Emergence of Food Production in Central Peru. Pages 181–207 in Stuart Struever, editor, *Prehistoric Agriculture*. Garden City, New York: Natural History Press.

Patterson, Thomas C., and Edward P. Lanning
1964. Changing Settlement Patterns on the Central Peruvian Coast. *Ñawpa Pacha*, 2:113–123. Institute of Andean Studies, Berkeley.

Patterson, Thomas C., and M. E. Moseley
1968. Late Preceramic and Early Ceramic Cultures of the Central Coast of Peru. *Ñawpa Pacha*, 6:115–133. Institute of Andean Studies, Berkeley.

Pezzia, Alejandro
1962. *La Cultura Nazca*. Lima: Cía. de Seguros y Reaseguros Peruano-Suiza.

Ponce Sanginés, Carlos
1948. *Cerámica Tiwanacota, Vasos con Decoración Prosopomorfa*. Buenos Aires: Emecé Editores, S.A.

1957. (Editor). *Arqueología Boliviana*. La Paz: Biblioteca Paceña, Alcaldía Municipal.

1961. Informe de Labores. *Centro de Investigaciones Arqueológicas en Tiwanaku*, Publicación 1. La Paz.

1964. Descripción Sumaria del Templete Semisubterráneo de Tiwanaku. *Centro de Investigaciones Arqueológicas en Tiwanaku*, Publicación 2. La Paz.

1970. *Las Culturas Wankarani y Chiripa y su Relación con Tiwanaku*. La Paz: Academia Nacional de Ciencias de Bolivia.

Posnansky, Arthur
1940. *El Pasado Prehispánico del Gran Perú*. La Paz: Instituto Tihuanacu de Antropología, Etnología y Prehistoria.

1945–1948. *Tihuanacu, The Cradle of American Man*. New York: J. Augustin, and La Paz: Ministerio de Educación de Bolivia.

Pulgar Vidal, Javier
1946. *Historia y Geografía del Perú: Las Ocho Regiones Naturales del Perú*. Lima.

Ramos de Cox, Josefina
1964. *Nota Sobre una Nueva Forma Cerámica y Material del Periodo Intermedio Temprano en la Costa Central del Perú*. Lima: Publicación del Instituto Riva Agüero, Universidad Católica.

Ravines, Rogger
1965. Ambo: A New Preceramic Site in Peru. *American Antiquity*, 31:104–105.

Regal, Alberto
1936. *Los Caminos del Inca en el Perú Antiguo*. Lima.

Reiche, Maria
1949. *Mystery on the Desert*. Lima.

Reichlen, Henry and Paule Reichlen
1949. Recherches Archéologiques dans les Andes de Cajamarca. *Journal de la Société des Américanistes*, 38:137–174. Paris.

1950. Recherches Archéologiques dans les Andes du Haut Utcubamba. *Journal de la Société des Américanistes*, 39:219–246. Paris.

Reiss, Wilhelm, and Alphons Stübel
1880–1887. *The Necropolis of Ancon in Peru*. 3 volumes. Berlin.

Roark, Richard Paul
1965. From Monumental to Proliferous in Nazca Pottery. *Ñawpa Pacha*, 3:1 92. Institute of Andean Studies, Berkeley.

Rosas La Noire, Hermilio, and Ruth Shady Solís
1970. *Pacopampa: Un Centro Formativo en la Sierra Nor-Peruana*. Lima: Universidad Nacional Mayor de San Marcos.

Rostworowski de Diez Canseco, María
1953. *Pachacutec Inca Yupanqui*. Lima: Editorial Mejía Baca.

1961. *Curacas y Sucesiones (Costa Norte)*. Lima: Imprenta Minerva.

Rowe, John H.
1944. An Introduction to the Archaeology of Cuzco. *Papers of the Peabody Museum of American Archaeology and Ethnology*, 27(2). Cambridge, Mass.

1946. Inca Culture at the Time of the Spanish Conquest. Pages 183–330 of part 2 of volume 2 in Julian H. Steward, editor, Handbook of South American Indians. *Bureau of American Ethnology Bulletin*, 143. Washington, D.C.

1948. The Kingdom of Chimor. *Acta Americana*, 6 (1–2):26–59. México, D.F.

1956. Archaeological Explorations in Southern Peru, 1954–1955. *American Antiquity*, 22 (part 1): 135–151.

1960. Cultural Unity and Diversification in Peruvian Archaeology. *Selected Papers of the Fifth International Congress of Anthropological and Ethnological Sciences*:627–631 [1956].

1962. *Chavin Art: An Inquiry into its Form and Meaning*. New York: The Museum of Primitive Art.

1963. Urban Settlements in Ancient Perú. *Ñawpa Pacha*, 1:1–28. Institute of Andean Studies, Berkeley.

Rowe, John H., Donald Collier, and Gordon R. Willey
1950. Reconnaissance Notes on the Site of Huari, near Ayacucho, Peru. *American Antiquity*, 16:120–137.

Ryden, Stig
1947. *Archaeological Researches in the Highlands of Bolivia*. Göteborg: Elanders Boktryckeri Aktiebolag.

Sauer, Carl
1936. American Agricultural Origins. Pages 279–297 in Robert H. Lowie, editor, *Essays in Anthropology Presented to A. L. Kroeber.* Berkeley: University of California Press.
1952. *Agricultural Origins and Dispersals.* New York: The American Geographical Society.

Schaedel, Richard P.
1948. Stone Sculpture in the Callejón de Huaylas. *Society for American Archaeology Memoir,* 4:66–79.
1957. (Editor). *Arqueología Chilena; Contribuciones al Estudio de la Región Comprendida entre Arica y La Serena.* Santiago: Universidad de Chile.

Spinden, Herbert J.
1917. The Origin and Distribution of Agriculture in America. *19th International Congress of Americanists, Proceedings:*269–276. Washington, D.C.

Squier, Ephraim George
1877. *Peru, Incidents of Travel and Exploration in Land of the Incas.* New York.

Steinmann, G.
1930. *Geología del Perú.* Heidelberg.

Steward, Julian H., Editor
1955. Irrigation Civilizations: A Comparative Study. *Social Science Monographs, I.* Pan American Union, Washington, D.C.

Strong, William Duncan
1943. Cross-sections of the New World Prehistory. *Smithsonian Miscellaneous Collections,* 104(2). Washington, D.C.
1948. Cultural Epochs and Refuse Stratigraphy in Peruvian Archaeology. *Society for American Archaeology Memoir,* 4:93–102.
1957. Paracas, Nazca, and Tiahuanacoid Cultural Relationships in South Coastal Peru. *Society for American Archaeology Memoir,* 13.

Strong, William Duncan, and John M. Corbett
1943. A Ceramic Sequence at Pachacamac. *Columbia Studies in Archaeology and Ethnology,* 1(2):27–122. New York.

Strong, William Duncan, and Clifford Evans
1952. Cultural Stratigraphy in the Virú Valley, Northern Peru: the Formative and Florescent Epochs. *Columbia Studies in Archaeology and Ethnology,* 4. New York.

Stübel, Moritz Alfons, and Max Uhle
1892. *Die Ruinenstaette von Tiahuanaco in Hochlande des alten Peru: Eine kulturgeschechtliche Studie auf grund selbstaindiger aufnahmen.* Leipzig: Verlag von Karl W. Heirsernann.

Stumer, Louis M.
1953. Playa Grande: Primitive Elegance in Pre-Tiahuanaco Peru. *Archaeology,* 6(1):42–48.
1954a. The Chillón Valley of Peru: Excavation and Reconnaisance, 1952–53. *Archaeology,* 7:171–178, 222–228.
1954b. Population Centers of the Rimac Valley of Peru. *American Antiquity,* 20:130–148.

Tello, Julio C.
1929. *Antiguo Perú: Primera Epoca.* Lima: Comisión Organizadora del Segundo Congreso Sudamericano de Turismo.
1931. Un Modelo de Escenografía Plástica en el Arte Antiguo Peruano. *Wira Kocha, Revista de Estudios Antropológicos,* 1(1):87–112. Lima.
1942. Origen y Desarrollo de las Civilizaciones Prehistóricas Andinas. *37 Congreso Internacional de Americanistas, Actas y Memorias,* 1:589–720. Lima.
1956. Arqueología del Valle de Casma. Culturas: Chavín, Santa o Huaylas Yunga y Sub-Chimú. *Publicación del Archivo "Julio C. Tello,"* 1. Universidad Nacional Mayor de San Marcos, Lima.
1960. Chavín, Cultura Matriz de la Civilización Andina. Revised and edited by Toribio Mejía Xesspe. *Publicación del Archivo "Julio C. Tello,"* 2. Universidad Nacional Mayor de San Marcos, Lima.

Thompson, Donald
1964a. Formative Period Architecture in the Casma Valley, Perú. *35 Congreso Internacional de Americanistas, Actas y Memorias,* 1:205–212. México, D.F.
1964b. Postclassic Innovations in Architecture and Settlement Patterns in the Casma Valley, Peru. *Southwestern Journal of Anthropology,* 20:91–105.

Tosi, Joseph A. Jr.
1960. Zonas de Vida Natural en el Perú. *Boletín Técnico,* 5. Instituto de Ciencias Agrícolas de la OEA, Zona Andina, Lima.

Towle, Margaret A.
1961. The Ethnobotany of Pre-Columbian Peru. *Viking Fund Publications in Anthropology,* 30. Wenner-Gren Foundation for Anthropological Research, New York.

Troll, Carl
1958. Las Culturas Superiores Andinas y el Medio Geográfico. *Revista del Instituto de Geografía,* 5:3–55. Lima.

Tschopik, Harry, Jr.
1946. Some Notes on Rock Shelter Sites near Huancayo, Peru. *American Antiquity,* 12:73–80.

Tschopik, Marion H.
1946. Some Notes on the Archaeology of the Department of Puno, Peru. *Papers of the Peabody Museum of American Archaeology and Ethnology,* 27(3). Cambridge, Mass.

Ubbelöhde-Doering, Heinrich
1957. Der Gallinazo-Stil und die Chronologie der Alt-

peruanischen Frühkulturen. *Bayerischen Akademie der Wissenchaften, Philosophische-Historische Klasse,* 9:1–8. Munich.

Uhle, Max
1913. Die Ruinen von Moche. *Journal de la Société des Américanistes,* 10:95–117. Paris.
1919. La Arqueología de Arica y Tacna. *Boletín de la Sociedad Ecuatoriana de Estudios Históricos,* 3:1–48. Quito.
1920. Los Principios de las Antiguas Civilizaciones Peruanas. *Boletín de la Sociedad Ecuatoriana de Estudios Históricos Americanos,* 4:448–458. Quito.
1924a. Ancient Civilizations of Ica Valley. *University of California Publications in American Archaeology and Ethnology,* 21:128–132. Berkeley.
1924b. Explorations at Chincha. *University of California Publications in American Archaeology and Ethnology,* 21:55–94. Berkeley.

Uhle, Max, and Alphons Stübel
1892. *Die Ruinenstätte von Tiahuanaco im Hochlande der Alten Peru.* Breslau.

Valcarcel, Luis E.
1924. El Cuzco Precolombino. *Revista Universitaria,* 44. Lima.
1934–1935. Sajsawaman Redescubierto. *Revista del Museo Nacional,* 3:3–36, 211–233; 4:1–24, 161–203. Lima.
1939. Sobre el Origen del Cuzco. *Revista del Museo Nacional,* 7(2):190–223. Lima.

Vargas Ugarte, Rubén
1942. *De la Conquista a la República (Artículos Históricos).* Lima: Librería e Imprenta Gil.

Vásquez de Espinoza, Antonio
1942. Description of the Indies (c. 1620). *Smithsonian Miscellaneous Collections,* 102. Washington, D.C.

Vavilov, N. I.
1932. The Process of Evolution in Cultivated Plants. *Proceedings of the Sixth International Congress of Genetics,* 1:331–342.

Villar Córdoba, Pedro
1935. *Las Culturas Prehispánicas del Departamento de Lima.* Lima.

Von Hagen, Victor W.
1955. *Highway of the Sun.* New York: Duell, Sloan and Pearce.

Wallace, Dwight T.
1962. Cerrillos, An Early Paracas Site in Ica, Peru. *American Antiquity,* 27:303–314.

Weiner, Charles
1874. *Pérou et Bolivie.* Paris.

Willey, Gordon R.
1943. Excavations in the Chancay Valley. *Columbia Studies in Archaeology and Ethnology,* 1(3): 123–196. New York.
1948. Functional Analysis of "Horizon Styles" in Peruvian Archaeology. *Society for American Archaeology Memoir,* 4:8–15.
1953. Prehistoric Settlement Patterns in the Virú Valley, Perú. *Bureau of American Ethnology Bulletin,* 155. Washington, D.C.

Willey, Gordon R., and John Corbett
1954. Early Ancón and Early Supe Cultures. *Columbia University Studies in Archaeology and Ethnology,* 3. New York.

Willey, Gordon R., and Philip Phillips
1958. *Method and Theory in American Archeology.* Chicago: University of Chicago Press.

Wing, Elizabeth S.
1972. Utilization of Animal Resources in the Peruvian Andes. Pages 327–351 of Appendix IV in Seiichi Izumi and Kazuo Terada, editors, *Andes 4: Excavations at Kotosh, Peru 1963 and 1966.* Tokyo: University of Tokyo Press.

Yacovleff, Eugenio
1931. El Vencejo (Cypselus) en el Arte Decorativo de Nazca. *Wira Kocha, Revista de Estudios Antropológicos,* 1(1):25–35. Lima.
1932. Las Falcónidas en el Arte y en las Creencias de los Antiguos Peruanos. *Revista del Museo Nacional,* 1:35–111. Lima.

Zuidema, R. T.
1962. Reflections on Inca Historical Conceptions. Pages 718–721 in *34 Internationalen Amerikanistenkongresses, Akten.* Vienna.

INDEX

Abiseo,11
Acarí, 195
Ai-apaec, 104, 188
Aija, 116, 118
Allita Amaya, 205, 207, 212
Allqo Machay, 162
Alto Ramírez, 212
Amano, Yoshitaro, 11
Amat, Hernán, 11, 205
Amato, 124
Ambo, 30
Ancón, 7, 8, 42, 52, 53, 72, 86
Andamarca, 55
Andean culture, 7
Anderson, Edgar, 35
Apurlé, 183
Arenal, 30, 36, 38
Arica, 211
Armatambo, 191
Ancón, 193, 195
Arqalla, 180, 199
Ascope, 102
Asia, 42, 44, 45, 47
Aspero, 40, 42
Atacama, 211
Atacameña, 211
Atarco, 155, 156, 157, 168, 174, 176
Atawallpa, 179, 217, 218, 219, 224
Auki Willka, 33
Ayacucho, 25, 26
Ayacucho Archaeological-Botanical
    Project, 10, 134
Ayampitín, 32
Aymara, 200, 202

Baessler, Arthur, 8
Ballesteros, Manuel, 11
Bandelier, Adolf, 7
Baños de Boza, 83, 86, 90, 92
Barreda Murillo, Luis, 56
Batan Urqo, 168, 177
Bat Cave, 35
Bennett, Wendell C., 9, 10, 12, 85,
    95, 96, 98, 111, 133, 140, 152, 155,
    182, 202
Bennett Stela, 140, 141
Bering Strait, 23
Bernedo Málaga, Leónidas, 207, 209
Bibar, Gerónimo de, 210

Bird, Junius, 10, 12, 41, 95, 205, 211
Bonavia, Duccio, 40, 149
Bosch-Gimpera, Pedro, 24

Caballuyoq, 199
Cabello Balboa, Miguel, 180, 195,
    215, 217
Cabeza Larga, 39
Cacha, 219, 220, 232
Cachi, 40,199
Cahuachi, 123, 124, 132, 133, 139
Caja, 136, 145
Cajamarca, 87, 147, 149, 157, 168,
    174
Cajamarquilla, 119, 166–168, 191
Calancha, Antonio de, 180, 188
Callaguaya, 201
Callango, 79
Cal y Canto, 228
Cana, 201, 203
Canario, 30, 32
Canchi, 201, 203
Canterón, 159
Capac Yupanki, 182, 218, 221
Capillayoq, 159, 160, 161
Caraponga, 191
Cardich, Augusto, 10, 22, 23, 29, 30,
    32
Carmenca, 145
Carrera, Fernando de la, 180
Casafranca, José, 70, 149
Casa Patak, 209
Caycho, Félix, 149
Central Andes, 4
Cerrillos, 59, 72, 83
Cerro Achona, 27
Cerro Blanco, 68
Cerra Colorado, 92, 93
Cerro Corbacho, 183
Cerro Culebras, 120, 121
Cerro del Oro, 152
Cerro Moreno, 212
Cerro Sechín, 69, 70
Cerro Soldado, 123, 124
Cerro Tortuga, 27
Cerro Trinidad, 86, 119, 121
Chakipampa, 153
Chanapata, 9, 55, 56, 57, 86
Chancay, 8, 119, 174, 179, 191–195

Chan-chan, 11, 166, 180, 183, 184–
    186
Chanka, 162, 180, 182, 198–200, 217,
    226, 228
Chankillo, 83
Chapi, 199
Charca, 201, 203
Chauchaq, 147
Chávez Ballón, Manuel, 57, 168
Chavín, 7, 8, 49, 54, 57–80
Chaviña, 127, 133, 138
Chavín de Huantar, 52, 59–67, 70,
    72, 80
Chavín de Moqekc, 166
Cheqnarapi, 206
Cheqo Wasi, 159, 160, 161
Chercana, 213
Chicamita, 166, 183
Chihua, 40, 47
Chilca, 37, 38, 39, 42, 47, 179
Childe, V. Gordon, 13, 36
Chillón, 42
Chilpe, 212
Chimo Capac, 183
Chimor. See Chimú
Chimú, 8, 163, 173, 179, 180–190,
    193, 232, 234
Chimú Capac, 166
Chincha, 8, 195
Chincha-Atacameño, 211
Chincha Islands, 102
Chiprak, 171, 229
Chipurik, 147, 149
Chiquitoy, 166, 183
Chira, 52
Chira Villa, 42, 44
Chiribaya, 205, 207, 210
Chiripa, 84, 86–87, 89, 90, 93
Chirisco, 213
Chivateros, 26, 27, 28, 30
Chivateros Red Zone. See Red Zone
Chocavento, 124
Choke Manco, 179, 191
Chongoyape, 72, 79
Chorrillos, 121
Chot, 181
Choy, Emilio, 13
Chucuito, 201, 202, 205, 206
Chullpa, 203

Chumbi, Pedro Cusco, 181
Chupas, 70, 72, 134
Chuquibamba, 174, 212, 213
Chuquitanta. *See* El Paraíso
Churajón, 205, 207–210, 212, 213
Churkampa, 162
Cieza de León, Pedro, 7, 159, 218, 223, 228
Clovis, 24, 27
Coe, Michael D., 54
Colinas, 52
Colla, 201, 205, 217, 218
Collagua, 201, 205, 213
Collao, 203, 205, 206, 212
Collier, Donald, 10, 133, 151, 173
Conchas, 44
Conchitas, 28
Conchopata, 138, 152, 162, 177, 198
Coras, 180, 198, 200
Corbett, John M., 9, 40, 119
Cordilleran Complex, 37
Core Tool Tradition, 24
Cortadera, 213
Cruz Pata, 137, 138
Cueva de las Lechuzas, 51, 54, 55
Cuis Manco, 179
Culebras, 42, 43
Cupisnique, 10, 40, 71–72, 75–76, 80, 106
Curawasi, 157, 168
Curayacu, 52, 53
Cursive, 174
Cusmancu, 182
Cuzco, 168, 214–215, 217, 218–221
Cuzqueños, 179, 188, 217, 218, 219, 223, 224, 228

Dauelsberg, Percy, 205, 211, 212
Dawson, Lawrence E., 11, 72, 90, 123, 127
de Candolle, Alphonse, 35
d'Harcourt, Raoul, 8, 119
Disselhoff, Hans, 12
Dollfus, Olivier, 22, 29
Dos Palmos, 123, 124

El Inga, 27
El Jobo, 30
El Paraíso, 44, 45, 52
El Pino, 191
El Purgatorio, 166, 183
Encalada, 191
Encanto, 37, 38, 39, 47
Engel, Frederic, 10, 23, 35, 36, 38, 39, 40, 41, 42, 44, 47
Epigonal, 8, 151, 174, 175, 192
Evans, Clifford, 10, 11, 35, 41, 51, 96, 99

Fell's Cave, 27
Flake and Bone Tool Tradition, 25, 26
Flores, Benedicto, 151
Flores, Isabel, 12, 205, 211
Flornoy, Bertrand, 147
Fonseca, César, 11
Ford, James A., 10, 11

Formative, 10
Friesenhahn, 24
Fung, Rosa, 10

Galindo, 183
Gallery of the Offerings, 62, 80
Gallinazo, 96–99, 106
Garagay, 52
Gateway of the Sun, 141, 142, 143, 145, 152, 163, 176
Gaviota, 44
Gayton, Anna, 9, 119, 121, 123
Gentilar, 211
Ghatchi, 28
Ghersi Barrera, Humberto, 205
Guañape, 51, 52
Guaylacan, 212
Guitarrero Cave, 26, 28
Guzmán L. de G., Carlos, 149

Hacha, 52, 54, 96
Hadden, Gordon, 11
Hammel, Eugene, 13
Hanan Cuzco, 214
Hatuncolla, 201
Hatun Wayllay, 163
Higueras, 145, 146, 147
Horco Pampa, 171
Horkheimer, Hans, 99, 102, 149
Hornillos, 212
Huaca Alvarado, 83
Huaca Chotuna, 101, 181
Huaca de la Cruz, 110
Huaca de la Florida, 86
Huaca de la Luna, 100, 102
Huaca del Dragón, 183, 186, 188
Huaca del Loro, 125
Huaca de los Reyes, 68, 69
Huaca del Sol, 100, 101, 102
Huaca Licapa, 97, 98
Huaca Negra, 41–42, 51
Huaca Pan de Azucar, 121
Huaca Prieta, 35, 41–42, 45, 51, 52
Huaca Singan, 188
Huaca Soto, 83
Huaca Trujillo, 120
Huactalacta, 209
Huamanga, 175
Huamaqueros, 32
Huancayo, 145, 146
Huancho, 191
Huanta, 27
Huantar, 116, 118
Huánuco Viejo, 224
Huapaya M., Cirilo, 10
Huarás, 85, 92, 116, 118
Huarcoy, 171
Huarmey, 42
Huarpa, 133–138, 152, 199
Huarto, 124
Huatanay, 234
Huaura, 175, 192
Huaycán, 191
Huaylas Yunga, 173
Huaytará, 224, 228
Humboldt Current, 3
Huruquilla, 212
Hutchinson, Thomas J., 7

Ica-Chincha, 195–197
Ica Vieja, 196
Ichubamba, 217
Inca, 162, 163
Inca Roca, 214, 215, 217
Ingenio, 168
Interlocking, 119
Inti, 219, 283
Intihuasi, 32
Iriarte, Francisco, 183
Isla, 72, 83
Izumi, Seiichi, 11

Jatun Marka, 200
Jauja, 224
Jaywa, 30, 37
Jaywamachay Cave, 28, 29, 32
Jijón y Caamaño, Jacinto, 8, 119
Juliana, 120

Kachakacha, 205
Kalafatovich, Carlos, 22
Kalasasaya, 89, 90, 141
Kekerana, 204, 205
Kelley, David, 40
Kidder II, Alfred, 9
Killa, 219, 232
Killke, 174, 215
Kipu Kamayoq, 231
Kojra, 206
Kosok, Paul, 126
Kotosh, 8, 11, 46, 47, 51, 54, 56, 59, 72, 145
Krieger, Alex D., 24
Kroeber, Louis A., 9, 12, 96, 99, 111, 119, 122, 123, 145, 151, 205
Kuelap, 147, 149
Kumun Senqa, 136, 137
Kuntur Wasi, 67, 72
Kutscher, Gerdt, 99, 106
Kuyu, 215

La Compañía, 162
La Copa (see Kuntur Wasi)
La Estaquería, 124
La Florida, 52
Lagunillas, 134, 135
Laka Kollu, 139, 142
Lanning, Edward, 10, 13, 26, 30, 38, 51, 120
Lanzón, 62–63
Larco Hoyle, Rafael, 10, 96, 99, 104, 106, 108, 110, 111, 112, 118, 149, 151, 173, 188
Las Haldas, 42, 43, 44, 52
Las Ventanitas de Otuzco, 171
Latcham, Richard E., 8
Lathrap, Donald, 11, 51, 54
Lauri, 192
Lauricocha, 22, 24, 25, 29, 30, 31, 32, 33, 47
La Vega, 162
Le Paige, R. P. Gustavo, 28
Lerma, 30
Lewisville, 24
Lima, 90, 115, 119–122, 152
Linares Málaga, Eloy, 12, 205

Los Chinos, 43
Lothrop, Samuel K., 133
Lucre, 174, 215
Ludeña, Hugo, 10
Lumbra, 191
Lumbreras, Luis G., 11, 133, 155, 205
Lupaqa, 201, 205, 218
Lurigancho, 191
Lurín Chincha, 195
Luz, 30, 31
Lynch, Thomas, 10, 26, 32

Maca, 213
Machu Picchu, 221, 222, 235
MacNeish, Richard, 10, 22, 23, 24, 25, 26, 27, 37, 40, 134
Mahler, Joy, 133
Makey, Carol, 11, 183
Malpase, 52
Manchán, 166
Manco Capac, 214
Mangelsdorf, Paul, 40
Mango Marca, 191
Mantaro, 180, 199
Maranga, 119, 120, 121, 122
Marcavalle, 56, 57
Marka Wamachuku, 169, 180, 182, 228
Markawra, 213
Masqo, 218
Matos Mendieta, Ramiro, 11, 26, 145
Maya, 8
McCown, Theodore, 9
Means, Philip A., 8
Media Luna, 83
Medina, Pío Max, 151
Meggers, Betty J., 11
Mejía Xesspe, Toribio, 177
Mendoza F., Rosa, 134
Menzel, Dorothy, 11, 72, 90, 127, 133, 152, 155
Mercaymarca, 206
Middendorf, E. W., 7, 8
Mina Perdida, 52
Minchan-çaman, 182
Miramar, 86, 120
Mito, 46, 47
Moche, 96, 99–111, 168, 173
Mochica. See Moche
Mocollope, 100
Mojocoya, 212
Mollebaya, 209
Mollo, 207, 212, 213
Moqeke, 68, 80
Morris, Craig, 11
Moseley, Michael, 10, 11, 28, 68, 183
Mostny, Grete, 211
Muelle, Jorge C., 13, 29, 176
Munizaga, Carlos, 205
Murra, John, 11, 201, 202

Ñam-lap, 181, 187
Ñawimpukyo, 134, 152
Nazca, 122–133, 138, 152, 155
Negritos, 51
Neira, Máximo A., 10, 12, 155, 203, 213
Neothermal, 29

Nievería, 119, 121, 174
Nordenskiold, Erland, 7, 8, 202
Núñez, Lautaro, 205

Ocucaje, 77–78, 88, 168
Ofrendas, 71, 72, 73–74
Okros, 138, 165
Ollantaytambo, 221
Olmec, 54, 57
O'Neale, Lila, 133, 151
Oquendo, 26, 27, 28
Otuma, 42

Pacaje, 201, 203, 218
Pacatnamú, 110, 166, 183
Paccaicasa, 24, 25
Pachacamac, 119, 120, 121, 152, 155, 157, 165, 166, 168, 174, 177, 223, 234
Pacha Kuteq Inca Yupanki, 162, 182, 195, 214, 215, 217, 218, 219
Pachamachay, 30
Pacheco, 152, 154, 168, 177
Pacopampa, 54, 55, 68
Paiján, 28, 30
Paita, 51
Pajatén, 11, 98, 149
Paleoindians, 24
Palli Aike, 28
Pallka, 68
Pampa de las Llamas, 166
Pampa de Tinguiña, 124
Pampa Ingenio, 125
Pamparca, 199
Panalagua Cave, 26
Pañamarca, 100
Paqallamoqo, 57, 86
Paracas, 72, 79, 83, 88, 90, 92, 115, 127
Paracas Cavernas, 87, 90
Paracas Necrópolis, 87, 90, 91, 127
Pardo, Luis, 221
Paredones, 196
Pariti, 155
Paroparo, 206
Patan Qotu, 180, 200
Pátapo, 183
Patasca, 85
Patterson, Thomas, 10, 26, 27, 28, 44, 120
Pezzia, Alejandro, 133
Phillips, Philip, 13
Piki, 37
Pikillaqta, 163, 168, 177, 215
Pikimachay Cave, 24, 25, 27
Pillucho, 199
Pinilla, 174
Piñiqo, 207
Pisquillo Chico, 191
Pizarro, Francisco, 218, 224
Playa Grande, 86, 119, 120, 121, 122
Playa Hermosa, 44
Pleistocene, 10, 21–23, 27, 28
Pocoma, 211
Pocsi, 209
Ponce Monolith, 141
Ponce Sanginés, Carlos, 12, 84, 139, 140, 141, 203
Poroma, 195

Posnansky, Arthur, 8, 139
Pre-Projectile Point Stage, 24
Presto-puno, 212
Proto-Chimú, 8, 99
Proto-Nazca, 8
Puente, 27, 29, 30
Puerto Hormiga, 50
Puerto Morrin, 81, 83, 85
Pukara, 37, 84, 88–89, 90, 92, 139, 145
Pukina, 200, 205
Pulgar Vidal, Javier, 3
Puma Qocha, 228
Punkurí, 68, 70
Punkurí Alto, 183
Putuni, 139, 142

Qaluyu, 55, 56, 57, 84, 88, 89
Qaqamarca, 199
Qasawirka, 145
Qawarikuna, 159
Qencha-qencha, 215
Q'eri Kala, 139, 142
Qoripata, 233, 234
Qosqopa, 155, 157, 174, 175, 213
Quaternary, 21–22
Quebrada de la Vaca, 228, 229
Quechua, 165
Quicapata, 135
Quiqché, 32
Quishqui Puncu, 30, 32
Qutimpo, 206

Raimondi Stela, 63, 79, 141
Raku, 71, 75
Ramos de Cox, Josefina, 10
Rancha, 84, 87, 135, 136
Ranracancha, 30, 32
Raqay Pampa, 135
Ravash, 147
Ravines, Rogger, 10
Recuay, 90, 92, 99, 111–118, 174
Red Zone, 26, 27, 28
Regal, Alberto, 162
Reiche, Maria, 126
Reichlen, Henry and Paule, 54, 147, 149
Reiss, Wilhelm, 7
Río Grande de Nazca, 38, 39
Río Seco, 42, 43
Ríos R., Marcela, 134
Roark, Richard P., 127
Robles Moqo, 152, 153, 155
Rocas, 71, 72
Rosas LaNoire, Hermilio, 11, 54
Roselló, Lorenzo, 10
Rostworowski de Diez Canseco, Maria, 215
Rowe, John H., 9, 11, 13, 43, 51, 54, 57, 63, 72, 83, 90, 123, 124, 127, 133, 145, 151, 180, 181, 188, 215, 221
Ryden, Stig, 203

Sacsahuaman, 8, 9, 174, 215, 220
Salinar, 81, 83, 85, 90, 92, 93
Saltur, 183
San Blas, 85

Sanders, William, 168
Sandia, 24
San Miguel, 211
San Nicolás, 162, 166
San Pedro, 195, 196, 211
San Pedro de Cacha, 168
Santa, 173
Santo Domingo, 162
Sauer, Carl, 35
Schaedel, Richard, 116, 118, 204
Senqato, 228
Sestieri, Claudio, 12
Shady Solís, Ruth, 11, 54
Shutuy Marka, 200
Sillustani, 203, 205, 206, 229
Solutrean, 24
Sono, Toshihiko, 11
Spinden, Herbert, 57
Squier, Ephraim George, 7
Steward, Julian H., 12
Strong, William Duncan, 9, 10, 12, 35, 41, 51, 57, 83, 96, 99, 119, 123, 124, 126, 133
Stübel, Alphons, 7, 139
Stumer, Louis M., 119, 191
Suchimansillo, 118
Suksu, 168
Supe, 8, 72, 79

Tacaraca, 234
Tajahuana, 83
Tallán, 187
Tambo Colorado, 195, 224, 225
Tambo de Calao, 196
Tambo de Mora, 195, 224
Tamboinga, 224
Tambo Viejo, 123–124
Tantamayo, 147
Tanta Orqo, 133
Tauri Chumbi, 191
Tauri Cusca, 191
Tauricuxi, 182
Tawantinsuyu, 201, 214, 216–235
Taycanamo, 181–182
Teatino, 174, 191, 192
Tehuacán, 41

Tello, Julio C., 8, 9, 12, 57, 62, 63, 68, 69, 72, 87, 92, 93, 111, 112, 123, 126, 132, 133, 151, 152, 163, 166, 173
Tello Obelisk, 63
Temple of the Crossed Hands, 46, 47
Temple of the Llamas, 51, 52
Thompson, Donald, 11, 166
Tiahuanaco, 139–145, 152, 176
Tilarniyoq, 30
Timirán, 213
Tolón, 50
Toquepala, 29, 30, 32, 33
Torrecitas-Chavín, 54
Tosi Jr., Joseph A., 3
Towle, Margaret A., 40
Tres Cruces, 209
Tres Ventanas, 30, 32
Trimborn, Hermann, 12
Troll, Carl, 3
Tschopik, Harry, 10
Tschopik, Marion H., 9, 203, 205
Tumibamba, 224
Tunasniyoq, 162, 198
Tupac Capac (Tupac Inca Yupanki), 182, 195, 218
Tutishcainyo, 51, 54, 72

Ubbelöhde-Doering, Heinrich, 11
Ubina, 201
Uhle, Max, 7, 8, 12, 99, 119, 121, 122, 123, 139, 151, 168, 205, 211
Umasuyo, 201, 203, 218
Ungará, 195
Urcusuyu, 233, 234
Urin Cuzco, 214
Uru, 200, 201, 202
Ushpa Qoto, 159, 161

Valcarcel, Luis E., 8, 11, 207, 214, 215
Valdivia, 35, 36, 38, 39, 40, 50, 51
Vásquez, 191
Vásquez de Espinosa, Antonio, 202
Vavilov, N. I., 35
Vescelius, Gary, 205

Vicus, 106, 111, 148, 149
Vilca, 218
Vilcashuamán, 224, 226–227
Villar Córdoba, Pedro, 8
Viñaque, 155, 157, 159, 176
Viracocha. See Wira Qocha
Virú, 96, 106
Virú Valley Project, 10, 12
Viscachani, 30, 32

Wacheqsa, 71, 75
Wachipayre, 218
Waira-jirka, 47, 51, 54, 55
Wallace, Dwight, 72
Wamantambo, 213
Wanka, 180, 198, 228, 230
Wankarani, 57, 79
Wari, 7, 119, 121, 122, 133, 151, 177, 181, 183, 199
Wariraxa, 112
Wari Willka, 162, 165, 171, 226
Warka, 213
Waru, 145, 174
Waskar, 217, 218
Watanabe, Luis, 68
Wayna Capac, 218
Waywaka, 168
White-on-Red, 81, 85
Wichqana, 55, 70, 80
Wiener, Charles, 7
Willey, Gordon R., 9, 10, 12, 13, 40, 81, 97, 119, 133, 151, 166, 183
Williams, Carlos, 10
Willkawaín, 85, 118, 162, 170, 171
Wing, Elizabeth, 54
Wira Qocha, 188, 198, 215, 217, 218, 219, 232
Wiraqocha Pampa, 162, 168, 169, 182

Yacovleff, Eugenio, 123
Yanamancha, 168

Zapallán, 191, 193
Zegarra, Jorge, 183
Zuidema, R. T., 214, 215